Staging the Savage God

Staging the Savage God

The Grotesque in Performance

Ralf Remshardt

Southern Illinois University Press
Carbondale

Southern Illinois University Press
www.siupress.com

 Cloth edition 2004.
Paperback edition 2016
Printed in the United States of America

19 18 17 16 4 3 2 1

Cover illustration: Alfred Jarry, *Véritable portrait de M Ubu*; from *Livre d'art* 2 (Apr. 25, 1896)

Library of Congress Cataloging-in-Publication Data
Names: Remshardt, Ralf, 1959– author.
Title: Staging the savage god : the grotesque in performance / Ralf Remshardt.
Description: Paperback edition. | Carbondale : Southern Illinois University Press, 2016. | Includes bibliographical references and index.
Identifiers: LCCN 2016020167| ISBN 9780809335510 (paperback) | ISBN 9780809388783 (ebook)
Subjects: LCSH: Drama—History and criticism. | Grotesque in literature. | BISAC: PERFORMING ARTS / Theater / History & Criticism. | PERFORMING ARTS / Theater / General.
Classification: LCC PN1650.G7 R46 2016 | DDC 809.2/915—dc23
LC record available at https://lccn.loc.gov/2016020167

Printed on recycled paper. ♲

In memory of Robert G. Egan and Bert O. States

To Caron, always

Contents

Figures

Acknowledgments

My gratitude goes to all those who have given counsel and encouragement while this book wound its way from infancy to maturity; special thanks are due Professor Bert O. States, Professor Simon Williams, and Professor Robert G. Egan of the University of California at Santa Barbara, as well as my friend and colleague Professor Joss Marsh of Indiana University. This book would not have existed without a fellowship from the German Fulbright Program at the outset, and a Research Development Award and a Fine Arts and Humanities Scholarship Grant from the University of Florida made finishing it possible. But the great undulating middle was held together by the unwavering support of my wife, Caron Cadle, to whom the book is lovingly dedicated.

Staging the Savage God

Introduction
Approaching the Grotesque

At the end of his autobiographical essay "The Tragic Generation," William Butler Yeats recalls a visit to the Théâtre de l'Œuvre in Paris in December of 1896 to see a play that left something of a lasting impression on him:

> The players are supposed to be dolls, toys, marionettes, and now they are all hopping like wooden frogs, and I can see for myself that the chief personage, who is some kind of King, carries for Sceptre a brush of the kind that we use to clean a closet. Feeling bound to support the most spirited party, we have shouted for the play, but that night at the Hotel Corneille I am very sad, for comedy, objectivity, has displayed its growing power once more. I say, "After Stephane Mallarmé, after Verlaine, after Gustave Moreau, after Puvis de Chavannes, after our own verse, after all our subtle colour and nervous rhythm, after the faint mixed tints of Conder, what more is possible? After us the Savage God." (Yeats 430)

Clearly, Yeats felt himself swept up in a moment of great importance in theatre history, a seemingly unprecedented moment of shifting and collapse but also of impetuous energy. Lacking a term, a theory to fit the occasion, he sought recourse in an archaic system of reference, and the speech of this eloquent poet turned to speechlessness. The "Savage God" Yeats saw hopping and strutting across the stage on Montmartre may have had a new guise and a new name—he was Alfred Jarry's King Ubu, whose perennial notoriety was born that night—but he was certainly not new to the stage nor merely a frontal assault on the symbolist ceremony of innocence. By all accounts, (Western) theatre takes its initial cues from a violent, irrational, mysterious, androgynous, and confounding deity from whom Ubu and many other figures have sprung: Dionysus, the original Savage God of the theatre. Whether one is persuaded by arguments linking the dithyrambic cults to the historical creation of tragedy or not, Dionysus stands at least as a powerful allegorical reminder of a savage impulse at the root of theatrical representation and of theatre's ancient connection to a set of images and tropes that could be called any number of things but that I have called, for the purposes of this book, the grotesque.

There is clearly a paradox at the heart of a book about the grotesque in performance, and it is not too soon to air it: performance is by and large self-articulating, an act that speaks for itself, but the grotesque, as Yeats's baffled reaction shows, is often beyond articulation, is unspeakable. Yet this book is as much about the grotesque as it is about performance; my central contention is that a simple syllogism makes them practically (and theoretically) inseparable: every performance is a kind of grotesque, every grotesque a kind of performance. The Savage God of the grotesque, Dionysus's progeny, is found somewhere in every act of performance. Such a notion extends the term "performance" beyond what some may find tolerable, encompassing not only dramatic performance (with which I am mainly concerned) but also the performances of carnival and monstrosity, the linguistic performance of metaphor and related tropes, performance art, and so on. The Russian director Vsevolod Meyerhold, whose biomechanical theatrical practice in the 1920s employed eccentric and *commedia dell'arte*–influenced styles of the grotesque (in his definition, "a deliberate exaggeration and reconstruction [distortion] of nature"), considered the theatre—the conventional cultural space of performance—to be a place enthralled by the grotesque:

> The theater, being a combination of natural, temporal, spatial, and numerical phenomena, is itself outside of nature. It finds that these phenomena invariably contradict our everyday experience and that the theater itself is essentially an example of the grotesque. Arising from the grotesque of a ritual masquerade, the theater inevitably is destroyed by any given attempt to remove the grotesque—the basis of existence—from it. (qtd. in Gorchakov 69)

All that possesses true theatricality, one might paraphrase Meyerhold, is also grotesque. It is this historically extensive and theoretically intensive relationship between performance and the grotesque that concerns me in this study. Readers will perhaps find that, in a book ostensibly devoted to the grotesque in performance, there is much reference to matters that do not directly bear on performance or the theatre. In my defense, I should immediately reveal that this is not intended as one of the many diligent studies that apply one particular definition of the grotesque (say, that of Mikhail Bakhtin) to one particular playwright or theatrical movement. Such studies are very helpful, and I have made use of them throughout. But the ambition here is to explore a larger context, to open up the field of the grotesque rather than to attain categorical closure, and that means importing into the discussion elements that at first glance seem extraneous, even strange. The book fits neatly neither into the category of theatre history nor of theatrical criticism or theory but aspires to be both and more: a consideration of the grotesque as a cultural phenomenon with, as Søren Kierkegaard might say, "constant reference to theatre."

"Grotesque" is an alarmingly archaic term with an alarming array of meanings. I may have to justify why I prefer vocabulary so apparently antiquated and forbidding when there is much more accommodating terminology already in circulation. To characterize disjunctions in drama and performance, playwrights have variously devised descriptors such as "pataphysical" (Jarry), "anti-Aristotelian" (Bertolt Brecht), "non-Euclidean" (Stanislaw Witkiewicz), "superrealistic" (Yvan Goll), "ridiculous" (Charles Ludlam), and so on; critics have been equally inventive: "absurd" (Martin Esslin), "dark comedy" (John Styan), "alogical" (Kenneth White), "non-matrixed performance" (Michael Kirby), and the like. Useful as these are under certain circumstances, they seem to me to have three distinct weaknesses. First, they are usually applicable only to drama *or* performance, not both. Secondly, they are typically more concerned with the structure of the work or performance than with the response to it. Third, they tend to be descriptive of a small segment of theatre (principally modern) but are impotent in the face of the totality of performance history. (The exception is Antonin Artaud's "Theatre of Cruelty"; his practice is the subject of my conclusion.) The grotesque, on the other hand, is a much more encompassing term, rigorously physical and concrete in its application but aesthetically and philosophically complex, and it trails a distinguished critical lineage from John Ruskin to Bakhtin and beyond.

Conversely, as much as the term opens up critical possibilities, it is subject to a fearful slippage of meaning. Writing on the grotesque cannot mean establishing inalterable knowledge about it—the topic has rejected such critical hubris for virtually hundreds of years. In the wry words of Geoffrey Harpham, one of the most eloquent apologists of critical failure in the face of this bewildering phenomenon, "[T]he grotesque is that sort of thing in the presence of which we experience certain methodological problems" (xxi). The grotesque will frustrate our desire to hold and name it; it will reside in persistent regression and dispersal from our cognitive faculties, in constant deferral. Coming to it with terms is not yet coming to terms with it. A potent stimulus to critical desire, the grotesque is also always the concept that got away.

Subterranean Etymology

The word "grotesque" unfailingly brings to mind a great variety of possible manifestations: the gargoyles perched atop the parapets of Gothic cathedrals, or the bewildering monsters of Hieronymus Bosch, or the cringing, abject humanity in Dante's *Inferno.* Some etymological excavation of the term will provide insights into its meaning.

"Grotesque" derives from the Italian word *grottesche,* which first designated certain wall paintings from Roman times uncovered in the fifteenth century. As late as the middle of the *quattrocento,* the great sites of the fallen Roman empire lay in scattered oblivion; swine, goats, and other livestock grazed in the ruins of the Forum. But around 1480, adventurers began to search among the relics and there discovered an imperial palace that had been overbuilt so often that it had sunk to subterranean levels, its long-sealed rooms in effect having become "grottoes" (as if the long history of the psychological and aesthetic suppression of this phenomenon had manifested itself coincidentally in a gradual physical submersion). This palace, the Domus Aurea, or Golden House, had been constructed for the emperor Nero after a fire in 64 C.E. had devastated the entire center of the city—the fire, to be sure, for which historical rumor holds Nero responsible.

The amateur archaeologists of the early Renaissance found a host of treasures in this forgotten jumble of ruins, including the famous sculpture of Laocoön. But their attention was captured by a phenomenon that seemed to mock and fly in the face of their classical aesthetics: the columns, walls, and ceilings were covered with ornaments in which an imagination—an unhealthy one, perhaps—was at work, uninhibited by classical reserve, indiscriminately mingling plants, beasts, humans, and architecture into a fantastical hodgepodge hitherto undreamt of in the art of (presumably) grave antiquity (see fig. 1). Since it was an art from the *grotta,* the underground, the neologism *grottesche* was soon adopted. The Domus Aurea became a premier tourist attraction of the Renaissance, and the designs, and their subsequent interpretation by such artistic luminaries as Pintoricchio, Michelangelo, and Raphael, sparked a veritable craze for grotesques that lasted into the seventeenth century.[1]

It is not, however, the fate of a relatively obscure and short-lived vogue that makes this story compelling but rather the fact that it contains in essence everything that distinguishes the grotesque, even in its vastly different modern forms. For instance, it seems significant that these

Fig. 1. Design (detail) from the Domus Aurea, first century C.E. From C. Mirri, *Le antiche camere delle Terme di Tito e le loro pitture* (Roma, 1776).

ornaments are connected to the name of Nero, who stands as a grotesque parody of the Augustan emperors in the period of Rome's accelerated decline, himself embodying the excesses and vacillations of a time out of joint. If Nero is etched into our historical memory, it is likely because of a single disturbingly incongruous (and historically apocryphal) moment of bathos we find ourselves compelled to call "grotesque": his singing of homemade poetry to the lyre as he watches the (allegedly homemade) conflagration of Rome. The grotesque artistic impulse seems strongest at such historical junctures and ruptures, in ages rich with uncertainty—compare only the dramatic works of Nero's erstwhile adviser Seneca. Kenneth Burke has remarked, somewhat tautologically, that "[g]rotesque inventions flourish *when it is easiest to imagine the grotesque,* or *when it is hardest to imagine the classical* (one may take either phrasing as he prefers)" (*Permanence* 117). For the literary products of the Neronian reign, particularly those of Seneca and Lucan, the label of classicism seems almost unimaginable. Their excesses of "hyperbolic horror," as Rainer Sell observes, betray the fierce discrepancy between the formal requirements of the tragic or epic mold and a shock content catering to "a public nurtured on the violent realism of gladiator games" (283).

In comparison, the ornaments of the Golden House seem easy to stomach. Yet the reception accorded to the ornamental grotesques, both in antiquity and in the Renaissance, was uncompromising, generating both high praise and strict rejection. This ambivalence in reaction, the mixture of attraction and repulsion, of emotional closeness and aesthetic distance, is still a hallmark of those phenomena we address as grotesque, and nearly their only predictable constant.

Further, we notice in the Roman ornamental grotesque and in its disinterment by the Renaissance a kind of metaphor of the unconscious and an allegory of alienation. That is to say, these designs were always alien, remote, and puzzling in some sense, and this comprised a large part of the fascination they exerted. Already in antiquity, they had come to Rome from somewhere else (perhaps Alexandria?) and had been imitated there. In turn, they became something strange to the Renaissance, something submerged by time and oblivion, which suddenly and unexpectedly confronted the eye. This variation on the strange—the alienation it arouses, espouses, and exposes—is central to grotesqueness. In Wolfgang Kayser's view, "The grotesque is the estranged world" (184). The historical coincidence that these shapes of the grotesque quite literally sprang from the underground allows us to read them as a metaphor of the unconscious as well, as its issues are by turns repressed and liberated. We are reminded that the grotesque touches the substrata of our own emotional and rational "underground," that it connects with the grottoes, caves, and sunken vaults of our being. The oneiric quality, too, is emphasized in their long sleep: *sogni dei pittori* (dreams of the painters) is what the sixteenth century called the grotesques (Kayser 22).

What the finding of the grotesques in the grotto so fortuitously exposes is the position of the grotesque in regard to the fundamental ideological dualism of the premodern age—the hierarchical division between the celestial and the infernal, the divine and the satanic. The grotesque has thus from the moment of its inception been charted into the lowest stratum of the epistemological geo/topography, in its debasement far from, and at odds with, the beauty, perfection, and holiness of the divine.

Defining the Grotesque

What, then, is grotesque, and what is "the" grotesque? Are the Neronian leaf creatures grotesque in the same way that Giuseppe Arcimboldo's composite paintings are, or performance artist Stelarc's suspension of his body by fish hooks is? Proposing any master example of the grotesque inevitably creates its own standards—and its own problems. (Georg Friedrich Wilhelm Hegel's famous dialectical theory of tragic collision would surely have been altogether different if his play of reference had been *Medea* instead of *Antigone.*) The term "grotesque" is often applied to a given context for intensely personal reasons in an attempt to communicate what a text, image, metaphor, or performance does to us. But the skip of the heart, the queasiness of the stomach, the fluttering of the breath, though legitimate objects of the poetic attention, are usually shunned in sound critical inquiry, too much do they seem quirks of the critic's body rather than issues of his or her mind. Walter Benjamin decries this inductive method in his prologue to *The Origin of German Tragic Drama,* and one does well to heed his warning that such a process leaves one "with nothing but some psychological data which, on the slender basis of an identity in the subjective reaction of the investigator or, at least, the ordinary contemporary citizen, are held to establish the similarity of things which are in fact quite different" (39).

But who could deny that, of all aesthetic encounters, it is the encounter with the grotesque that is virtually defined by such a slippage of reason and language? In his book about Francis Bacon, one of the most celebrated grotesque artists of modernity, the critic Ernst van Alphen noticed first a speechlessness, an incapacitation and paralysis that befell him when he viewed the canvasses: "This inability to reflect upon the very aspects of works that touch one most seems to be caused by a momentary *loss of self.* The capacity to reflect seems to be temporarily narcotized, so that the intensity of the experience itself precludes reflection upon one's emotional state" (9).

What, then, is the investigator to do with an aesthetic phenomenon that aims inexorably for those uncredentialed strata of his being? The literary scholar is at a loss. He may either engage in strict textual analysis and uncover structural, rhetorical, or symbolic meanings while jeopardizing his grasp of the larger questions at hand. Or he may choose the opposite route and risk being called unduly subjective and esoteric, which can today be accomplished by adherence to any number of critical schools. Sir Ernest Gombrich, whose intellectual presence will be found to pervade this study at several points, remarks on the peculiar fusing of form and content in the grotesque that subverts the conventional framework of analysis:

> If we find it hard to come to terms with the tradition of drollery and the grotesque, the fault may lie in the way we have been taught to approach the visual arts. As long as we divide the field between formal analysis and iconography, the area . . . will inevitably elude us. (*Sense* 273)

For the theatre scholar, especially if she is concerned with performance theory, a certain amount of slipperiness in her subject comes with the territory. She is, after all, the chronicler of an occasion that, in the poignant words of Herbert Blau, "exists most substantially in the rehearsal of its disappearance" (*Blooded* xiv).

This may be the opportune place at which to—as a point of reference—interject a brief definition of the grotesque as it is reflected consensually in the most prominent critical studies on the subject.[2] German critic Christian W. Thomsen provides this summary definition:

> [The grotesque] makes the known strange through the interplay and mixing of heterogenous parts into new and autonomous entities (vegetable-animal-human-mechanical-automatic). It partially or completely revokes or reverses recognized norms and consciously disappoints expectations. It intends to baffle,

> intimidate, and shock the viewer or reader and to stimulate his own (critical) thought process.[3] (200)

Thomsen here gives the most concise rendering of the constitutive elements of any aesthetic phenomenon, the elements of production, reception, and efficacy. But each one by itself does not necessarily describe the grotesque. The productive or "poetic" aspect of making the known strange is quite reminiscent of the concept of estrangement that Victor Shklovskii advanced in his famous 1917 essay, "Art as Technique," as the foundation of *all* artistic production. Any genre principled on the inversion of norms, such as the "world-upside-down" satire, could fulfill the second, receptive or "aesthetic," aspect without so much as verging on grotesqueness. Thomsen also omits the problem of grotesque laughter (to which I will return in chapter 2). As for the efficacious or "cathartic" part of the three-step, the stimulation of critical thought through shock tactics is a familiar objective of avant-garde art, much of which cannot legitimately be called "grotesque." I am not trying to disqualify Thomsen's definition; it very much serves its purpose as a point of departure. But an airtight definition remains maddeningly elusive.

Jean Baudrillard, speaking of the inescapable paradox of the modern ethnologist who is forced, in observing, to destroy the condition of the observed, muses that "every science live[s] on this paradoxical slope to which it is doomed by the evanescence of its object in the very process of its apprehension" (13–14). Describing the grotesque is not so serious an issue, but it is subject to a similar dilemma, for once one has hauled the huge and unwieldy critical apparatus, clanking and rustling with terms and distinctions, near what one suspects to be the habitat of the phenomenon, it has almost always shied away already, or else has transformed itself into something perfectly harmless, such as the absurd or the macabre. The critic soon learns that the grotesque is always on the verge of transformation (because in the last analysis, it is itself metamorphosis, or, rather, *performs* metamorphically), and it possesses a core instability that resists and even mocks definition; close scrutiny invariably tends to unravel all but its most flagrant examples. And so the critic must convert from a hunter to a gatherer and cultivate the furtive glance rather than the rapacious gaze.

A variety of aesthetic and literary concepts can serve to elucidate the grotesque. The grotesque re-presents, or re-represents, an already known quantity, as Kenneth Burke says of the metaphor, "*in terms of* something else" (*Grammar* 503). There is, as we will see, a sympathetic relation of the grotesque to the metaphor—the grotesque also performs metaphorically. Metaphor and its sister tropes always harbor the potential to become grotesque, especially if they are literalized, that is, if their component parts are brought together not only on the plane of the rhetorical imagination but also in the field of concrete aesthetic experience. One such field is the canvas of a painting. Another is the stage of the theatre, or any liminal space in which performance takes place.

The grotesque work advocates the possibility of an aesthetically representable truth, even if a crisis of representation is the result of the pursuit. Robert Penn Warren acknowledges that "we may say that the grotesque is a 'truth' drawn out of context, isolated, brought to a sharp individual focus. By the same token, paradoxically, to assert the grotesque may be to assert a 'truth' that, in its natural context, is ignored" (246).[4]

This is indeed the paradox. The grotesque is largely about perspective and perception. Its steadfast refusal—in nearly any of its forms—to accommodate ready interpretations makes it a mode in which light is cast on the act of perceiving itself, as the moment of the aesthetic and semantic transaction, a transaction that in the case of the confrontation with grotesqueness becomes an "agony," in the sense of the struggle or *agon.* Thrown back by an uncompromising object of attention upon our own devices and reminded of the fickleness of our senses, we become self-conscious. Says Harpham, "Looking at ourselves looking at the grotesque, we can observe our own projections, catching ourselves, as it were, in the act of perception" (43). Perceiving one's own perceptions is a vertiginous act and, what is more, one that is perhaps philosophically dangerous, a prelude to what van Alphen had called the "loss of self."

But if the grotesque confounds and questions the perception, it implicitly dissolves the perceiving self. This movement toward self-recognition of the aesthetic apparatus, then, seems indissolubly connected with the perception of the grotesque, but it also diminishes or vanquishes the grotesque response, which is principally an unreflected, direct, naive response. Grotesqueness, it appears, is an ephemeral attribute in the work of art, eliciting a response it refuses to sustain. With all but a few exceptions that seem to reach and hook into our nervous essence, grotesqueness is transitory both as concerns the immediate act of seeing and the emotional response and in the historically variable elements it chooses in order to attain its effect. Grotesque objects do not usually remain grotesque under the steady gaze. We cannot peacefully contemplate a manifest sensual contradiction, just as we cannot, as Gombrich says, "strictly speaking, watch ourselves having an illusion" (*Art* 6). We are mentally unequipped for the persistence of indeterminacy—successful survival dictates that we make up our minds—and are inclined to impose interpretations. And at the moment where pure perception gives way to the mechanism of reflection and interpretation, the mind can usually provide the safety of nomenclature, context, irony, or any of its many forms of distantiation that are inimical to the grotesque. Yet the grotesque does not become impotent in the face of reason; even when the critical faculties are engaged, Frederick Burwick finds, the imagination may restore the grotesque: "The very tension between the disbelieving reason and the excited imagination may heighten the grotesque" (15). The theatre makes particular use of this believing disbelief; as action-in-time, "rehearsing its disappearance," it holds, as I hope to show, both a special aesthetic license and a structural preference for the grotesque.

As for historical variability, the grotesque in concept and affective response shows itself subject to ongoing revision over time. It may resolve itself in a change of cultural assumptions or the substitution of one historical discourse by the next—indeed, this type of radical revision increasingly seems to take place within a single life span. The grotesque, one could say, is often an unrecognized reality, or a necessary but latent possibility of reality.

The process of revolutionary revision is a systemic quality of the sciences, as Thomas Kuhn has demonstrated in *The Structure of Scientific Revolutions.* In his "Discourse on Language," Michel Foucault calls Gregor Mendel, the pioneer of genetic science, "a true monster" to his time because he "was not *dans le vrai* (within the true) of contemporary biological discourse" (*Archaeology* 224). Mendel's ideas, in other words, were monstrous, grotesque to his contemporaries, who had no thoughts to think them in. What is true for Mendel is doubly so for Charles Darwin.

But other examples indicate the converse—what is not grotesque to a certain age may become so for another. The nightmarish paintings of Bosch have come to epitomize visions of the grotesque for us only because we lack familiarity with their iconic vocabulary and do not necessarily share the moral assumptions of the artist and his medieval constituency. There is evidence that our modern (mis)reading of Bosch is very much at odds with his original intentions and that what arouses in us a sense of the grotesque, like the Hell scenario in *The Garden of Earthly Delights,* may have been designed to inspire a satisfaction with just punishment meted out for the flagrant display of sinning shown in the central tableau of the same painting. To all appearances, Bosch was not so much a complex, troubled visionary as a stern moralist, and his prominence in the canon of the grotesque may be due, as Kayser frankly admits, to "our ignorance" (181). If this is so, it is a productive ignorance and one that need not be discounted. For while we look at Bosch differently than did his original clientele, our own reading is no less valid; we are simply addressing a grotesque pertinent to our own cultural disposition.

But there is an even lower and more fundamental structure of epistemological treachery that has not yet been addressed. That is, not only do the objects in our pool of grotesques constantly change but also the very sense of what it means to call something grotesque is unceasingly evolving. To assert that there is something "essentially" or "immutably" grotesque would be to fly in the face of that historicist criticism that sees art as the outcome of an ever-changing interplay of social and intellectual forces. I have no quarrels with that position; indeed, the notion of the changing form and purpose of grotesque representations informs this study. To say that there are reappearing structures in which this mode expresses itself, or that it is predominant at times of historical rupture, is entirely consistent with the idea of its contingency. We do well to recognize with Roland Barthes that the dichotomy between formalist analysis and historical criticism is a false one and that "the specific study of forms does not in any way contradict the necessary principles of totality and History" (*Mythologies* 112). Grotesqueness—if the seeming paradox must then be expressed—is both historically indifferent and historically particular.

"Incongruity" and violent contradiction are often tagged as fundamental strategies of the grotesque. As common sense tells us, there is no stable quality of incongruity and contradiction, because they are invariably tied, in an oppositional relation, to whatever is regarded as congruous and conventional. This in turn is regulated by the governing rules of a society's discourses (its *episteme,* in Foucault's familiar term), so that in consequence, when an age reaches a point of discontinuity or rupture in which it rearranges the rules of these discourses, it is quite possible that what was previously mutually exclusive is thrust into a taxonomic proximity that erases all sign of grotesqueness and that, conversely, previously sympathetic elements are divorced into widely heterogenous fields of order.

Any rapidly evolving discourse, such as social politics or the *système de la mode,* is quite an unstable or superficial grotesque, and its emphasis will be strongly satirical or caricaturistic. That grotesque, on the other hand, which constitutes itself from discourses that undergo few, if any, shifts and to which we might ascribe a deeper, more "archetypal" quality that appears nearly inviolable or intangible (human life and body, blood relations, and the like) is closer to the hypothetical "core" of grotesqueness—a core that exists only as a modulating field, for, as we can assume with some certainty, there is nothing truly static. We may call these two distinct variants the "weak" and the "strong" grotesque, although they will almost invariably be found in shadings and mixtures. Some of the strongest grotesques touch on those archetypes in which the holy or sacrosanct is inscribed: mother and child, the suffering Christ, and so on.

Obviously, in the perception of the grotesque, a stable and a less stable discourse can contextualize each other according to the preoccupations of the age. In the case of the Renaissance *grottesche,* the harmony of the natural order and the integrity of the body (a stable discourse) superseded the ornamental fashion (a transitory discourse) to produce, in their violation, a "strong" grotesque in some Renaissance minds. To us, these *grottesche* are "weak" grotesques because our predilection to read art as allegory is diminished; thus, they primarily signify as ornaments rather than herald a rupture in the order of existence. We recall that these grotesques were perceived as disturbing because they mingled stylized foliage with human and animal shapes. It takes an unshakable faith in natural (or God-given) hierarchies to be perturbed merely by the juxtaposition of distinct categories of living things. As far as we can see, these grotesques had no determinate meaning whatsoever; they were merely playful and fanciful. It is not that they were meaningless per se (there is surely no such thing) but that they teased an allegorical, heraldic, or metaphorical reading and yielded no satisfying response to this approach. And in the age of rigid decorum and abundant, even obtrusive, allegory, the simple absence of concrete signification became grotesque.

The Grotesque Is/Is Not the Postmodern

As inhabitants of postmodernity, on the other hand, we are disconcerted by other things: our tolerance for interpretational difficulties is considerably higher. We perhaps possess, in the familiar term of John Keats, a greater "negative capability," that is, a higher mental resistance to the disorderly. Ours is an age in which the multiperspectivity of cubist art or the mind-bending paradoxes of quantum mechanics have become pop clichés, accepted with a passing nod and no longer disruptive to our thought process. Our mental safety sometimes seems to have become nearly impregnable to an aesthetic challenge. The Nietzschean "transvaluation of values," the Herculean project of early modernity, seems no longer possible. There is much to be said for the notion that the postmodern sensibility is wholly inhospitable to the perception of the grotesque because it has systematically leveled hierarchies of meaning and values to create a cultural pastiche of universal equivalence (or indifference), a carnival of non-essentiality, in which the quotation mark reigns supreme. Or, to return to the arguments of Baudrillard, reality has been replaced wholesale by its simulation:

> The reality of simulation is unendurable—more cruel than Artaud's Theatre of Cruelty, which was still an attempt at a dramaturgy of life, the last flickering of an ideal of the body, blood and violence in a system already sweeping towards a reabsorption of all the stakes without a trace of blood. For us the trick has been played. All dramaturgy, and even all real writing of cruelty has disappeared. Simulation is master, and nostalgia, the phantasmal parodic rehabilitation of all lost referentials, alone remain. (72)

It has become exceedingly difficult, if not impossible, to produce the artistic stimulus, that "writing of cruelty," that will yield the grotesque response. Popular culture, having absorbed and commodified the rebellious impulses of various sub- and countercultures, now delivers an incessant drone of vacuous scandal and transgression as norm: a culture where androgyny and body-piercing, relegated only thirty years ago to the margin of the freak shows, have become markers of suburban chic. In much of popular culture, the true grotesque has been supplanted or partially erased by products of a "false," conventionalized grotesque that supplies grinning terror as a superficial thrill—to wit, the nearly unending stream of identically plotted horror, slasher, and chainsaw massacre movies—crudely perverted wish-fulfillment fantasies in which critical thinking is not awakened but anesthetized. Mark Edmundson, in his recent *Nightmare on Main Street,* is only one of a number of cultural critics who diagnose America's malady as an addiction to the Gothic, or rather to the twin currents of Gothic shock and promises of facile transcendence, in an effort to stave off that most unwelcome threat to late consumer culture: uncertainty, confusion, the encounter with the grotesque. Writes Edmundson:

> With the Gothic, we can tell ourselves that we live in the worst and most barbaric of times, that all is broken never to be mended, that things are bad and fated to be, that significant hope is a sorry joke, the prerogative of suckers. The Gothic, dark as it is, offers epistemological certainty; it allows us to believe that we've found the truth. (68)

Are we unshockable, or have our criteria merely adapted themselves to a new ethical habitat? Perhaps the grotesque needs for its survival the kind of force that is now unachievable solely through the aesthetic experience, and I will argue that transcending the limits of mere representation is a common factor in many instances of the grotesque. Since we often cannot muster the requisite naïveté (being seen as naive, writes Edmundson, was "one of the worst things to be in '90s culture" [36]), our perception of the grotesque in art may often be pious pretense or historical reminiscence ("I *should* feel shocked/confounded/uneasy here") rather than honest response. Having witnessed much performance art meant to elicit such shock, critic Cynthia Carr reveals that often, "'transgressive' performances do nothing for [her] personally, and shock for the sake of shock does nothing at all" (157).

Just as one might argue that the postmodern excludes the grotesque because it can no longer perceive it as grotesque, one might be tempted to declare the postmodern identical to the grotesque, under the theory that they share their most salient feature, the willful mixture of antithetical terms and objects. After all, postmodernism "veers toward open, playful, optative, provisional . . . , disjunctive, or indeterminate forms, a discourse of ironies and fragments, a 'white ideology' of absences and fractures, a desire of diffractions, an invocation of complex, articulate silences" (Hassan 93–94). In its disjunctive nature, its emphasis on play, its often radically ironic stance, its apparent self-subversion (or what Ihab

Hassan calls "the impulse of self-unmaking" [86]), the grotesque seems at home in the postmodern. Is the grotesque then the postmodern?

On the contrary, it would seem to me that the notion of postmodernity as a pervasive supertext of the age is largely an academic conceit that responds to a thoroughly commodified social environment. If the postmodern condition, roughly, is marked by the absence of the genuine and the breakdown of a determinate relationship of signs and meanings, the presence of grotesque works is a sure sign (if such a thing exists) that this condition obtains only superficially. One of the fundamental assumptions of this study, then, is that the grotesque is indeed still an active mode of the aesthetic experience and, moreover, a necessary one. More than that, grotesque art—*ex negativo*—recovers a quality postmodernity is thought to have all but obliterated: an ethical sense (even if the very term "ethics" has sometimes become an embarrassment to the academy).

This does not simplify the theory of the grotesque. Arthur Clayborough has noted (without apparent dismay) that "[i]n theory . . . there is nothing which might not be regarded as grotesque from some standpoint" (109). The sheer quantity of examples will inevitably frustrate the extrapolation of a master concept (that is, how is the grotesque, "grotesqueness," as a field of signification, described; what are its irreducible requisites; what are its culturally predicated variables?). The profusion of possible examples and shades of meaning demands that critical sacrifices be made and delineations established so as to decide which phenomena to welcome into the term and which to exclude.

How to articulate these criteria of inclusion and exclusion has long been a chief topic of criticism about the grotesque. The case is far more complex than Peter Fingesten will have us believe when he suggests that form and subject matter "must come together in a very specific manner" in the genuine grotesque, all other manifestations being but "quasi-grotesques" (420). That is, he suggests that a work of art—or a play, or a performance—cannot be grotesque if its form is not appropriate to its content. But especially in drama with its strong generic strictures, I hope to show that the mutual *inappropriateness* (or impropriety) of content and form, a damaged dialectic, is often the sign of the grotesque.

It follows that writing about the grotesque is largely an exercise in exclusion, although by no means an arbitrary one. That holds true for this study as well: although there are many incidents of performance and many more plays that might qualify for discussion in this context, I have resisted the temptation to be encyclopedic and have instead emphasized the analysis of selected works and forms that seem to me to point to the most specific and interesting problems of the grotesque in theatre and performance. Quite deliberately, readings of canonical works *(The Bacchae, Titus Andronicus, Ubu Roi, Hamletmachine)* are counterposed to interpretations of noncanonical works (*The Tutor, Chronicles of Hell, AC/DC,* and others). This means for some readers that they will most likely be missing their favorite dramatic grotesque and for others that they will object to the occasional obscurity of my choice of subjects or my frequent reliance (which as a lapsed Germanist I freely concede) on sources from the Central European dramatic traditions.

The grotesque, as I have said, has no historically indifferent, precast form; as such it is in direct opposition to whatever is regarded as classical, eternal. This fluidity has made it practically inaccessible to a literary criticism bent on proper factual reasoning: there was no language for the grotesque. There still is none, for the grotesque dodges language, but it can be surrounded by terms. Thus, this study employs a polyglot criticism, encouraged by the steps toward interdisciplinarity in the humanities that have made every humanist a specialist in his own field by virtue of being a scavenging dilettante in every other. The languages of gestalt psychology, anthropology, psychoanalysis, genre theory, tropology, dramatic analysis, and even theology are invoked here at different times, all to shed light on the recesses of the grotesque, none ultimately to be proposed as the single key.

There are four main parts to the book, each with a particular emphasis. In the first chapter, the grotesque is interrogated primarily as a visual mode, concentrating on perception and the body, monstrous and carnivalesque, in their performative aspects. The second is theoretical in outlook, both inventorying critical approaches to the grotesque and establishing the outlines of a theory with regard especially to the generic properties of drama. In the third chapter, the emphasis is on the classical theatre as it is threatened with self-consumption when grotesque structures intrude into the tragic form. The fourth chapter concentrates entirely on the postclassical theatre, from the modernist trope of the *Kunstfigur* to the characterology of the grotesque. Finally, the conclusion attempts to unravel the paradox of the grotesque theatre.

What is a monster? A being whose duration is incompatible with the existing order.
—Denis Diderot, *Elements of Physiology*

1 The Sense of Disorder
Art, the Body, and Performance

The Perils of Perception

> Supposing a painter chose to put a human head on a horse's neck, or to spread feathers of various colours over the limbs of several different creatures, or to make what in the upper part is a beautiful woman tail off into a hideous fish, could you help laughing when he showed you his efforts?

This is how Horace opens his *Art of Poetry,* urging the neophyte artist to steer clear of "sick man's dreams" and "idle fancies" (79). The type of laughable incongruity Horace hopes his adherents can avoid in the composition of verse—one to which we might attach, *avant la lettre,* the term "grotesque"—is poignantly invoked as a series of disjointed images focusing on the disturbed integrity of the body and on the impermissible amalgamation of human and beast. But roughly a century later, just such ridiculous monstrosities sprang from the painters' brushes onto the walls of Augustan buildings in Pompeii and Rome. Vitruvius, in his *De Architectura,* grimly castigates what he perceives as flagrant decorative aberrations, complaining of a plethora of odd formations "without rhyme or reason." He sees strangely shaped leaves and columns grow into animal heads and figures, mingling the organic with the architectural with previously unimaginable license, and exclaims:

> Such things . . . never existed, do not now exist, and shall never come into being. For how can the stem of a flower support a roof, or a candelabrum pedimental

> sculpture? How can a tender shoot carry a human figure, and how can bastard forms composed of flowers and human bodies grow out of roots and tendrils?[1] (qtd. in Kayser 20)

Here, we are at the heart of the classicist fallacy that what cannot be may not be, a view the grotesque is destined to clash with across the ages. The point is that these "bastard forms" *can* grow exactly where they *do* grow, namely in ornamental representation. (Vitruvius compares these supposed miscarriages of proper taste to the low satyric style of drama, which recalls Tertullian's later diatribes against the stage on similar grounds of "untruthfulness.")

A third text voicing eloquent dismay at the disorder created by the grotesque stems from the twelfth century. Even before the Augustan *grottesche* had been rediscovered and sparked a fashion, Romanesque stonemasons decorating the cloisters and churches of the High Middle Ages had dreamt up a style of decoration that gave free rein to the imagination and that bears witness to the irrepressibility of the grotesque impulse. In a climate given to pious introspection, though, such extravagance seemed frivolous and pointless, and so the learned St. Bernard of Clairvaux, in a letter to an abbot, demanded:

> [W]hat is the point of such ridiculous monstrosity, the strange kind of shapeless shapeliness, of shapely shapelessness? . . . You can see many bodies under one head, and then again one body with many heads, here you see a quadruped with a serpent's tail, here a fish with the head of a quadruped. Here is a beast which is a horse in front but drags half a goat behind, here a horned animal has the hindquarters of a horse. In short there is such a variety and such a diversity of strange shapes everywhere that we may prefer to read the marbles rather than the books. (qtd. in Gombrich, *Sense* 255)

St. Bernard's ascetic sentiment, informed by scholastic dialectics and a certain clandestine pleasure in description, is less censorious than amazed at the sheer teeming variety of disorder, and it pays indirect homage to the diverting and engrossing force of strangeness that is apt to take the monastic mind off books (and the rules and limitations inscribed in them). How little weight his admonition was subsequently to carry can be seen in a review of the Romanesque and Gothic sculptural art of the High and late Middle Ages, which seems to breed fantastic beasts and gargoyles in every cornice and crevice, with demons and chimeras leering from portals, buttresses, arches, and spires.[2] In antiquity, the chimera itself symbolized, as Paul Diel explains, the externalization of the peril of "imaginative exaltation" that dwelt inside every human mind. The chimera is thus synonymous with the perverse imagination (9). Creative exuberance and aesthetic anarchy are inseparable from the medieval grotesque, which in Frances Barasch's words "represents an expression of imaginative freedom that was not permitted in other art forms of the period" ("Definitions" 60). It took Renaissance boldness for Sir Philip Sidney to declare the poet's very prerogative as making things "quite anew, forms such as were never in nature, as the Heroes, Demigods, Cyclops, Chimeras, Furies, and such like," his freedom roaming the "zodiac of his own wit" (23).

Still, the classical and medieval revulsion against manifestations of the grotesque must seem excessive in light of the marginality of the grotesque and its unquestionable dialectical role in affirming the power of the center—quite literally so, for many late medieval breviaries, prayer books, and books of hours were illuminated by imaginative artists with strange shapes and demons in the margins, as a sort of running commentary and counterpoint to the text proper. Such illustration is the product of a period that was prepared to accommodate expressive insubordination and teasing drollery between the printed letters and the fringes of the book, because the center of signification (the sacred text) was so persuasive and incontrovertible that its power was enhanced, not diminished, its sublimity exalted, not tainted, by these miniatures. Michael Camille notes that these marginal illustrations, many of which are notably grotesque and preoccupied with the body, served a function similar to the (equally marginal) medieval theatre: in both "the body becomes an amorphous changing shape, a signifier of difference, transforming people's notions about boundaries and roles" (192). In Martin Schöngauer's famous sixteenth-century engraving of the temptation of St. Anthony, the seemingly airborne saint hovers in the center of the drawing, assailed but unfazed by a host of repugnantly monstrous spirits around him. The picture's very structure recaptures the admiration of that age for the immovable holy center of virtue that renders demonic temptation marginal and impotent (just as Salvador Dali's treatment of the same subject, in which the saint is squeezed, prostrate, to the edge of the frame by overpowering apparitions, may stand for the loss of faith in the modern age).

However, Horace, Vitruvius, and St. Bernard are also keenly aware that the pictorial is always in some sense a threat to the real, that image-making, as E. H. Gombrich observes, "is beset with dangers. One false stroke and the rigid mask of the face may assume an evil leer. Strict adherence to conventions alone can guard against such dangers" (*Meditations* 8). The exposure to the grotesque calls the entire conceit of perception into question by breaking down its sensual and intellectual components and manifesting its attendant fragility. Far from being a simple transaction in which an objective external reality meets the *tabula rasa* of the individual mind, perception turns on a complex and as yet incompletely understood set of preexisting conceptual frameworks, visual schemata, assumptions, and expectations, constructing reality as much as perceiving it.

A degree of orderliness in the environment is necessary for the orientation, well-being, and, ultimately, survival of any life-form; where it is not already supplied by nature, the mind must generate it by implicit patterning or volition. The desire to produce orderly arrangements, says Rudolf Arnheim, "is inbred by evolution" (*Entropy* 3). If this is so, the challenge of aggravated disorder would seem not only to elicit severe discomfort but also to engage—even in some remote and rationalized form—the archaic mechanism of self-preservation as well. The mind craves order and takes quite violent exception to chaos if its limits of tolerance are overstepped. Arnheim cites experiments by Else Frenkel-Brunswik that found that "people whose social insecurity made them demand clear group distinctions were disturbed by a set of line-drawings in which a cat gradually changed into a dog" (*Toward* 103). The disharmonic creations of the grotesque provoke such vituperation in Horace, Vitruvius, and St. Bernard because they resist, in effect, any effort at classification. The unclassifiable is ominous and must be laughed or ruled out of existence.

Cognitive psychology suggests that art's intellectual purpose as a mode of order-production is complemented by its emotional function of tension-reduction. In *Psychology and the Arts,* H. and S. Kreitler observe that a spectator seeks out a work that produces tension but anticipates a final reduction of tension as her state of diffuse, cue-less arousal before her confrontation with the work is aesthetically refocused (Crozier and Chapman 12). The seeming contradiction, of first inducing tension to obtain relaxation, stems from the fact that the simplest, least tension-laden visual structure would tend to be the one with the highest degree of homogeneity or entropy and that in art this natural trend toward the entropic and redundant must be counterbalanced by what Arnheim calls the "anabolic establishment of a structural theme" (*Entropy* 52)—what the work is "about." We might say that a harmonious (or "beautiful") work of art reduces tension, not by negating, but by "thematizing" it; the anabolic component supplies the necessary classificatory knowledge. One of the earliest systematic theoreticians of the grotesque, Heinrich Schneegans, attributes to the "monstrous impossibility" of the grotesque an unresolved "feeling of aversion" (29). In other words, the grotesque work of art does not seem to contain the anabolic tendency, conceived as a "pattern of forces" (Arnheim, *Entropy* 33), in equal and ordinate measure. A glance at almost any drawing by Francisco Goya or James Ensor will reveal how the tension generated by the work is uncompensated by an indwelling clarity of structure and referentiality; an uncomfortable surplus of tension remains.

In *The Object of Performance,* Henry M. Sayre has made a useful distinction in an attempt to classify the types of ambiguity typically found in modern and postmodern works of art: he distinguishes between undecidability ("the undecidable is a function of the audience—the myriad responses the audience is capable of recognizing as the potentialities of the work") and indeterminacy ("the indeterminate is a function of the work itself, its internal contradictions and ambiguities") (26). The grotesque, whether in art or in performance, I would argue, resides typically in the first category, not the second. A merely indeterminate work allows the perceiver to dismiss it outright, to refuse engagement. The undecidable work, on the other hand, has moved past this first screening; the problem is no longer that of the work but is the *audience's problem.* It cannot be dismissed because it is not simply "outside" or "objective." I would suggest that any instance of performance is at its core undecidable and thus distinct from any other aesthetic experience. As David George (who prefers the term "ambiguity") explains, "[A]ll performances create a here which is not 'here,' a now which is not 'now,' restlessly slicing time and space into layers of 'difference'" (74). It is precisely because performance is a "problem" for the audience on a perceptual level that the theatre and the theatre's ritual precedents have resorted to such conscientious framing of the performance event in time and space and depend on an act of volition to minimize the extent of undecidability, demanding, in Samuel Taylor Coleridge's familiar phrase, "the willing suspension of disbelief."

But the process of aesthetic perception is far more complicated than functional reductions would have us believe. The human intellect is not helplessly at the mercy of an apparently undecidable aesthetic structure, and the grotesque is typically a transitory phenomenon that unfolds its greatest force in the initial confrontation.

In the terms of information theory, representations with the lowest degree of informational redundancy lend themselves most easily to the occurrence of the grotesque. The grotesque gravitates toward a state of zero-redundancy; this corresponds naturally to the greatest amount of surprise. It is instrumental to survival for the mind to rest assured that most of the world is highly redundant most of the time. Such economy of comprehension is built into, for instance, a frog's eye, which detects the movement of prey only. The grotesque thwarts this project purposely; it bars itself from rapid comprehension and categorization by proving strongly disorderly (though not random) in the initial stages of perception. We are alarmed and even vaguely threatened, as Frenkel-Brunswik's insecure subjects are, or as the frog would be if it suddenly saw the world turning.[3] But in this equation, a low factor of redundancy and a high factor of surprise (or "improbability") are tantamount to an abundance of information and thus to an increase of "knowledge" (which is clearly an inappropriate way of describing what transpires when we read Kafka or look at Bosch for the first time). It becomes quite apparent that such a simple algorithm, or indeed the lean terminology of information theory itself, will not do the trick of unlocking the grotesque response.

The act of seeing, as indeed all aesthetic perception, is a temporal and complex act. Perception is informed by what Gombrich calls a "prognostic character" of inference based on an inborn "sense of order," according to which the visual image is scanned with a host of specific expectations and frames of reference assembled from experience and necessity, which will allow the subject to eliminate indeterminacy (*Sense* 107). When we speak of a painter "leading the eye," we are aware that each picture has one or several obligatory paths that the viewer's gaze must follow to extract its information coherently. Indeed, physical eye-movement analysis testifies to the fact that our perceptions are constructed through an integration of discrete samples of the picture and are biased toward the "loaded" parts of the picture in which the most useful information can be accumulated—we read an image very much like a text.

Part of this act of reading is the expectation that the content of the margin does not contradict the center. While an image or object is being scanned, the center and the periphery are indeterminate, one becoming the other and vice versa. The rapid succession of such momentary glances will form the overall cognitive concept, which then clarifies the structural center of the thing at hand (which is a result, we may assume, of its anabolic components). But as Bernard de Clairvaux or our other classical authorities scan the objects of their concern, their gaze is rebuked. The eye is misled, not led. Horace's legitimate expectation that a beautiful woman's top half may end in a bottom half of the same species is painfully contradicted. The margin mocks the center, and the center cannot hold: "There is nothing to hold on to, nothing fixed, the *deformitas* is hard to 'code' and harder still to remember, for everything is in flux" (Gombrich, *Sense* 256).

The constructional flaw in the human perceptual apparatus may well be the fact that perception is necessarily sequential, that we can only perceive in time, even if the object of perception is static; there is, so to speak, a "perception gap" between our knowledge of the phenomenal presence of an object and our full recognition of its visual qualities. This disparity will not usually come into play in aesthetic perception because the static object will "hold still" until it is fully identified. We habitually, instinctively flesh out the imperfections of our straining senses with a number of guiding hypotheses as to what we will perceive—intellectual anticipation fills in the perception gap. In aesthetic perception, this behavior is justified and even accommodated by the generic properties of the objects—indeed, anticipating the ways in which pictorial or poetic genres constitute the representation (and thus construct perception) is an important element of our delight in art. In this there is security, as we feel our anticipation vindicated and sometimes pleasantly disappointed (or reappointed).

But when the aesthetic object wreaks havoc on the expectation, when something radically intrudes into and interferes with the closure of perception, when the "perception gap" is suddenly and painfully foregrounded and made conscious, we can almost be certain that we are in the realm of paradox and possibly of the grotesque. The perception gap becomes the space wherein the grotesque work stages itself, demanding constant negotiation from the viewer, building its dynamic tension out of its ability to artfully elude his grasp.

Much of the sensual and cognitive paradox of the grotesque is so difficult to describe and categorize because it is so "messy": there are few clearly determinate points in pictorial representation, and even fewer in literature, where we can securely grasp the moment of becoming grotesque (or of un-becoming it). Therefore, we may take as analogies pictures like those of Giuseppe Arcimboldo that are not necessarily grotesque but display very similar dynamics concerning our aesthetic behavior toward them and have the added advantage of being clearer in their ambiguity and more persistent in their paradox. The viewer of an Arcimboldo painting must make a constant choice as to which version of the picture she will accept as "reality" and is consequently put to the task that in conventional (nonambiguous) art the painter has already solved: setting priorities or privileging one version over another. When gestalt psychology posits that only one version of a drawing may be perceived at any one time to the exclusion of all other possibilities, it fails to account for that moment of uncertainty in the viewing of an Arcimboldo canvas, which Roland Barthes describes so aptly as a hesitation between coding and decoding, in which "our eyes retain the tracery of the first meanings" even as they decode the second ones: "[I]t is because everything signifies, *on two levels,* that Arcimboldo's painting functions as a rather alarming denial of pictural language" (*Responsibility* 137 and 134).

In most of the works of Arcimboldo, the choices are fairly clear; the ambiguities are, so to speak, unambiguous (without being trivial). In the image *Winter*, I am either looking at a trunk of a tree or a portrait of a man (see fig. 2). But by their construction they reveal, as Gombrich says, "the hidden complexity of all picture reading" (*Meditations* 155). Arcimboldo's art, which Barthes apostrophizes as "a kind of structural monster" (134), rests on his use of two strategies of grotesque image-making, hypertrophying and animation. With these strategies, the grotesque mode rehearses the breakdown of physical distinctions and assaults the integrity of bodies and spaces, of space and nonspace (figure and ground, ground and underground), and of the living and the dead.

Horror vacui, the term by which art critics have referred to the mania for ornamentation on archaic vases that seemed to stem from a "fear of leaving empty spaces," designates a peculiar compositional feature of

Fig. 2. Giuseppe Arcimboldo, *Winter* (1653). Kunsthistorisches Museum, Wien.

the grotesque that is already evident in the original *grottesche:* the compulsion to fill every available surface with decoration. Virtually every square inch of the walls of the Domus Aurea was ornamentally articulated, presaging a grotesque that willfully employs compositional excess to achieve its aims. Excess is the scourge of proportion and classical harmony: Aristotle, in the *Nicomachean Ethics,* calls a thing beautiful if it is not possible either to take away or to add anything. If it cannot stop growing, a thing is grotesque. Indeed, the hypertrophying of the grotesque exhibits the impulse to transcend the frame and spill into realms that are no longer aesthetically regulated or controlled.

The paintings of Hieronymus Bosch and Pieter Breughel are already filled with such a degree of detail that they create the impression of a chaotic simultaneity of life (and afterlife), but it is the mannerist and baroque impulse that caters to the fullness of excess. The result is a school of composition that overwhelms the viewer with sheer profusion: a swarming, uncontained, boundless, self-propagating disorder that in Arcimboldo's paintings Barthes calls a "*malaise* of substance" (*Responsibility* 146).

Images are not the only things capable of free proliferation. The verbal grotesque rests on a similar formal principle of accumulation. In François Rabelais's *Gargantua and Pantagruel*, we find unending hyperbolic word cascades in a deliberate parody of ostentatious learnedness and the scholastic habit of *enumeratio.* It finds its disturbing modern equivalent in the verbal fulminations and massing of epithets of certain protagonists in the plays of Michel de Ghelderode, or more famously in the wrenching logorrhea of Lucky's monologue in Samuel Beckett's *Waiting for Godot.* In the stream of an unhinged consciousness, words become detached from meaning and take hold of the speaker in a grotesque reversal of mystical utterance, and an anarchic *parole* of sound and fury displaces its *langue.* When Caryl Churchill creates a child-eating demon in her play *The Skriker,* the creature becomes doubly grotesque in its manic vaudevillian patter, speech that seems to overflow with references and puns almost to the point of self-engorgement:

> When I go uppety, follow a fellow on a dark road dank ride and jump thrump out and eat him how does he taste? toxic waste paper basket case, salmonelephantiasis, blue blood bad blue blood blad blood blah blah blah. I remember dismember the sweet flesh in the panic, tearing limb from lamb chop you up and suck the tomorrow bones. Lovely lively lads and maiden England, succulent suck your living daylights, sweet blood like seawater everywhere, every bite did you good enough as good as a feast. (31–32)

In the theatre, excess is a constant possibility; as a living thing, performance invariably strains the boundaries imposed upon it. The baroque age in particular, with its immense appetite for ornamentation and its *horror vacui,* produced a theatre of profusion. In baroque tragedy, for instance, a massing of objects often underlines the emblematic import of the plays, as when an initial stage direction in a sixteenth-century German play reads: "The stage is filled with corpses, pictures, crowns, scepters, swords. Above the stage the heavens open up, under the stage hell gapes."[4] But baroque *teatrum mundi,* in its infatuation with the great mechanical spectacle it inherits from the courts of the Renaissance, is a theatre in which the thrill of the presentation of the spectacular and teeming is counterbalanced by the thrill of containment. The intermezzi of designers like Bernardo Buontalenti or Ludovico Burnacini are a tribute both to the celebration of self-conscious scenic craftsmanship at its apex and to the overriding urge to cram the known and unknown world, storms, ships, demons, and all, into the confines of a proscenium arch and make it heed the beck and call of the master of ceremonies—*decorum vincit omnium.* The more ghastly and frightening the pageant, the more the theatre, by extension, seems in control even of those phenomena beyond the perimeter of the theatre proper, because it stands symbolic both of the social and philosophical attitudes and the instrumental *puissance* of the age.

Modern theatre has rediscovered the perils of the baroque impulse but not its comforts. In Ghelderode's *Chronicles of Hell,* the stage direction demands "piles of baroque objects" lining the walls in disarray; "heaven" is represented only by shabby portraits of clergymen, "hell" by a demonic mob in a courtyard below. The frame begins to break down; control becomes impossible. In Eugène Ionesco's entropic farce *The New Tenant,* chairs begin to fill up the entire stage and finally the world itself. But the theatre of the avant-garde is connected to this impulse of the grotesque most closely through the Artaudian demand for a "total theatre," where the theatrical performance spills into the spectatorial space—physical and sensual—until all difference is obliterated. This transgressive nature of the modern theatre will be the topic of subsequent chapters, but here we can already recognize in it a version of *horror vacui,* the hypertrophying aspect of the grotesque that often signifies the uncontrollable and monstrous and seems to belong to the mode's most archaic roots.

One of the foremost narrative strategies of fantasy and the fantastic, animation, the projection of life into inanimate objects, is a related topos. By its very nature, animation trespasses against the categorical sense of order, for it dissolves the vital difference between living and dead;

it enfranchises the dead in the realm of the living and conversely implicates the living in the realm of the dead. While this poses no problem for a fundamentally animistic or pantheistic mindset, modern Western thought is unaccustomed to it; it has set up elaborate rituals for the denial of death and clings to a fiction of instrumentality that pretends that all objects are subservient to human purpose. In this context, animation becomes the first indication of an uncanny and rebellious, grotesque universe. In grotesque animation, the object itself is invested with life and, furthermore, with a degree of menace or malevolence that presages the (demonic) revolt of things.

In the realm of objects, we instinctually, paranoically, sense an opposition to life, an unformed, erratic conspiracy, a revolution waiting daily to erupt out of triviality. Wolfgang Kayser calls this the "malice of the inanimate object," in which we find that "the small, apparently familiar things in constant use, turn out to be strange, evil, and possessed by hostile demons" (111). The pictorial vocabulary of animation owes much to Bosch, in whose canvasses things develop an independent life and march in an infernal parade of mocking and retribution against mankind, animated by a sometimes obscure moral vision as if they were allegorical actors in a hermetic morality play. It is not until the nineteenth-century French illustrator Grandville created pictures for a Swiftean satirical fantasy of the machine age that animation finds a modern form. Here, in his series of bizarreries, *Un Autre Monde* (1847), every object springs to life and, in a sudden metonymical emancipation, takes the place of its master. One particularly vivid tableau depicts steam-powered "metal musicians" or robotic instruments performing a symphony. Superficially charming, fantastical vignettes, these pictures radiate an unease with the progress of the industrial age that will finally supplant the optimism of transcendental idealism with the philosophy of alienation: the symphony played by the machine musicians is significantly called "Le Moi et le Non Moi" (The I and the Non-I), but there is no "I" to play it. In his seminal essay "Paris, Capital of the Nineteenth Century," Walter Benjamin analyzes this unease in Grandville in the context of a blossoming consumer culture:

> The enthronement of merchandise, with the aura of amusement surrounding it, is the secret theme of Grandville's art. This is reflected in the discord between its utopian and its cynical elements. Its subtleties in the presentation of inani-

> mate objects correspond to what Marx called the "theological whim" of goods. . . . [Grandville] presents them in the same spirit in which advertising—a word that is also coined at this time—begins to present its articles. He ends in madness. (*Reflections* 152)

Performing automata had created sensations in the courts and salons of the seventeenth and eighteenth centuries as privileged toys, but the nineteenth century democratized them and so reinforced in their demotic also their demonic quality: performing automata were featured in the Universal Exhibitions in Paris in 1867, 1878, and 1889. The purpose of the automata was not so much to perform a particular task (speaking or playing chess) but to perform a Cartesian drama of counterfeit being to the pleasure and awe of the "machines made of earth," as René Descartes had called humans. What fascinated spectators about them was in a sense the same unresolved contradiction of presence and absence, being and nothingness, that informs performance as such. André Pieyre de Mandiargues wrote: "In fact, I think what those people are looking for is not so much an accurate imitation of life as a kind of mask, a pretense which leans toward mockery, almost a brilliant joke produced at the expense of life, as the theatre often is for theatre-lovers" (qtd. in Beaune 474).

The anxious modern reinterpretation of this archaic mode of animist thought is surely a backlash against rationalism (and increasing rationalization), but it often uses, as in Grandville, the rational-mechanical idiom. It is no mere coincidence that the theatre of the Grand Guignol in late-nineteenth-century Paris, product of a scientific society, is simultaneously enamored of complex mechanical stage effects and pervaded with a paranoiac relation to objects. Farce provides its undergirding, but farce, properly viewed, is the dramaturgy of alienation.

This idea can further be extended to the silent film era: film is the first medium in which the object can function as an autonomous actor, and Benjamin, quoting V. I. Pudovkin, noted that film is "capable of demonstrating how matter plays tricks on man" (*Illuminations* 249 n). In the experimental scenes and films of the Italian Futurists, one finds a "Drama of Objects"—although it is unclear how one is to imagine in practice "a discussion between a foot, a hammer, and an umbrella" or a stage direction that demands that "the chairs leave the room" (Kirby and Kirby 133, 295). Of course the decontextualized object obsessed the surrealists who—taking their cue from the Comte de Lautréamont's "fortuitous meeting of a sewing machine and an umbrella on an operating table"—sought to produce, in Max Ernst's words, "the effects of a systematic bewildering" (Breton 275).

The theatre has shown the revolt of the objects in simple dystopian visions such as the robot revolution in Karel Capek's *R. U.R.*, or used the theme in a satirical manner, such as in Bertolt Brecht's *Respectable Wedding,* where the furniture collapses under the wedding guests, its glue being no better, Brecht suggests, than that which holds the general state of *petit-bourgeois* affairs together. Indeed, there is an entire quasi-genre of the "theatre of objects," as Hans Hoppe has called it, which reflects a reorganization of the traditional subject-object relation in the experience of alienation and the objectification of humans. The beginnings of these new forms of scenic action are perhaps in expressionism, but they find eloquent articulation in Ionesco, who remarks:

> Nothing is barred in the theatre: characters may be brought to life, but the unseen presence of our inner fears can also be materialised. So the author is not only allowed, but recommended to make actors of his props, to bring objects to life, to animate the scenery and give symbols concrete form. (*Notes* 28)

Animation is perhaps a particularly romantic theme; E. T. A. Hoffmann's *Sandman* may also be the quintessential narrative of mechanical animation in the early nineteenth century—and closely linked to that of galvanic animation in *Frankenstein.* As a strategy of the grotesque, animation is the obverse of that other standard of romantic grotesque iconology, the man-as-puppet, the objectified and manipulated human. In both incarnations, though, it draws on the irrational fear of becoming engulfed by an object world empowered by the ubiquitous machine that has (in a Heideggerian turn of phrase) superseded its mere "toolness."

The Body, the Face, and the Mask

We believe the sky is going to fall on our head if we meddle with the body.

—Performance artist Orlan, "I do not want to look like . . ."

If there is a single place in and upon which the grotesque sensually manifests its contradictions and to which it returns even in its most sophisticated forms, it is the body—not the body of mythical beasts, but the human body. As an icon of cultural signification, the human body has no equal. Language is pervaded by images of the body, and body-terms govern our thought. The body is the foremost image of language when it must speak of concrete wholeness, holiness, and the inviolate: the *corpus delicti;* the body politic or social; the body of Christ (in its literal resurrection, its metaphorical extension to the community of the faithful, and their symbolic ingestion of the host); bodies of water and celestial bodies.

In both Western and Eastern thought, and to a surprising degree of mutual similarity, the living body is representative of human potentialities and depravities (in the Aristotelian scheme, it is the outward material expression of the form of the soul, while the gnostics looked upon it as a demonic corruption and bestialization of the divine spirit, as a vastly inferior appendage). It is also the symbolic topos upon which the map of the cosmos is inscribed—man was widely believed to reflect the structure of cosmic creation in his physical appearance, pursuant to the general synecdochic logic of the ancient Emerald Table: "The thing that is on high is like the thing that is below." Kenneth Burke calls such representations of the macrocosm through the microcosm an "ideal synecdoche" (*Grammar* 508). Indian Vedic literature contains a mythic cosmology of the human body and describes it in terms of the caste structure, projecting the Brahmins onto the head, the warriors into the arms, and so forth, just as yogic philosophy divides the body into hierarchical "Lotus centers" (Campbell 64–65). Conversely, Platonic philosophy (in *Timaeus*) and its Neoplatonic derivatives think of the universe as a living creature with soul, body, and reason. Finally, the epistemological habits of the Middle Ages foster an emphatically allegorical view of the body as a polysemic signifier almost to the point of semantic dismemberment. The beginnings of medical science mingle with cosmology and mysticism in the sixteenth-century author Jakob Böhme's *Aurora,* in which the biblical notion of the likeness of man to God is worked out in fine detail. In Böhme's vision, the entire body in all its parts signifies heaven and earth, the interior representing the "deep between the stars and the earth," and each element attached to an organ, such as the heart to fire, the breath in the windpipe to air, and so forth (Wayman 182).

Böhme's body cosmology, one of many similar conceptions that associate the body's regions with humors, elements, continents, zodiacal signs, and planets, testifies to the centrality of the corporeal in Neoplatonic metaphysical thought up to the threshold of the modern age. But even if we accept the idea that the modern ideology of the body has permanently removed it into bourgeois subjectivity, both erasing its objective status as the synecdochic reflection of the metaphysical and displacing it as the site of unmitigated punishment, labor, and lust, I would argue that it has survived this culturally instigated repression with sufficient traces of its erstwhile ontological preeminence intact to continue to serve as the primary indicator of the kind of contradiction or alienation expressed in the grotesque. The grotesque, in other words, "embodies" its concerns quite literally; it is part of what one might call the "anthropic" character of this mode that it inscribes its tensions onto the body, confident that the body is still a symbolically mapped microcosm, even if in now faded writing. Consequently, the grotesque deformations of the body, "strong" grotesques in my sense of that term, point in some manner to deformations in the order of existence. I do not necessarily construe a causal relationship between the medieval body cosmology and the modern corporeal images of the grotesque, but I think that both practices, sometimes interdependently, advertise the immediacy and polyvalence of the signifier "body."

The grotesquely deformed body also challenges another fixed system, that of physical harmony and proportion. To fulfill the demands of total harmony, the Vitruvian body (which remained the effective model for centuries) must adhere to certain numerical proportions: the head is one-eighth of the total height; the face and the hand are one-tenth each; the foot is one-sixth; the cubit one-fourth, and so on (Arnheim, *Toward* 111–12). Resting on the principle of *congruentia,* a code of proportion and numerical relation traceable to pre-Socratic times, the ideal of the mathematically describable harmony of the body makes its strongest impression, again, on medieval aesthetics, where it naturally intersects with the notions of body cosmology. Umberto Eco believes that the desire to frame aesthetic phenomena in numerical equations (as for example in Boethius's theory of musical harmony) derives from a quest for order in a time of barbaric dissolution, ironically the very motive that the *incongruentia* of the grotesque persistently reverses (Eco 30).

For the premodern age, the harmonic perfection of the body, its "unity in variety," was living proof of the symmetry of divine creation, and physical beauty was an index of the transcendental essence of things. Thus the body was saddled with the attainment of an ideality of form that thrust it toward the eternal, just as the ephemerality of the flesh, its inevitable bulging, shriveling, and aging, pulled it toward the demise it is always already marked with. Endless allegories of *vanitas* and dance-of-death scenes manifest this intrinsic ambivalence toward the body—as the map of the universe, temple of the soul, and isomorph of divinity, but also as the seat of vices and object of corruption—which medieval philosophy was unable to resolve. Scholasticism dialectically asserted the necessity of the ugly, nonideal, and grotesque (partially because its mere existence made it part of blessed creation and therefore in a sense "beautiful," and partially because it served as a *tertium comparationis* by which true and divine beauty was exalted) but also maintained a pervasive system of moral allegory in which goodness corresponded to beauty and deformation to moral depravity. This aesthetics was divested of its moral qualities and codified in the Renaissance view of the classically harmonious and static body encapsulated in Leonardo's famous *homo quadratus* figure.

If the language of the human body is the preferred vocabulary of the grotesque, the face is its exclamation mark (being, as Antonin Artaud has put it, "an empty power, a field of death" [*Artaud Anthology* 229]). The prominence of the face as a semiotic field is no secret to art history (compare Leonardo, to whom we owe a series of "grotesque heads" and who divides the face into four distinct fields in his *Treatise on Painting*) or to the theory of acting. But it is equally important in the nonaesthetic realm. Gombrich notes that the face is among the most privileged motifs of the visual world and that we respond strongly to its variations: "Our whole perceptual apparatus is somehow hypersensitized in this direction of physiognomic vision," which may at times assume "pathological forms" (*Meditations* 6).

The inherent problem of physiognomic perception is the face's almost inextricable mixture of essential, unchanging, "eidetic" features that designate character (or its dominant "key") and the superimposed, accidental features that express momentary emotions. Classical physiognomics (as opposed to pathognomics) has always maintained this distinction and preferred the former to the latter as the "true" form of the face (Magli 90–91). (We may be able to explain the grotesque gargoyle whose face is frozen in a twisted, leering position as an inversion of this traditional hierarchy: the accidental has superseded the essential.)[5]

It is no surprise that there have been repeated attempts to systematize human expression, most notably by the court painter of Louis XIV, Charles Le Brun, who, following the logic of Cartesian mechanics, saw the face as a kind of instrument board with the mouth or the eyebrows as indicators. Gombrich calls this mechanization of the face in Le Brun's theory "chilling," which alerts us to the fact that there is a certain inviolability, even sacredness, to the image of the human visage that, when offended, generates severe emotional repercussions ("Mask" 3) . We recall Barthes's "unease" concerning Arcimboldo's portraits, which refuse to be semiotically arrested: "These composite heads are heads which are decomposing" (*Responsibility* 143).

Arnheim mentions a picture by Henri Toulouse-Lautrec, in which a figure's face in profile is cut off by the frame, and he terms this effect "disturbing" and "violent." This is no actual, physical amputation of the face but merely an unconventional intersection of the represented subject (a man) and the arbitrary limits of the representational space (the picture frame). Yet the effect is nonetheless unsettling because it violates the integrity of the face and literally constitutes an act of defacement (Arnheim, *Power* 60–61).

The "faceless man" is the protagonist of a curious but persistent subtopos of modernism, which, as Willard Bohn has remarked in a detailed study, "has exercised a strange fascination on his audience" throughout history and "continues to arouse intense emotions in readers and spectators alike" (15). For instance, a 1914 poem by Guillaume Apollinaire, *Le Musicien de Saint-Merry,* features an enigmatic "man with no eyes no nose and no ears," an image that seems to have exerted a great influence on surrealists such as Giorgio de Chirico. Bohn detects a sexual connotation (the "man," who has only a mouth and who leads a procession of prostitutes, is a "phallomorphic" [63] image, a reflection of Apollinaire's own problematic sexuality). Later, Apollinaire transformed the poem into a pantomimic scenario, *A quelle heur un train partira-t-il pour Paris?*, which contains the following stage direction:

> *The Man* with no eyes, no nose, and no ears advances slowly, entering on the right and playing his flute. He has no mouth but plays the flute through an opening in his throat covered by a rubber or metal washer, like those applied to horses following surgery on their respiratory tracts. . . . While he continues to play, various *women* gradually gather around him: a woman with no head, a woman with no arms, a blue woman, a red woman, a bald woman, a smartly dressed woman, a little girl, an old woman. (Bohn 57)

The total absence of the face is incompatible with the fully articulated human form, which challenges us to read the image as a whole and yet withholds any trace of animate humanity; the experience is primally uncanny and grotesque. Apollinaire and de Chirico identified with the faceless figures and mannequins they created, but, as Bohn notes, subsequent generations have typically had the opposite reaction, following a "general pessimistic shift in the collective modern psyche dating from the First World War" (153). This important shift will be addressed in more detail in chapter 4 when I turn to the modernist *Kunstfigur.*

The strategies of caricature have traditionally been equated with the grotesque. Caricature deals in excesses and protrusions; it is fond of violent disproportion and exaggeration of defects. The face is the caricaturist's primary target and place of operation, his physiognomic laboratory, because it is a marvel of semiotic compression: anything may be projected onto the face and everything reflected by it. The political cartoonist can, as Gombrich felicitously formulates, "mythologize the world of politics by physiognomizing it" (*Meditations* 138). The obverse of this power of revelation in the face is its susceptibility to those potent "natural metaphors" of bestialization that aim at immediate negative emotional reaction and of which the Nazi caricatures of the stereotypical Jew made such disconcertingly effective use.

But one cannot simply assume that caricature and the grotesque are completely synonymous. Although they share common strategies of deformation, there is a distinct difference in attitude. Caricature is a game with the possibilities of physiognomic expression and a (clandestine) love affair with its object, which it teases into extremity. It needs a certain degree of intimacy with its target, a form of symbiosis. As opposed to the grotesque, caricature may initially defamiliarize its subject, but it never radically estranges it. Its very mission is to produce the typical and epitomic, the immediately recognizable and categorizable; its exaggerations and deformations are not disquieting but, on the contrary, reassuring, for they feed a repetitious iconic-metaphorical vocabulary of political and social discourse.

The producer of caricature may still produce the grotesque—many of Goya's works walk a fine line. Honoré Daumier, too, was an artist whose work had emancipated itself from humor and whose creations, in Charles Baudelaire's opinion, were "often terrifying in their intensity" (Gombrich, *Art* 355). Elsewhere Baudelaire calls caricature "double: the drawing and the idea; the drawing is violent, the idea biting and veiled." To this aggressive double signification, he concludes, the uninitiated mind must react with "uneasiness," even "fear" (Baudelaire 145). Primarily, however, the object of caricature is to expose its referents in search of a consensus, and it assumes that its audience is sophisticated enough to be in on the joke. The grotesque, in theory at least, renders its audience unsophisticated in the initial encounter; this is a great part of its effect. Thus, the projects of caricature and the grotesque are fundamentally at cross-purposes.

The use of the animal metaphor in the depiction of the face is a preferred method of caricature and satire, which draws on an established typology of human traits and similar presumed characteristics in animals. As a literary method (for example, in Ben Jonson's *Volpone* or Jean de la Fontaine's *Fables*), this is unproblematic so long as the analogy is conventionally stable, but this *homme-bête* trope has a second, deeper level that questions human identity in the mirror of the beast. Patrizia Magli observes: "It is a paradoxical situation, for if man can recognize himself through the animal, the latter returns man to animality at the very moment in which its form surfaces in a recognizable way on a human face" (100). Wherever hierarchical categories of order (animal realm, realm of man) come so perilously close as to intersect, the grotesque can make an inroad. Immanuel Kant attributes "revulsion" to those incidents of behavior where we see "the animal too much protruding from the human" (Burwick 47).

An illustration in J. C. Lavater's *Physiognomische Fragmente* (1775–78) gives a good example of the status of the grotesque as an intercategorical mode, shown through the metamorphosis of the face (see fig. 3). In twenty-four steps, the drawings chart an (imaginary) sequence of development from a frog's head to the head of the *Apollo Belvedere.* Here we can very much catch the grotesque in the making, as it were, in that space where the head has ceased to be a frog but has not yet become a human head, producing several strange intermediary creatures that display both human and reptilian features but cannot be resolved into either category. The drawing makes it easy to discern exactly the moments of transition, and it calls attention to the precise elements that contribute first to the dissolution and subsequently to the restoration of the sense of order as we follow the shift from batrachian monstrosity to hideous human and then to god. The sequence is of course meant not as a study of biological evolution but as a pictorial experiment that confirms Lavater's ideas about the "line of animality."

If read against its flow, from god to frog (as Grandville did in a famous parody), the sequence also demonstrates quite well the coincidence

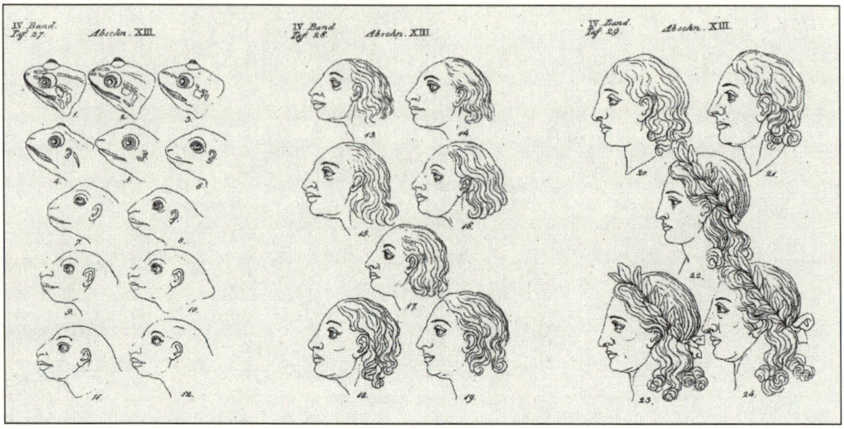

Fig. 3. J. C. Lavater, Physiognomic study. From J. C. Lavater, *Physiognomik: Zur Beförderung der Menschenkenntnis und Menschenliebe* (Wien, 1829).

of the grotesque with what one could call "lower-order intrusions," the usurpation of a higher order within a discourse by an incontrovertibly lower, or inferior, one. For Lavater and his contemporaries, Apollo represents the apex of ideality in the discourse of physiognomy, which is here eroded and corrupted by an inferior species of fauna. Ironically, Lavater's imaginative morphology sets out to prove the categorical discrepancy between the species and accomplishes precisely the opposite.

In the seventeenth century, Charles Le Brun conceived a number of famous physiognomic studies in which he contrasted animal and human heads, emphasizing their characteristic similarities. His "three eagle heads and three human heads in relation to the eagle" is a fine example, translating, in a half-playful way, the eagle's beak into the "aquiline" features of a vaguely Roman-looking youth (see fig. 4). Yet Le Brun succumbs to a remarkable reversal, which Jurgis Baltrusaitis brings to our attention in his essay on animal physiognomy. The animals, notes Baltrusaitis, are drawn from life, vigorously and with Le Brun's characteristically superb draftsmanship, even though they display a marked element of human intelligence.

> The men, on the other hand, are strongly bestialized, their features enlarged and deformed. . . . Yet the heads are not overdone, they are not caricatures. It is very seriously done. . . . Through this demanding and methodical transfiguration we arrive at an equivocal humanity that is tinged with something evil and terrible, a humanity that escapes words or understanding. (Baltrusaitis 22)

Fig. 4. An engraving after Charles Le Brun by André Legrand, *Three eagle heads and three human heads in relation to the eagle* (c. 1820). Réunion des Musées Nationaux/Art Resource, New York.

Le Brun's drawings, to the modern eye, seem to partake of both a fascination with and a fear of that unthinkable—"grotesque"—idea that Charles Darwin later systematized: that the dogma of a separate creation of man and beast, which had been central to medieval and early Renaissance thought, was indeed untenable; that the literary *homme-bête* trope (of which the animal fable is a benign subcategory) was more than a moral metaphor; that there was forensic evidence of the beastliness of man. Le Brun seems to contemplate that notion playfully, but he has transgressed the threshold separating man and beast, and there appears a portent of the terror and revulsion this vision will evoke in times to come.[6]

The sculptor Rubek of Henrik Ibsen's last play, *When We Dead Awaken,* a character himself endowed with grotesque vision, is an accomplice in spirit to Le Brun. He fashions portrait busts of his wealthy patrons, insinuating behind the "striking likeness" of the sitter qualities only he can see, "something hidden, something sinister":

> [D]own at the deepest core are respectable and worthy horse faces and the stubborn muzzles of mules—lop-eared, low-browed dog skulls, and pampered pig snouts—and every so often, the heavy, brutal semblance of a bull. . . . All the animals that human beings have distorted in their own image. And that have distorted human beings in return. (1036)

Gaston Bachelard seems best to pinpoint the shift in the *homme-bête* trope when, in discussing the bestiary of Lautréamont's *Maldoror,* he writes: "La Fontaine has written of human psychology in the form of an animal fable, but Lautréamont has written an inhuman fable by reviving those brutal impulses that are still potent in men's hearts" (3).

The incursion of the animal into the human realm as a disturbing other is catalyzed by the fundamental anthropocentricity of traditional art and discourse that with Darwin begins to see a revision in the direction of a "biocentric" discourse, as Margot Norris calls it. Biocentricity describes a phase of modernism in which the critique of the anthropocentric ideology found expression in the works of certain artists and writers (Friedrich Nietzsche, Franz Kafka, Ernst, D. H. Lawrence) who appropriated the voices and gestures of beasts to announce their own scandalous animality. Such art subverts the entire duality of culture and nature, human and creature, consciousness and instinct, thinking and being—in short, the formative undergirding of the kind of rational-scientific system the Enlightenment had sanctioned—and creates strategies that allow "the animal, the unconscious, the instincts, the body, to speak again" (Norris 5). But biocentricity also throws the doors open to the forces of dehumanization, to "pure peril and shuddering risk," for as José Ortega y Gasset remarks, the tiger "cannot be detigered," but man is "always on the point of not being man" (Ortega 190). This is the art of the grotesque.

The theatre has historically preferred to translate the face into the mask. In the mask, the face is doubled and denied in a peculiar dialectic; the mask "always points to two subjects, namely the one it means and the one it conceals" (Fischer-Lichte, *Semiotik* 1:108). Through the mask, character is strengthened and defined to the point of complete unambiguity. At the same time, the actor is engaged in a constant struggle with the mask. Patrice Pavis writes:

> The mask fixes an essential part of the body, forbidding it to speculate on physical and psychological modifications. In contrast, however, other parts of the body are freed; at the same time, we are free to shift our eye from the carved face that looks fixedly back at us to the body and our newly aware sense of its slightest vibration. Mask and living matter unceasingly do battle until the spectator can no longer distinguish inanimate from human. (59)

Such a commingling of the animate and the inanimate—as the previous section showed—is fundamentally grotesque. Where Pavis understands the aesthetic momentum created by the masked actor as one of freedom, both for the actor's body and the observer's eye, the inevitable *agon* of living and nonliving in the mask performance has been read in the context of the neoprimitivist leanings of modernism (one need only think of the masks in paintings by Edvard Munch, Ensor, or early Pablo Picasso) as a *threat* of the mask to the face. The semiotician B. L. Ogibenin observes that the mask represents a "deformation of the traits of a human face . . . which conserves the general similarity between the mask and the face, although the entire appearance of the mask indicates that it must be understood simultaneously as another face, *opposed to the human one*" (5). In that sense, the masking of the actor recapitulates the manner in which the social mask submerges the "authentic" human face in contemporary society, a theme that preoccupied particularly the Italian movement of the *teatro grottesco.*

This conception of the mask is modern; in the word *prosopon* of the Greek theatre, the conviction still resonates of an essential identity of face and mask, actor and character. The Greek spectator would not have felt what we may feel: that the mask suppresses, even victimizes, the living actor. To be sure, I am not speaking here of some kind of melodramatic combat of the actor with his mask onstage but rather of a metaphor, embodied in the mask, that encapsulates a deep division between freedom and determinacy, the animate and the inanimate. In this spirit,

Michael Goldman compares the "uncanniness" of the mask with that of the actor: both represent "a mingling of the animate and the inanimate, a projection of human energy beyond normal bounds" (9).

Masks juxtapose beings and objects separated by differences. They are beyond differences; they do not merely defy differences or efface them, but they incorporate and rearrange them in unprecedented fashion. In short, they are an aspect of what René Girard has referred to as the "monstrous double" (*Violence* 167). Such an incident of the mask as monstrous double is recounted in Rainer Maria Rilke's *Notebooks of Malte Laurids Brigge,* one of the seminal novels of modernism, in which the protagonist tries on a disguise in front of the mirror only to be overwhelmed by it: "[It] imposed on me an image, nay, a reality, an alien, unbelievable monstrous reality, with which, against my will, I became permeated: for now it was the stronger, and it was I who was the mirror. . . . I lost all knowledge of myself, I simply ceased to exist." Geoffrey Harpham, who quotes the passage, finds in it "an exemplary fable of the act of reading" (109), but more directly it is an exemplary fable of the art of acting and its concurrent endangerment of the self. In acting's always threatening extermination of selfhood, its cannibalism of identity, there is a terror that concerns the grotesque. Consequently, two of modernism's foremost writers of the theatrical grotesque, Alfred Jarry and Yvan Goll (see chapter 4), insisted on masking their actors. For Jarry, the actor's job was to "depersonalize" himself, to let the effigy of the character take over, as if the "solid structure of the skeleton" were protruding from the "surrounding animal flesh" (Jarry, *Selected Works* 73). Goll wanted his audience, confronted by the mask's uncanniness, to "learn to scream again"; in the mask, actor and character would both cede to the play of "naked instincts" (Goll, *Dichtungen* 65, 79).

We can call the body and the face the *sine qua non* of the grotesque—if Gordon Craig wanted to refine the actor's physique to supple perfection and Beckett perhaps to abolish it altogether (leaving, as in *Not I,* the merest trace of a face), they are going against the grotesque agenda of the theatre. Precisely the body's capacity for incapacity, its deviations from the classical ideals that it both summons up and unstoppably ages away from, its jerking and stumbling and flailing in violent mockery of the harmony of the motion of the spheres, open the path for the performance and the performer of the grotesque.

Carnival and Performance

In carnival culture, the grotesque assault on the sense of order culminates; it is the performance of ordered disorder. Carnival and the saturnalian modes of literature and art align themselves with performance not only because performance is a steady component of carnival nor because both are equally subversive and transgressive within the boundaries of the permissible but also because they emphasize and indeed exhume, in their own (laughing) ambiguity, a culture's ambiguities about itself. As a "dialogic" or "heterogloss" mode (the terms that the carnival's chief theorist, Mikhail Bakhtin, applies to literary artifacts that break down the monolithic narratives of authority), carnival, like performance, will not surrender to univocal analysis. Moreover, in this nexus of carnival and performance, a reconceived, reconfigured body plays a signal role.

Michael Bristol, in a study drawing on a large body of sociological and ethnological research, concludes that the festival has three functions: its unselfconscious ritual character, its character as a durable strategy for maintaining social cohesion, and its self-conscious pragmatic character of altering the status quo (25). This last, critical aspect is represented by the carnival's master trope, its predilection for reversal. Indeed, all that seems irrevocably fixed by divine and secular order is fair game for the carnivalistic spirit. The carnival is the fitting expression of an age that tends to think in terms of analogies and sympathies, where cosmological, spiritual, and social hierarchies all partake of the same structure. As Jan Kott writes in an essay on that carnivalistic play *A Midsummer Night's Dream:*

> In "serio ludere" the top is only "mythos"; the bottom is the human condition. The signs and emblems of the bottom are the earthly probation of the signs and emblems of the top. "Venus celestis" is merely a projection, a mythical image of "amore bestiale"—the untamed libido. . . . Having its origins in Saturnalia, "serio ludere" is a festive "parodia sacra." (38)

"Top" and "bottom" being thus connected, carnival finds its sport in their reversal and a play on their inherent ambiguity. Typically, this temporary upset and inversion of values will include the roles of the sexes, political and ecclesiastical authority, social identity, and even language. Numerous carnival traditions feature analogous practices to "misrule." A pronounced incidence of inversion is the Feast of Fools, which is, though not strictly carnival, certainly a "carnivalistic" affair. On such occasions, even the minor clergy would turn the tables on their employers by electing a Pope of Fools from among their ranks, dressing him in garments turned inside out and celebrating a gibberish mass (Tuchman 32). As the grotesque springs from an inversion of standards, there is a tendency to include such expressions of medieval misrule and carnival in discussions of the grotesque, particularly the greatly popular topoi of the *mundus inversus,* or "world upside down." Here we typically see a wife bossing her husband around, children acting like parents, horses on top of their riders, pigs in pulpits, and the like.

In truth, as may be seen from a comprehensive collection of such topoi in illustration (Lever and Tristan), the *mundus inversus* motif tends to be almost tiresomely repetitive; only a handful of inverted relationships compose the canon. They are ultimately safe (because they are limited and guarded) reversals of the most typical social hierarchical structures. These comic inversions of the established order are permissible, even officially encouraged in the imagination, but it is their ridiculous, not their revolutionary, aspect that is stressed. They are a weak and ultimately harnessed grotesque, meant to convey not a message of insurrection but a sense of absurdity that confirms the "natural" order in the act of violation—which is as husbands, parents, riders, and priests would have it. (The pig in the pulpit—or for that matter any animal impersonating a dignitary—may come closest to being truly subversive in nature because it rests on analogy rather than opposition. The porcine monk is a staple of medieval satire. But wherever legitimate inversion fantasies come so close to a revelatory quality that they may cause genuine disrespect for authority, censorship tends to strike swiftly.)

Maurice Lever remarks in an essay on the iconography of the *mundus inversus* that its ideological status is notoriously uncertain and that it can serve both "reactionary thinking and revolutionary thinking" (Lever and Tristan 179). Natalie Zemon Davis dissents in her study of early modern France, suggesting that the repetition of the *mundus inversus* motif (at least as far as "unruly women" are concerned) finally whittled away at the hegemonic structures long enough to have an evolutionary—if not a revolutionary—effect on women's social standing (151). That may be true, but contemporary critics find themselves much less impressed with the putative ethos of rebellion in the carnival code than did Bakhtin (for whom such an assertion was also a cathartic reverie amidst Stalinist repression, his concept of "grotesque realism" no doubt being a rejection of conformist socialist realism). Terry Eagleton observes caustically: "Carnival, after all, is a *licensed* affair in every sense, a permissible rupture of hegemony, a contained popular blowing-off as disturbing and relatively ineffectual as a revolutionary work of art" (148).

On the one hand, the anarchic impulse tends to pose a threat to the integrity of authority; on the other hand, the cathartic factors within the practices of carnival keep it from becoming that threat. The Church was well advised not to ban the excesses of carnival (although there was no scarcity of attempts to that effect). In many ways, the carnival became affirmative of faith and obedience, not their denial. Indeed, the anarchy of carnival is itself replete with a certain orderliness, a counterformality and regulated misconduct, as the democratic processes that are often still a part of the festival stand to prove (the election of the Lord of Misrule, the King of Fools or Beans, or the Prince and Princess of Carnival). Joseph Roach has stressed the peculiar symbiosis of carnival and the law in his historical analysis of Mardi Gras, which he regards as not so much "an occasion for seeking release from a way of life, it would seem, but an institution dedicated to its perpetuation." Once it becomes cozy with the prevailing power structure (or is in fact merely one of its masks), carnival can experience a secondary subversion from within by a "hidden carnival," as Roach shows. In Mardi Gras, the hidden carnival is created by those excluded from the official celebrations, mostly blacks (Roach 46 and 50–51).

Like the grotesque, carnival grows from a fundamental dialectic of law and transgression and appears perpetually vulnerable to self-negation, the tensions it creates sustainable only as fierce bursts of anarchy or within an occasion already subsumed from its inception, by a structure of order that produces it simply as its necessary other. The anarchy of carnival and its propensity for violence should not, however, be understated; the threat of mayhem (always greater to the individual reveler than to the social fabric) is close to its core; carnival no doubt has "a sinister side" (Bristol 51), where festive abuse is on the cusp of brutality and playful reversal funnels into armed revolt, as in a case that Emanuel Le Roy Ladurie documented for the town of Romans in 1580. Conversely, one may read into the promiscuous sexual couplings, heavy drug use, and murderous rampages of the Manson "family" in 1969 "the characteristics of a daemonic carnival" calculated to confront a rigidly hypocritical society with its unacknowledged darker side (Bernstein 370).

For Bakhtin, however, carnival is still free from these problematic accretions; it is the epitome, indeed "the symbol and incarnation[,] of the true folk festival" (220). Bakhtin's theory of carnival is now conventionally cited as critical commonplace; his definition of the grotesque, though often used with considerable imprecision in the many studies that quote it, has emerged as the preponderant manner of looking at the phenomenon. In the following, I want to rethink Bakhtin without rejecting him. I hope to make clear that Bakhtin's view, if particularly evocative, is only one part of the spectrum of grotesqueness. Bakhtin, for whom carnival reflects a "double aspect of the world and of human life" (6) outside of the officially sanctioned, takes a structural approach centering around an analysis of his exemplary novelist, Rabelais. The affect of laughter is at the basis of carnival; all of the activities connected with the feast have their origin in "one culture of folk carnival humor" (4). Laughter, as a term of popular and festive self-expression, enables a temporary liberation from prevailing orthodox truths and an established order, a suspension of hierarchy and norms, and yet is essentially regenerative: "Folk humor denies, but it revives and renews at the same time. Bare negation is completely alien to folk culture" (11).

Bakhtin's critique has opened up a redefinition of carnival as a potential oppositional system characterized by the presence of laughter within any system of law(s) from which laughter is banished. But laughter is not an individual emotional response in Bakhtin; it is a category of collective ideological resistance—a force of history, not of psychology. To laugh carnival laughter in the vein of Bakhtin is to refuse, refute, and begin to dismantle a coercive logic of order, of "thusness," to place oneself (momentarily) outside of social, and indeed epistemological, rules and forces. Carnival laughter as an articulation of resistance does not outlive the Middle Ages unchanged, but it does survive. Bakhtin charts its decline especially into the rational eighteenth century, until humor, irony, and sarcasm, those "genres of reduced laughter" (120), are the only pitiful remains of the carnival spirit in romanticism. But it is also carnival laughter that burst forth from the Théâtre de l'Œuvre in 1896 at the first appearance of Père Ubu, or from Zürich's Cabaret Voltaire in 1916. Some of modernism's defining moments are marked by carnival laughter, appropriated by a community of intellectuals and artists who strain as much against the tyranny of the norm and the authority of State and Church as did their forebears in the medieval marketplace.

Intimately connected with the etiology of laughter in Bakhtin's theory is the body to which it finds recourse as a physical affect and in which it is finally grounded. The grotesque body is the comic body—laughable and racked by laughter alike, laughing its guts out. In the unofficial history of the Middle Ages, Bakhtin discovers also an alternate tradition of the body and the face; indeed he reads carnival praxis, as Renate Lachmann says, "as the realization of a myth whose focus is the body" (148). Ostensibly providing an analysis of Rabelaisian writing in its time, Bakhtin's project is far broader: it is nothing less than a materialist rereading of the grotesque body images of the Middle Ages and early Renaissance in an attempt to salvage a positive, popular, universal body that has been suppressed by the modern, individualistic interpretation of corporeality. The grotesque body is Bakhtin's utopian super-sign into which all folk activity is subsumed and through which it is expressed. This is no single, delineated body but a *genus:* "the body and bodily life have here a cosmic and at the same time an all-people's character." The popular forces Bakhtin discovers appropriate the established symbolic hierarchy of the body, its vertical division into higher and lower strata, for their own purposes and challenge the authority of the body's bipolar structure and the fixed assignations of spiritual and material realms (by implication redrawing the map of the world): "The essential principle of grotesque realism is degradation, that is, the lowering of all that is high, spiritual, ideal, abstract; it is a transfer to the material level, to the sphere of earth and body in their indissoluble unity" (19). This is a body in flux, a body of excess, constantly exploding into new orifices, ingesting, protruding, indecorously spilling into the environment with its unbounded mutability. This unruly body, the body of misrule, undermines fixed notions of identity and brazenly collapses the polarities of self and other, of body and world, of up and down.

Consequently, the lower stratum of the body, the suppressed place of defecation, copulation, pregnancy, and birth, gains prominence, and the act of grotesque degradation initiates a double movement of destruction and regeneration that repeats the larger rhythms of existence. Part of an eternal cycle of self-destruction and self-renewal, the grotesque body is devoid of all classical stability and timelessness. It is "a body in the act of becoming. It is never finished, never completed; it is continually built, created, and builds and creates another body" (Bakhtin 317). Bakhtin locates this unceasing, persistent ambivalence of the body in a surprising image:

> In the famous Kerch terracotta collection we find figurines of senile pregnant hags. Moreover, the old hags are laughing. This is a typical and very strongly expressed grotesque. It is ambivalent. It is pregnant death, a death that gives birth. There is nothing completed, nothing calm and stable in the bodies of these old hags. They combine a senile, decaying and deformed flesh with the flesh of new life, conceived but as yet unformed. (25–26)

This brilliant notion of the collective body, as much an unabashed celebration of mythical golden-age wholeness as an ideological critique of the "new canon" of private post-Renaissance physicality, is the centerpiece of Bakhtin's book and the complex that is of most interest to this investigation of the grotesque in performance. For Bakhtin's vision of the anti-canonical body born from carnival can be a guidepost to our explorations of the grotesque body, particularly in modernism, only if we expand its purview beyond Bakhtin's original intent. We need to ask, for instance, what the hidden aspects of this grotesque body are: what happens to this defiantly vigorous corpus on Ash Wednesday, the day of the corpse? Bakhtin's carnival body is death-less because for him all decay is only the prelude to renewal. The crux of Bakhtin's approach, as Lachmann points out, is that he "formulates a myth of ambivalence that denies the 'end' by sublimating death in and through laughter" (124). But the ravages of Nazism and Stalinism, the horrors of pogroms and purges that made the twentieth century history's largest cemetery, the very excesses of destruction that caused Bakhtin to fantasize about a historically intangible, indestructible folk-super-body (effectively his way of distancing, even exorcizing the carnage), are what must prompt the postmodern critic to restore history to Bakhtin's ahistorical body, that is, to stop laughing and return to it its death. For seen in concert with the body at Auschwitz, or rather with the piles of bodies too numerous to count, Bakhtin's notions of joyful "degradation" and of the collective universal body take on a troubling hue; seen through the lens of Guernica or My Lai, the pervasive images of the "gaping mouth" or bulging eyes acquire an aspect of horror. To the (post)modern spectator, such primary signs of Bakhtin's carnival code can easily collapse into their opposite, like actress Helene Weigel's celebrated "silent scream" in the 1949 *Mother Courage*—a carnival image suddenly returned to its precise historical moment, a double death-moment. My intention here is not to moralize about Bakhtin (he is not to blame for these associations) but rather to insist that the "double body" of grotesque imagery has itself another body double unacknowledged by Bakhtin but implicit in carnival's dangerous side. We find this double in other, hidden spaces such as the underground, the chthonic realm from whence the grotesque is always born, and even in the literal underground, such as the Paris Métro, about whose inhabitants Herbert Blau is prompted to write:

> This is the underworld . . . where eating, drinking, defecation, and the imminent throes of death may remind us that the word *somatic,* from the Greek root *soma,* originally designated a *corpse.* It has been translated as *body,* but it designates rather what remains of the body when its life-force and vital functions are gone, and there is only the inertial figure, waste matter, or at best . . . an effigy. (*To All Appearances* 93)

The dismemberment of bodies in carnival has its "somatic" counterpart in emerging Renaissance practices of anatomical study and pathology (Bakhtin mentions an autopsy of a hanged man carried out by Rabelais in 1537). But where carnival *sparagmos*—its Dionysian heritage—is a joyous negation of structures and of closure and finitude, the anatomical spirit is excited exactly by the finite moment of death, and the procedure of autopsy makes sense only with a body that is the very opposite of the carnival body: solitary, reified, self-enclosed. The invasion of the knife through the epidermis and the extrusion of the intestines mirror the carnival body's interchange with the material world—Ewa Kuryluk writes that "the way corpses and anatomical parts are displayed in a prosectorium has . . . a slightly theatrical character. . . . In this scientific grotto of curiosities the inside is turned outside and dark secrets of the organic become disclosed as the bodily cave is opened up" (28). At the same time, the autopsy makes a mirthless mockery of the cycle of protrusion and ingestion in "grotesque realism." Like the carnival body, the corpse is ambivalent, not because it is living and dying like the terra-cotta hags (it is irremediably dead), but because it resists its objectification, its conversion into the general body of the anatomist by stubbornly asserting an individuality it can no longer lay claim to. In her essay "'Still Life with Corpse,'" Katharine Young describes her observation of two autopsies, one of the body of a woman whose garishly painted toenails attract her attention, the other of an old man:

> These irruptions of subjectivity through the discourse of objectivity attest to the fragility of the framing of the body-as-object. The toe, that particular gnarled and wrinkled toe with its modest indulgence of feminine vanity, is a

> locus of personhood. This allusion of the corpse to its own personhood, this insistence on its presence, is attested to by the curious gentleness of the pathologist's pat on the head of the old man, administered with the kind of cheerful absent-minded tenderness with which one pats a child, without any particular expectation of response. . . . Attempts to reach through the frame to the person, or to break out of the frame by the person, trouble the distinction we are culturally concerned to maintain between subject and object, self and body, life and death. . . . The corpse remains incorrigibly carnivalesque. (128–30)

It is the ineluctable, persistent trace of personhood—paradoxically most in evidence in the phase between death and decay—and the body's quite ineradicable inscription with the history of a lived life that haunt Bakhtin's theory because it refuses to countenance them.[7]

Much as his notion of carnival as a phantasmal enactment of collective liberation is seductive, Bakhtin's theory of the grotesque hides precisely what it seems to reveal. Bakhtin's grotesque realism is itself a grotesque in the sense that it represses another order of reference—call it danger, death, decay, finitude. It is the element that within the revolt of carnival revolts against itself. This element is, first and foremost, the grotesque's ethical side, and it comes most strongly to the fore in performance, which in turn may perhaps be seen as the most ethical of the arts (after all, Aristotle's term for dramatic character in his *Poetics* is *ethos*). For performance is inescapably bound to double business between now and not-now, as if at every moment shattering the deadness of indifferent space and trailing behind it the comet-trace of its continuous demise. In that it is the simultaneous reminder and defier of death; it is always, in Julia Kristeva's sense of the term, *abject.*

The problematic collision of Bakhtinian medievalism and the modern bodily canon can perhaps best be interrogated by looking more closely at a genre of performance that began articulating itself in the early 1960s and saw its feverish apogee in the half-decade between 1970 and 1975: body art. From the early 1960s to the mid-1970s, a period associated with radical social changes in most Western societies, art moved away from its material orientation and closer to a concern with ritual, narrative, and performance. Performance art gained ground when "art" was no longer circumscribed by the separation of artist and object, when—as happened in the 1960s—the art *object,* as Sayre writes, "had become, arguably, dispensable" (2). The key to artistic expression then migrated from the finite, immutable "work" to the malleable, transitory, and risky moment of performance.

This transformation was momentous; revisiting what Blau has called modernity's "almost ceaseless discourse on the body" (*To All Appearances* 89), performance-based art redefined modes of art perception and consumption because it put before the spectator an object not other than himself (a sculpture or canvas) but *like* himself (the artist), while often permissively or overtly exhorting him to read the artist as part of the object or process. That this is essentially the same thing that happens in theatre does not minimize the disturbing aspects of performance art. Frequently bare of the generic or conventional strictures (plots, characters, physical stages) that allow theatre to pass safely through our perceptual crises, performance art aggravates the grotesque nature of performance by placing the entire weight of the event on the sense-making apparatus of the perceiver: into the realm of pure experience, from which there is no distance. More than in object-based art, the spectator of performance is invited, even forced, to be party to the making of art; in some cases, she is—wittingly or not—herself the object (as in Vito Acconci's *Following Piece* [1969], where the artist pursued uninitiated pedestrians).

This frequent subject/object ambiguity of performance art should remind us of the carnival code. There too, spectator and performer are often indistinguishable and interchangeable and event boundaries are uncertain. The stringency of subjectivity itself stands in question as the possibility of objective spectatorship gives way to communal experience and unregulated exchange. Consequently, a critic like Sally Banes has used Bakhtinian language to describe the emerging genre of performance in her chronicle of Greenwich Village in 1963, calling the "effervescent" body of these artists "first and foremost a body of carnivalesque performance" (193). And indeed, performers such as Carolee Schneemann, whom Sayre rhapsodizes as "postmodern art's greatest artist of the body" (100), in her exuberant alimentary spectacle *Meat Joy* (1964) summoned the entire gamut of Bakhtinian banquet imagery in an "apotheosis of libidinal plenitude" (Banes 216). Schneemann and Alison Knowles, who specialized in "feeding pieces" and similar fare, pushed performance free of its framing strictures in the most primal way, by centering it on the act of material exchange, on nourishment (manifesting perhaps literally art's proposed function in the psychic economy), and thus rendering their audiences part of that Bakhtinian circulation of matter that brooks no isolation. Understanding the performance became, literally, "digesting" it.

If in these gustatory gestures we recognize an effort to recapture the celebratory spirit of carn(iv)al desire, they are in their conscious overflow and breach of boundaries also a calculated affront to the rationale of representation. The grotesque agenda thrives on this simultaneous promise and threat of performance to neglect the recognition of civil margins of comfort, and the history of performance art in the 1960s and 1970s can also be read as a continuous battle of escalation in the bid to pierce through the ever-expanding buffer zone that the rapid reabsorption of all provocation extruded around the savvy spectator. Receptiveness to the threat of performance, sensitivity to shock, became a moving, elusive target.

Fairly successful at generating such shock were the Viennese Actionists (Herrmann Nitsch, Otto Mühl, Rudolf Schwarzkogler, and Günter Brus), who in the early 1960s formed a loose group united by disenchantment with formalism and traditional painting. Intent on overcoming the "picture plane" of representative art, they progressed from tachist paintings to a series of provocative "material actions" *(Materialaktionen)*. The very idea of the material action was a violent and expressively excessive coagulation of separate matter, often in the form of using and abusing naked human bodies or animal carcasses in rituals frequently composed of degradations—Mühl chose the untranslatable Viennese idiom *Versumpfung*—or counterfeit crucifixions, with the help of materials such as paint, flour, blood, eggs, meat, mud, brain matter, saliva, and so forth, applied to space and bodies with artful anarchy. The Actionists invented a highly theatrical aesthetic of ceremonious self-abuse, spattering themselves with lambs' blood and other organic materials (Nitsch, who invented the term "O[rgies]. M[ysteries]. Theatre" for his displays),[8] painting their bodies and confronting them with instruments of incision (Brus in his *Self-Mutilation*), or staging mock-amputations of body parts (Schwarzkogler, who left the question of whether he had indeed cut off his penis tantalizingly open; he hadn't). The group was mainly concerned with creating a spectacle of physical risk and shock, a dramaturgy of the organic, not with truly putting themselves in harm's way. Operating within the painfully repressed society of postwar Austria, they knew their symbolic invocations of blood, slime, filth, and anguish were as potent as reality and that the sacerdotal manner of presentation and the co-optation of religious iconography could create strong grotesques in an arch-Catholic country. Mühl wrote in a 1964 manifesto:

> [T]he material action is painting which has grown beyond the picture plane. . . . [T]he theatre still frequently uses symbols which are supposed to illustrate a story. [T]he material action uses symbols which are themselves the story, the sequence and mixture of symbols as realities existing for themselves. [T]hey do not want to explain anything, they are what they appear . . . the bodies and things which we usually see and evaluate as the objects of our purposes are radically devalued by the material action. . . . [H]umans appear not as humans, as persons, as sexual beings, but as bodies with certain characteristics. [I]n the material action, they are cracked like an egg and show their yolk. (qtd. in Schwarz 270)

Significant in this programmatic statement are the forced breakdown of the symbolic aesthetic frame associated with the theatre and the systematic degradation of the body-as-object, which is invoked with more than a hint of Bakhtinian glee. Indeed, one may see a pronounced carnival aspect to these performances, which became—like carnival—a constant irritant to the suspicious authorities (police raids were an expected, even legitimizing, component of Actionist events).

But soon these elaborate simulacra of violence and *sparagmos* seemed insufficient. As the cultural climate hardened in the early 1970s, the ritualistic and orgiastic *Materialaktionen* and the Dionysian frenzy of the O. M. Theatre with its faith in cathartic action[9] gave way to an aesthetic of the isolated, distressed body that seemed to be "a grotesque inversion of the birthing rituals of the sixties, with their synesthetic imagery and collective swapping of body parts" (Blau, *To All Appearances* 98). The protagonists of this new body art seemed to feel, whether they articulated it or not, that in spite of all phantasmal desiring, they were condemned to exile in the body of the new canon in which "no signs of duality have been left" and which is "self-sufficient and speaks in its name alone" (Bakhtin 321). Body art of the 1970s consequently sought to develop an escape from the impasse of the artists' entrapment in a symbolic economy, the exchange of commodities and signs, by having defiant recourse to the solitary body they still knew they possessed, or had "at their disposal," even through the constant "backwash of meaning" (Barthes, *Responsibility* 132).

Some performance pieces, it seemed, were investigations *coram publico* of whether the body in an age of increasing mediatization and physical attenuation still existed at all. Vito Acconci would apply differing degrees of stress to his body, for instance stuffing a hand into his mouth until he choked (*Adaptation Studies,* 1970) or grinding cockroaches into his stomach flesh (*Rubbings,* 1970) in an attempt to ascertain fundamental ontological questions: "I used the body as a proof that 'I' was there—the way a person might talk to himself in the dark" (qtd. in Linker 22). Submission to physical extremity became a way to authenticate the experiences of the body and thus of body art. The California artist Chris Burden achieved notoriety with a string of performance pieces in which he had himself shot in the arm with a .22-caliber rifle (*Shoot,* 1971), placed under a tarpaulin in the middle of busy La Cienega Boulevard in Los Angeles (*Deadman,* 1972), and crucified on a Volkswagen Beetle (*Transfixed,* 1974). Using pain or fear in a work, Burden declared simply, "seems to energize the situation" (qtd. in Carr 17). Dennis Oppenheim lay on the beach with a book on his stomach to obtain a controlled sunburn (*Reading Position for a Second Degree Burn,* 1971) and had himself stoned (*Rocked Circle Fear,* 1971). Gina Pane—*nomen est omen*—gargled with milk until it mixed with blood in her throat (*Sang, Lait Chaud,* 1972) and climbed a ladder with protruding blades (*Escalade Sanglante,* 1971). The Australian artist Stelarc repeatedly had himself suspended on wires by fish hooks pierced through his skin and flesh (for example, *Event for Stretched Skin,* 1976), declaring that "everything beautiful occurs when the body is suspended" (qtd. in Carr 12).

Any such catalogue of self-abuse of course is easily mistaken for a litany of increasingly desperate attention-getting stunts, and indeed getting the jaded art audience to look at all (instead of, in Brecht's immortal phrase, "gaping romantically") was bought at the cost of escalating peril to life and limb that often smacked of a Barnum-and-Bailey-esque need to outdo the rival sideshow.[10] But body art, even in its more questionable excesses, was concerned with a very different dynamic between performance and audience than the merely exhibitionist meeting the prurient or voyeuristic—and where it suggested such a dynamic, as in Acconci's infamous *Seedbed* (1971), in which gallery visitors walked over a ramp under which the artist was masturbating while speaking his fantasies into a microphone, it at least made it highly problematic. In some sense, subjecting the artist to danger or pain was only body art's method of creating its true end-product: the spectator *in extremis.* When Cynthia Carr uses the now loaded term "terrorism" to descibe Chris Burden's work (24), she means that it poses a visceral threat to the audience's autonomy. In one piece, Burden lay on the floor of a gallery, exposed electrical wires and buckets of water next to him. Had any audience member chosen to spill the water—or spilled it accidentally—Burden would have been electrocuted. The real threat to the artist was small, but the degree to which it compromised the audience's safety margin by making them potential killers was commensurately greater. The most consequent body art pieces took this step of reconfiguring the artist/audience relationship in terms of a sacrificial logic in which the performer/outsider/*pharmakos* implicated the spectators in a host of impulses impermissible in quotidian life: violent, murderous, taboo. Marina Abramovic, in her infamous *Rhythm 0* performance in the Galleria Studio Mora in Naples (1974) (see fig. 5), lay still for six hours as the audience was exhorted to use any of a number of tools and instruments of torture on her naked body. Only when an audience member threatened to pull the trigger on a loaded revolver did a fight break out and the performance was stopped. *Rhythm 0* was calculated to provoke this crisis because it thrust the audience into an exceedingly perilous space between observation, performance, and violent domination.

Body art such as that of Abramovic aimed at being truly transgressive, that is, at shattering the boundaries between performance and the spectators' reality; breaking down reserve and distance; denying them the power to code, interpret, and evade; rejecting the prurience of the merely aesthetic; and drawing them irresistibly into a dangerous conspiracy of acquiescence with the work, an area of ethical threat. Of these performances, she says: "I asked the audience to experience the raw power of confrontation" (Abramovic 21)—confrontation not so much with the work as such but with what the work might unsettle in oneself. Erika Fischer-Lichte describes the audience reaction to body art:

> On the one hand, the spectators feel shocked and deny what they see; on the other, they are fascinated because someone violates him/herself voluntarily and because the action conjures up taboos of torture and physical punishment. Spectators are fascinated and shocked by their own curiosity since, according to cultural norms, they should feel disgust or horror. ("Performance Art" 35)

Performance, it was hoped, would eventually cast off all pretense and undo itself by arriving at a place (that holy grail of modernism, that Artaudian utopia that seemed to elude the "conventional" avant-garde

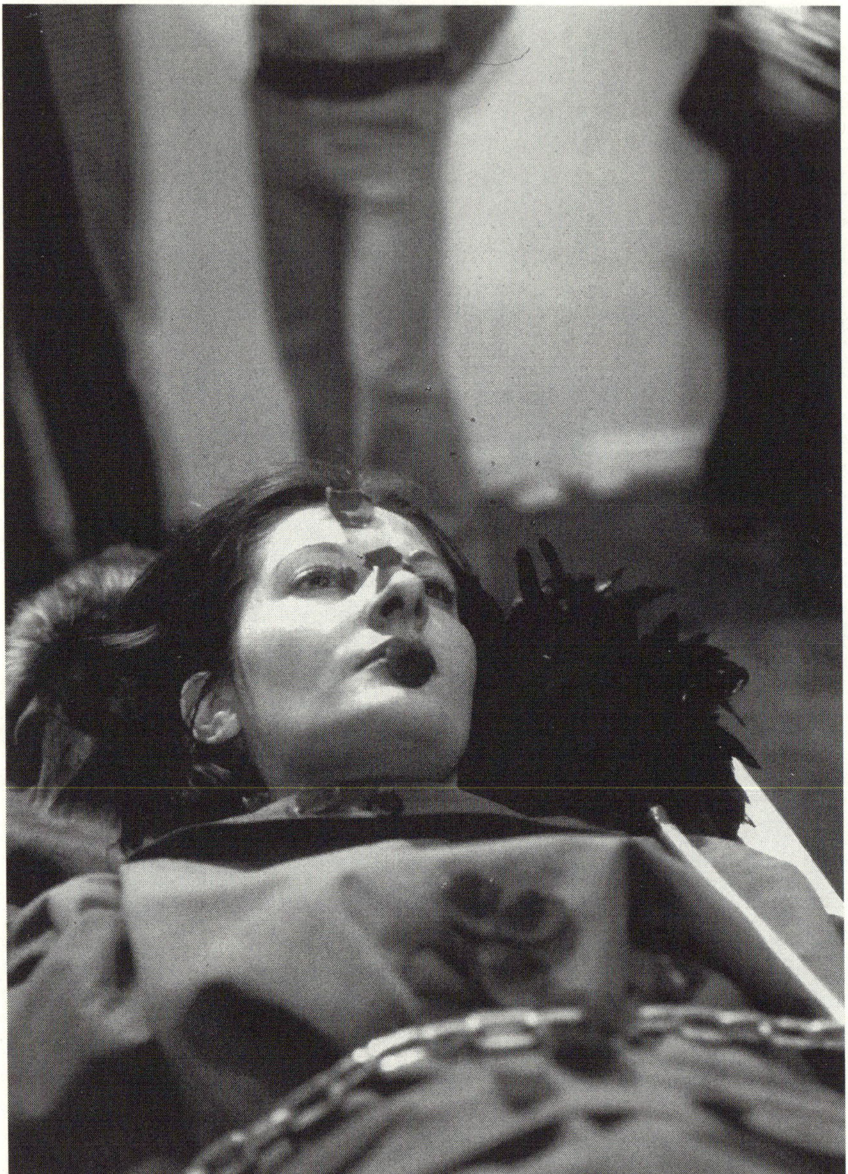

Fig. 5. Marina Abramovic, *Rhythm 0* (1974). ©2003 Artists Rights Society (ARS), New York/VG Bild-Kunst, Bonn.

theatre) where action was no longer a symbolic quotation but authentically, irreducibly itself and the divide between art on the one hand and true life on the other effectively evaporated. Just like Mühl's material actions, in which "the symbols . . . are themselves the story," for Abramovic, "[i]n performances, things are not symbols. There is always a very minimal construction. If we say we are doing a wall piece, hitting a wall, then we are doing that activity" (qtd. in MacRitchie 30).

Most of the body artists—if they had formal training at all—came from art, not from theatre, and there was a naive quality to their revolutionary discovery of the body as object and canvas. They were, first of all, not bound to the conventions of the space and time of theatrical performance. Performances could take place (and did) in lockers, streets, warehouses, or an exotic locale such as the Great Wall of China. Almost always, body art had an aspect of "ordeal art," and the primary way to communicate an ordeal vividly to the audience is to stretch its duration. The performance piece *Nightsea Crossing* (1982–86) by Abramovic and her companion Ulay consisted of seven agonizing hours in which the artists sat across from each other in absolute immobility, even trying not to blink, a feat they repeated ninety times.

But as much as body art was an attempt to transcend the mere representation of the body for the body's pristine presence, stripped of all that was accidental, social, or symbolic (Stelarc referred to himself in suspension simply as "the body," a pure physical object, declaring himself concerned only with "cosmic, superhuman, extraterrestrial manifestation" [qtd. in Carr 12]), the project was destined to fail. And if it was hoped that these woundings and piercings of the flesh, like some rite of cultural passage in reverse, could break open the body again to "show the yolk," to emulate with sympathetic magic the carnival semiotic that "stages the penetration of the outside into the bodily insides as a spectacle" (Lachmann 151) so that art, and body art in particular, could again become, as Chris Burden said in a carnivalesque formulation, "a free spot in society where you can do anything" (qtd. in Carr 20), that too was largely illusory. The violence, as Anthony Kubiak has recognized, was not only self-inflicted but also often self-referential:

> The violence of body art is hardly a transgressive act when the state no longer inscribes its laws into the flesh but incites the artist, like Kafka's jailor [in *In the Penal Colony*], to write them there himself. Far from resisting the systems

> of information and representation that confine and brutalize her body, the artist is eventually absorbed into the fictions of myth and law, this time by her own hand. (145)

The problem occurred exactly because the agenda (and I am loosely ascribing a homogeneous "corporate" agenda to these artists) was contradictory; what was at odds, we might say, were carnival code and sacrificial code. The first belongs, in Bakhtin's scheme, to the realm of folk culture, the second to that of official ecclesiastic culture (the coercive power of most social control roots in the theology and ideology of sacrifice). Carnival is laughter; sacrifice is terror(ism).

Significantly, the primary psychophysical determinant of Bakhtin's theory is practically absent in body art—it eschews laughter. Nervous guffaws at some Actionist slaughter are cited with contempt by the practitioners; disbelieving laughter from a witness to one of Stelarc's suspensions is seen as a sacrilegious response. Body art is a serious, often solemn, sometimes hysterical task, frequently preceded by manifestos and followed by press conferences, enclosed in galleries and lofts, self-conscious to a fault. Listening to Chris Burden's earnest explanations of his self-destructive projects, such as in his *Documentation of Selected Works, 1971–1974*, one finds it difficult to deny a strong impression of the banality of such radical gestures in the context of a thoroughly desensitized media environment.

If anything, "classical" body art, such as it was, not only did not signify a return to the carnival body but also starkly advertised the impossibility of such regress. It seemed that the more it attempted to unlock the "pure" potentialities of the body, to escape the studied sexlessness, painlessness, and pleasurelessness of postmodern corporeality, the more it caught itself up in objectifications and the farther it drifted from any truly radical origin. Performance art's "ethos of play," as Blau writes, created a "movement of supplementarity that . . . occupies the absence of a center, dispersing (after arousing) nostalgia for origins in a field of infinite substitutions" ("Surpassing" 92).

In the carnival code, the body becomes everything, it *overwhelms;* in the sacrificial code, nothing, it *disappears.* Blau recognizes this key ambiguity when he remarks: "[T]here is in the extremity of postmodern performance, along with valorization of the body, a utopian desire to do without it entirely. Or to claim it doesn't exist" ("Surpassing" 94). The body of the postmodern performance artist is often the thoroughly modern, individuated body *posing as* the carnival body, and that means inescapably creating a layer of fiction, or displacement, as one struggles toward authenticity.[11] In this incongruity, perhaps, the grotesque momentarily appears: are we witnessing "pain" or pain, the possibility of "death" or death, "danger" or danger? For a moment, that moment of "undecidability," the audience's *cordon sanitaire* is pierced and the performance generates, as Sayre says, "the condition of conflict and contradiction which presents no possible 'solution' or resolution" (xiii), especially if things "go wrong" as in *Rhythm 0* (even if they "go right" by "going wrong"). The performances—all performances, but these in particular—rest ineluctably on certain "subjective constructions," as Fischer-Lichte remarks:

> While during the performance, for a fleeting moment, signifier and signified seem to merge, before and after it, in the subjective constructions of the performers and the spectators, they irretrievably fall apart. In this respect, one might even discover a potential utopia in the performance. ("Performance Art" 34)

What could this utopia better be compared to but the total congruence of signifier and signified in the carnival code in which "the boundaries between play and life are intentionally erased" (Bakhtin 258)? But such a boundary violation is utopian only from one point of view (that of Bakhtinian medievalism); from another (that of modernity), it also marks the terrifying collapse of difference and is substantially grotesque. To be truly utopian, the body art performance would need to be able to count on an *objective* consensus with its audience, as in a ritual or shamanic ceremony or sacrifice. But although body art performances typically use the symbolic vocabulary of ritual, they are often deeply personal, even hermetic actions. For the spectators of such actions, the immediate confrontation with the anguished body forces a search for interpretation that itself becomes anguished as it "falls apart," and they are remanded to the spectacle of the flesh, to pure fascination or pure revulsion, a reaction strongly at odds with the aesthetic frame of the event. In the disjunction between what the event proposes to do (create ritual cohesion and/or legible meaning through the instrument of the body) and what it does (thematize the ambivalent spectatorial reaction as the event's *true* meaning), body art creates a particularly modern, that is, anti-Bakhtinian, version of the grotesque. It confirms my previous assumption that, in principle, all performance is grotesque. Body art, certainly, is performance at its most extreme, where it tends to unravel *as performance.* But at the same time, centering on the body as a vehicle of performance, it reverts to and locates itself entirely in performance's most intimate physical territory, proposing that as the "object of performance," the body is simultaneously inescapable and unendurable.

Staging Monsters

Recent poststructuralist theory has concentrated on the forms of otherness, or heteromorphy, to describe the delineations of self and the constitution of difference in the formation of consciousness, gender, race, and history. The grotesque naturally feeds on structures of opposition, on questions of identity and difference, and its apposite discipline may well be that science of otherness, teratology, the study of monsters. But the monster is not only *different*; it is virtually a *performance* of difference, if we recall the derivation of that term: the bringing-forth of form. Thinking of the long association of monstrosity with sideshows and chambers of horror, one cannot escape the connection between aberration and exhibition and the immediate—if often pathological—relationship of objectification and enthrallment that the entirely extraordinary generates (note that Trinculo's first thought in *The Tempest,* after stumbling upon Caliban, is to exhibit him—a fair Renaissance impulse). It should become apparent in the following that there is indeed an essential affinity between performance and monstrosity.

Myth in particular is fertile in producing monsters, and the sheer variety of monstrousness makes classification difficult, but we may distinguish between natural and supernatural monsters and regard aberration as the common denominator: the monstrous is what is in some sense *in*human. Yet the grotesque is not particularly interested in the entirely alien that makes its home in the realm of the fantastic but rather in a brand of the monstrous that is well designated by Harpham's phrase "corrupted or shuffled familiarity": that in which, distorted, we see our world and in which, disappearing, we see ourselves (5).

This is not the space to deliver a thorough inventory of monsters or the monstrous but rather of attitudes toward monstrosity and to hint at what (and how) it *means.* Ambroise Paré, in his 1573 treatise *Des monstres et prodiges,* writes in full earnest: "There are several things that cause monsters. The first is the glory of God. The second, his wrath. The third, too great a quantity of semen. The fourth, too little a quantity. The fifth, the imagination" (3). This undifferentiated etiology of monstrosity may strike us as comical, but it represents the state of thinking on the verge of the scientific age. Though it need not be a hieroglyphic prefiguration of catastrophe as in the apocalyptic beasts in the Book of Revelation, Paré understands that a monster always signifies something and that therefore the actual and the imaginary aberration share the same semiological status: mythical creatures, birth defects, and exotic animals populate his pages in a kind of taxonomical carnival.

Mythology has created innumerable monsters in a great variety of strangeness and numinosity. The Egyptian gods Molos and Bes are headless; the Roman god Janus two-faced; the guard dog of Hades, Cerberus, three-headed; and so forth. But the grotesque is more narrowly interested in the monstrosity that holds a warped mirror to humanity. Girard observes: "To pontificate on the subject of monsters is in effect to take them seriously, to enter into their game; it is to be duped by their appearance instead of recognizing the human being who lurks behind the monstrous form" (*Violence* 253). The very topography and imaginative geography of the medieval world mirrored in their shape the paradigms of the grotesque—the further to the margins one ventured, the greater and ghastlier the monsters one was bound to encounter. The world resembled the pages of illuminated manuscripts and incunabula: it was like a text in which letter and meaning were eternally determinate and stable at the center but which at the edges faded into enigma and chaos. Particularly, a breed of anthropoid monsters was believed to live beyond the horizon, on the edges of the earth or in the mythical Antipodes where all was reversed. Only voyagers and seafarers might encounter them and return with their embellished tales of men with beastly shapes and appendages; wild men, hermaphrodites, and mermaids; one-legged (sciapodic) or monocular (cyclopic) quasi-humans; or people with faces on their breast (sternophtalms), almost inevitably of the cannibalistic persuasion. Diligently illustrated encyclopedias of oddity reported the finds, one plagiarizing (and seeking to outdo) the other, from Lambert de Saint-Omer's *Liber floridus* (1120) to Conrad Lycosthenes' famous *Prodigiorum et ostentorum chroniconquae* (1557). William Shakespeare's Othello is yet such a traveler and he parlays his tales into erotic capital when he tells "of the Cannibals that each [other] eat, / The Anthropophagi, and men whose heads / [Do grow] beneath their shoulders" (1.3.143–45).

The sternophtalms and other humanoid monstrosities always amount to a scrambling and rearranging of the human physique, disproportionately privileging one part or omitting another. The monster is invariably the human *manqué;* no attention is paid to the plausibility of its deformation nor to the mere functionality of its imaginary extremities—it is a pure suffering allegory of want. Few representations are as candid in revealing the full anthropocentric conceit of the age.

A pre-Enlightenment time, firmly believing in the efficacy of divine communication, would paradoxically be less unsettled by the monstrous than a rationalist period. For in the earlier humans, the monstrosity provokes no interpretive impasse—it is clearly so unnatural that it can only come from God, that is, be a celestial sign or portent. The monster is not wholly and entirely "other," not *totaliter aliter.* It is always readable, and indeed cries out to be read, for allegorical wisdom is always contained in, and must be extracted from, any unusual apparition. Contemporary wisdom had it, after all, that the monster was *non contra, sed supra naturam.* This belief is echoed, for instance, in Shakespeare's *Julius Caesar,* where Cassius muses that the sudden appearance of a "monstrous quality" in normal things springs from a heaven that "hath infus'd them with these spirits, / To make them instruments of fear and warning / Unto some monstrous state" (1.3.68–71). Stephen Greenblatt writes:

> Prodigies could be viewed both as signs—monitory messages to be read by those who understood the art of divination—and as wonders—marvelous instances of the inexhaustible variety of things. Prodigies challenge the classification of things, but they do not make classification itself impossible. . . . Where the modern structuralist understanding of the world tends to sharpen its sense of individuation by meditating upon the normative, the Renaissance tended to sharpen its sense of the normative by meditating upon the prodigious. (76–77)

The monster's Latin root is *monstrare* (to show, expose), but there is an echo, too, of *monere* (to warn). Thus, the monstrous draws attention to itself not only for its abnormality but also because it has been inscribed with a message from the hand of the divine. While it must still be read and understood (for which there are authorities and procedures), one can rest assured of its sign-ness, and therefore ultimately of its well-considered participation in the mutual discourse of God's history. Thus, if Hans Sachs, in an anecdotal poem of 1557, "reads" the birth of an apparently hydrocephalic child as a warning to the sundry "heads" of state to resist pride and folly, he does so in the secure assumption that this type of visual pun is part of God's vocabulary. In his influential *Cannochiale Aristotelico* (1645), Emanuele Tesauro explicitly included monsters among the "jokes of Nature." Monsters were in his view "nothing but mysterious hieroglyphs and facetious images devised by Nature for the purpose of either deriding or educating mankind" (qtd. in Bompiani 392).

Most Renaissance thinkers were not inclined to doubt that moral misconduct finds immediate and retaliatory expression in the flesh. Infinitely refined, this belief has remained a constant of the grotesque: monstrosity still means a challenge to the ethical integrity of the universe. But following the advent of Baconian empiricism, this indicatory power of the monster became sublimated by ethical, economical, and scientific forces. In Michel de Montaigne's essay on the cannibals (1580), the monstrous other stands as a model for a lost, utopian innocence, even a repository of the Golden Age. These cannibals are pre-Rousseauian *hommes sauvages* whose aberrant behavior is less barbaric and repugnant to the liberal stoic Montaigne than that of his countrymen. Here teratology turns into a form of didactic ethnology.

A plague of stranded whales, "sea monsters," on the Dutch coast, also in the latter half of the sixteenth century, gave rise to ominous fears and oracular rantings, not the least reason being the association with the tale of Jonah and the fact that the mouths of great "fish" had been a medieval iconic commonplace for the mouth of hell. But the whales were soon discovered to be at least as useful as fearsome, and they assumed "twin capacities as symbol and commodity" (Schama 143) until the mercantile impulse won out over the exegetic impulse and spawned a profitable whaling industry. (On the other end of the spectrum of mercantile instinct stands the logic of colonialism and slavery, which intentionally *preserved* the notion of an inhuman otherness of its victims to justify its ends.)

The rise of scientific naturalism in the eighteenth century achieved the logical repatriation of the monstrous into the mainstream by addressing it as a necessary aberration. J.-B. Robinet claimed in 1768 "that far from disturbing the order of things, [monstrosities] contribute to it. It is only, perhaps, by dint of producing monstrous beings that nature succeeds in producing beings of greater regularity and with a more symmetrical structure" (qtd. in Foucault, *Order* 155). Or, as Foucault paraphrases, "the monster provides an account, as though in caricature, of the genesis of differences" and thus becomes useful for the project of order (*Order* 157). The entire age of rationalism indulged in a pruriently ambiguous passion for the aberrant, both laying the foundations of a solidly empirical psychology, physiology, and anthropology and treating madness and monstrosity as a sentimental spectacle (tours of bedlams and charnel-houses were greatly *en vogue* among the middle classes).

Romanticism finally permits the erstwhile absolute exteriority of the grotesque outsider to collapse into utter interiority; it invents the sentimental or pathetic monster (Victor Hugo's Quasimodo; Mary Shelley's Frankenstein monster) in whom the other is recast as a perverted and victimized projection of the better self. The monstrous that was previously a *heterotopos*, a something and somewhere else, is suddenly strongest within us. This last, literary sublimation notwithstanding, the monstrous maintains a link with the portentous, an aura of the grotesque. Arnheim remarks that the monster "carries the threatening message that nature can go out of joint":

> [T]he birth of a monster is a failure of nature herself and threatens our faith in the basic soundness of what grows. . . . Distortions are comments on nature that may provoke indignation. But the monster creates anxiety because it shows reality itself at a fault. (*Toward* 256)

Monstrosity is more than a mere chance aberration; it invites chaos and plunges into namelessness, insofar as it "changes the quality of the things to which God has assigned a name": it is "metamorphosis" and "transmigration" (Barthes, *Responsibility* 147).

In the premodern understanding, the monster signaled an alterity that appeared menacing but finally comforted, because it was only a variant in an unfathomable divine universe (and tangible proof of God's power to break the rules) and also a signpost for the borders of normalcy. Scientific skepticism having displaced the faith in its revelatory function, the monster now continues to signify in a metaphysical vacuum where neither its specific ominousness nor its complete randomness can quite be believed: "In spite of the pressure applied to the enigma of monsters by an analytical philosophy, they resisted the collapse into simplicity" (Stafford 259).

Persuaded by the enduring perception of monstrosity as a physical manifestation of larger, hidden meanings, we should now look more closely at the apparent sympathies between monstrosity and performance. Notably, premodern teratology conceives of the monster in the twofold manner of Horatian aesthetics—*prodesse et delectare*—and by thus invoking use and delight (or, perhaps more clearly, significance and fascination) implicitly associates monstrosity with the realm of art. Indeed, according to Marie-Hélène Huet, many accounts of teratogenesis point to a common causative in the birth of prodigies: the maternal imagination. The mother's (forbidden) subconscious desires or her impressionability create the unnatural offspring, suggesting a "complex relationship between procreation and art," one that reverses the common mimetic process, for "in cases of monstrous procreation Nature imitates Art" (Huet 7). (It is no surprise that the exercise of the female imagination, her refusal to be the mere receptacle of the father's semen and thus her rebellion against her own passivity, should be thought productive of hideous results. Even a play concerned with monstrosity such as David Pomerance's *Elephant Man* indirectly summons this myth, if in its sanitized Victorian version: Merrick's mother is said to have been knocked down by a circus elephant prior to his birth. The resulting "impression" on her physical imagination presumably led to his deformities—a tale that, as Arnold Davidson remarks, "conceals, and not very well, the fantasy of bestiality" [53].)

The combination of the (frequently suspect) productive imagination creating something close to but distinct from nature with the Horatian imperative to instruct and delight aligns monstrosity with theatre. It may be suggested that all theatre is based as well on this double discourse of showing *(monstrare)* and warning *(monere),* of aesthetics and ethics, of presence and (absent, implicit) meaning. Plays, we might say, are the prodigies of art, the theatre the realm of the unnatural—partly because, paradoxically, it comes so close to nature.

In 1850, the painter Eugène Delacroix declared the new process of the daguerreotype to be false exactly because of its great verisimilitude, and therefore monstrous: "The monstrosities it presents are justifiably shocking, even though they are, literally, those of nature itself" (qtd. in Huet 188). What we have here is the recoil from the uncanniness of the too-lifelike. Theatre has experienced such recoil throughout its history, celebrated not only in numerous anecdotes (the purported horror of spectators at the Aeschylean Eumenides; Garrick's spine-tingling encounter with Old Hamlet's ghost; and so on) but also in theatrical theory from its very beginnings: from Plato's insistence on the malignant persuasiveness of theatre to Aristotle's conviction of its purgative powers. The highly charged, potentially corrupting influence of all-too-lifelike mimesis and its purported ability to hijack the viewer's ethical reasoning is of course the very substance of Plato's argument against the theatre, and he seeks to banish it from his ideal republic, to relocate it beyond the confines of culture (just as the monster, in Barbara Stafford's words, is always "situated . . . not within culture but beyond culture" [256]). The antitheatrical prejudice (to use Jonas Barish's phrase) has found a constant way to ensure that the points of contact between civic culture and the counterfeit, monstrous culture of the theatre have remained few by locating it "beyond culture," or at least in those zones—such as the "liberties" of Elizabethan towns—where it shared its space with other cultural exiles: brothels, inns, leper colonies, scaffolds.

Among the arts, theatre alone has had and maintained such a "prodigious" status, defiantly intercategorical: inanimate (as literature) but alive (as performance); true, but false; now, but not-now; here, but not-here. The nexus of theatre, the grotesque, and the unnatural was made explicit by the director Vsevolod Meyerhold when he called theatre, as a thing outside of nature, "essentially an example of the grotesque." Especially in the theatre's nucleus, in the act of performance itself, there has always been more than a hint of monstrosity, or what Michael Goldman apostrophizes as the "terrific" quality of performing, the "compelling strangeness" and "terribilità" of the actor (7). What is "terrific" is that the monster and the performer are always simultaneously denizens of two realms of classification and so ineluctably intercategorical; the monster's taxonomic impertinence is replaced in the actor by mimetic impertinence. It is the monsters' propensity, like the actors', to "shamelessly exhibit themselves" (Stafford 254), and condemnation of that shamelessness (or "immodesty" or "wantonness") that seems to add a provocative quality of defiance to the already dangerous impulse of exhibitionism is a cardinal factor in almost all antitheatrical screeds of the sixteenth and seventeenth centuries.

The peril of mimesis, or impersonation (where, if we reason parallel to the grammar of "insemination," part of another persona is inserted into the inviolate self), is perhaps best illustrated at its extreme edges, where it collides with pathology. In his book *The Man Who Mistook His Wife for a Hat,* the neurologist Oliver Sacks recalls a gray-haired woman in her sixties whom he observed on the street in New York and who was afflicted with a particularly bewildering variety of Tourette's syndrome. She was instantaneously, automatically, and convulsively mirroring every passerby in ever more rapid succession and finally, in a kind of frenzied feedback, imitated even the reactions of the observers to her "performance": "This grotesque, involuntary resonance, or mutuality, by which *everyone* was drawn into an absurdly amplifying interaction, was the source of the disturbance I had seen from a distance. This woman who, becoming everybody, lost her own self, became nobody." As the pressure in her built up, she desperately turned into a side alley, where Sacks witnessed her cathartic expulsion of the multiple acquired *personae:*

> She delivered one vast, pantomimic egurgitation, in which the engorged identities of the last fifty people who had possessed her were spewed out. And if the taking-in had lasted two minutes, the throwing-out was a single exhalation—fifty people in ten seconds, a fifth of a second or less for the time-foreshortened repertoire of each person. (122–23)

It is of course unlikely that such a mimetic crisis would occur in the theatre, because the theatre presents an institutional frame to prohibit the threat of rampant, incontinent mimetic neuroses and to ensure a distance between actor and character, performer and performance. But Sacks's story is also a kind of allegory of the uncanniness of acting and the monstrosity of performance.

In the freak shows and sideshows that endured into the early twentieth century (and that have recently experienced a renaissance of sorts), scientific sublimation notwithstanding, the archaic *frisson* of monstrosity remained essentially intact, covered now only by a thin veneer of sentimentality. But for the objects of these displays, the "monsters," there had been a longstanding, peculiar economy in place, at the root of which was the transformation of the mere prodigy into the (often skilled) performer of his or her own monstrosity. At least until the early modern period, this transformation conferred a kind of legitimacy upon the aberration, which is demonstrated in the curious but quite logical fact that St. Wilgeforte, the patron saint and protectress of monsters, was thought through her intercession either to restore normalcy to her wards or to assure their prosperity as performing monsters (D. Williams, "Wilgefortis" 173). Such prosperity and the celebrity that accompanied it could often be prodigious itself: Lazarus Coloredo, who had a parasitic twin growing from his navel, toured Britain for many years in the mid-seventeenth century with his servants as a licensed performer, receiving paying visitors at his quarters (Park and Daston 20–22). He was thus a legitimate colleague of the licensed actors of the Jacobean theatres. Significantly, Coloredo was that most popular, most grotesque variant of freakdom, the "double monster." Double monsters are exquisite perceptual conundrums because in them, the fundamental spiritual equation of personhood, of one soul to one body, breaks down: Which of the two heads can be said to *be* the person? Whom does the body *belong* to? The double monster manifests a constant, disturbing dissolution of the integrity of identity. To many antitheatrical critics, actors, too, are double monsters by virtue (or vice) of role-playing engaged in a satanic deconstruction of sanctified categories. From antitheatrical pamphlets such as William Prynne's (prodigiously sprawling) *Histriomastix* to the encoding of acting as quintessentially transgressive in plays such as *Twelfth Night* or *The Duchess of Malfi,* theatrical performance is encrusted with an "ontological subversiveness" (Worthen 18) that in the eyes of a suspicious world slyly undermines social norms, gender roles, familial stability and the distinctions between sanity and madness, truth and fiction, and so on.

Like theatre, the display of the monster summons a moral discourse. *Performare* means to put forth form. Both the monster and the performer emerge from formlessness but never quite leave behind the chaos that has birthed them; instead, they hover tantalizingly forever on the edge of unraveling, kept from collapse only by their "terrible" energy, as they dazzle the categorical multitude. For the performing monster and the "monstrous" performer, the challenge is nearly identical: to convert their unnatural, abhorrent quality into something acceptable and remunerative without abandoning its substance. Monster and performer both must inhabit a dangerous and shifting middle ground as producers of a prodigious semiosis between acceptance and rejection, sympathy and terror, in the intercategorical territory of the grotesque.

All your life you live so close to truth, it becomes a permanent blur in the corner of your eye, and when something nudges it into outline it is like being ambushed by a grotesque.

—Tom Stoppard, *Rosencrantz and Guildenstern Are Dead*

2 Theories

Romantic Negotiations

Summarizing the motivation of the modernist artist, Frederick Karl notes the prominence of "disregard for authority," the "temptation to test out chaos and the demonic," and the "thrust toward reordering of objects in our perception" (367–68). He is speaking, by implication, of the grotesque.

As a force of renewal and revolution, this grotesque is the perennially modern. It is most in evidence in those works of art with which the eye and the mind have not yet caught up, which they have not yet successfully colonized and domesticated. George Santayana claims that the grotesque is "novel beauty," but any sense of beauty is by definition conventional. If every novelty is a convention in the making, the grotesque is the not-yet-made, or even the un-made convention. From the point of view of historical aesthetics, the grotesque could then be seen as a point of crisis toward which any movement gravitates, but one which is also the point of its fulfillment; the moment at which, while outrunning its subsumption into the canon of regulated representation, it arrives at the precipice of its own impossibility and possible extinction.

The concern of this chapter is in a sense hybrid; while it moves toward a general theory of the grotesque and finds the un-made conventions in the making, its true (but sometimes hidden) referent is the dramatic grotesque in particular, and it will address some vital concerns of dramatic genre and structure. The first part, concerned with the vagaries of the grotesque in romantic and postromantic theory, shows a considerable deepening and stretching of the term and its adjuncts. Through a complex interplay of espousal and resistance, the aesthetics of the nineteenth century in effect marked the grotesque as the major clandestine paradigm of romantic (and, by implicit extension, modern) poetics.

From the end of the eighteenth to the beginning of the twentieth century, forms of the grotesque surface frequently in both artistic works and in writings on aesthetics. The appearances of the grotesque in art were almost always subject to controversy, and the aesthetic tracts of the time seem less an attempt to formulate the theory of beauty and its sensible appearance than to alternately deny, disguise, and reconsider the theory of the nonbeautiful and to police its intercourse with the aesthetic domain.

One finds that—particularly in the terminology of the romantic period—the ugly corresponds to (and contrasts with) the beautiful, whereas the grotesque is linked to the concept of the sublime. For the purposes of the following discussion, though, which traces the invasion of traditionally marginal forms into the canon of the arts in the nineteenth century, the grotesque and the ugly are compatriots, a collegiality abetted even more by the fuzzy terminological habits of the period, which often do not distinguish well between them. The systematic aesthetics after the Cartesian revolution set out to forge a new, "objective" framework for the appearance of the beautiful according to the neoclassical mode, in which taste and reason became the arbiters. Neoclassicism first had to repress the demonic (virtue became synonymous with beauty in the writings of Berkeley and Shaftesbury), efface the ugly, and subject art to the reign of moral purpose. The aesthetics of the beautiful assumed the role of a censoring superego of artistic practice. If grotesque forms were permitted, it was only when they were firmly subordinate to these rules. But "the shifting of a convulsive order from the physical plane to the moral one," which as Paul Ilie observes is inherent in the grotesque from Dante to the baroque, is "absent in its subsequent Romantic forms" (38). Thus, where deformity and the ugly are concerned, modern aesthetics are founded upon a reconsideration of this a priori allegorical function, a move that liberates the nonabsolute to search for new areas of signification but also renders it potentially dangerous, since nothing vouches for its functional marginality any longer.

The primary theorist of nineteenth-century aesthetics, Georg Friedrich Wilhelm Hegel, expressly takes up the grotesque only in the passages on the "fantastic symbolism" in Indian religious art in his *Aesthetics* (1835), and his discussion is replete with ethnocentric preconceptions that today are abhorrent, to mention only his unquestioning assumption that the Indian sculptures are per se artistically inferior. But the analysis is only ostensibly about Indian art (although Hegel might deny that); it really concerns the aesthetic Original Sin. Hegel perceives the grotesqueness of the Indian temple sculptures as the result of a problem-solving strategy gone awry. The problem in question is that the "intuited identity" between the divine realm and the reality of existence, what we might call mythical congruence, has been ruptured. This is, to use a Lacanian analogy, a kind of "mirror stage" of culture, in which otherness, difference, and separation from the divine, the *manque à être,* are first perceived. At this stage of "cleavage between the hitherto united aspects, i.e., the battle between meaning and shape," man is born into art and becomes subject to desire, the desire to "heal the breach again by building the separated parts together in a fanciful way" (Hegel 1:333).

The Indian artists, however, ignorant of those classical principles of composition that may achieve the reconstitution of the broken unity, respond with a "fermenting imagination," with an "unrest of . . . fantasticalness," in short, with confusion and excess. But since neither the meaning (the Absolute) nor the shape (the symbolic artwork) yet represent a totality in themselves, they cannot interact dialectically:

> In their confused intermixture of finite and Absolute . . . they fall, despite all their exuberance and magnificent boldness of conception, into a monstrous extravagance of the fantastic which runs over from what is inmost and deepest into the most commonplace present in order to turn one extreme directly into the other and confuse them. (Hegel 1:335)

This critique of the unmediated coexistence of the trivial and the sacred, or of the laughable and the profound, is already a hardly veiled anticipation of Hegel's commentary on such German romantic authors as Jean Paul and Ludwig Tieck, whom he castigates in similar terms. In the Indian sculptures, though, the dissonance is more glaringly obvious to the naked eye:

> In order, as sensuous figures themselves, to reach universality, the individual figures are wildly tugged apart from one another into the colossal and grotesque. For the individual figure which is to express not itself and the meaning appropriate to it as a particular phenomenon but a universal meaning lying outside its own, does not satisfy contemplation until it is torn out of itself into monstrosity without aim and measure. (1:338)

Hegel is here painting a grotesque kinetics of desire, in which the statue, in its vain attempt to symbolically reach and capture the universality of heaven, stretches itself out of all proportion, into "the most extravagant exaggeration of size." He sees as symptomatic the impulse I have previously described as *horror vacui*—here the desperate attempt to substitute quantity for essence: "the multiplication of one and the same characteristic, the many heads, the mass of arms, etc." (Hegel 1:338).

Even though Indian art in Hegel's analysis "does not get beyond the grotesque intermixture of the natural and the human" (1:341), he acknowledges that it strikes a "note of sublimity." But the sublimity is necessarily false, because it pretends to a false reconciliation. While true sublimity is indexical, meaning that it points to what cannot be represented, and by that makes the Absolute present to consciousness in its necessary sensuous negativity, the Indian art "does not succeed in positing negatively the phenomena that it presents" but rather "thinks that the difference and contradiction between the Absolute and its configuration has been obliterated and made to vanish" (1:340).

If in classicism the Idea has found complete harmony with the appearance and can indeed realize itself as fully in it as the sensual medium allows, the romantic art form, as the next historical step, again forces a separation of the Idea and its manifestation: "The romantic form of art cancels again the completed unification of the Idea and its reality and reverts, even if in a higher way, to that difference and opposition of the two sides which in symbolic art remained unconquered" (Hegel 1:79). For the "spirit" of the Absolute is intrinsically progressive and strives to attain more than merely its expression in the corporeal realm, which is not its true essence. In romanticism, "spirit is pushed back into itself out of its reconciliation in the corporeal into a reconciliation of itself within itself." In this process it "wins in itself its objectivity" (1:518).

Spirit and art have become separate totalities without an essential mutual link, and the "new [romantic] art" is not charged with "the immersion of the inner [the Spirit, the Absolute, God] in external corporeality" as was the classical mode but can merely indicate "the withdrawal of the inner into itself" (Hegel 1:520). This is an aesthetics of negativity, of absence, but it is not a negative aesthetics. For, as Hegel makes clear *à propos* the appearance of the divine (the true Absolute) in classical and romantic art, the Greek statues of the gods harbor a "defect" in that they are unable to show "the expression of the [god's] soul in its simplicity."

Romantic, or Christian, art alone, *because* it is unable to supply a sensuous positivity of the divine, can disclose God's "inner being to man's inner being" (1:521)—by virtue, apparently, of failing to disclose his outer being. This purpose, however, in Hegel's view, is just as well or better served by religious or philosophical thought; the sensual realm is quite secondary and even distracting to it. Art, as Hegel unambiguously puts it, has become "superfluous" (1:535).

Thus, romantic art has only a tenuous connection with the Ideal and therefore itself becomes subjective; mired in its "finite deficiency and determinacy" it can "give unfettered play to the bold lines of the ugly" (Hegel 1:527). Indeed, if we assume the ideal bond between the Spirit and the artistic work to be metonymically constructed (that is, that the work strives to render the abstract Spirit as a concrete particular), the correct trope for the appearance of the Spirit in romantic art would be the *catachresis.* Originally, catachresis is the apparently inappropriate or arbitrary substitution, in speech, of one thing for another; the widest, most radical extension of metaphor that brings the expressive capacity of language nearly to the breaking point. Candidly called *abusio* in its Latin form, it is the most subjective of tropes, the one in which according to Paul De Man "something monstrous lurks" because "it can dismember the texture of reality and reassemble it in the most capricious of ways" (qtd. in Harpham 174). Grotesque art in romanticism stands in this "catachretic" relation to the Spirit, which in it suffers the *abusio* of unfettered and willful subjectivity. Of course, catachresis is also the most adventurously productive figure of speech, and it is in this dichotomous state of the destruction and revolution of signification that the grotesque breeds.

Hegel, as Christian Thomsen observes, "recognizes very acutely the mixture of metaphysical, rational, irrational, of sublime and extremely sensuous worldly elements in the grotesque" (67). But the grotesque is also always in some sense a catastrophe for the Hegelian system, because it is the true presence of what should not be, a vehement subversion of his peculiar sense of order that turns on a faith in the progressive self-revelation of the Absolute in history. Is not the grotesque, which Hegel always shows from the point of view of human failing, in this context also indicative of an impotence of the Absolute to manifest itself, a failing of what cannot fail? This heretical idea is nowhere expressed, but its mere possibility (it is, after all, only a dialectical extension of Hegel's system) accounts for the vigorousness with which all representations of the ironic, grotesque, and ugly are exorcized.

The only true poetics of the grotesque in romanticism, and the dramatic grotesque at that, is to be found in the manifesto that prefaces Victor Hugo's play *Cromwell* (1827). Hugo intended the lengthy and sometimes rambling discussion in the preface to illuminate the ideas the play was meant to embody, but *Cromwell* itself is now forgotten (it was regarded as unstageable because of its scenic demands and the size of its cast and did not see its premiere until 1956). The *Préface de Cromwell,* however, remains a mainstay of French romantic theory. Hugo thus stands as paradigmatic of the dilemma of romanticism: that its theories have consistently overshadowed its products, though—in accordance with the strange but universal law of revolutionary thought—never to the detriment of the credibility of the former.[1]

Although opposite in practically every conceivable respect to Hegel, Hugo reiterates two of Hegel's central precepts. One is the division of human history into three successive, ascending stages of development. The other is the conviction that the drama is not only the culmination of the romantic (third) period but also the superior generic form per se. But the similarity between Hugo and Hegel ends with this superficial description. To Hegel, drama represents the "most perfect totality of content and form" and "must be regarded as the highest stage of poetry and of art generally" (2:1158). But Hegel has the classical Greek drama in mind, and he advocates its traditional separation into comedy and tragedy, indeed, sees it as indispensable to its dialectical purpose. For Hugo, the drama must supersede this unnatural separation: "[A]fter these abstractions there remains something to represent: man; after these tragedies and comedies, something to write: the *drame*" (Hugo 167).

Consequently, Hugo's historical succession of the "primitive," "ancient," and "modern" periods finds only in the last step, in which the force of Christianity dominates, the rationale of all history and the pinnacle of art. Hegel categorically denies romantic art the ability to summon and manifest the divine: it exists in abjection and superfluity, in what I have called a catachretic state. But Hugo reverses this notion. In his opinion, Christianity revolutionizes art as it had previously sent religion into a tumult that upset the ancient world. With its spirit of melancholy and attitude of meditation, Christianity overcomes and defeats the one-sided classical adoration of beauty, subsuming it into an overarching vision of the interconnectedness of things:

> Christianity leads poetry to truth. Like it, the modern muse will view things from a higher and broader vantage point. She will see that everything in creation is not humanly *beautiful,* that the ugly exists beside the beautiful, deformity beside gracefulness, the grotesque on the reverse side of the sublime, evil with good, light with shadow. (Hugo 158)

Here is, in a nutshell, the aesthetic attitude of which the *drame* shall become a formidable instrument, aided by the "fruitful union of the grotesque type with the sublime type" that "produces the modern genius" (Hugo 159). Inherent to it is a democratic perspective, a gesture of poetic justice as poetic *égalité,* in short, the roots of the ideology of realism. A simple phenomenological observation suffices for Hugo to dispel millennia of beauty-worship: "The beautiful has only one type; the ugly has thousands" (162). Antiquity, Hugo decrees, is not free of the grotesque, but the grotesque is not free *in* it: it is "timid and always seeking to hide itself" there. "In modern thought, however, the grotesque plays an important role. It is found everywhere; on the one hand, it produces the deformed and the horrible; on the other the comic and buffoonish" (160). Hugo advances no theory of what is grotesque; instead he apologetically posits its existence and the necessity of its representation in art. If anything, his taxonomy of things grotesque is regressive as measured against Hegel. The grotesque is the result of a melancholy inventory of reality, not of a monstrous failure of reconciliation between the finite and the Absolute.

The French author suppresses (or at least understates) the new complexity of the term that results from romantic self-disjunction. This suppression derives from the indwelling paradox of his theorizing, a par-adox that is played out again and again in subsequent views on the grotesque and that manifests itself in the binarity of the *grotesque horrible* and the *grotesque bouffon.* The paradox stems from the fact that the grotesque is by nature aggressive, unbending, anarchic, disruptive, and unregulated. But Christianity can impossibly tolerate such a mode, for Christianity exists by a set of rules and a strict teleological agenda; and although it releases the grotesque into art in the first place, it must then discipline and rein it in again. In other words, Hugo is (without seeming to appreciate this problem) seeking that aesthetic *contradictio in adiecto,* the tame grotesque.

On the one hand he sets the term free by demanding an inner totality of the work of art under the auspices of Christianity. Drama would be "the grotesque, joined with the sublime," "[t]he soul within the body," "tragedy beneath comedy" (187). On the other hand, while he casts scathing aspersions upon the "pedants" who would see only beauty represented in art, he unwittingly reverts to the profoundly classicist assumption that beauty reflects itself in the "lower" styles only to be all the more admired in the contrast; thus the grotesque "seems to be a stopping point, a point for comparison, a point of departure, from which one approaches the beautiful with a fresher and keener perception. The salamander sets off the water-nymph; the gnome heightens the effect of the sylph" (161).

It follows that the peaceful coexistence of grotesque and sublime, grace and deformity, in Hugo's theory, and the insinuation of an autonomy of the lower aesthetic phenomena, is only apparently a democratic proposition. The grotesque is rapidly reassigned familiar positions and functions within the theological and aesthetic discourse, positions reminiscent of the very Augustinian Neoplatonism it seemed at first to transcend:

> In effect, in the new poetry, while the sublime represents the soul as it is, purified by Christian morality, the grotesque will play the role of the animal in man. . . . In this partition of mankind and creation, to the latter will fall passions, vices, and crimes; it will be lustful, servile, gluttonous, miserly, perfidious, mischievous, and hypocritical. It will be, in turn, Iago, Tartuffe, Basile; Harpagon, Polonius, Bartholo; Falstaff, Scapin, Figaro. (Hugo 162)

Conspicuously absent from this list are characters like Christopher Marlowe's Tamburlaine or Barabas, Shakespeare's Aaron or Tamora, Molière's Don Juan, and other true monsters of dramatic history. The ambiguity they spell has no place in Hugo's *drame;* the "animal in man" is obviously a comical or ridiculous animal, meek before the gravity of the Christian sublime, for "the grotesque is comedy" (166).

It would be unfair to label Hugo entirely regressive; he does allow the horrible element to intrude with a Richard III or Mephistopheles. But the ultimate movement of sublimation (the analogue, in art, of salvation) always remains active in this aesthetics of grace: "A deformed, horrible, hideous thing transported with truth and poetry into the domain of art, will become beautiful, admirable, and sublime, without losing any of its monstrousness" (Hugo 194 n).

Hugo's great service to the grotesque is to rescue it from the charge of unfounded subjectivity and to install it in the objective realm. His disservice is that he cannot resist overmoralizing it and consigning it to the play of conventional values. It is astonishing that a poetics so grounded in conservative precepts was received as a revolutionary manifesto. But by way of explanation, Arthur Clayborough notes that in nineteenth-century France, the grotesque "acquires revolutionary overtones" merely by being associated with "objective reality" (13). And Frederick Brown paraphrases the dismay of the bourgeois *arrivistes* at the political implications of an unbound grotesque, as they read it into the *Préface de Cromwell:* "Without genres to distinguish high from low, there could be no foundation on which to predicate distinctions of breed, no *essential* hiatus between the orders, no structure consecrating power and property. Everything would fuse. Everything would be possible" (112). The grotesque, in a period predicated on ideals of harmonic hierarchies defined by apodictic gestures of power, presents a deep affront where it resists being relegated to the margin. All of a society's discourses, as the critics of Hugo well noted, are inextricably meshed; challenge the wisdom even of a generic convention and turn it upon itself, and the authority of historical interpretation, the authority of orthodox seeing and knowing, the authority of political action, and finally, *affreusement,* the nation itself is challenged.

The aestheticians following Hugo do their best to hedge against "everything becoming possible." An exception is Charles Baudelaire, never suspect of conservative sympathies, in his essay "Of the Essence of Laughter" (1855). Baudelaire's grotesque (or "absolute comic") springs from man's satanic conviction of his superiority over nature. He acknowledges its code-breaking subversiveness: "Fabulous creations, beings for whose existence no explanation drawn from ordinary common sense is possible, often excite in us a wild hilarity, excessive fits and swooning of laughter" (151). Baudelaire's compatriot Gustave Flaubert on the other hand, in his travelogue *Par les champs et par les grèves* (1848), sounds like a latter-day Vitruvius when he goes so far as to deny the legitimacy of such fantastic mirth-inducing beings, of "impossible existences, revelations that cannot be grasped" (qtd. in Bompiani 400).

The aesthetic theories of the romantic and postromantic period leave the grotesque entangled in a complex maze of terms, alliances, and modifiers, in which it is often unnamed and never completely realized: the sublime, parody, irony, pain, alienation, paradox, failure. Its continuing crisis of legitimacy as the bastard concept of art and literary criticism has left it, like Edmund in *King Lear,* slyly aggressive, amoral, and ambivalent about itself, half beholden to the "plague of custom," half responsible only to "nature."

The nineteenth century, explicitly or not, yearns for the final synthesis of the conscious and unconscious mind in art, for an absolute and unalienated aesthetic being in which "instinct" and "intention" coalesce. But the synthesis has not taken place, nor can it ever: universal poetry is always *becoming* (or, in the pessimistic view, always on its way out, like in Friedrich Nietzsche's view of tragedy). And the subject always desires to heal the primal psychic displacement and constitutes itself from out of that desire. This is nowhere better expressed than in one of the paradigmatic texts of the nineteenth century, Heinrich von Kleist's "On the Marionette Theatre," which places man, always abject, midway between the unconscious marionette and the supremely conscious god. Psychically and poetically, man needs recourse to the intentionally mediated recuperation of the instinctual and of the absolute. The grotesque is such a mediation; its voluntary disjunction of content and form attempts to open a gap that allows a view onto what is invisible or inaccessible to a philosophy of harmonic representation. The obverse of the dream, which casts into discordant symbols the undertow of the narrative of life, the grotesque constructs the discord to enter the passage in reverse and find what is beneath and beyond.

As it emerges from the theories of the nineteenth century into its modern interpretation, the philosophy of the grotesque is part of the theoretical conflict between consciousness and expression that modernism addresses in a variety of ways. But the grotesque in art seems to contain two distinct directions of attack: First, it is the parodic revelation of the discrepancy between matter and form that the doctrine of beauty suppressed. Second, it provokes the urge to overcome and replace representation itself with essence, to substitute the rich totality of the signified for the poverty of the signifier, to eliminate form in favor of the presence of pure matter (this is, we may presume, the ultimate aim of Hegel's Indians). Grotesque art is always cognizant of the futility of the latter project, because it itself is the result of that failure, which causes it to double back with a vengeance upon its objects in savage parody. It is thus a kind of double parody, sprung from two sources; one the ironic decree that the poles of the world (mind and matter, Apollo and Dionysus, finite and infinite) shall not meet in harmonic identity, and one the horrified disappointment that they cannot meet. But parody, as Jean Baudrillard observes, makes "obedience and transgression equivalent, and that is the most serious crime, since it *cancels out the difference upon which the law is based*" (40). It is this crime that gives the grotesque its standing in what the romantic theorist Friedrich Schlegel called the "criminal codex" of modernity.

Yet this pays attention only to its sense of mission, its earnest intents, so to speak. There is also a ludic or playful element to the grotesque that remains in place vestigially from its older incarnations and of which its "humorous" or "caricaturistic" features are the trivialized form. Modernity reinvests this playful tendency with new meaning. The true extent of this play of the grotesque is that it eschews an orderly metaphysical, aesthetic, and social structure already in place by the decree of centuries of philosophical work (and its correlation in art); it is a play that is the joyous and painful affirmation of the loss of security. For the grotesque is always the midwife at what Jacques Derrida describes as a "birth" of a new form of interpretation born of play, a birth of "the as yet unnamable which is proclaiming itself and which can do so, as is necessary whenever a birth is in the offing, only under the species of the nonspecies, in the formless, mute, infant, and terrifying form of monstrosity" (*Writing* 293).

The Problem of Grotesque Laughter

One paradox of the grotesque is that its structure is assumed to be quite simple, but the responses to it are highly complex. The objects of the grotesque occasion, so much is critical consensus, a severe and strongly ambivalent affective or emotional conflict: terror tempered by ridicule, or comic surprise mingled with a sense of the uncanny. But as we saw in the discussion of the nineteenth-century approaches, it is not, on the whole, the *terror* of the grotesque that poses critical problems; it is the *laughter.*

Assessing the role that laughter might play in the grotesque is difficult, since there is no definitive psychology of laughter. Yet, as Baudelaire writes in "Of the Essence of Laughter," "There is only one proof of the grotesque, which is laughter, a burst of instantaneous laughter." Baudelaire describes this laughter tantalizingly as "profound, axiomatic, and primitive" (152). Ignoring for the moment Baudelaire's moralizing premise that the comic is the mark of Satan in humans, we may agree with him that laughter, a certain kind of laughter, is the sign of the grotesque and that defining it by our response is as good an approach as any to this chimeric phenomenon. Moreover, I would propose here that the way in which it manages laughter, indeed stage-manages it, is in fact one of the primary structural determinants of grotesque art. Yet critical consensus seems to break down here, and several important modern theories of the grotesque ignore the aspect of laughter altogether. Even where they take it into account, like Mikhail Bakhtin, it appears, as we saw, inadequate to a modern theory. Bakhtin's laughter is mainly cathartic and inextricable from its alliance with the comic: "[The] grotesque image cannot be understood without appreciating the defeat of fear. The people play with terror and laugh at it; the awesome becomes a 'comic monster'" (91). Bakhtin is expounding on a comic concept of grotesqueness that is obviously festive and cathartic, in which laughter is emancipatory, not so much defensive as transformative, a universalizing gesture. I have previously noted the problems of omission with that approach: it is clearly a premodern affect, historically conditioned to premodern fears, and it subsumes the grotesque-as-terrible entirely into the comic, if for the opposite political reasons than the romantic theories.

As we have seen, aesthetic theory, especially in the nineteenth century, was at great pains to associate the grotesque with the comic and to tolerate its presence in polite company only if it donned the fool's cap; it was often referred to only in its hyphenated form as the "grotesque-comic." The first, albeit unsystematic, study of the subject was Karl Friedrich Flögel's *Geschichte des Grotesk-Komischen* (*History of the Grotesque-Comic,* 1788). Even Hugo, or the Hegelian Karl Rosenkranz, who wrote an "Aesthetics of the Ugly," finally always insisted on a redemption of the grotesque through humor.

But the discrepancies between ridicule and the comic are not so easily explained. Baudelaire, who is persuaded that the sinful human assumption of one's own superiority over nature is at the root of grotesque laughter, delivers a version of the ridicule-hypothesis, and he bluntly challenges the reader: "Find another plausible explanation if you can" (152). In so doing, I am inclined to follow Eugène Souriau and Hans Robert Jauss, who describe the ridiculous as part of an empirical (*lebensweltlich* is Jauss's term) response but the comic as an aesthetic refinement of the same impulse (subject to a *révision réflexive,* in Souriau's words) (Jauss, "Zum Problem" 361). If the laughing response to the grotesque then is indeed ridicule, it is at its root a pragmatic response, that is, directed at something perceived as real rather than represented and drawing on the atavistic (or "primitive") stratum of laughter as defense or rejection rather than the civilized and gentle laughter of correction. Laughter here functions, in Julia Kristeva's words, as "a way of placing or displacing abjection" (*Powers* 68). The laughter of ridicule is thus the impulse in which the first onslaught of the grotesque, its terrible immediacy and presence, is distanced and aesthetically and morally framed (as something "other" and "inappropriate"). Speaking of the plays of Seneca, Rainer Sell concludes that "[h]yperbolic horror seems to create laughter when the reader, listener, or spectator can no longer relate the manifestation of horror to a system of human values or a familiar pattern of human behavior" (290).[2]

It is clear that laughter is a persistent problem for the theory of the grotesque, which likes to either cede the field to it or make it disappear. Kristeva, correctively glossing Bakhtin, speaks of carnival laughter as "no more comic than tragic; it is both at once, one might say that it is *serious*" (*Desire* 80). In the further pursuit of this "serious" laughter of the grotesque, we should remember that both the grotesque and the comic rely largely on a similar operation: the use of incongruity or incompatibility, or what Arthur Koestler describes as "the sudden bisociation of a mental event with two habitually incompatible matrices" (59). Kenneth Burke, in fact, calls the grotesque "the cult of incongruity," but he stipulates: "The grotesque is the cult of incongruity *without* the laughter. The grotesque is not funny unless you are out of sympathy with it (whereby it serves as an unintentional burlesque). Insofar as you are *in* sympathy with it, it is deadly earnest" (*Attitudes* 58). Burke points to the paradox of laughter in the grotesque, but he is too quick to evade the problem. We have the key here, it seems, in the terms "acceptance" and "rejection," two terms around which Burke builds an entire system of analysis. Could it be that the binarity Burke suggests is in fact a dialectic—that the grotesque is by definition such a work that we are by turns in sympathy and out of sympathy with its content, that by its form it solicits acceptance and rejection, not in perfect suspension but in rapid oscillation? Is the grotesque work one that is intent on breaking down this a priori dichotomy from which we typically derive a sense of safety and stability of perspective in the realm of art?

The key is perhaps that grotesque laughter is not the laughter of humor; it is always inappropriate laughter, and therefore it both does and does not belong to the grotesque. One is, in other words, simultaneously in sympathy and out of sympathy with the grotesque; this is an essential part of its aesthetic definition. We can see inappropriate laughter as a relative of black humor or the macabre, which enables certain transgressions against established codes of piety (especially those connected with death) and then recodifies these transgressions. But the laughter of the macabre is relatively more orderly than that of the grotesque due to this implicit recodification; it is completely purposeful in respect to its function in the psychic economy and does not force an emotional ambivalence it cannot resolve. The grotesque sometimes tests the limits of even these amplified boundaries; it is literally "sick" humor, humor too diseased to allow for easy reconciliation.[3]

Burke is right in observing that sympathy with the grotesque (that is, closeness) prohibits any hilarity. Cognitive incongruity and categorical confusion are more painful than comical, and studies that focus exclusively on that element will tend to downplay the role of laughter. In illustration of the notion of inappropriate laughter, let me quote the venerable A. C. Bradley on the porter scene in *Macbeth,* even though the occurrence is "grotesque" only in Bradley's looser sense of the term:

> The Porter does not make me smile: the moment is too terrific. He is grotesque; no doubt the contrast he affords is humorous as well as ghastly; I dare say the groundlings roared with laughter at his coarsest remarks. But they are not comic enough to allow one to forget for a moment what has preceded and what must follow. And I am far from complaining of this. I believe that it is what Shakespeare intended, and that he despised the groundlings if they laughed. (329)

Bradley's chastisement of the groundlings for their "inappropriate" laughter may offend our democratic sensibility, but it emphasizes an important fact: that the capacity for laughter always depends on a *partial* viewpoint. The Bradleian groundlings, in their mirth over the scene at hand, are oblivious of "what has preceded and what must follow"; they are momentarily given over to a comedic mood that shrinks the surrounding poetic universe to the size of a punch line. This comedy is in a literal sense irresponsible, unrespondent to the grisly deeds done and the unraveling of a world to come (the tragic mood, in this same sense, is always overrespondent, enlarging the individual deed to encompass universal significance). But Bradley's pronouncement that Shakespeare loathed this irresponsible hilarity I think is utterly wrong; on the contrary, I assume that it is exactly the author's intention to intoxicate his audience with comic mood and then to sober it, within a scarce minute, with "horror, horror, horror." As a matter of fact, this is probably one of the most concise examples of the tragicomic mechanism at work in Shakespeare, the same mechanism that pervades *King Lear,* in the words of G. Wilson Knight, with "ripples of impossible laughter" in which the pathos, far from being minimized, is "redoubled" (137–38).

The point is that the genuine grotesque appeals to our Bradleian instinct and our groundling instinct at the same time, to the overrespondent and the irresponsible, forcing closeness and distance simultaneously. Thus the grotesque brings out what Roland Barthes calls "the great secret of every vital semantics": that distance and proximity are both in their own way "promoters of meaning" (*Responsibility* 141). But this doubling of meaning results in a conflict of emotions. Northrop Frye has found that the motivation for laughter in a group is its potency to displace or dispel a threat to the community: "[In laughter] some kind of deliverance from the unpleasant, even the horrible, seems to be very important. We notice this particularly in all forms of art in which a large number of auditors are simultaneously present, as in drama, and, still more obviously, in games" (46). Thus we have in it a kind of emotional expurgation, a sacrificial rite (for the horrible in drama and games is most often embodied in a symbolic substitute) that needs the communal forum to be efficacious. If aesthetically refined catharsis entails, as Jauss puts it, "self-enjoyment through the enjoyment of what is other" (*Aesthetic Experience* 92), then the catharsis that laughter aims at entails, on a raw psychic level, self-assurance through the assurance that the object of ridicule is other.

We may speak of the contradictory expression of both a social and an individual (or a public and a private) impulse in which the grotesque attempts to snare us. In Henri Bergson's theory of the comic, which is really a theory of the ridiculous, laughter is an intellectual and above all a social response; it is "always the laughter of a group." Bergson's famous formula for detecting some form of rigidity in the realm of *élan vital,* the "mechanical encrusted on the living," is productive of laughter only by categorically ruling out compassion or closeness (64, 84). This laughter is a type of communal self-assurance that obeys the logic of the masses; it is groundling laughter, sharp, irresponsible, and humiliating. In the grotesque, the "Bradleian" conscience, which is the overrespondent conscience of individual endangerment, of the isolated, self-reflexive emotion, returns us from this judgmental glee to confront us with the mechanical as a terrible allegory of our own lives. But in the process, both partial responses are transformed; the laughter is neither solely that of ridicule anymore, nor is the terror that comforting terror of tragedy. Each becomes tainted with the other without dissolving into its opposite—terror shades laughter as laughter shadows terror. Thus it is this frightful familiarity as well as uncanny uncommonness that create the terror that laughter must defuse. This seems like a paradox (and it is) because both closeness and distance, or closeness-in-distance, the own in the other, breed terror. The paradox may be explained by having recourse to Sigmund Freud's analysis of the uncanny. In his essay, Freud plays on the etymological ambivalence of *heimlich* (homely, but also secret or hidden) and *unheimlich* (uncanny): "[T]he *unheimlich* is what was once *heimisch*, familiar; the prefix '*un*' ['un-'] is the token of repression" (*Standard Edition* 17:245).

Laughter has a special function in the theatre that has remained remarkably stable from the satires of Aristophanes to the farces of Georges Feydeau. The optimistic genre of comedy, through which a community practices self-affirmation and periodically reratifies its value system, is its material manifestation. By definition, such laughter is appropriate, a defense of the boundaries of proper conduct. Where it is not, we have a good chance of being in the presence of the grotesque. The grotesque in the theatre may be most effective where we are given a surrogate in the form of an onstage audience in whom our worst instincts—our social instincts of aggressive ridicule for the *pharmakos* or victim—are embodied in grotesque magnification. The terrible transformation of benevolent villagers into murderous accomplices in Friedrich Dürrenmatt's *The Visit* or the crowd in Bertolt Brecht's *Mahagonny* that responds with loud and prolonged (inappropriate) laughter to the announcement that Joe has been killed in the boxing ring are good examples.

To René Girard, laughter is a "bizarre affection," inherently contradictory and serviceable to any number of causes, an emotional conundrum in which survival instinct and endangerment (or "threat") are simultaneously expressed:

> A man will not laugh . . . unless there is an actual threat to his ability to control his environment and the people in it, even his own thoughts and his own

> desires. A man will not laugh, however, if that threat becomes too real. The conditions necessary for laughter are therefore contradictory. The threat must be both overwhelming and nil; the danger of being absorbed into the pattern that has already devoured the victims of our laughter must be both immediate and nonexistent. In order to "have a good laugh," we must always come out "on top," even as we are constantly threatened to "go under." ("*Double Business*" 130–31)

There are probably two distinct ways in which laughter can work in the grotesque, and they are dependent on the distribution of the latent and the manifest element. Simply put, if the horrible aspect is dominant or manifest, laughter will almost always be a mechanism for counteracting the horror. When the comical element is dominant, horror becomes a response to the callousness of one's own laughter. Either way, the grotesque structure must assure that the distribution of the elements is adequate to guarantee that neither impulse takes over too quickly and that there is a responsive interdependence of laughter and horror.

If John Ruskin is correct in assuming that the objects of grotesque horror, contemplated correctly, would "cease to be grotesque and become altogether sublime" (150), then there must be an element of arrested judgment, of perspective held hostage, in the confrontation with the true grotesque. Ruskin suggests that there is a way of looking past the contradiction in the object by which everything blossoms into transcendent sublimity (a good *précis* of the favorite nineteenth-century post-Hugo position). But we must then conclude that grotesque perception is, in a sense, a "wrong" perception from the standpoint of sublimity, one that cannot avail itself of the mitigating circumstances that transform its object and elevate it, like a child awakened from nightmares by the flick of the light switch in the bedroom. This fierce contiguity of the grotesque perspective lends it an aspect of truth that is of necessity partial, ephemeral. There is no grotesque *sub specie aeternitatis.*

This "hostage taking" of the perspective in the grotesque presents a key to the copresence of horror and ridicule that marks its effect. For now we may be able to construct not only a simultaneity of the two impulses but a true dialectic. Taking my cue from Immanuel Kant's observation in his *Critique of Judgment* that we cease to perceive things that disgust us as aesthetic objects, I will assume that this reaction is stimulated when the aesthetic object trangresses against the limits of aesthetics and demands a closeness that is no longer amenable to a disinterested contemplation. The force of its persuasion, in other words, is such that it almost comes into *being* rather than remaining in appearance, not because it is actually so real or threatening, but because it has access to an emotional stratum that is commonly identified with a real threat. It is only logical that, as a defensive countermove, the subject will seek to muster an affect that is in turn identified with the conversion of life into spectacle, reality into aesthetics, an affect that will release the hostage perspective. This affect is laughter, the social affect. Of course, how complex this interplay becomes before it again allows emotional equidistance depends entirely upon the particular structure of the grotesque work involved.

But the laughter of the grotesque is not, as I have noted, merely adversarial, that is, generated by the audience to "defuse" the insistent aesthetic object; the most successful grotesque will incorporate the laughable into its own structure and play it against the horrific in such a way that we are horrified to laugh where we do and amused that we are horrified where we are. Exposure to the grotesque creates an oscillation of acceptance and rejection; it consists of giving in to and repudiating the seduction of the grotesque object. This entails not a simple ambiguity that results from a loss of center and structure but a complex and playful ambiguity, a movement of being confounded and being liberated in which the empirical and the aesthetic attitude dominate in turn.

Simple catharsis, in the sense of the unilateral purification of emotions, cannot then be the objective of the grotesque work, for catharsis presupposes clear structures in which one's own emotions may be objectified. But the emotions of the grotesque are "kinetic emotions" in the sense that James Joyce speaks of them in *A Portrait of the Artist as a Young Man.* The character Stephen Dedalus there argues that tragic emotion is "a face looking two ways, towards terror and towards pity"; tragedy, as a "proper art," thus arrests the emotion and renders it "static":

> The feelings excited by improper art are kinetic, desire or loathing. Desire urges us to possess, to go to something; loathing urges us to abandon, to go from something. These are kinetic emotions. The arts which excite them, pornographical or didactic, are therefore improper arts. The esthetic emotion (I use the general term) is therefore static. The mind is arrested and raised above desire and loathing. (186)

Dedalus's view is positively neo-Kantian; "desire" is the Kantian "interest," which may play no role in the perception of the artwork; "loathing" is the Kantian "disgust" that must not be aroused by the representation. To his list of improper arts Dedalus might have added the grotesque, which is (as concerns the emotional response it evinces) perhaps a strange mixture of the pornographical and didactic, the province of desire *and* loathing. If the grotesque is indeed an "improper art," then the laughter of the grotesque is improper, or perhaps inappropriate, laughter, not because it is morally wrong, but because there is nothing that is "proper" (Latin *proprius*) to it, because it lacks the "objective correlative" (in T. S. Eliot's noted term) of the comic object.

Underlying the ambiguous reaction to the grotesque is the conflict of the private and the public (communal and personal), which is both engendered by and represented in the appearances of the grotesque. This theme is like a leitmotif in all considerations of the mode: Bakhtin, with his public and universal carnival body, emphasizes the collective moment, just as Wolfgang Kayser isolates the personal factor (the notion of privacy and its exacerbations in the alienated and abject subject being, arguably, a modern invention).

But nowhere can the contrast, even the utter disparity, between our public and private being be so provoked as in the *theatron,* the "seeing place," where our isolated sensibility as a "spectator" battles our communal identity as part of an "audience" (as we, in turn, observe with this doubled, schizophrenic attention the actor in his role, the ultimate public/private paradox). Because of this double manner in which the theatre constitutes us, it is more potent than any other branch of fiction in the business of catharsis (understood as the promise to reconcile, for an instant, this ontic incongruity that it has thrown into relief); but it is also the most disturbing in its refusal of the cathartic experience.

If I contend that the grotesque play (so long as it does not simply parade "grotesque" incidents for shock value) is unwilling to effect catharsis, this is very much a logical consequence of the preceding argument. For in tragedy catharsis must in essence be understood as the transmutation of the personal emotions of pity and fear into a kind of communal acquiescence in tragic fate. Catharsis can be seen as a function that momentarily erases the emotionally overextended private persona in order to restore in it a balance of distance and closeness. The objective of the grotesque is precisely to deny such a balance, for in this balance the harmony of private and public self, of reality and representation, and of self and world is announced and consecrated. Thomas Scheff also argues for a kind of emotional equidistance that the cathartic work of art achieves. Grotesque works—he does not use the term but cites Seneca, Grand Guignol, and so on—are incapable of generating such a balance:

> The effect of these [plays] is to provoke strong feelings without resolution, leaving the audience stranded, therefore, at the end with feelings of anxiety, fear, and grief. Such dramas lead the audience to an emotional response, but it is emotional distress, rather than discharge. (153)

I do not, however, quite agree with Scheff that the plays one would have to call grotesque are necessarily "underdistanced from emotion"; I have instead asserted that their emotional signature is an irresolute mixture of closeness and distance (or, in Scheff's terms, perhaps a simultaneous "overdistance" and "underdistance").

Although I quoted Baudelaire earlier and agreed with him that the grotesque is marked by a peculiar type of laughter, it should be clear that my thinking on the grotesque is quite different from Baudelaire's. For Baudelaire, one of the most distinctive signs of the "absolute comic" is that it is "unconscious of itself." This is clearly not true for grotesque art as I have defined it here. Indeed, I have posited a necessary self-consciousness of the artwork that creates an equally self-conscious response—laughter made uneasy by its awareness of its own impropriety or inadequacy. There is certainly a side to this laughter that wants to be "profound, axiomatic, and primitive," for therein lies safety. But in the disruption of this safety, in the manner in which it takes laughter to task, the grotesque work claims its deeper purpose. In grotesque plays, as coming sections will show, the moment of laughter coincides not with an occasion in which a crisis is mastered (as in conventional comedy) but in fact with an occasion of impossible representation and "improper" response that first makes an aesthetic crisis visible (and risible) and through it points to an ethical failure. Grotesque art thus creates such self-conscious laughter to mark the boundaries of the generically manageable and the aesthetically representable in the culture from which it springs, yet the laughter is always a token of a boundary already violated. Thus our laughter becomes an echo of the original transgression, simultaneously rejecting and endorsing it.

Bending Genre

Genre is the fortresslike warrant of propriety in the realm of drama in the face of all that might challenge it. Aristotle admonishes that "something merely monstrous" has no place in tragedy, "for not every kind of pleasure should be demanded of tragedy, but only that which is proper to it" ("On the Art of Poetry" 49). However, in trying to determine how generic theory might treat the grotesque, we encounter the persistent stumbling block of generic criticism, its reluctance to acknowledge new expressions. The grotesque is one of a handful of formal problems in relation to which, to quote Frye, "we find ourselves in the position of the Renaissance doctors who refused to treat syphilis because Galen said nothing about it" (13).

Though not in itself a genre, the grotesque is closely tied to generic problems. Genre, which can be described as a conventionalized way of dealing with actuality, is a manner of "framing" events such that we are clearly aware of what is included in and what is excluded from our "horizon of expectations" (to borrow a term from reader-response theory). Genre is a type of representational insurance; the security it provides lies in its tacit elimination of chaos. Certain things that typically happen in detective fiction are unthinkable in the pastoral novel, and vice versa. We are left with a small pool of possible operational permutations; most possibilities of variation are simply excluded by virtue of a set of hard-and-fast rules.

The grotesque is antigeneric mostly because it is anticonventional. Genre treats actuality, or converts actuality, in a largely prescribed and understood conventional manner. As an instrument of literary economy, or expressive shorthand, genre can count on a set of assumptions it need not expressly manifest, and one of its salient feats is the exclusion of certain combinatorial, symbolic, or narrative possibilities (there will be no comedic *ad spectatores* in a Henrik Ibsen drama, nor will a picaresque hero be inclined to shoot himself in abject depression). As in the eidetic operation of phenomenology, every genre "brackets" certain elements of actuality to arrive at its own verity. Since antiquity, genre has been construed to serve a predominantly hygienic function; its rules have been seen as a veritable *cordon sanitaire* against the invasion of alien elements.

That classicist attitude perpetrated the fiction of the timelessness of generic forms by clinging to the prescriptive nature particularly of the Aristotelian canon. There is of course no timeless genre; even the "master" genres of epic, drama, and poetry are informed by a limited and limiting set of historically motivated assumptions according to which they are constructed and which they have far outlived, even if they concurrently seem to echo "eternal" modes of human expression. Subgenres such as tragedy, or the sonnet, are even more clearly products of a certain fixed epistemology.

The literary genre has consequently become a holdout against historical progression, surviving long beyond its period of greatest "maturity," or ideological congruence with its age. It is necessarily almost always unsynchronized with the laws of perception of any age but its own. Paradoxically, this "inadequacy" of genre is not at all detrimental but rather one of the foremost productive forces of literature.[4] At the same time, it is exactly the steadfast refusal of genre to conspire with actuality that makes it susceptible to the parodic, and consequently to the grotesque.

Grotesqueness, of course, means a deliberate skewering of the combinations of plot and symbolic elements a genre permits. It is a force against the grain of genre. In that function, it has as much need of genre as any other form of literature, because it exists in an aesthetic universe that, as Tzvetan Todorov has shown, cannot avoid being in some form generic.[5] Carl Pietzcker argues that the grotesque "awakens certain expectations" in the viewer or reader that he or she will be able "to interpret what it presents with the help of certain categories," and then disappoints these expectations. Thus, the "normal and common," says Pietzcker, "necessarily belongs to the grotesque" (204–5). Normalcy, however, is not a meaningful category of art criticism, for what is normal in a work of art is always determined by its genre. We can attribute to the grotesque work an implied genericity that it must first formulate to then seize upon generic expectations. This does not mean that in principle the grotesque is restricted to appearing *within* works of a certain genre; it must only ensure itself of an environment defined by generic rules. The museum is such a space (much of contemporary installation art is constructed around the compelling generic power of the museum space). A split hog's carcass, for instance, while unremarkable when on display in a butcher shop, can become grotesque when put on display in a gallery, which is a space in which bodies generically mean something else. This proclamatory quality of generic space—the museum in effect claiming, "All within me is art"—is present, in a slightly more diffuse way, in the theatre as well. The theatre's incessant generic assertion may be phrased as: "All within me is a lifelike allegory of life." Such generic self-confidence is a powerful provocation to the sense of the grotesque.

As a mode, the grotesque is thus parasitical to genre—it affixes itself to the para-site of genre, the site at genre's edge, its blind spot, whence it can be unraveled and turned against itself. Thus the grotesque, in its effort to transcend genre, or regulated representation, injects a kind of "operational negativity," a "scenario of deterrence" into its host that tries to "regenerate a moribund principle by simulated scandal, phantasm, murder—a sort of hormonal treatment by negativity and crisis" (Baud-rillard 36). I am here borrowing terms of Baudrillard's that were written for an entirely different context, but his observation seems eminently applicable, for instance, to Antonin Artaud's agenda of unleashing an aesthetic pestilence on the theatre space in hopes of recovering the theatre's lost, archetypal, and dangerous "double," true reality, and the double of that double, the true theatre. To inscribe forcefully the heavy hieroglyphs of his new theatre, Artaud had first to dispense with the airy allegories of the old by exploding them from within.

Being thus corrective of genre's exclusionary tendencies but dependent on the existence of genre, the grotesque betrays an ambivalent attitude toward its host structure; it becomes an impulse directed at generic *execution* in the double sense of the term: perpetuation and destruction. This is why Baudrillard's analogy seems appropriate here: in the very process by which it questions the validity of generic representation, the grotesque also revalidates the genre by "scandalizing" it.

Comedy and tragedy are notoriously rigid frames, reinforced by the reception of the Aristotelian critique that made tragedy out to be a kind of catharsis machine, inevitably producing sublimity where the correct elements were combined. This means that dramatic genre is by tradition far more strongly tied to a notion of efficacy than any other poetic genre. In tragedy (as well as in comedy), drama presents a paradigmatically solved conflict. The drama consists of this conflict—the deliberate provocation of a potentially entropic crisis—and its rechanneling into the Procrustean bed of a genre endowed with a certain formal arrogance. The arrogance of tragedy is that it is, as Walter Kerr says, "born of certainty" (275), a certainty that may also be described as the conviction of its own a priori power to sublimate or sacralize the critical events. Comedy is perhaps less stringent, but it nonetheless parallels tragedy's paradigmatic self-confidence as a genre. In both genres, we could say, crisis is treated much like an illness, to be cured either homeopathically (tragedy) or allopathically (comedy). The grotesque—to remain within the metaphor—favors the creation of a crisis that does not yield to the conventional (generically prescribed) cure. Arguing from within the traditional context of dramatic structure, it subverts it by signaling the presence of a virulent crisis but confounding the generic immune system. The grotesque thus has a highly developed sensitivity to the shortcomings and limitations of genres, their own submerged perceptual crises.[6]

It is unnecessary for the grotesque to invent these generic crises; they are already structurally present. The generic base and point of reference of the grotesque in modern drama, this much should be certain, is not comedy but tragedy—tragedy that has become suspect, untenable, embarrassing. Tragedy is a genre that is simultaneously open to the notion of human freedom and to the determinism of fate—this is its potential Achilles heel. Because we tend to favor the ideal of freedom as more consistent with the generic representation of ourselves, fate as a mechanical operator within the living is suppressed. The "hormonal" treatment of the grotesque for tragedy may thus consist of crossing it with farce, or rather, of making tragedy admit that in the mechanism of fate, it harbors within itself the "horribly attenuated" view of human life that farce represents (Bentley 247). Eliot's reading of Marlowe's *Jew of Malta* "not as a tragedy, or as a 'tragedy of blood' but as a farce" would concur with this notion (*Elizabethan Dramatists* 63).

Luigi Pirandello referred to the works of the Italian *teatro grottesco* as "transcendental farce": "The farce of the Grotesque includes in its tragedy its parody and its caricature, not as extraneous superposed elements, but as its own shadow, the awkward shadow of every tragic gesture" (Valency 96). For the generic disruption of tragedy, sometimes no more is necessary than a sort of kinetic exacerbation or extravagance that counteracts tragic dignity and gravity. In the words of Eugène Ionesco, "Take a tragedy, accelerate the movement, and you will have a comic play" (*Notes* 236). And Senecan tragedy, in an attempt to convey a feeling of moral chaos, "resorted to the adequate literary means—namely the grotesque—in a genre that, by tradition, was not capable of expressing 'total moral disorientation'" (Sell 287).

The fact is, however, that tragedy as a form is not brittle, and it may be stretched far until its limits are reached. The Fool's scenes in *King Lear*—a play often labeled "grotesque" because of the emotional turmoil it induces—work for the tragedy, not against it; they subvert no pieties but strengthen them implicitly. If we take the play as a Beckettian scene, as Jan Kott has urged, we are deaf to at least half of its meaning. When

Lear finally arrives at his "Thou'lt come no more, / Never, never, never, never, never" (5.3.308–9), Cordelia's death has not been depleted of significance but filled entirely. *Lear,* since it rests on a vindication of filial loyalty that is nowhere questioned, is as immune as tragedy may be to the grotesque, short of having Cordelia herself become the monster. But such sturdiness is not a given. When the world of the Andronici in *Titus Andronicus* falls apart (a question that I will pursue in the next chapter), it is a much flimsier tragedy that succumbs to the grotesque, one that would rather have been a romance in the first place.

The injection of the grotesque into the bloodstream of genre is thus a veritable inoculation that, by taking the generic form to its extremes, also fortifies it against its own imminent obsolescence. This is the foundation, for instance, of Dürrenmatt's grotesque dramaturgy that categorically denies that the tragic prerequisites of "guilt, despair, moderation, lucidity, vision, a sense of responsibility" are anywhere present in the "Punch-and-Judy show of our century" and that therefore the tragic can be reconstituted only "out of comedy": it can only be brought forth "as a frightening moment, as an abyss that opens suddenly" ("Problems" 136).

There is no rule that in the theatre the grotesque must already be inscribed into the play-text; it can just as easily be a function of the *mise-en-scène.* Ionesco suggests "playing against the text":

> A serious, solemn, formal production or interpretation can be grafted onto a text that is absurd, wild and comic. On the other hand, to avoid the ridiculous sentimentality of the tear-jerker, a dramatic text can be treated as buffoonery and the tragic feeling of a play can be underlined by farce. Light makes shadows darker, shadows intensify light. (*Notes* 25)

In Peter Brook's notorious 1968 staging of Seneca's *Oedipus,* the bloody tragedy concluded with the unveiling of a giant golden phallus, and actors began to dance around it as a Dixieland band broke into the (appropriately phallic) tune "Yes, We Have No Bananas." Some critics found this ending distasteful or frivolous since it created "a last wrenching disjuncture . . . converting the somber moment into farce" (Motto and Clark 18). But Brook was merely—even if through a *coup de théâtre* of questionable validity—emphasizing the ludicrous side of the Oedipus fable by confronting it (and the audience) with the oversized symbol of its own "hidden" meanings. The farce is an integral part of *Oedipus,* the obverse side of its reveling in Grand Guignol gore. Of course, Seneca's version—

particularly in the anatomically explicit adaptation by Ted Hughes—accommodates this farcical ending more easily than Sophocles'.

The rereading of classical texts and their scenic exploration for unacknowledged grotesque structures is of course a frequent occurrence in the contemporary theatre, although one must distinguish carefully here between the arbitrary imposition of an incongruous interpretation that subverts the play simply by refusing to take it seriously and one that subverts it by taking it very seriously indeed. The destruction of tragic pieties under the onslaught of the grotesque vision is exactly what serves to regain a sense of the pure tragic itself. Modern tragedy thus becomes possible only by suffering its own defeat.

Kayser has noted that "the history of the grotesque in the field of drama is largely one with that of tragicomedy" (54). This is a reasonable but essentially fallacious assumption; nothing is gained toward the explication of the grotesque by equating it with a generic construct as overused and underdetermined as tragicomedy. While the occasional cohabitation of the grotesque mode and the tragicomic structure in the same dramatic vehicle cannot be denied, I am here interested in revealing their difference.

The tradition of tragicomic criticism has been to distinguish with precision between Sidney's proverbial "hornpipes and funerals," that is, to single out which instruments play the comic dominant, which the tragic subdominant. This task was formerly eased by the clear distribution of each part by character position and plot: royalty demands tragic treatment, a peasant provokes comedy, love is an occasion for mirth, death for high seriousness, and so on. In modern tragicomedy, these realms are hardly separable, and if they are, they may go contrary to convention: death becomes a comic occurrence, survival a tragic mistake.

Tragicomedy is a generic descriptor without the advantages of strict genericity and identity, an already compromised term without manifest content. If, as I said, genre has a specific historicity, then tragicomedy's historical place is the Renaissance. But there already, it is defined *ex negativo:* constructed not in the spirit of a positive expression but a default consequence of the increasingly intolerable separation of tragic and comic realms. It is meant to exhibit, as Dr. Johnson says of Shakespeare, "the real state of sublunary nature" (Johnson 266), a notoriously fickle determinant. Tragicomic theory has been in the process of constant updating and revision; thus it *appears* modern. This is an illusion: tragicomedy—as opposed to the grotesque—will at any moment only admit to the representation of what is generically plausible, that is, *what it is already possible to represent;* it is the codification of the logically and aesthetically permissible in the field of a consensual perception of "realism."

Thus tragicomedy, in its seeming progressiveness, is a truly conservative generic construct, in the sense that it rescues what it purports to supersede: tragedy and comedy. In Karl S. Guthke's considered view, what is essential for the modern tragicomedy is not merely the alternate representation but "the reciprocity of the interaction of the tragic and the comic" that leads to a "heightening of effect": "[I]t may well be that the tragic is more tragic and the comic is more comic in the tragicomic fusion." For Guthke, the grotesque is different from tragicomedy, for the grotesque world "has gone so mad that it is impossible to understand its madness," while the tragicomic world is always "still intact" (58–59, 75).

But Guthke's distinction seems based on a matter of degree rather than on a firm differentiation, and so an exemplary analysis may be in order. Since Kayser sees the beginnings of the grotesque-tragicomic symbiosis in the drama of the *Sturm und Drang,* let me briefly consider a signature play from that period, Jakob Michael Reinhold Lenz's play *The Tutor, or The Advantages of Private Education* (1774). Lenz finally called his play "a comedy" after changing the genre designation several times to "tragedy" and "tragicomedy" (*Lust- und Trauerspiel*). Lenz's dramaturgical creed is summarized in his statement that "comedy is a picture of human society, and when that becomes serious, the picture cannot become hilarious" (qtd. in Huyssen 114). Henry J. Schmidt also notes Lenz's social motives in choosing genre: "The situations he creates resist generic classification because he wants to overcome the traditional elitism of these categories" (71). In spite of the fact that writing tragicomedy was Lenz's stated intention (he took his cues from Plautus and Shakespeare), the play itself rejects the notion that the tragicomic structure can accommodate the grotesque; indeed, the main grotesque incident in *The Tutor* appears to undercut the entire assumption upon which the tragicomedy relies.

The protagonist of Lenz's play, Läuffer, candidate of theology and son of a sniveling and subservient pastor, is in the employ of the brash and authoritarian Major von Berg and his snobbish wife to tutor the pair's dull son, Leopold, and his romantically inclined sister, Gustchen. Läuffer's station in the major's house amounts to little more than bondage; his salary is surreptitiously cut, and his employers cast constant aspersions on his competence. The volcanic major jealously guards Gustchen's presumed virtue, fancying her "the very image of me" (Lenz 7). His "treasure" of a daughter, however, trysts clandestinely with her cousin Fritz, son of the major's more enlightened brother, Councillor von Berg. When the councillor intrudes on the couple's overheated Romeo-and-Juliet attitudinizing, Fritz is sent away to university. Subsequently, Läuffer displaces Fritz in Gustchen's not overly fastidious attentions, at which point social satire derails into tragicomedy. Gustchen discovers that she is pregnant with Läuffer's child and both flee, he finding refuge in the house of the overbearing and loquacious teacher Wenzeslaus, she with a blind woman where she bears the child.

In a parallel plot, Fritz goes to debtor's prison for his reckless friend Pätus, duels, and is cursed by his father (and later pardoned). To aggravate matters, Gustchen attempts suicide by drowning but is rescued by the major (who eventually forgives her). Gustchen and Fritz are thus projected into the tragicomic horizon where their by turns magnanimous and desperate actions bear witness to the potentially tragic integrity of character that their nobility generically demands. In seeking to drown herself, Gustchen chooses the act of self-annihilation (perhaps modeling herself on Ophelia), an act that fully conforms to the tragic notion of preserving freedom in necessity and dignity in guilt. That she is rescued by her father—in keeping with tragicomic theory—does not compromise her tragic being but only heightens it, while at the same time her rescue opens the avenue of reconciliation that allows for the comic ending.

Läuffer, however, is entirely alienated from these generic proceedings and has no recourse to their logic. He is unsynchronized with the play, being first a comedic figure trapped in an environment that demands tragic action, then a tragic figure in a play that suddenly turns to comedy on him. When by chance he is shown his child by the blind woman, he perceives his likeness in the infant, calling it a "most frightening enigma" (40), and faints. In his next scene, he has succumbed to the grotesque consequence of his state of powerlessness; his friend Wenzeslaus finds him in bed and, on inquiring after his health, receives the reply: "I don't know if I've done the right thing—I've castrated myself" (42). Läuffer's self-emasculation is terrible in itself, but it becomes simultaneously funny when Wenzeslaus, in his religious fervor, praises the sublimity of the act: "What!—castrat—my heartiest congratulations! You splendid young man! A second Origen! Let me embrace you! What a precious stroke of genius! I cannot hide it from you, I almost cannot resist the heroic impulse to imitate you. So right a deed, valued friend!" (42). The cataclysmic self-castration of Läuffer is the grotesque affirmation of his social position and a terrible travesty of the task of cultural sublimation, but it is in a deeper sense the *reductio ad absurdum,* in the flesh, of his psychic being. Läuffer (the name means "runner") is metaphorically implicated in an entire carnival of displacements and attempted sublimations that whittle away at his identity until it seems present only in distorted reflections of his self (father figures, the "enigmatic" child, the paternalistic *doppelgänger* Wenzeslaus).

He is troubled by visions that seem to deny the spiritual rewards of self-mortification that religion promises: a painting distresses him in which the evangelist Mark "looked not a bit more human than the lion that sat beside him" (47); we are clearly in the realm of grotesque signification. Läuffer's self-castration is only the radical upshot of so many metaphorical castrations that have already been performed upon him; early on the councillor comments on his station: "He's relinquished all the privileges of a man; if he can't live according to his principles he can't call himself a man" (11). And at Wenzeslaus's, he prophetically gives himself the pseudonym "Mandel" (meaning "almond"—the almond tree in baroque iconology is the *emblema emblematum* of Christ's "bittersweet" death—but the word can also be read as "little man").

The deed by which he attempts to recuperate his identity permits him to become neither tragic nor comic; Lenz supplies the requisite comedic counterbalance by letting Läuffer fall in love with the innocent girl Lise, but this is only a painful reminder of what is no longer possible for the emasculated protagonist, namely the sexual consummation that comedic fertility demands. Läuffer is truncated, reduced, dehumanized ("O homuncio, homuncio!" Wenzeslaus appropriately cries out [51]), and his last words in the play are again a bid for paternal approbation, this time from Lise's father. The dramatic rhythm of this tragicomedy allows most of its characters to fall comfortably first into the one category, then into the other—by constructing the "tragic" dilemma out of resolvable misunderstandings—but Läuffer is denied this freedom. He comes to be, by virtue of an act that emanates simultaneously from utter necessity and comic inadequacy, generically suspended in a perspective of grotesque compulsion. Self-castration, of course, is also a motif of "sacrifice," and one particularly prevalent in late-eighteenth-century Pietism, and so Läuffer's grotesque fate is tied to a crisis of representation that is both mimetic—the radical act is not shown, cannot be shown—and generic. The self-castration is essentially a muted *sparagmos*.

The last two scenes display a sped-up version of the tragicomic structure in their predictably tearful redemption of all compromised characters from tragic abjection. Läuffer is absent from these scenes. He cannot fit into them because he does not partake of their logic. The indebted Pätus reveals that he has won the lottery. Fritz first believes Gustchen dead, then finds her alive. Even Pätus's formerly monstrous father (who "set aside his humanity for a while and degenerated into a wild animal" [55] and whose abused mother—how else?—the blind woman turns out to be) is infected by the pervasive magnanimity of the ending. Fritz adopts Gustchen's illegitimate child, which he declares "the image of his mother," thus denying Läuffer's likeness, and he destroys the last vestiges even of Läuffer's spiritual paternity by promising the boy (in a would-be jesting tone that at this point is terrifying) that he shall never let him "be educated by a tutor" (55).

With these last words of the play, all is resolved as regards the conventional tragicomic structure, were there not the liability of the castrated tutor. But the same words double as an affirmation of Läuffer's castration, his effacement and annihilation as a human being and character. The happy equilibrium of the play's tragicomic structure is bought with the grotesque extermination of the protagonist. Lenz has thus undercut the foundational economy of tragicomedy with the grotesque treatment (I cannot resist the irony of calling it, in Baudrillard's term, "hormonal") in a manner that calls the tragicomic horizon itself into question. In the words of Girard, the anguished protagonist in Lenz finds himself in a "psychotic situation where the imaginary reigns as master, but where, conversely, it no longer finds intelligible expression, permitting the subject to insert itself into the symbolic order." Lenz's grotesque writing, Girard surmises, "is not essentially a critique of social structures but rather one of the organization of the ego" ("Lenz" 23). Schmidt, too, feels that calling Lenz's dramaturgy tragicomic is inadequate, since every action seems "as if it were a hologram that changes appearance when viewed from a different perspective": "His dramas somehow manage to stage *themselves* against the grain, leaving their audiences with vacillating judgments" (72). Indeed, in this antigeneric self-fashioning, Lenz's tragicomedies become undecidable, grotesque artifacts.

In Brecht's later adaptation of *The Tutor* (1950), by contrast, Läuffer is already merely the didactically viewed type in a social situation that is unequivocally corrupt. He is endowed with mechanical movements that illustrate (but trivialize) his lack of freedom; castration figures only as the symbolic *mise-en-scène* of false acquiescence—the spectacle of a lonely self-emasculation was hardly fit to cause great emotional distress to an audience that had just survived a vicious war. Consequently, the powerful ambivalence that is the hallmark of Lenz's play is lacking; Brechtian distantiation does not embrace the grotesque for its own sake.

A cursory analysis of *The Tutor* such as the one above cannot, of course, conclusively prove the separateness of tragicomedy and the grotesque; it merely suggests their ideological incompatibility and their divergent taste for what is "realistic." I agree with the assessment of Arnold Heidsieck who claims that "[t]he grotesque form excludes tragedy, comedy, and also tragicomedy," although I differ as to the reasons. Heidsieck sees the foundation of tragicomedy in its insistence on the "trans-social heteronomy of man, the insuspendable determinacy of social processes," against which the grotesque asserts their radical arbitrariness (82–83). I would argue that the grotesque aims at a different stratum of truth, one—whether socially determined or not—that is not already known and therefore a priori accessible to the generic idiom but one that is only discovered in the grotesque event itself, as it confronts genre with its own reluctance to transcend the very limitations that constitute the truth peculiar to it (and thus its innate falsity).

In summary, the grotesque, as considered in the context of generic representation, is a mode operating within genre as an agent of what is *outside* it. Therefore, its shape depends on the shape of the genre itself. If there is a genre in which the grotesque mode seems at home, it may be farce. The formal properties of farce harbor a certain sympathy for grotesque expression—the theatre of farce emphasizes the animality or "thingness" of man; it is, as Eric Bentley says, "the theatre of the human body": "It is a theatre in which, though the marionettes are men, the men are supermarionettes. It is the theatre of the surrealist body." Bentley detects in farce a "double dialectic," "a contrast between either the gravity or the gaiety on the surface and whatever lies beneath":

> What do gravity and gaiety have in common? Orderliness and mildness. What lies beneath the surface, on the other hand, is disorderly and violent. It is a double dialectic. On the surface the contrast of gay and grave, then, secondly, the contrast of surface and beneath-the-surface. The second is a larger and even more dynamic contrast. (252, 242)

But farce is also at its base a cynical genre, one that has—in contrast to both comedy and tragedy—no true pieties. The "disorderly and violent" stratum Bentley discovers there is not its nemesis nor its thorn in the flesh, not its unacknowledged or disturbing other (as in tragedy and comedy), but its very motor force. Farce is blunt, but not sincere. It has no teleology, holds out no hope for the better. It is the theatre of the triumphant undisplaced id. The mind trained on pure farce is imperturbable; to it, the grotesque is an almost sentimental notion. Farce is perhaps the generic form of a grotesque that can fully salvage itself in laughter, that goes not the path of Pentheus but of Dionysus the Eternally Unscathed, Eternally Resurrected. Thus, it is formally close to the grotesque in many ways, and yet the grotesque has no interest in farce per se (although, as I have said, it can use farce as a *means* by projecting it into the tragic horizon).

The grotesque must cease to exist (or be effective) when it becomes generic and predictable. Being saddled with the mandate to arouse certain responses, it must be a chameleon mode, constantly amending its strategy. However, it can hardly help falling into the generic trap, since that seems to be the eventual fate of all art. There are certain elements that are generically connected with the grotesque (the man/machine dichotomy; the man/beast dichotomy; the deformed body; and so on) because they remain effective in spite of their generic status. But even the grotesque can easily be imitated and lapse into pastiche. Like truth, the grotesque is always an endangered species.

Radical Metaphor and *Mise-en-Scène*

> *The best way, it seems to me, to realize [the] idea of danger on the stage is by the objective unforeseen, the unforeseen not in situations but in things, the abrupt, untimely transition from an intellectual image to a true image . . .*
>
> —Antonin Artaud, "Metaphysics and the *Mise en Scène*"

There is no trope more ambiguous or risky than metaphor. It constructs, as Gerard Genette has said, a "gap" between what is said and what is meant (48). But it (often) neglects to give this gap a semantic stability and so permits the grotesque to insinuate itself. Metaphor asks of the user that it be read in one way only: from what is said to what is implied. To comprehend metaphor correctly, we must turn a blind eye to its literal meaning. But metaphorical or figurative meaning always travels both ways. It cannot be contained, and the literal meaning always in some sense "haunts" the abstracted semantic end product. Not every metaphor is grotesque, but every incident of the grotesque is in some sense a collapsed, or effaced, or literalized, metaphor. What I am interested in here, however, is the *mise-en-scène* of metaphor.

Metaphor, like the grotesque, is a combinatorial way of seeing. Both have their root in the imagistic or visual realm, and both have emancipated themselves from a context in which they were regarded as purely ornamental (neoclassicism, for instance, thought of figures of speech as linguistic adornments) to reveal their participation in the formation of epistemology. We may think of a metaphor as an irregularity (or, in astrophysical parlance, a "singularity") in the smooth texture of linear, denotative discourse. It exerts a gravitational energy that pulls in and fuses distinct significative realms, just like the grotesque does in the smooth (or smoothed) texture of perceived reality. In exploring the close relationship of metaphor and the grotesque, I want to show that the grotesque is precisely not what it appears to be when considered as a mere style, namely arbitrary, mannered, and marginal, but is on the contrary central to human thought and connected with the entire task of dialectical thinking, which is, as Plato says in *Phaedrus,* "to see 'a One and Many' in nature" (*Dialogues* 269).

It has been observed in a variety of contexts, perhaps nowhere better than by Derrida in *Margins of Philosophy,* that thinking is inextricable from metaphor ("inextricable" is an implicit metaphor, "implicit" is another, and so on). Metaphor is anything but ancillary to thought; it *is* thought, and every meta-metaphorical attempt to expose the figurative in philosophical discourse will again be caught up in a figure ("expose" and "caught up" are figures). Figurative thought is unremitting; indeed, it forms the very historical foundation of human culture. Hayden White, paraphrasing an argument in Giambattista Vico's *New Science,* writes: "The origins of human knowledge, and *a fortiori* of human society and culture, are to be found in the onomathic powers of primitive men, the power of 'naming' objects, of distinguishing them from other objects, and, in the process, endowing them with specific attributes" (204). This original metaphorical-tropological operation, the "projection onto the unfamiliar of attributes felt to characterize the familiar," is quite similar in intent to Kayser's formula summarizing the intent of the grotesque artist "to invoke and subdue the demonic aspects of the world" (188). The unnamed world is necessarily "demonic" (if not grotesque). It abounds with sound and fury but, for lack of signifiers, cannot signify. Only the name, the appellation, can render its otherness, its out-there-ness, internal; only the name can create a "belonging" of the world to humans, which is the correlative to the biblical injunction in Genesis to subdue it and exercise dominion over all its parts (an action typically symbolized by Adam's naming of all living things).[7]

But while "primitive" or "onomathic" metaphorical behavior is a way of world-acquisition, metaphor itself is a two-edged sword; it not only invokes what is "out there" into the circle of the familiar but also in turn extends and semantically surrenders this own to the other. This trade-off is part of the economy of naming and describing; it is the basis of what I referred to in my first chapter as "animation." E. H. Gombrich reminds us that the force of metaphorical habit is especially strong as concerns objects with a functional analogy to the human body. Thus, "we are particularly prone to project faces into any configuration remotely permitting this transformation" (*Sense* 171).

Language reveals this pattern of animist thought in its repleteness with body-terms: we speak of clock "faces" and "hands," "spines" of books, the "mouth" of a river, and so forth. In normal discourse, the metaphoricity or connotative reading remains hidden behind the denotative function of the term as signifier, but this kind of absentminded metaphorical habit is simply the grotesque waiting to be unleashed; now not because the demonic is unnameable but because it inhabits the analogues of our own body and stares back at us with our face.

In his germinal essay "On Truth and Lie in the Extra-Moral Sense," Nietzsche argues that human culture, now so far from onomathic innocence, is mired in "a moveable army of metaphors, metonymies, anthropomorphisms, in short, a sum of human relations" that are accepted as truth; but the seeker after such truths is really only looking for "a metamorphosis of the world into man" and a "feeling of assimilation" (*Werke* 3:1022, 1024). Metaphor is thus a kind of white magic of truth production that can convert anything alien into human semblance (or, rather, cloak its strangeness in the familiar). It is a shamanistic trope, complicitous with animation. But there is also its "forbidden" and Promethean side, its black magic aspect, so to speak. José Ortega y Gasset, in his essay on the dehumanization of art, restates this double nature of metaphor as "a tool for creation which God forgot inside one of His creatures when He made him," a tool that is simultaneously "the most radical instrument of dehumanization." In Ortega's opinion, this double nature emanates from the tabooistic origins of metaphorical speaking (33, 35).

In his *Cannochiale Aristotelico* of 1645, Emanuele Tesauro compares the process of metaphor to the symbolic and heraldic practice of his day, casting it as a kind of poetic creation by *fiat,* analogous to the divine creation. Emblematic metaphor, says Tesauro, can "produce being from nonbeing; it causes a lion to become a man and an eagle a city. It grafts a woman onto a fish and produces a mermaid as the symbol of the seductress. It joins the bust of a goat to the rear of a snake and creates the Chimera as a hieroglyphic of insanity." But by so doing, the heraldic-emblematic iconography combines "substances which nature has studiously separated" and "turns nature upside down," invariably producing "grotesque metaphors" (qtd. in Bompiani 392–93).

Renaissance scholars like Tesauro sensed the element of danger this alchemical antinaturalism of the symbolic image may introduce, which could be defused only if it was kept in a rigid symbolic—or, better yet, allegorical—relation to its object. But the more complex the meaning at which the heraldic composition aimed, the more it had to condense its metaphorical image to achieve its highly charged signification and, consequently, the more the symbol could get "out of hand," or as Barthes says of Arcimboldo, "hypertrophy" with signification.

Tesauro resides on the fringe of the Renaissance, where the formerly "plethoric" idea of existence, which sustained a safe textural network of unending resemblances, is exploded; where "resemblances and signs have dissolved their former alliance; similitudes have become deceptive and verge upon the visionary or madness; things still remain stubbornly within their ironic identity: they are no longer anything but what they are" (Foucault, *Order* 47). On the verge of modernity, metaphorical thinking becomes a liability because its many possibilities are not contained in a structure of analogies indefinitely folding back upon themselves. In the dawning *episteme* of rationalism, metaphor in its search for resemblance also invokes the dialectics of identity and difference, and it is by suddenly exposing the identity in difference and the difference in identity that its formerly reassuring properties are bound to become unsettling.

Our mind, in short, needs metaphorical thinking and is simultaneously endangered by it; this "uncanniness" of the metaphorical construction can be suppressed only by surrounding ourselves with dead or gravely ill metaphors, such as, indeed, everyday thought and speech are riddled with. But dead metaphors are a provocation to the grotesque, and so it seeks to revive them. This it can do because metaphor (like the grotesque) engages in principle, as Kenneth Burke says, in "a constant reordering of categories": "Indeed, the metaphor always has about it precisely this revealing of hitherto unsuspected connectives which we may note in the progressions of a dream. It appeals by exemplifying relationships between objects which our customary rational vocabulary has ignored" (*Permanence* 90). The heuristic function is part of any but the most conventional metaphorical utterance. Metaphor restores on the plane of language the primal attraction that disparate things of the actual world harbor for one another; it reunites separated meanings out of spurious similarity. Through metaphor they find their surprising (but never illogical) common ground. In Paul Ricoeur's words, "metaphor is that strategy of discourse by which language divests itself of its function of direct description in order to reach the mythic level where its function of discovery is set free" (247). However, the range of discovery in poetic metaphor is limited: the "mythic level" is bounded by genre and convention. As a device, it aims at a fusing of heterogeneous images that may be novel but that fall within a certain degree of pragmatic or poetic consensus. Poetic metaphor reacts to anticipation and confounds expectation only politely. It acts within the limits of the permissible and linguistically warranted and provides a context in which its literal reading is suppressed in favor of a figurative interpretation. There is little chance for interpretive catastrophe, for instance, in Hamlet's "slings and arrows of outrageous fortune."[8]

The grotesque, however, is serious about metaphor; it takes what is essentially a sophisticated trope—so sophisticated, indeed, that cognitive psychology has only a vague understanding of its functioning—and deliberately regards it naively, or incorrectly, or primitively, in hopes perhaps of traversing the graveyard of commonplace metaphor and restoring its onomathic origins. The grotesque takes metaphor *literally.*

In principle, metaphor is the simplest linguistic indicator of sublimation. One object is replaced by another, and the choice of the replacing object, as in Freudian theory, is largely dependent on some feature of similarity within the greater difference that makes the substitution both useful and novel. The vehicle becomes, in Freudian parlance, "overdetermined" by the effacement of the tenor(s), and in this overdetermination lies an avenue for the grotesque. In the metaphor "John is a lion," "lion" may stand for strength, boldness, ferocity, and blondness, all of which are plausible, but the overdetermined character of the vehicle "lion," its inevitable semantic surplus, allows for an interpretation in which monstrosity is bred, for it suggests that John has a tail or claws.

In relating it to the unconscious, and particularly to Freud's concept of dreamwork (dream condensation being the obvious analogue), Jacques Lacan sees metaphor as one side of the "effective field constituted by the signifier," a field defined by the essential self-reference of signification in the endless chain of signifiers that drives the Symbolic Order of human cultural and psychic existence. Metaphor, for Lacan, is "the precise point at which sense emerges from non-sense," and it is the obverse of wit in the Freudian sense of the term (158). We can then perhaps reverse Lacan's formula to say that the grotesque metaphor is the site where apparent non-sense emerges from sense. Radical (or grotesque) metaphor is the reversal of the metaphorical process in that it does not mean something *other* than what it literally says; it literally says what it means, and this meaning is part of *another* order of speaking, or rather, of showing.

Only the "radicalization" of metaphor turns it from rhetoric into spectacle; radical metaphor is the *mise-en-scène* of metaphor, but it is also the putting on trial, or putting to the test, of metaphorical thinking. This is precisely what takes place in the case of Läuffer in *The Tutor.* In a play such as Sophocles' *Ajax,* Athena becomes the agent of radical metaphor when she projects the Greek hero's unspoken metaphorical transformation of his adversaries into beasts onto his conscious mind and thus onto the scene in a grotesque parody of sublimation. Observes Michael Davis:

> One can imagine Ajax's hatred for the Greeks expressed to himself in terms that portray his enemies as less than humans, as sheep for example. Athene simply makes this internal metaphor of anger and enmity real. Ajax was about to treat the whole Greek army as though they were beasts. Athene turns beasts into his enemies. ("Politics" 145)

Ajax's actions, under the force of radical metaphor, are indeed "apparent non-sense" (so much so that this act of madness, pursuant to a heroic code of ethics that is intolerant of self-contradiction, precipitates his suicide). But in another stratum of truth production, the one at which the grotesque aims, a surprising, horrific, and ridiculous "sense" has been made of Ajax's heroism. Ajax, in the last analysis, dies of this ridicule, the "mockery" and "indignity" of his situation, the farce injected into his tragedy. By causing him to slaughter sheep, Athena reveals the bestiality of the heroic enterprise, the latent truth beneath the martial metaphors (although from the perspective of the warlike goddess, this result is the inadvertent by-product of Ajax's humiliation; her primary aim is the punishment of hubris).

Radical metaphor is the concrete fixing of the virtual. It functions much in the same way as those fairy tales in which some powerful and inscrutable agency—often a genie or some form of enchanted marine life—grants the fulfillment of any wish uttered by some fortunate beneficiary. In those instances, language becomes (in the familiar term of J. L. Austin) thoroughly "illocutionary," that is, it performs an act through mere utterance. But these tales are often undisguised admonitions to "watch one's language," for a seemingly harmless turn of phrase may have devastating consequences when it meets with the bafflingly laconic literal-mindedness of the wish-fulfiller.

In one particular Oriental fairy tale, a barren woman begs the gods to bless her with a child, "and be it as small as a bee." In response, the prankish deities—giving little heed to the distinction between comparison and metaphor—cause an entire beehive to grow in her womb, and she gives birth to a swarm of bees: a grotesque consequence if properly imagined. Characteristically, when Georg Büchner wants to convey the sense of a grotesque universe in *Woyzeck,* he does it by giving the grandmother a fairy tale in which the most terrible metaphorical imagination about the world—that the moon is no more than a piece of rotten wood and the stars gnats pinned to the heavens—turns out to be literally real. (Fortunately, most fairy tales are not constructed to follow up meticulously on the narrative havoc they often wreak on their subjects—their treatments will usually prefer the schematic over the realistic mode and thus eschew the overtly grotesque.)

The comparison with the fairy tale brings another aspect to light: the grotesque is not only radical metaphor but radical *ironic* metaphor, a sort of recombinant trope. In radical ironic metaphor, what is literalized or reified is exactly what *should not* be there (an ironic presence) but what the semantic surplus of the metaphorical construction "advertently," so to speak, brings into play. The bee-bearing woman, wishing for one child only, is suddenly gifted with a great quantity of offspring (a grotesque proliferation) because the primary logical ground of the metaphor, "smallness"—as expressed through the vehicle "bee"—also entails a secondary ground, "multitude": bees in linguistic metaphors may come singly, but in radical metaphor, metaphor that is truly literal-minded and unforgiving, they come in great numbers. The gods of the fairy tale, by being thus unwavering in their interpretation, are part of a latent universal irony in which our expectation that we can make partial or exclusionary sense of things, that we can maintain a single perspective in spite of the fact that we play with the dangerous poly-perspectivism of metaphor, is reflected grotesquely back at us.

These same deities are at work everywhere in Franz Kafka's universe. Kafka's *Metamorphosis* is a kind of *locus classicus* of the grotesque because its structure is so transparent and so arresting at once, and because it seems to supply just the right amounts of fearfulness and ludicrousness, an equal measure of each. It is also an excellent example of radical metaphor. Gregor Samsa's fate may be a literary metaphor, in the loose sense in which we use the word, for alienation. But the tone of the narrative is emphatically nonmetaphorical. Gregor is not merely compared to vermin, nor is he fantasizing or dreaming that he has become a bug (indeed, Kafka makes sure to note that he has just *woken* from "uneasy" dreams, which such a transformation would surely generate, and is wholly present in the world of the story). Yet the story's guiding notion has its origin in the linguistic faculty of comparison, which can equate a character with the bug's most salient feature, its repulsiveness. Gregor, it so happens, bears the burden of language's obsession with tropes—he gets caught in one.

The disturbing quality of Kafka's narrative, as has often been noted, lies primarily in the uncompromising manner in which he maintains the frame of an unviolated reality, adding detail upon detail with great circumspection without deviating from the fantastic premise. Only in this way can he make the vermin-in-Gregor take the place of Gregor: metaphor cannot simply remove itself into the plane of language and signal its customary playfulness (saying, in effect, "Just kidding!") because in this meticulously constructed reality, nothing exists that is not reified. In this sense, Kafka's prose is "theatrical"—there is no narrative reprieve. The theatrical aspect of Kafka's prose has in fact been forcefully suggested by James Rolleston, who finds the "theatrical analogy" in *The Metamorphosis* "so obvious as to be for the most part unnoticeable," organized mainly around "[t]he split between human mind and insect body [that] compels Gregor to look at his existence from the outside, to formulate a role, a pattern of living for himself." Indeed, says Rolleston, *The Metamorphosis* might almost be called "Play of Gregor" (53, 67).

The generative rules of Kafka's parabolic universe insist that any incipient bug metaphor will become a bug, just as the letter of the law will become a lethal inscription on the body (see *In the Penal Colony*). But Stanley Corngold insists that Gregor's transformation is incomplete and that the potency of Kafka's story lies in the fact that it concerns itself not with the result but with the *process* of literalization:

> It appears, then, that the metamorphosis in the Samsa household of man into vermin is unsettling not only because vermin are disturbing, or because the vivid representation of a human "louse" is disturbing, but because the indeterminate, fluid crossing of human tenor and material vehicle is in itself unsettling. (56)

Let me invoke, for the sake of contrast, a second version of metamorphosis: in Ionesco's *Rhinoceros,* the image of grotesque transformation is placed inside a closely discursive play. The scene of Jean's transformation into a rhinoceros at the center of the play theatricalizes the disturbing coming-into-being of the latent animality, the otherness or "rhinocerocity" that befalls all but one of the play's characters. Wrapped into the stage action of Jean's disappearance into and reappearance from his bathroom—a practical necessity in order for the actor to apply successive layers of rhinoceros makeup—is the dialectic of presence and absence through which the "grotesque" transformation progresses. The practical *mise-en-scène* happily coincides with the structure of the parabolic meaning: Jean's absence from human company (his friend Berenger) hastens his transformation, and he brings into its presence a confirmed otherness.

But, unlike Kafka's story, *Rhinoceros* is a parable that can be satisfactorily resolved or filled with referential meaning: substitute Nazism (or Vichy-ism, collaboration) for the rhinoceros, and the play becomes a transparent argument about the seductiveness of totalitarian mass movements. Its putative vitalist or biocentric proposition (Jean's insistence on amorality, "nature," and "primeval integrity," which echoes Nietzsche or the Comte de Lautréamont) is really a repudiation of aggressive animality, which it reveals to be not an individual metamorphosis but an element of political mythology. No such referential substitution is possible in Kafka's case; the image of the vermin is not substantially a metaphorical-allegorical image like the rhinoceros; it is metaphorical-catachretic and so irresolvable or undecidable.

Ionesco makes sure the perspective is maintained through Berenger, the untransformed, the holdout for human values. The metaphor that the play radically deploys could read: "Berenger watched the increasing inhumanity around him with distrust; to him they were all becoming rhinoceroses." The analogous metaphor in Kafka is: "Gregor had become an insect"—here, metaphoricity is so hidden as to be almost absent. In the Ionesco play, the rhinoceros topos is subject to progressive allegorization; it is deliteralized bit by bit. Ionesco's parable illustrates the effects of a rapid paradigm shift: Berenger falls out of normality and becomes a "monster," but the play as such does not buy into this new perspective. At its heart is a solid, quite conventional humanist sentiment. (What rescues it finally from being merely an allegory and permits it to unfold a certain grotesque quality is the undeniable physical presence of the rhinoceros *onstage.*) The "beautiful" rhinoceros heads that appear at the end ironically signify nothing more than the conventionality of beauty in the field of powerful persuasion and the fickleness of isolated judgment. But no authorial irony rescues Gregor Samsa; he remains imprisoned in his self-consciousness, not one iota less literal.

In Ajax's metaphorical substitution of the sheep for the soldiers he intends to punish, there is an indication of a "sacrificial substitution" in Girard's sense of the term (only that it takes place outside of the ritual context and is thus attributed to madness). The radical metaphor of *The Metamorphosis* could be construed as representing just such a substitution within what Girard, in *Violence and the Sacred,* calls a "sacrificial crisis." Sacrificial substitution, like metaphorical substitution, demands a balance of similarity and difference between the victim, the surrogate, and the community; it entails "a degree of misunderstanding." When this balance is upset, orderly sacrifice becomes impossible and a sacrificial crisis results: "The sacrificial crisis can be defined as . . . a crisis affecting the cultural order. This cultural order is nothing more than a regulated system of distinctions in which the differences among individuals are used to establish their 'identity' and their mutual relationships" (49). In Kafka's story, the sacrificial ritual is efficaciously carried out (Gregor's family appears markedly purified, relieved at the end); but it is grotesque in the radicalism with which the surrogate (Gregor) is not *replaced by* but instead *transformed into* the sacrificial victim. True difference—which is necessary for the sacrifice—has given way to the "monstrous double"; this is the form of the perpetual sacrificial crisis of modernity inscribed in the radical metaphor of the grotesque.[9] Many of Kafka's narratives are incidents of an unsolved "sacrificial crisis": *The Trial, The Castle, A Hunger Artist, In the Penal Colony.*

The context of the application of a radical metaphor is utterly significant to its function; context is important to the emotional effect it produces, which can range from the purely comic to the purely pathetic. The device of the "concretization of metaphor," as Edith Kern has called it, is ubiquitous in comedy, for instance in Molière (517). Kern refers us to the passage in *The School for Wives* in which the innocent Agnès is told that she has "wounded" Horace by looking at him. In her simplicity, she takes the metaphor literally: "Did I drop something on him unaware?" The effect here, of course, is merely comic. It is the perfect illustration, in fact, of Henri Bergson's observation that an idea expressed becomes comic in proportion to the degree with which our attention is fixed on the material aspect of a metaphor.

It is undoubtedly true that the mistaking of a figurative for a literal meaning is an instance of linguistic incompetence worthy of ridicule, as in Agnès's case. But the semantic problem here remains firmly embedded in language and does not carry beyond it—it is a correctable error, since the actual meaning of the metaphor is distinct and apparent. In fact, what happens here is that Agnès, the character, becomes subject to a kind of grotesque perspective that we do not share because we are easily capable of resolving the ambiguous metaphorical structure that, for the moment, escapes her. It is this contrast that produces the comedy. As Jerry Palmer has demonstrated, metaphorical construction in general can be found at the basis of most jokes or gags, a circumstance linked to their shared conflation of the plausible and the implausible: "[I]n the structure of the joke, as in the structure of the metaphor, there is a moment of the perception of semantic anomaly and a moment of the perception of something which resolves this anomaly" (69).

The less we are forced by the structure of the work to leave the "semantic anomaly" unresolved, it seems, the more easily we can view it comedically. But this notion is not equivocal; an odd variant of the instance of radical metaphor is the scene at the end of Kleist's *Penthesilea* where the eponymous Amazon heroine commits suicide with an imaginary dagger she has conjured up from the depths of her feverish and guilty imagination:

For now I will step down into my breast
As into a mine and there will dig a lump
Of cold ore, an emotion that will kill.
This ore I temper in the fires of woe
To hardest steel; then steep it through and through
In the hot, biting venom of remorse;
Carry it then to Hope's eternal anvil
And sharpen it and point it to a dagger;
Now to this dagger I do give my breast:
So! So! So! So! Once more! Now, it is good.
She falls and dies. (267)

The dagger fashioned from the ore of her self becomes literal enough to fulfill its fatal mission, yet the literalization is neither comic nor truly grotesque but rather pathetic. The key is probably that, in contrast to all other radical metaphors discussed here, this one does not substitute a lower for a higher order (sheep for soldiers, insect for Gregor, bees for baby, and so on). Rather, it is an instance of poetic sublimity; there is no essential incongruity, no semantic surplus or overdetermination, no "predicative impertinence" (in the term of Jean Cohen [Palmer 62]) between the "emotion that will kill" and the metaphorically constructed dagger that the grotesque could exploit. The one is perfectly represented by the other. Nonetheless, there is a stratum of grotesque imagery in *Penthesilea,* associated with the equation of love and battle, coming to a head in Penthesilea's killing of Achilles in which she is unable to tell "kisses" from "bites." The implicit conflation of the erotic and the cannibalistic prompts the critic Günter Blöcker to note that *Penthesilea* is "a drama of love that could have been written by Baudelaire" (151).

A last example will demonstrate the complex interaction of culturally predicated tropes for the *mise-en-scène* of the grotesque vision. In an interview with the weekly *Der Spiegel,* dramatist Heiner Müller remarked upon the function of metaphorical writing: "If you translate an idea into an image, either the image will go askew or the idea will be exploded. I prefer the explosion" (qtd. in Weber 18). Such an explosion of the idea occurs in his short farce *Heartpiece* (1981), an example of the staging of radical metaphor in which a character, simply named "One," offers to "put his heart at the feet" of character Two. Two, unconvinced by One's protestations that his heart is "pure," extracts it with a penknife, only to find that it is nothing but a brick. "But it beats only for you," declares One (Müller, *Hamletmachine,* 119–21). In fact, Müller's playlet employs a metonymical/metaphorical double structure in which the conventional metonymical signifier for the emotions, the heart, inhabits several dead figures of speech: "I will lay my heart at your feet," "My heart is pure," and "You have a heart of stone." The grotesque literalization revives the dead metaphors by taking the "false" semantic content of each metaphor—long erased and repressed by the conventional, nonliteral reading of its meaning—to be its ultimately true content. As a consequence, a penknife is necessary to reveal one's (One's) emotions.

The play is clearly reminiscent of Müller's teacher Brecht, in whose *Baden Play of Acquiescence* (1929) a similar clown scene plays an integral part. There, two clowns, purporting to be helpful, by and by dismember their everyman victim, Herr Schmidt, in a series of amputations. *Heartpiece* is, as grotesque displays go, highly stylized, and yet the lapidary manner in which it converts metaphor into spectacle conveys a sense, emotionally abbreviated though it is, of the horrible and the ridiculous. Its first performance in 1981 did not, however, occasion faintings, as Brecht's play did in 1929. Composer Hanns Eisler describes the scene when the clowns came to saw off Schmidt's feet:

> These feet were very apparently stilts made of wood. But the rough joke turned to horror in the minds of many spectators. Some fainted, even though only wood was sawed and it was certainly no naturalistic presentation. I sat next to a well-known music critic who fainted. I helped him outside and brought him a glass of water. When I told this to Brecht, he said, "That's just too silly; the man doesn't faint in a symphony concert where there's always sawing, namely of the violins"—Brecht hated violins. (qtd. in Steinweg 34)

Critic Franz Norbert Mennemeier has expressly characterized Brecht's piece as an "unusual variant of a 'theatre of cruelty'" and as "one of the few totally ruthless, original avant-garde plays in German literature" and sees in it "the concrete reflection of the catastrophe hidden in modern history and society." But he adds—correctly, I think—that part of the play's "unbearable" quality lies in the tension between the radical revelation of the terrible as content and the "strictly anti-mimetic presentational style" in the form ("Bertolt Brechts 'Theater'" 75–76, 81).

The visceral reaction to Brecht's clown play is interesting in light of the fact that there is an abundance of reports of actual dismemberments and executions from antiquity to early modern times from which the mention of spectatorial empathy is conspicuously absent. This fact is further testimony to the power of metaphorical thinking. Compare for instance the words with which Raphael Holinshed in his famous *Chronicles* describes the execution, in 1586, of the Babington conspirators who were accused of having plotted to assassinate Elizabeth I. After being hanged, the first man's "traitorous heart [was] taken out and thrown into the fire" and his head impaled, and as for his coconspirators, "these venomous vipers were thus hewn in pieces, their tiger hearts burned in the fire, and the sentence of law satisfied" (917). This "sentence of law" is full of figures: the condemned men are a priori dismembered into metonymies (traitorous hearts and heads) and displaced into metaphors (vipers and tigers), and this prefiguration is so strictly controlled by the punitive logic of the time that sets the parameters of the spectacle of execution that to the spectators, only the metaphorical meaning, not the suffering man, exists. As Karen Cunningham remarks: "Such exhibitions serve their public function only if the condemned seem to be (that is, are legally defined as) wholly other" (211). So persuasive is this objectifying power of the legal tropes that the would-be regicide Damiens, who was horribly executed in 1757 for an attempt on the life of Louis XV, is reported to have observed with a certain interested detachment the tortures visited upon his own body, as if he were in this extremity "wholly other" to himself. Samuel Taylor Coleridge already knew: "Persons conversant with deeds of cruelty contrive to escape from their conscience, by connecting something of the ludicrous with them: and by inventing grotesque terms: and a certain technical phraseology to disguise the horror of their practices" (544). In the metaphorical framing of the event as meaningful spectacle, the horror of the situation is de-realized, just as conversely a kind of actual horror is re-presented, even in a stylized spectacle, to the mind that maintains no faith in the complete coincidence of metaphorical expression and meaning, to which the punitive metaphors have no absolute power of displacing the raw horror of the moment. More simply, a successful execution, in respect to its managing of the metaphorical frame, is a successful sacrifice, while in the plays the *mise-en-scène* of radical metaphor points to a sacrificial crisis and thus a crisis of the cultural order.

Francis Barker remarks that the texts of Jacobean drama reproduce a "spectacle of a corporeality which is quite other than our own" (22). The modern body, however—that which we recognize as our own onstage—"cannot realize incarnationally the central significations which the older body . . . was able to bear out"; in this older body, we find no instance of what we could call metaphorical quarantine—it was unequivocally the site of total embodiment, a site at which any distinction between vehicle *(physis)* and tenor *(psyche)* was groundless. Barker writes:

> Judicial tortures bore down on it, and the mortification of the flesh was merely the starkest form of an ethic which never had to divide itself: the ancient pseudo-separation of the body and the soul, scourging one to liberate the other . . . was predicated on their real inseparability. (63)

In the playlets of Brecht and Müller, this older body is restaged in a modern context, and we are made horribly aware that it could be ours.

The grotesque, then, is paradoxically possible in a theatrical display like *Heartpiece* or Brecht's clown play where it seems absent (at least for the contemporary onlooker) in the empirical spectacle of execution because of the divergent manner in which radical metaphor works in both contexts. In the latter, metaphor controls the demonstration with a firmness approaching moral allegory. In the former, it forces a literalist reading without supplying the legalistic or moral-aesthetic frame that warrants such a reading; as a consequence, as Barthes says of Arcimboldo, "the metaphor turns on itself, but according to a centrifugal movement: the backwash of meaning never stops" (*Responsibility* 132).

The Grotesque in Dramatic Structure

The grotesque structure plays obsessively with incompatibility, incongruity, and paradox. Yet all attempts to define it in terms of specific structural clashes of opposites (the fantastic and the realistic, the tragic and the comic, illusion and anti-illusionism) are strangely unenlightening; the grotesque is clearly not satisfactorily explained as a mere *coincidentia oppositorum* but must be regarded as a *transformation* in which the elements of the opposition themselves become so problematic as not to respond to their previous appellations. The grotesque structure seems best described by negativity, as a structure of productive omission. What is omitted? In the most general terms, mediation. Just as the metaphorical structure omits the ground of the comparison, thus creating a "perspective by incongruity" (K. Burke), the grotesque omits the mediating element that allows for adjustment and distantiation and forces a literal interpretation that appears by turns necessary and intolerable.

Margot Norris supplies an important clue when, on seeing pictures by Max Ernst, she observes that her "visceral shock had been triggered as much by the violent distortions of form as by the content of the scenes, that is, by the violence to representations rather than in them" (16). Form and content are mutually inextricable in the grotesque structure. The disjunctive content, as a matter of fact, must be physically reflected in the formal composition in some manner to warrant the term "grotesque" at all. "The art of the grotesque," writes Vsevolod Meyerhold accordingly, "is based on the conflict between form and content" (139). The mutual reflexivity of form and content in the grotesque mode is almost as strong as in the classical mode, in which, ideally, a total functional identity of form and content prevails (see Hegel's theory of drama). The grotesque is thus *the* anticlassical impulse.

In drama, the minimal formal requirement would seem to be that the grotesque plays adhere to a kind of fractured form, to what Volker Klotz has designated as the "open" or "a-tectonic" dramatic form. But in fact, a surprising number of grotesque plays operate (often parodically) out of a strictly controlled formal structure that is—like genre—the objective equivalent of an illusion of order against which the grotesque militates. Representing the grotesque content is always an act of "dismembering the real," the *sparagmos* of an orthodox perspective, and the dismemberment of reality in turn is the perennial content of the grotesque, hence the seeming paradox that in the grotesque structure, the content is adequately represented by a form that is a form of misrepresentation, and therefore always inadequate.

Since it is originally a plastic or visual mode, the grotesque tends toward concretion. Distortion, disproportion, and disfiguration, which are closely associated with the shape and misshape of the human body, are the fundamental structural expressions of the grotesque. But next to disproportion, a second, less concrete form of the grotesque is systemic excess, the extreme and seemingly unaccountable or irrational disproportion of one element over another in a dynamic system such as a play. This is a grotesque form that often prevails in the dramatic system in conjunction with the first. For example, the grotesque heroine of Dürrenmatt's *Visit,* Claire Zachanassian, is herself a disfigured assemblage of artificial limbs with a retinue of blind eunuchs, but her stage appearance is only the concretion of her idiosyncratic or monstrous interpretation of justice (which is fed by an excessive thirst for personal vengeance) and of her subsequent irrational usurpation of the dramatic world.

The symbolic practice of drama encourages such a parallelism of grotesque expression between deformation and excess. The connection is strongest in frankly allegorical drama (the vice or devil figure of the medieval mysteries in whom the evil he works is plainly embodied) and weakest in realism, which often wholly forgoes the plausibility-shaking opportunity to impart concrete indications of grotesque excess to character physiognomy. Ibsen, for example, allows only for the most sketchy hints at the customary appearance of the melodramatic villain in Judge Brack in *Hedda* (moustache, heavy eyebrows), a slightly ridiculous dirty red wig for old Ekdal in *The Wild Duck,* or a walking stick—the limp conventionally denoting inherent corruption—for a character like Kroll in *Rosmersholm.*

Kenneth Burke provides another way of speaking of this sphere of excess via the "ratios" that inform dramatistic analysis in his *Grammar of Motives.* His key terms (scene-act-agent-agency-purpose) allow for ten potential combinations in which certain ratios of one motivating element to another within a system such as a play are established and explored (for example, the scene-act-ratio, or the act-agent-ratio). Without delving into the minutiae of Burke's approach, it should be noted that these terms, though seemingly emergent from a logic of causality or rationality (scene is the "background" to act, agent is a priori to act or agency, and so on), can and must be taken to such extremes of definition that they include their opposite. Burke speaks here of the "paradox of substance," "substance" being a word that etymologically designates both essence and context and is therefore in a sense its own negation.[10] In each of the terms of Burke's dramatistic pentad, and in their respective ratios, there is a "strategic moment, an alchemic moment, wherein momentous miracles of transformation can take place" (*Grammar* 24). This precarious moment provides for the grotesque, which infuses the paradox of substance into the dramatic structure by inverting or disrupting ratios—by becoming, literally, "irrational."

Paradox or logical incongruity is the third structural form of the grotesque, and, compared to deformation or systemic excess, it is also the sensually weakest form, being furthest from the manifest grotesque image. There have been attempts to classify modern drama with the epithet "alogical" (a term already used by Yvan Goll in 1922 to designate his style of drama and echoed in spirit by Stanislaw Witkiewicz's almost contemporaneous proposal of a "non-Euclidean" dramaturgy).

The movement from intellectual paradox to visible deformation denotes concretion or increased aesthetic presence. To return to my previous example: in *The Visit,* the sphere of paradox, the ideological sphere, consists of the insertion of Claire's private revenge into the absolute idea of justice and the insidious interpenetration of publicly professed morality and private corruption, the common good and individual evil. We are here, in other words, dealing with abstractions and concepts, or with what Aristotle calls the realm of *dianoia,* or thought. The layer of systemic excess is formed by Claire's "irrational" usurpation of the dramatic action (which is, moreover, a parodic rehearsal of the very genre in which individual excess is defeated and balance restored, tragedy). At the center, however, stands the deformed character of Claire herself, "like an old stone idol" (101). Or again, in Ionesco's *Rhinoceros:* the latent animality manifests itself first in deformation (Jean turns into a rhinoceros), then in systemic excess (rhinoceroses take over the city). Finally, the intellectual paradox becomes apparent (humanity, in the play, is revealed to be a precarious function of statistical normalcy, not a moral absolute).

The logical and the perceptual structures of the grotesque run at oblique angles, or even exactly counter to each other; for the ultimate poetic and thematic justification for the grotesque play may lie in the paradox contained in it, the logical or ethical discrepancy it displays in grotesque images. But it is the grotesque image itself, the deformed character, that we perceive first and most strongly. We are charged, in the face of the powerful image, to reconstruct the logical ground or reasoning behind it, but the true raison d'être of the grotesque image is precisely to *prevent* such rationalization. In this insistent and unreformed sensuality, after all, lies its distinction from other aesthetic modes.

It appears to me that the grotesque can be structurally achieved by using two separate directions of attack, from two different sites of origin: from the "lower orders" of the suppressed and from the "higher orders" of myth. If these designations seem esoteric at first, I will explain them shortly, but it should be kept in mind that these are not necessarily two distinct types of the grotesque, only two separate means of systematizing its structure.

We in fact experience "lower-order intrusions" all the time. Take for instance what you might call the "butterfly effect." Our mentally "smoothed" image of a butterfly excludes (forgets, represses) the manifest ugliness of the animal's torso, captivated by the beauty of the wing markings. The insect itself, sans wings, is not grotesque; what is (momentarily) "grotesque" is the perception of a composite image, the butterfly seen in total, in which a culturally neglected order of discourse (associated with entomology or lepidopterology) intrudes into the predominant one (associated with aesthetics) and confounds the conventional way of seeing. What is "grotesque" is the transformation of a "smoothed" butterfly into a "rough" one by suddenly replacing what we could call "art-vision" with "bio-vision."

Rudolf Arnheim describes the hierarchy of orders in his essay on proportion. "Organized wholes," says Arnheim, "grow by differentiation of a germ structure, and each detail is determined by the law of the whole":

> This means they have layers of order, which descend from the highest and simplest to more and more complex ones. The order found at each level is true. The edge of a knife is straight even though under the microscope it reveals its irregularities. And when the statistician "smooths" a curve, he is not cheating but trying to clean the intrusions of lower orders off the higher one. (*Toward* 116)

Arnheim's statistician corresponds to our proponent of generic correctness, for the prominent feature of genre is that it yields statistical probabilities for action and reception by offering a "smoothed surface." And if, as Arnheim perceptively states, "the order found at each level is true," then the grotesque, which makes it possible to see two hierarchies of order from the same perspective, is obviously out to replace the simplified or "smoothed" concept of truth with a more complex, synthetic one. Indeed, the beauty of the butterfly wings is "true" in Arnheim's sense, but the synthetic perception of the entire butterfly is "truer." The forgetfulness with which we see the butterfly (or, to invoke larger dimensions, the slaughter of warfare) is the same forgetfulness Nietzsche cites as endemic to the production of conventional "truth"—a kind of truth that in Nietzsche's uncompromising analysis is really an illusion.[11]

Such an intrusion of a lower order into a higher, more "sublimated" order is one of the primary figures of the grotesque. It is repeated in any number of manifestations that duplicate this essential structure: ornament into image (as in the *grottesche*), subconscious into consciousness, myth into realistic narrative, farce into tragedy, and so on. But none of these intrusions are grotesque per se; they must express themselves in the grotesque idiom, through the concrete deformation that is their sensuous and aesthetic analogue. What makes the trope so persuasive is that we are not seeing here the intervention of something inherently alien or other. Rather, it is an unrecognized or unacknowledged isomorphy or the concretion of a latent analogy or similarity. As such it is not really an active intrusion or incursion—since it is already there—but rather the manifestation of a latency into consciousness via the grotesque work.

I use the term "latent" instead of "unconscious" because it encompasses not only the objects of pathological repression but also that which is merely hidden, forgotten, or excluded (although a Freudian might, with reference to the *Psychopathology of Everyday Life,* argue that there is nothing that is "forgotten" that is not also repressed). The manifest intrusion of a lower order is a reminder of some neglected or dismissed connection that the grotesque image forces into view in a manner that makes it difficult to relegate it to a mere aberration. Even neurophysiology knows of types of lower order grotesques: Oliver Sacks, for example, cites a case of Tourette's syndrome, a disorder in which the (phylogenetically) primitive strata of the subcortex generate violent involuntary tics and spasms that overlay and disrupt conscious and controlled behavior. Tourette's is "a sort of possession by primitive impulses and urges" that, as Sacks remarks, can result in symptoms "of quite terrible grotesqueness and violence" (*Man* 92, 120).

But the grotesque demands attention as the concretion not only of latent lower orders but also of a different kind of latency, one we would perhaps have to call "higher orders." In his book on the avant-garde, Renato Poggioli writes:

> The distortion of effigies and the human body sometimes functions as the "objective correlative" of the sense of the unspeakable and transcendent proper to the mystical vision, as in the case of El Greco. . . . The paradoxical task of such a distortion is a transfiguring figuration. (177)

This is an interesting term. Poggioli points here to an aesthetic problem that is analogous to the artistic rendition of the Absolute in Hegel's theory—the paradox of lending of concrete shape to the elusive and unspeakable. What are the manifestations of Indian symbolic art Hegel finds so distasteful if not instances of "transfiguring figuration"? The grotesque, then, as Carl Skrade categorically states, "demands theological consideration" (14). Drawing on Rudolf Otto's *Idea of the Holy,* which examines concepts of numinosity and emphasizes the notion of God as the *totaliter aliter,* the entirely or wholly other, Skrade claims that the numinous and holy may appear in the form of the grotesque: "In the artistic expression of the grotesque we find a call to hope and health as man is presented *sub specie mysterium tremendum et fascinans,* as a being caught up under the fearful and fascinating experience of the numinous, beyond all that is necessarily so" (79). Like Victor Hugo's, Skrade's view of the grotesque is unnecessarily inclined toward simple moral judgments and makes the questionable claim that the grotesque can ever show anything that is "wholly other." However, grotesque mysticism cannot represent the *totaliter aliter.* The latent "higher order" that the grotesque, in its disfigurations, transfigures (because it can never adequately represent or "figure" it) should perhaps be called the realm of the mythical. Myth is the locus, as Frye remarks, of an "implicit metaphorical identity" of all things where the "radical form of metaphor, 'A is B,' comes into its own" (134, 124). But if in myth everything is transmutable into its opposite or other, it is only another (namely literary) way of speaking of a quasi-Platonic infinite contiguity of things, ideas, and identities outside the realm of concrete representation. This is the state of things preceding representation, the a priori state Ludwig Wittgenstein means when he asserts in his *Tractatus* that "[t]here is no order of things a priori." In the same paragraph, Wittgenstein announces: "Everything we see could also be otherwise. Everything we can describe at all could also be otherwise" (153 [5.]634).

The grotesque, then, organizes the infinite (mythical) contiguity of things "otherwise," that is, contrary to the order of things a posteriori, the rational or common-sense order. Arthur Schopenhauer, with a nod to Kant, says of religion that it reaches for "an entirely different order of things, an order of *things-in-themselves.*" This is also true of the mystical grotesque, which is the grounding, in the sensual idiom, of what is beyond the senses. Like religion it maintains "some absolute inconsistencies and contradictions"—or at least appears to—because it must be true only *"sensu allegorico"* (Schopenhauer 166). Paradox is often the first way of speaking of (or looking at) the incommensurable and transcendent before the "transfiguring figuration" of the grotesque brings it to our senses. Mystics, for instance, tend to speak of God in paradoxical terms. In the early medieval *Liber XXIV philosophorum,* we find a description of God as "an infinite sphere, whose center is everywhere and circumference nowhere" (Campbell 44).

There is a pervasive atmosphere of grotesque mysticism in some of the ecstatic "annunciation" plays *(Verkündigungsdramen)* of German expressionism or those of Oskar Kokoschka and Ernst Barlach, in the work of Michel de Ghelderode, in Jean Genet, and even in a play such as Heathcote Williams's *AC/DC,* which will be discussed in chapter 4. But its foremost theatrical manifestation is perhaps not to be found in the drama but in that approach to acting that attempts the radical spiritual transfiguration of the performer as expressed through the "sacrifice" of the body: the "holy" theatre of Jerzy Grotowski.

It could be argued that the true grotesque, that which creates and sustains horror and ridicule in equal measure, must simultaneously bring into play higher and lower orders until they become nearly indistinguishable, so that the transfiguration of the numinous supplies the terror *(tremendum et fascinans)* and the eruption of the suppressed evokes derision. In a certain sense, the grotesque enacts the reciprocal transformations of Mircea Eliade's "sacred" and "profane" and demonstrates their essential similarity. As in the case of the black hole or "singularity" of astronomy, into which cosmic matter is attracted with such fierce gravitational pull and so condensed at the center that light itself can no longer escape, only to be spewed out again in a supernova when the mixture becomes unstable, the lower and higher orders that the grotesque invokes are aggregate aspects of each other, fused in the gravitational field of a perspective. Dürrenmatt seems to envision such a singularity when he speaks of his grotesque ideas dropping "like bombshells" (or meteors) into the world and "poking holes into the landscape" ("Problems" 136). This is the "landscape" of the grotesque play.

The grotesque brings into expression both the beast-in-man and the god-in-man in their respective and mutual incongruity. Classical drama is fond of placing its characters in such a double jeopardy, in which the bestial and the numinous simultaneously bear down on them. Ajax's grotesque slaughter of the sheep, for instance, originates both from latent lower orders (as a concrete metaphor of men-as-animals, war-as-butchery, in which he himself is implicated) and from the higher "orders" of the goddess Athena. Similar patterns are apparent in Euripides' *Orestes* and *The Bacchae.*

Jean-Pierre Vernant, in an excellent essay on *Oedipus Rex,* characterizes the function of successful sacrifice or scapegoating as a "delimitation" of the community against what I have called lower and higher orders:

> In the person of the ostracized, the city expels what in it is too elevated, what incarnates the evil which can come to it from above. In the evil of the *pharmakos,* it expels what is vilest in itself, what incarnates the evil that menaces it from below. By this double and complimentary rejection it delimits itself in relation to what is not yet known and what transcends the known: it takes the proper measure of the human in opposition on one side to the divine and heroic, on the other to the bestial and monstrous. (491–92)

Characters like Oedipus and Ajax, then, embody in conflation the hidden and unacknowledged isomorphies of humanity with the bestial and the divine, its most extreme extensions that it must crop in order to safely occupy the middle ground upon which community can flourish. But the significant paradox out of which the grotesque is born is already implicit in Vernant's passage: because what is human is the mathematical median or statistically smoothed generic mean, so to speak, of these excesses or extremes, there is an essential reciprocity between them. The extreme cannot be expelled without risking self-annihilation, and yet its presence cannot be tolerated either. The grotesque in much of ancient drama (as we will see in the next chapter) is the visible manifestation of this paradox of expulsion, which is congruent with Burke's "paradox of substance" and with the paradox of representation: in each we are faced with the aporia that figure and ground, essence and context, content and form, inside and outside are both inextricable and irreconcilable.

The other tradition of drama that is built on the intersection of myth and the mundane is the religious drama of the Middle Ages. But the Corpus Christi and passion plays, expressions of a totalizing theology in which sacred and profane freely intersect, nonetheless never voluntarily surrender to the grotesque. In its strict allegorical separation of realms, it creates an effective generic barrier. Typical is for instance the play *The Crucifixion of Christ* by the anonymous York Realist, in which Christ's tortures are represented in grim detail, exacerbated by the ludicrous incompetence of the executioners, who have bored the holes incorrectly into the cross. Christ's familiar plea for forgiveness for his tormentors ("What they wirke wotte they noght" [1.261]) is thrown into a radically ironic light by the fact that these soldiers "know" very well what they "work" (technically) and are unjustly proud of their handiwork (in contrast to the pinners and painters who played them; there is a satire on sloppy workmanship embedded in the sacred proceedings) but are devoid of the knowledge that counts.

We have here, in other words, the gruesomely and comically enacted collision of a divine and a human agenda; but from a transcendent perspective (a perspective that the audience itself is encouraged to adopt), these agendas coalesce seamlessly. There is no salvation without Christ's suffering and crucifixion, and the more he is seen to suffer, the more radiant and powerful divine grace appears. The primary purpose of this juxtaposition is to make the medieval congregation understand the humanity of Christ and through this humanity again remind them of his divinity. The York Realist's dramaturgy makes good didactic sense, but it makes no grotesque in the sense developed here. The deformations presented are already superseded by the implications of the very spectacle that brings them forth. In other words, there exists no "sacrificial crisis," no paradox of expulsion—the crucifixion play is archetypal mimesis of a successful sacrifice. To the commonplace observation that Christian tragedy is a contradiction in terms, we may add that a grotesque that works completely within the precepts of Christianity is (at least) difficult to imagine. This, of course, is also the enduring problem with Victor Hugo's approach.

The modern theatre thrives on forms of grotesque mysticism, from drama that has a manifest metaphysical content or theme (as in August Strindberg and much of expressionism, Ghelderode, some of Jean-Paul Sartre and Beckett, Dürrenmatt, and so forth) to theatre that attempts to recover the authority of ritual. Some of this will be the subject of the following chapters, but here I simply want to draw attention to Bruce Wilshire's remarks on theater as an explicit metaphor in which meaning is compressed:

> We can . . . say that the world as it is experienced is protometaphorical in its structure. That is, a thing which corresponds to another—or symbolizes another—stands in for that in our experience. . . . Theatre as explicit metaphor

> sums up, condenses, and thematizes these protometaphorical correspondences, so that the world is mapped into a "world." . . . There is transfusion of energy from theatrical "world" to world, and from world to "world." . . . The power of theatre as metaphor is the power of meaning compressed: world compresses into "world," with energy flowing continuously back into world. (239–41)

There is a suggestive analogy between the transactions of the world of experience and the "world" of the theatre and my model of latencies that are "compressed" into or "mapped" onto the grotesque. If the grotesque is, as I have said, in a certain sense a *mise-en-scène* of metaphor (or even protometaphor), then it can also be understood as a type of theatre, *sensu allegorico* (and the theatre, in turn, as a type of grotesque). This is the area that remains to be examined in the following chapters.

How are these considerations of the grotesque in genre and structure applicable to the drama and theatre? The guiding paradigm by which the grotesque in drama and theatre is identified would have to be, in its widest sense, interrupted, aborted, trans- and deformed *play,* play that becomes uncontrollable and serious: *serio ludere,* play that refuses to be sequestered but rather springs to life. In an essay on the Théâtre Alfred Jarry, Artaud asserts "that with each performance we are playing a serious game, that the whole point of our effort resides in this quality of seriousness" (*Selected Writings* 156).

Metaphor is linguistic play that, literalized, becomes serious. Play is present on every level of drama and theatre: as a theme of drama, as the form of drama, as the essence of acting, as the substance of theatrical perception, as the foundation of theatre in its conversion of reality into an orderly plot and a controlled spectacle with beginning, middle, and end. Even the sacrificial ritual, if we follow Girard, is premised upon the "pretense" of the identity of victim and community and thus, like theatrical role-playing, begs some suspended disbelief. In all of these forms of play, the grotesque extracts the other, hidden side and demonstrates the problem of maintaining order, or hierarchies of order, and of separating the subreal, the real, and the superreal, the fictional and the nonfictional. A universe subjected to grotesque restructuring works perhaps much like the world of Tom Stoppard's *Rosencrantz and Guildenstern Are Dead,* where death lurks behind every door out of (the) play.

Drama is a threat to things as they are.

—Georg Kaiser, preface to *Methusalem,* by Yvan Goll

3 Classical Grotesque

The drama of the grotesque, it would appear, is not so much a genre in itself, or even a relatively homogenous body of work, but a potentially large number of plays that in some radical and unexpected manner challenge accepted canons, ideologies, and generic constructs and to which we react in the manner that I have discussed in chapters 1 and 2. What links these widely divergent plays is perhaps the single theme in which José Ortega y Gasset sees the common thread of all drama, the endangerment of the characters as human beings. He writes: "[U]nlike all the other beings in the universe, man is never surely *man;* on the contrary, *being man* signifies precisely being always on the point of not being man, being a living problem, an absolute and hazardous adventure, or, as I am wont to say: being, in essence, drama!" (189). The endangerment of humanity that the serious play of the grotesque is so inclined to represent would, then, be nothing other than an extreme expression of the project of all drama, namely, to interrogate the constitution of the human condition at the point of its greatest crisis, were it not that the grotesque drama has left behind the comforts of genre, within which such interrogation habitually takes place.

A play that parades grotesque incidents of dehumanization, however, is not yet a grotesque play unless it can establish the grotesque vision as the prevailing one. Gotthold Lessing, in his influential aesthetic treatise *Laokoon, or, On the Limits of Painting and Poetry* (1766), posits that the distinction between pictorial and poetic works of art consists in their difference in regard to temporality—poetry unfolds in time, whereas sculpture and painting exist only in space. The drama, for his purposes, is a subcategory of poetry, even if its theatrical representation is oddly spatio-temporal. Ugliness, Lessing finds, is permitted in dramatic poetry where it is an ephemeral impression soon erased by the progress of the plot in time, but it cannot easily be tolerated in imagery or sculpture, where the impression is permanent. Thus, says Lessing, Virgil in his *Aeneas* may speak of the agonized Laokoon's scream, but the expression on Laokoon's face in the eponymous sculpture must be muted to silent suffering; the sculptor must "reduce" the expression of pain, "soften shrieks to sighs," and avoid at all costs the "hideous contortion of the countenance" lest, as in the face of a gargoyle, the accidental supersede the essential (17).

Those "masters of propriety," the French, are to be thanked that "no such ridiculous and intolerable characters as a moaning Philoctetes or a shrieking Hercules will ever again appear on the stage," notes Lessing with relief. In an argument that takes its cues once again from Plato, he concedes that in narrative art such "transitory impropriety" is occasionally justified, but the drama, because it actually represents and does not just relate an incident, should be confined "more strictly within the limits of material art" (11, 23). Friedrich Schiller, very much in line with Lessing, also suggests in his "Reflections on the Use of the Vulgar and Low Elements in Works of Art" that tragedy has a certain hygienic obligation:

> [E]ven in the serious and tragic there are certain places where the low element can be brought into play. But in this case the affair must pass into the *terrible*, and the momentary violation of our good taste must be masked by a strong impression, which brings our passion into play. In other words, the low impression must be absorbed by a superior tragic impression. (470)

In this view, drama may present the ugly or the grotesque if it safely removes it or converts it into sublimity. Perhaps we can, then, broadly define the grotesque drama in opposition to Lessing and Schiller: drama is substantially grotesque only if there is no "removal" of its disturbing qualities, either by a sudden reversal of the catastrophic plot (as in comedy and melodrama) or by the force of catharsis (as in tragedy). Further, the grotesque perspective comes even more strongly to the fore if the "removal" is attempted but unsuccessful, if a genre like tragedy, known for its sanitary habits, is unable to clean up convincingly after itself. This idea informs the following discussions.

Given that the response to the grotesque is often psychologically fragile and wanes precipitously with prolonged exposure as the viewer's consciousness struggles to make sense of the grotesque effect, grotesque dramaturgy must labor to sustain it. There are two potential solutions to this problem. One is to make grotesque drama short so as to forestall all emotional accommodation; this has been a trusted method from the Greek satyr plays (of which Euripides' *Cyclops* is our only extant example) to the silent "grotesque" film comedies, or one-reelers. In fact, the silent film "grotesque" has at least three elements in common with the dramatic grotesque: first, a type of kinetic eccentricity that exposes the body as a mechanically dominated object (in the Bergsonian sense); second, a type of disjunctive narrative or diegetic flow that goes beyond purely linear mimesis and affords the temporal and logical ellipses typical of montage; and third, a type of character—the manipulated innocent—who is nearly devoid of initiative or self-assertion in the classical character vein, a merely reactive character who persistently invites the wrath of a material world unleashed. This connection between the grotesque in modern drama and the silent film is further underlined by the fact that for at least two of the playwrights discussed in the next chapter, Yvan Goll and Michel de Ghelderode, the figure of Charlie Chaplin's tramp represents a key to the modern condition. (Goll wrote a "film poem," the *Chaplinade;* Ghelderode dedicated his *Don Juan* to him and claimed the descent of his prototypical innocent hero, Pantagleize, from Chaplin.) The influence of Chaplin is of course traceable in Samuel Beckett, Bertolt Brecht, and Heiner Müller as well.

In the modern theatre, most plays that explicitly carry the generic descriptor "grotesque" are one-acts, a form (like early film) derivative of music hall, burlesque, and vaudeville. Goll reasons in the programmatic preface to his play *Methusalem, or the Eternal Bourgeois* that the grotesque in large doses is unendurable: "The drama stops because you have tired, grown old in a single hour, and because truth, the most potent poison for the human heart, may only be swallowed in very small doses" (*Dichtungen* 80). Some remarks by Peter Szondi may elucidate why the (largely modern) form of the short one-act is so suitable to the idea of the grotesque. In the one-act, Szondi observes, tension is no longer a product of interpersonal conflicts but rather is already present in the ineluctable catastrophe toward which the situation is heading:

> Catastrophe is a given, lurking in the future: gone is the tragic personal struggle with a destiny whose objectivity humans could . . . resist through their subjective freedom. What separates the individual from destruction is empty time, time that can no longer be filled by an action, time that encompasses a pure space stretching out toward catastrophe and within which the individual is condemned to live. Thus, even on the level of form, the one-act proves to be the Drama of the unfree. (55–56)

The other dramaturgical answer to the problem of the transitoriness of the grotesque response is the escalation of the grotesque action, a progression from "normalcy" (or its generic equivalent) to disruption and the continuous (self-)creation and (self-)revelation of the grotesque world and its characters. In other words, the action that the grotesque drama imitates is the forced intrusion of lower orders (or the transfiguration of higher orders), the acceleration and spreading of excess, and the aggravation of paradox as it is expressed with increasing vehemence in the space-time of the stage. The grotesque drama, instead of ending in the resolution of crisis and in dénouement, builds inexorably toward a cataclysmic epiphany that signals merely the end of (the) play, not its resolution.

In the first section of this chapter, Friedrich Nietzsche's idiosyncratic construction of tragedy and his polemic against Euripides in *The Birth of Tragedy* gives me the opportunity to reread *The Bacchae,* the first stage appearance of the Savage God, as the original pattern of grotesque dramaturgy. In the second part, I consider a play nearly twenty centuries old, the *Thyestes* of Seneca, then the stepchild of Shakespearean tragedy, *Titus Andronicus.* Both plays are bound together superficially by a common theme: they revolve to some degree around cannibalism. Yet it is not their mere sensationalism and indulgence in unsavory practices that compel my attention here but rather that in a deeper sense they are plays that take human experience to the limit of the generically representable, tragedies that in their grotesque occurrences devour themselves (becoming "self-consuming artifacts"). Together with *The Bacchae* (which also contains incidents of *omophagia*), they compose a trio of premodern "impossible tragedies." They serve as a means of analytically locating the grotesque in classical and neoclassical drama primarily in the subversion of genre.

Dismembering *The Bacchae*

Nietzsche's *Birth of Tragedy Out of the Spirit of Music* (1872) would seem a promising candidate for the derivation of a dramatic theory of the grotesque since the familiar conceptual dyad of the Apollinian and the Dionysian emphasizes a return to the dark, terrifying, destructive forces of the god of chaos, excess, and intoxication. But the Dionysian in Nietzsche's theory stands not for disjunction but for an "overwhelming feeling of unity" (*Birth* 59), not for individuation but for a transcendence of the *principium individuationis.* And dreams, that simulacrum of a grotesque symbol structure, are to Nietzsche an Apollinian principle. In the following, my aim is to reconsider *The Birth of Tragedy* in order to find the true place of the grotesque in (or beneath) its argument.

On the surface, *The Birth of Tragedy* no longer aligns itself with the previous concepts of romantic aesthetics but completely invalidates and replaces them. Yet underneath we find that the unambiguous, clear, typical characteristics of the Apollinian are equivalent to those articulated in the older theories of beauty, while the principle of terror and the loss of self of the Dionysian are prefigured in the romantic sublime. By preferring the Dionysian-Sublime, Nietzsche remains firmly in the romantic tradition. (Indeed, he takes up again the romantic lament at separation from the Absolute, individuation, the loss of metaphysical connections: "[W]e are . . . to regard the state of individuation as the original and primal cause of all suffering, as something objectionable in itself" [73].)[1]

At the same time, aesthetics is here being developed on grounds that are much more frankly proto-psychoanalytic than all previous theory; the Dionysian has many aspects of the id-function, just as the Apollinian in turn reflects characteristics of the superego. Their mutual agonistic history seems to recapitulate metaphorically the repressive/sublimatory movement from Freud's "oceanic" original state to the present discontents of civilization; Nietzsche's theory of art after all proposes "redemption from the 'ego'" (48) as its aim. Nietzsche, in other words, has charged the Dionysian and Apollinian as hyperterms that in some manner incorporate and represent every binarity of occidental metaphysics: speaking and writing, instinct and thought, content and form, subject and object, essence and appearance, and so on.

Like the god as whose disciple he presents himself, Nietzsche wears a series of masks in *The Birth of Tragedy.* It is no secret that his construction of the etiology of the dithyramb is often highly problematical and sometimes completely wrongheaded, as contemporary philologists were not remiss to point out. However, the historical aspect of the book is a mere surface pretext that gives way to its prophetic aspect, the rebirth of tragedy. The substratum of the essay is its philosophical tier, where Nietzsche launches an investigation into the relationship of art and consciousness in modernity and clandestinely comes to conclusions that belie his later panegyric to Wagnerian music-drama. The problems inherent in his theory are buried in the manner in which Nietzsche constructs the relation between Dionysian and Apollinian in tragedy.

Benjamin Bennett, in somewhat of a dithyrambic mood, celebrates the Apollinian and the Dionysian as a "true dialectical relationship": "The clash of the two drives tends not to weaken but to intensify and purify them until, at their highest level of purity, they merge into the dialectical synthesis of tragedy" (235). Nietzsche's dramaturgy, Bennett suggests, provides for what one might call an ideal classical union of humanity's matter (the Dionysian) and form (the Apollinian) analogous to the implicit dramatic program of German classicism, as first expressed (but not realized) by Schiller. This union, according to Bennett, is to be found in the experience of tragedy, which is not conceived as a *representation* of human self-affirmation but which is "to *be* the achievement of a human wholeness which had not yet existed prior to performance." The burden Bennett places upon tragedy is consistent with Nietzsche's radical aesthetic code: if life is to be evaluated solely on aesthetic grounds, then art must be the fulfillment of the highest human aspirations. Thus, Bennett argues, "what Nietzsche does in theory is to *free drama from the idea of representation*" and enable it "boldly to *create new states of self-consciousness* by the mechanism of the theater" (238). This attempt to overcome representation, we recognize, puts Nietzsche's program into the grotesque discourse; it is the same trans-mimetic impulse that later inspires Antonin Artaud or body art.

But the problem is that taking Nietzsche at his word—as Bennett does—invariably falsifies him, for Nietzsche's argument is nowhere really on the surface of the text. What is more, Bennett ascribes to the self-proclaimed pessimist Nietzsche (and inscribes into his theory) what has to be most abhorrent to him, a kind of didactic optimism more in concert with Schiller. This misreading is not surprising, since it rests to some degree on Nietzsche's own misapprehension. In *The Birth of Tragedy,* two poles form the structure of the Nietzschean dialectic *beneath* the Dionysian and Apollinian, poles we could perhaps designate as ontological and teleological. One is the apprehension of "eternal contradiction" (*Birth* 45) as the condition of existence, the other the faith in art as salvation or transport from this abjection. But how can art, which is "mere appearance," effectively ease or erase this primal disjunction? Through tragedy, according to Nietzsche. The Dionysian is essential to the epistemology of this operation. In the Dionysian state, man experiences a lethargic immersion in communal intoxication, the surrender of ego and self-consciousness. In this egoless, paralinguistic condition he has access to the *eidos,* the "essence of things." For this insight he pays, once having reemerged into consciousness, with "knowledge," in particular the knowledge of "the horror or absurdity of existence." Such knowledge induces nausea, inactivity, the entire existentialist dilemma as Nietzsche sees it reflected in *Hamlet* (60). (He almost seems here to anticipate a Lacanian insight: "The unconscious is knowledge, but it is a knowledge one cannot know one knows, a knowledge which cannot tolerate knowing it knows" [qtd. in Felman 166].)

The purgation, or sublimation, of this *nausée* is possible only by repeating the communal experience of the Dionysian suffering in symbolic form, the form of tragedy. But the symbolic, the realm of illusion, image, art, is the province of the Apollinian. Here is where the theory Nietzsche advances becomes increasingly problematic, for to create drama, the Dionysian state must mirror itself; indeed, Nietzsche describes the primitive chorus of satyrs as the "mirror-image in which the Dionysian man contemplates himself" (63). We are faced with a "magic transformation":

> In this magic transformation the Dionysian reveler sees himself as a satyr, *and as a satyr, in turn, he sees the god,* which means that in his metamorphosis he beholds another vision outside himself, as the Apollinian complement of his own state. With this new vision the drama is complete. (64)

But Nietzsche is playing with his terms; for if the reveler sees himself, as Nietzsche says, then no true transformation has taken place, only a projection. There is still an ego that is doing the seeing of both self and god, and this ego is Apollinian. This "new vision" is essentially the self-division of the Dionysian, its birth into irrevocable consciousness. What has transpired is the fundamental *parabasis* of the constitution of drama, an act of (radical) irony. In the parabasis, ritual (the unself-conscious) becomes drama (the entirely self-conscious). Nietzsche does not seem to fully appreciate the precariousness of this construction; everything in his theory indicates that he believes in the possibility of arresting the ironic, of stopping the parabasis, of controlling the Apollinian.

Nietzsche glosses over this most glaring internal problem of his aesthetics—the inadequacy of the representation of the Dionysian through the Apollinian. In this context, he takes up again that exact dilemma of philosophical idealism that we traced in Georg Wilhelm Friedrich Hegel and saw remedied by an uneasy truce in Victor Hugo in the previous chapter: the paradox of the figuration of the Absolute in the finite. And wherever we encountered this aporia of representation in the nineteenth century, it expressed itself in some manner of the grotesque.

Peter Sloterdijk, in an illuminating analysis of *The Birth of Tragedy*, has put his finger on the defect of Nietzsche's argument when he speaks of "a sort of Apollinian catch mechanism" that will ensure that "the Dionysian element is never in power as such":

> In truth, the polarity between Apollo and Dionysus is not a turbulent opposition that vacillates freely between two extremes; we are dealing much more here with a stationary polarity that leads to a clandestine doubling of the Apollinian. The Apollinian Unified Subject *(Eine)* makes certain, through the mechanism of the silently established axiom of balance, that the Dionysian Other never comes into play as *itself*, but only as the dialectical or symmetrical Other to the Unified Subject. An Apollinian principle governs the antagonism between the Apollinian and the Dionysian. . . . Apollo is, even within Nietzsche himself, the ruler in the antithetical relationship with his Other. (124–25)

We could thus say that Apollo is always already waiting at the point of synthesis, like the tortoise in the fable. The "redemption in illusion" that Nietzsche hopes for in tragedy is also necessarily an illusion of redemption. When he apostrophizes the "manifestation and projection into images of Dionysian states" as the "essence of tragedy" (92), Nietzsche has implicitly subverted his own project. In this transference or translation of the Dionysian revel into Apollinian terms, he is already past the point at which pure tragedy can be saved. What in his theory appears as balance is thrown off balance precisely *because* it appears, because signification is introduced, because representation has corrupted the *Ur*-moment of the Dionysian. Tragedy is always already lost (*sous rature,* if you will), and from this instant of its nascency out of whatever the dithyramb had been into what is now unequivocally a stage, its trajectory is set and its demise sealed. The birth of tragedy, to paraphrase Beckett, is a birth astride the grave.

Tragedy—this is the fundamental problem in Nietzsche, who laments the moment at which he believes the inexorable flow could have been arrested—cannot contain or sustain myth, because it is already beyond myth, and this beyond is marked by thought. As the stage forms, the thinker has already entered, and in this thinker Nietzsche should recognize not only Euripides or Socrates or the authors of bourgeois tragedies, or indeed all of post-Platonic thought, but also himself.

In truth, it is Nietzsche's own construction of the aesthetics of tragedy, its systemic and ineradicable flaw, that suffocates the Dionysian element. In staging the tragedy of tragedy, Nietzsche also restates the tragedy of modernity, complete with attendant "metaphysical comforts" that he flies in *ex machina* from Bayreuth.[2] Most intriguing in his cast, however, is not Richard Wagner but the culprits he fingers for tragedy's premature demolition, the villainous duo of Euripides and Socrates. In Nietzsche's passion play of tragedy, Socrates is that oddest of demons, a demon out of a surfeit of consciousness and a lack of intuition. He is the satanic intellectual, the casuistic Mephistopheles to Euripides' Faust, and the grotesque of modern man. Nietzsche had earlier characterized the satyr of the Dionysian chorus as the archetype of man compared to whom civilized humanity is "shriveled into a mendacious caricature" (61). To Nietzsche, Socrates *is* that caricature.

Note the language of the grotesque Nietzsche employs in his description of Socrates: the Greek philosopher's overpowering rationality is a reversal of the natural order, a "hypertrophying" and "excess" of his logical faculties, the result being "truly a monstrosity *per defectum*" (88). In his implicit grotesqueness, Socrates is "thoroughly enigmatical, unclassifiable, inexplicable"; he is outfitted, to emphasize his degenerate monstrosity, with "one great Cyclops eye" that incomprehendingly surveys the tragic art (89)—a simile that summons another grotesque vision, that of Nietzsche/Ulysses gouging the eye of Socrates/Polyphemus with a stake hardened in the fire of Wagnerian music. Finally, Socrates is implicated, by a cunningly placed industrial-mechanical metaphor, in the creation of the aberrations of technological society. Nietzsche sees "the enormous driving-wheel of logical Socratism in motion . . . *behind* Socrates" that must be viewed "through Socrates as through a shadow"—as though, Oz-like, the philosopher were but an insubstantial projection or marionette of this logical juggernaut machine that he invented but that now in turn animates him (88–89). Thus he is answerable, by guilty association, for the "disaster slumbering in the womb of theoretical culture" (112), a disaster against which Nietzsche prescribes the resurrection of tragedy as a panacea.

The direct culpability for the demise of tragedy in this text is fastened on the dramatist Euripides, whose foremost crime is to bring "the *spectator* onto the stage" (77), a charge I attempted to deflate above by exposing the inescapable necessity of such a development. Euripides too is implicated in the rise of technical civilization. Nietzsche transfers the metaphor of *deus ex machina,* which he regards as the playwright's folly, explicitly to the "machines and crucibles" (109) of the technical age, completely mistaking the fact that in Euripides the creaking machine that suspends the god also *suspends* the serving of justice or logic; it is no declaration of faith in the prevailing of reason, nor is it instrumental optimism. Euripides is heir to a tragic system that is, by Nietzsche's very own description, already programmed to unravel; he merely exploits this self-destructive tendency of tragedy to become the first modern dramatist and the first dramatist of the grotesque.

In some of Nietzsche's judgments on Euripides we hear the Hegelian condescension toward whatever is not "pure." Euripidean drama as a thing "both cool and fiery" (84) is a febrile web of impurity, of incompatibles and irresolvables. Nietzsche accuses Euripides of "audacious reasonableness," forgetting that Euripidean reason is thin and that through its cracks it purposely reveals, as in his *Orestes,* a universe of tortured irrationality and sometimes random chaos. In claiming that Euripides "did not understand tragedy" (81), being, as he was, preoccupied only with what the rational mind could fathom, Nietzsche paints Euripides' faith in the power of *logos* as so strong that he ignores how Euripides emphasizes time and again the fragility of all signification in his plays. One need think only of the famous parody of the Aeschylean recognition scene in Euripides' *Electra,* where Orestes declares: "How then can man distinguish man, what test can he use? . . . We can only toss our judgments random on the wind" (ll. 373, 379). And Electra agonizes: "What sign do you see? What can I know and trust?" (l. 527). While Nietzsche is celebrating the possibility of resurrecting, in Dionysus, the oneness of unconscious irrationality and condemning Euripides for his petty logic, Euripides is waiting this side of modernity with his implicit distrust in the rational and the irrational alike. Where Nietzsche claims that the credo of "aesthetic Socratism" (read: Euripides) is essentially the tenet of Enlightenment thinking, "To be beautiful everything must be intelligible" (*Birth* 83–84), the postmodern Euripides seems to be retorting: "Nothing is intelligible, and very little is beautiful. In fact, most things are grotesque."

While Euripides is charged with assassinating the original Dionysian myth and replacing it with a worthless simulacrum that precipitates the "suicide" of Greek tragedy (75–76), it does occur to Nietzsche that he is, perversely, the only tragedian to actually represent the god Dionysus himself onstage (he also appears, of course, in Aristophanes' comedy *The Frogs*). Nietzsche constructs the circumstances of this apparent contradiction as a kind of melodramatic deathbed conversion: recanting and repenting in his dotage, Euripides attempts to restore the Dionysian in *The Bacchae* in what Nietzsche reads as a "glorification of his adversary." But, alas! it is too late, for his fiendish plot to alienate tragedy from myth and to destroy it has already borne fruit. Thus Euripides kills himself "like a giddy man who, to escape the horrible vertigo he can no longer endure, casts himself from a tower" (82). Exclaims Nietzsche:

> What did you want, sacrilegious Euripides, when you sought to compel this dying myth to serve you once more? It died under your violent hands—and then you needed a copied, masked myth that, like the ape of Heracles, merely knew how to deck itself out in the ancient pomp. . . . And because you had abandoned Dionysus, Apollo abandoned you: rouse all the passions from their resting places, and conjure them into your circle, sharpen and whet a sophistical dialectic for the speeches of your heroes—your heroes, too, have only copied, masked passions and speak only copied, masked speeches. (75–76)

Nietzsche's language is nothing if not evocative; he uses, in his own famous phrase, an "army of metaphors" to indict Euripides on a variety of offenses: degeneracy, insincerity, forgery, violence—indeed, theocide (or at least mythocide). Nietzsche sees Euripides' art as a direct commentary on his life: he fancied himself an unbending Pentheus, had the power of the god not been so great; instead, he finally became the careful Cadmus—a convert to the god out of prudence.

In Nietzsche's reading, consequently, *The Bacchae* is an impotent propitiation a little like Claudius's prayer: "My words fly up, my thoughts remain below: / Words without thoughts never to heaven go" (*Hamlet* 3.3.97–98). It is nothing but Euripides' cheap attempt to save his soul, or at least hedge his bet. Moreover, it is a deliberate forgery of the authentic myth of the god who in Nietzsche's model can deliver humanity from the *principium individuationis,* the horrible Apollinian individuation that marks the original sin of human consciousness. Dionysus, to Nietzsche, is more than the symbolization of an abstract principle; he is a veritable self-portrait—Nietzsche's *Ecce Homo* ends with the words: "Dionysus versus the Crucified!" That made Euripides' transgression all the more grave, and yet one cannot shake the feeling that Nietzsche's attacks on Euripides are so vituperative partly because the playwright mirrors his own intellectual vacillations and critical temperament.

But I believe that we must read *The Bacchae* against Nietzsche to realize that, far from being a recantation of Euripides' principles, it is their most consequent elaboration. For in *The Bacchae,* the contradictory Dionysian entity comes into its own; Euripides' Savage God is both the archaic and terrible deity and its Apollinian representation, both the intoxicator by raw divine power and the Socratic seducer by illusion, deception, and dialectical wit. He is as paradoxical as deity gets, *tremendum et fascinans* because he is not *totaliter aliter* but rather a violently oppositional aspect of the very human community from which he demands sacrifice and which he is yet willing in turn to sacrifice to his own conceit. This monster of nature, born from the "male womb" (*Bacchae* l. 527) of Zeus, is also the master of ceremonies for the funeral of the tragic and the birth of the grotesque.

The play has sometimes been regarded as the Manichaean struggle between chaos and order, but Pentheus is as unadmirable a representative of Hellenic culture as anyone in Euripides' plays, and he too is implicated in monstrosity:

> [B]orn of the breed of Earth,
> spawned by the dragon, whelped by Earth!
> Inhuman, a rabid beast,
> a giant in wildness raging,
> storming, defying the children of heaven.
>
> (ll. 540–44)

A thoroughly ambiguous world is put into play onstage, in which the adversaries are in another sense mutually indispensable others (Dionysus, at first called "The Stranger," is also Pentheus's alter ego or *doppelgänger*), and the theatre, which is after all the site of their conjunction, must negotiate whether these "two modes of being in the world," as Mircea Eliade has called the sacred and the profane, can be reconciled any more (14).

The supposed incursion of ecstatic Dionysian cults into the mainstream of Greek culture is the mythological-historical foil of *The Bacchae*, and in the etiology of the cult we recognize the determined (and largely successful) attempts of fifth-century BCE Athens to guard against the perceived excesses of Dionysian worship by creating sublimatory rituals to supplant the violence of the prehistoric myth. But to the modern, post-Freudian eye, the play is set, on another level, in the space of the unconscious, as a *mise-en-scène* of analysis and repression. Charles Segal observes:

> In the case of the *Bacchae* in particular, Euripides seems to be using the stage itself as a kind of dream world where our most buried fears and fantasies—particularly of an oedipal nature—can be acted out. The space of the dramatic representation thus becomes a privileged space in which . . . we can evade the censor and view things that we do not normally allow ourselves to see, hear things that we do not normally allow to be spoken. (295)

This dreamwork, however, which in psychoanalytic terms is the exact analogue of Nietzsche's tragic formula—the transliteration of the Dionysian Unconscious into the grammar of the Apollinian Dream—also implies the multiple displacement and condensations, the distortions of the "dream" content in the symbolic language of the play's substratum. In short, read in this manner, *The Bacchae* addresses the problem of representation, the very dilemma posed by the incompatibility of form and content, essence and appearance, immanence and transcendence, which has dogged aesthetics at least since the eighteenth century. And it rehearses this aporia by casting it into a grotesque metaphor, a metaphor that is all the more powerful because it is drawn from the foundational myth of theatre itself, the myth of Dionysus.

This metaphor is made concrete in the *sparagmos*, the tearing apart of Pentheus, which is in a sense the most drastic dramatization (or radical *mise-en-scène*) of the problem of representation. For Pentheus is the signifier made to stand, by the logic of Dionysian ritual, for the signified god, and his dismemberment signals (in a double sense) the catastrophe of representation: textual and theatrical. In Euripides' text, and on Euripides' stage, the relation in this fundamental signifying act of theatre is already less determinate than in older tragedy. The suffering imposed on Pentheus is not the communal, affirmative suffering of the god (the god does not suffer but instead triumphs adversarially in the gruesome excess of his revenge). It is, rather, the suffering of individuation; Pentheus's identity has been systematically stripped and annihilated, without being replenished by that of the god. The *sparagmos* is only the extreme physical confirmation of a state of alienation from his culture, his origins, his sex, and his ego. Northrop Frye remarks: "*Sparagmos,* or the sense that heroism and effective action are absent, disorganized, or foredoomed to defeat, and that confusion and anarchy reign over the world, is the archetypal theme of irony and satire" (192).

The sacrifice is thus devoid of ritual meaning; it is not a vicarious repetition, but a parody of Dionysus's primal dismemberment. Moreover, it is a violent travesty both of Sophocles' *Oedipus* (for Pentheus is not, like Oedipus, a true *pharmakos* or scapegoat effecting genuine purification) and of the Oedipal situation as constructed by psychoanalysis. Pentheus's involuntary transvestism, the unspeakable indignity of dying in women's garb, even introduces an incongruously comical note into the proceedings. Jacques Lacan might have a great deal to say about the fact that the son is outfitted by the god as a mirror image of his mother, Agave (thereby stripped of his symbolic Phallus), and that in that disguise his mother deludedly reads him as the completely Other, the beast or lion, which is one of the masks of Dionysus, who is the play's symbolic Father (and the symbolic lover of the mother whom he has "seduced" with his ritual). The drama rests on an entire network of such *méconnaissances,* mutual readings and misreadings that play off of the Oedipal structure.

Dionysus's self-representation, too, is precarious. His vacillating identity as effeminate youth and as powerful animal (leopard or bull) is his tactical strength but also his strategic weakness: no one, including his followers, can quite "figure" Dionysus out in this play. It is a given of his cult that the god is typically most powerful when he possesses his adherents, that is, is manifested through a medium in *ek-stasis* who is not herself but not the god either; as concerns his own worship, the god consequently must disappear in order to appear, a true paradox of substance. A newcomer to the Pantheon, he also poaches on the territory of other gods (he has reportedly "usurped even the functions of warlike Ares" [l.

301]). Even the fundamental truth-claim of his divinity, the myth of his genesis, is damaged by misperceptions and garbled by imperfect transmission and indeed is a myth inherently rife with misrepresentations (Zeus masquerading for Semele, showing Hera a counterfeit Dionysus, and so on). Euripides' Dionysus is a god very much in doubt, and *The Bacchae* is first a drama about the crisis of representation playing itself out on several levels. As such it is deficient not out of weakness or willfulness, as Nietzsche claims, but out of the necessity of its representational paradox, in the sense that Jacques Derrida, glossing Artaud, speaks of the classical theatre as "a mark of cancellation that lets what it covers be read," as "the margin of an aberration whose meaning and measure are visible only beyond birth, at the eve of theatrical representation, at the origin of tragedy" (*Writing* 236).

Above and beyond, but manifestly linked to, the crisis of representation enacted in *The Bacchae* is what René Girard has defined as the "sacrificial crisis." Although he is fundamentally interested in broader anthropological questions, Girard's analysis of the Euripidean drama corroborates my own. The role of ritual sacrifice, according to Girard, is the substitution of channeled and controlled violence visited upon a sacrificial victim for the indiscriminate violence of a cycle of mutual vengeance that is likely to escalate in a prelegal society. This sacrificial substitution may experience a crisis of efficacy resulting from an effacement of the distinctions upon which it is founded—the clear boundaries between victim, substitute, and society; it then becomes "a crisis affecting the cultural order" (*Violence* 49). I have emphasized the seeds of the grotesque contained in such a breakdown of the categories of difference in the previous chapter; Girard notes its generic/genetic connection to tragedy, which is "a child of the sacrificial crisis" (65).

Tragedy, then, redresses the sacrificial crisis by displaying first the symmetry of antagonistic violence and finally its conversion into the "unanimous" violence of the purifying sacrificial act; such is the case in *Oedipus Rex.* But in *The Bacchae,* the structure is founded on that deritualized vestige of the sacrificial rite, the festival, and moreover on "a festival that goes wrong" (Girard, *Violence* 127). In contrast to *Oedipus,* the antagonistic violence in *The Bacchae* has no concrete aim other than the assertion of divine power; "but behind that divinity there lies only violence" (143). So similar (and essentially interchangeable in this impossible sacrifice) are Dionysus and Pentheus, so much caught in a "double bind" (147) of mutual mimetic desire, that they have mutated into each other's "monstrous double": "The unity and reciprocity that the enemy brothers have rejected in the benign form of brotherly love finally impose themselves, both from without and within, in the form of monstrous duality—the most disquieting and grotesque form imaginable" (160). The presence of the monstrous double that, as Girard points out, permeates *The Bacchae* thus initiates a crisis of representation—who doubles whom?—within which the sacrificial crisis cannot in fact be unequivocally resolved but only paradigmatically displayed or displaced in the grotesque *sparagmos,* the tearing apart of Pentheus. This is my conclusion, not Girard's, who however does acknowledge that Euripides' tragedy "never succeeds in finding its equilibrium": he speaks, appropriately, of a "shaking of degrees" in this play that "blunts all distinctions and multiplies all meanings, allowing none of them to remain unshaken" (138). If all tragic heroes before the advent of Euripides—to follow Nietzsche's reasoning—are versions of Dionysus, then perhaps Pentheus is the model for the postclassical (grotesque) hero-victim. As for Dionysus, he reflects the other side of the grotesque, the implicit animality within culture about which Nietzsche writes in *Beyond Good and Evil*: "Almost everything we call 'higher culture' is based on the spiritualization of *cruelty,* on its becoming more profound: this is my proposition. That 'savage animal' has not really been 'mortified'; it lives and flourishes, it has merely become—divine" (158). Dionysus and Pentheus are two sides of the grotesque character: victimizer and victim; the victorious and horrible impulse of chaos behind the human mask and the defeated force of an illusory cultural order. They mark the complementary poles of a world defined in hunter/prey relationships. And yet it is not an arrested dialectic; even if Dionysus seems to triumph unequivocally, he has also lost the game, for what he most desired, the willing submission of Pentheus to his godhood, he has accomplished only through violent coercion, that is, not at all.

Penthean and Dionysian aspects, sometimes in separation, often in extreme conflation, inform almost every grotesque play, every grotesque characterization. Pentheus's savage death in *The Bacchae* stands as a paradigm of the release of Apollinian control, for the peril of role-playing, for the parlous transformation from acting to embodiment, for the unclear limits of fiction. In its depiction of the release of the lower orders of a chaotic and willful Dionysian force into the perimeter of a stage held and circumscribed by the oneiric laws of Apollo, *The Bacchae* is perhaps the original pattern of grotesque dramaturgy.

It is surely not coincidental, for instance, that a modern play such as Friedrich Dürrenmatt's *Visit* mirrors *The Bacchae* so closely: Claire, like Dionysus an implacable divinity (she reminds the town schoolmaster of "an avenging Greek goddess" [26]), returns to her native soil to seek redress for a slight, accompanied by an entourage entirely under her spell. Her opponent is her former beau Alfred Ill, "the most popular personality" in town, next in line for the mayorship, who is finally dispatched in a *sparagmos* in the town hall at Claire's behest. Dürrenmatt satirically transmutes Dionysus's natural force into the force of finance but preserves much of the grotesque problematic of *The Bacchae.*

The Bacchae is one of a handful of landmark plays that have the power to call everything into question, but very few successful stagings exist. However, Klaus Michael Grüber directed a remarkable production of the play at Berlin's Schaubühne theatre in 1974 (see fig. 6). Grüber's *Bacchae* (part of an "Antiquity Project" at the Schaubühne) was called to double duty: to provide a semblance (this in itself a paradox) of the violent immediacy of the Dionysian ritual in and for modern civilization, and to retrieve the symbolic meaning of the play into the present without giving in to faddish updatings. The notion to strip *The Bacchae* of its discursive layers and reduce it to a ritualistic core was no longer novel in 1974; the experiments of Grotowski and Schechner were by then well known. Grüber instead treated its ritualism self-consciously, stressing the close mutual relation of order and chaos (in a brilliant theatrical image, the Bacchae tore away the stage floor to dig up the earth, the "lower orders" of unruly Dionysian nature, underneath; Pentheus's crews restored order with a street-sweeping machine) and their irresistible attraction (a strong homoerotic subtext in the Pentheus/Dionysus scenes underlined the mutual mimetic desire). In the ensemble discussions during rehearsals, it became clear to the actors that *The Bacchae* is a profound challenge to theatrical representation itself, and they imagined a "grotesque" image to illustrate that challenge:

> Is it at all possible that the theatre can go back beyond the theatre, beyond that which began in Greece as the play of mimesis? Is not really every going-back also a mimetic going-back, because all seemingly immediate processes are already being represented in the medium of mimesis? To make clear that the

Fig. 6. Euripides, *The Bacchae.* Schaubühne Berlin, 1974. Photo: Helga Kneidl.

> reality of theatre rests on transformation, imagination, and mimesis, one could imagine the grotesque situation that one first presents the audience with the victim of a car accident, then removes him and substitutes him with an actor who plays the dead man. The moment of transformation is the actual reality of our practice. (Iden 181)

These actors understood that *The Bacchae* is a play about that bold and precarious transformation with its ineluctable shading of grotesqueness, the transformation of the *sparagmos* into *mimesis,* as is the theatre itself.[3]

While in *The Birth of Tragedy* Nietzsche largely thinks against Hegel and the Idealistic positions of the nineteenth century, he fails to extricate the grotesque entirely from its inferior and oppositional state; or, rather, he demonstrates by indirection that it not only cannot be set free but that confinement and suppression are part of its essence. The sublime, in Nietzsche's words, is "the artistic taming of the horrible" (*Birth* 60), and Apollo is the ubiquitous agent of such sublimity. In the grotesque, some of the primal savagery of the horrible is restored.

The seeds of the grotesque in Nietzsche's theory, then, are not contained within the Dionysian or the Apollinian themselves but in their irreducible difference, which is muted and finally unacknowledged in the surface discourse of *The Birth of Tragedy.* In other words, it is exactly the aporia of tragedy, its inability to make good Apollinian work of the amorphous Dionysian force that creates the dramatic grotesque in *The Bacchae.* The grotesque itself is the surprising, cataclysmic revelation of this paradox, literally embodied by Euripides' stage image of the *sparagmos.*

In *The Actor's Freedom,* Michael Goldman claims that there is a potential *sparagmos* in every play: "[S]omewhere in every play something threatens to tear the principal character apart" (17). As *The Bacchae* demonstrates, the aim of the dramatic grotesque is always to find out and enlarge that potential moment.[4]

Tragic Self-Consumption

The problem of tragic structure and mimesis that *The Bacchae* displays like a wound continues into the genre's further history. Frye places Senecan tragedy and its Elizabethan offspring firmly into what he calls the "sixth phase" of tragedy, a liminal phase bordering on irony and satire (where, incidentally, he locates the forms of the grotesque). Tragedy of the sixth phase dwells on "a world of shock and horror in which the central images are images of *sparagmos,* that is, cannibalism, mutilation and torture"; sixth-phase tragedy not only contains shocking incidents but "shocks as a whole" (Frye 222).

In Shakespeare's work, there is a pervasive imagery of cannibalism that haunts particularly the later plays as the token metaphor of cultural dissolution. In *Othello,* Emilia remarks wryly (and with not a little premonition) to Desdemona that for the lower orders of humanity, love is not about romance but consumption:

> 'Tis not a year or two shows us a man:
> They are all but stomachs, and we all but food;
> They eat us hungerly, and when they are full
> They belch us.
>
> (3.4.103–6)

In *King Lear,* Albany, aghast at Lear's tiger-daughters, prophesies:

> If that the heavens do not their visible spirits
> Send quickly down to tame [these] vile offenses,
> It will come,

> Humanity must perforce prey on itself,
> Like monsters of the deep.
>
> (4.2.46–50)

There are echoes here of the metaphor of the "universal wolf" that Ulysses warns will make prey of all things when degree is upset and power has degenerated finally into mere will and "appetite" (*Troilus and Cressida* 1.3.120ff.). Caliban, of course, has long been thought to be an anagrammatic transformation of "cannibal." Shakespeare is here part of the mainstream of the culture/nature discourse of his time; cannibalism is a prominent cultural taboo and an example of ultimate transgression, bearing repeated literary invocation from Pliny and Juvenal to Michel de Montaigne and Jonathan Swift. Girard emphasizes that there can be a sacrificial aspect to cannibalism, but this applies only where there is a firm ritual framework and where the victim/scapegoat/meal is an aspect of the other, such as a defeated enemy (*Violence* 274–76). It is far more problematic in such instances as the one Plutarch cites, where the "cannibal feast" is prepared in Dionysian ecstasy and the victim is a child or relative to the eater, an aspect not of the other but of the self (Frazer 339). This is the case in the two plays to be discussed here.

Cannibalism is an extremely ambivalent motif, and it shares with other forms of the grotesque the simultaneous invocation of sublime or holy and inferior or infernal realms: the symbolic "eating of the gods" is a frequent archaic ritual of participation in the divine that still informs Christian practice in one of its paramount rites, the taking of communion, and yet the act of cannibalism proper is indicative of utter depravity and inhumanity. It is rather unsurprising that there is a pervasive sympathy between the topos of the cannibal and the art of the grotesque; thus we find the cannibal motif in Dante's tale of Ugolino; we see monsters feasting on men and men gnawing at one another in Hieronymus Bosch and Pieter Breughel; Francisco Goya provides a horrific illustration of Saturn eating his children; and so forth.

But there is a comic dimension to the topos that accounts for its frequent use in political satire and caricature; gastric imagery per se is associated with comedy, and the banquet table is a comedic location (although there is an ominous countertradition from Belshazzar to Macbeth). It is indeed quite obvious how the grotesque structure is recapitulated in the act of cannibalism: in eating a fellow man, I reduce him to a lower order (food) and concurrently contradict a sublimated perception of corporeality by valuing the body not for its human aspects (beauty, strength, sexual attraction) but for its protein content. Art tied to the motif of cannibalism invariably produces a "strong" grotesque, perhaps the strongest imaginable. There is no need, of course, for the "eating" to be utterly literal. Actual ingestion is only the most immediate expression of the transformation of man into meat, which may even be accomplished by the radical metaphorical/metamorphic power of mere verbal invective, as when Hal's abusive words to Falstaff can be read as a "reverse-transubstantiation in which man becomes flesh" (F. Barasch, "Definitions" 64).

Harold Skulsky, while investigating the cannibal/demon motif in Ben Jonson's *Volpone,* has attempted to shed light on our continuous fascination with the taboo against eating others. He finds that demonic possession and cannibalistic ingestion stand in close mutual relation, both hinging on what he calls "primitive having." The body, argues Skulsky, is an exception to the rules of "having" because we cannot possess it but rather coincide with it. Therefore, as concerns the body, the absence of "having" produces a void that longs to be filled:

> One morbid way of fighting *vanitas*—filling the void—is Falstaff's: to stuff it. A still more morbid variant is Shylock's or the legacy hunter's: to fill one's void (in fantasy at least) with another person's flesh or "substance." The converse way of fighting *vanitas* is Volpone's; to fill other people's voids with one's own "substance" or power—that is, to possess them demonically. (300)

But both versions—possession and cannibalistic ingestion—are subject to a traumatic, archaic fear: the fear of "finding oneself the container of something malignant, intelligent and alive" (Skulsky 301)—a fear brilliantly tapped in films such as Don Siegel's *Invasion of the Body Snatchers* or Ridley Scott's *Alien.*

It is fairly evident that this idea is particularly applicable not only to dramatic action and plotting but also to the theater itself, because in the art of acting this exact double movement of "possession" by the part and "ingestion" of the character routinely takes place. The character's substance momentarily fills the void of the actor, and the actor seems always on guard lest the character come too much "alive" in him and he himself be consumed, like the unfortunate woman observed by Oliver Sacks. For the actor is already "taken in" by the spectator (and must often feel in the face of a hostile crowd that they will "eat him for lunch," or some such cannibalistic metaphor). The actor never escapes.

Conversely, theater whets the audience's appetite for a "cannibalism of empathy," as the Brechtian Heiner Müller puts it, which often yields a less than nourishing meal (Müller, "Brief" 107). But in his First Manifesto for the Theatre of Cruelty, Artaud envisions the "cannibalism" of the spectator pouring out, "on a level not counterfeit and illusory, but interior" (*Theater* 92). For one who admired Seneca, as Artaud did, the cannibalistic play may present a prelude to the "true illusion" of a cannibalistic theatre, a theatre that is itself, in Bert States's words, a "rather predatory institution" that "consumes nature" and looks "objectively at the subjective life of the race as something prepared for the community out of the substance of its own body" (13, 39). The theatre with its insatiable mimetic appetite is pervaded by such structures of mutual consumption. It is small wonder that such a cannibal medium would delight in the cannibal theme and in characters starved for substance, characters of excess, not merely ready to chew the scenery but to eat the scene. Hypertrophying, systemic excess, and monstrous incongruity are, as we found, signs of a grotesque world, and the grotesque character is always in some sense in an excessive, irrational relation to the dramatic environment in which she finds herself, in such a way that she assaults its very categories of ideology, genre, and representation. But far from destroying the theatre, as we will see, such characters strengthen it because they flush out (and flesh out) its grotesque essence.

The list of works touching on the subject of cannibalism could easily be extended beyond the three plays discussed here: it is treated romantically (in the double sense) in Heinrich von Kleist's *Penthesilea,* in which the heroine "devours" her lover Achilles, and played in the Gothic-macabre vein in Stephen Sondheim's *Sweeney Todd.* In Eugène Ionesco's *Jack or the Submission,* the character Father Robert praises his daughter to the recalcitrant Jack in culinary terms: the bride-to-be has "a tongue the color of tomato-sauce, pan-browned square shoulders, and all the meat needed to merit the highest commendation" (92). The plays of Fernando Arrabal's "Panic Theatre" abound with cannibalistic tableaux (especially *The Architect and the Emperor of Assyria*), and in Edward Bond's *Early Morning,* cannibalism becomes the central motif in a revisionist view of British history. Finally, fairly typical of the contemporary theatre is Nicky Silver's farce *Fat Men in Skirts* in which young Bishop Hogan, product of a loveless marriage, proceeds to kill and consume both his parents and the father's girlfriend. In Silver's warped and vacuous middle-class society, casual cannibalism is just one more way of "stuffing the void."

The most radical treatment of the theme of cannibalism in antiquity remains Seneca's *Thyestes.* Seneca's plays seem as timely and paradigmatic again for the twenty-first century as they were for the first. In this, if little else, we share the sensibilities of the Renaissance. Without Seneca, the modern grotesque play is unthinkable—Alfred Jarry acknowledges this by having his Ubu paraphrase Seneca's Latin in *Ubu Cuckolded,* much as Renaissance protagonists were wont to. If Seneca's plays show a disastrous event "pursued ruthlessly to its end," as one critic remarks (Watling 25), one is reminded of Dürrenmatt's claim that the plot of a truly grotesque play must always take the "worst possible turn" (*Physicists* 95).

Artaud considered Seneca "the greatest tragic writer in history." He wrote to his friend Jean Paulhan that "[t]here is no better *written* example of what can be meant by cruelty in the theater than *all* the Tragedies of Seneca, but especially *Atreus and Thyestes.*" For Seneca's sake, Artaud was even prepared to put aside his dislike of the literary text since he detected beneath Seneca's syllables "the transparent surge of the forces of chaos" (Artaud, *Selected Writings* 307). Segal believes that Seneca's rhetoric of violence

> has a modern descendant in the atmosphere of unreality and nightmare which pervades the novels of Kafka, Canetti, and Wiesel and a still living cousin in the element of the surreal and incredible that attaches to the (alas) nonfictional accounts of the tortured from Argentina to Algeria, from Auschwitz to the Gulag. (336)

And William Calder observes that Seneca's "portrayal of transcendent evil" in *Thyestes* has made him "a prophet for our unhappy century" (195). Renewed theatrical interest in Senecan tragedy (by Peter Brook and others) bears out this judgment of Seneca's modernity.

Thyestes opens with the voices of the netherworld; the allegorical character of Fury, like a master of ceremonies (and with a confident theatrical sensibility), sets the stage for the next installment in the Thracian tragedy of the accursed House of Atreus, while the ghost of unhappy Tantalus himself (unlike ghosts in Thomas Kyd and Shakespeare) exhorts his sons to practice restraint, not revenge. These warnings go unheard.

Tantalus, made clairvoyant by suffering and repentance but powerless to prevent the repercussions of his own outrageous deed, gives a first introduction to the peculiar topography of Seneca's inverted world when he cries to all condemned souls to be "content with [their] afflictions" (Seneca 48). Suffering in inferno is preferable by far to dwelling in the upper world: not Hades but Mycenae is hell.

The presiding demon of this hell is Atreus, Seneca's ultimate villain and model of character pathology, who is plotting revenge against his brother, Thyestes. As a kind of overture to the play's moral problem, Atreus first issues an idiosyncratic interpretation of kingship through which he constructs the persona he will assume in the ensuing action. Kingship, above all, is a question of power. The king, to Atreus, is not a representative of justice or repository of law; justice, it is obvious, is a trifling thing to this monarch. He may, in his first lines, invoke the "sacred law" (53) his brother has broken by stealing his wife, throne, and the golden ram to which he lays claim. But such rhetoric of moral indignation is purely perfunctory and is roundly subverted by the contempt he displays for the "luxuries" of sanctity, piety, and trust (55). The true king, as whom Atreus casts himself, is above (or below) the law; the regal prerogative on which his authority is founded is the exercise, with total impunity, of arbitrary violence. What is more, he argues like a true proto-Machiavellian when he exults that his subjects are compelled "not only to endure but to approve their master's actions" (54)—this fondness for exacerbating physical by mental cruelty, of coercing acquiescence, also determines the method of his revenge.

Atreus by no means represents "motiveless malignity" (in Coleridge's famous term)—by mythological and dramatic standards, his reasons for taking revenge are sound, for he has indeed been grievously abused. But he is *willing* to become pure evil, he aspires to it, and the solid justification for vengeance that Thyestes' actions have given him in a sense stands in the way of this absolute self-fulfillment. Casting aside all pieties, Atreus thus sets out to reorder the dramatic universe in a way that negates the structure of causality on which it is based, to bypass the perpetual exchange of horrible deed for more horrible deed that the curse of Tantalus imposes, not by putting an end to the spiral of violence but by throwing it open to something so unspeakable and unimaginable, "beyond the bounds of human nature" (57), that it becomes transcendent. This deed has no more need of the feeble appellation "revenge"; it is unequivocally and self-confidently a "crime" that Atreus contrives, a "better crime" than all preceding ones (and he is in contention with a host of choice abominations). Indeed, it is the perfect crime, "wonderful" and perverse, with a consummate beauty all its own: that Thyestes, "happily, with eager appetite," eat his own children (57).

The gruesome irony of such a crime is boundless: it is in the worst tradition of the Atreides, having its precedent in the consumption of Pelops by the gods, but it greatly refines that atrocity and, being "more terrible than any ordinary act of man" (57), lends the perpetrator himself an aspect of divinity, much like Dionysus affirmed his status in the sheer excess and cruelty of his revenge. This deed is thus uniquely suited to Atreus's (and Seneca's) purpose: to put into scene an apocalyptic drama. Atreus is, together with Dionysus, the prototype of the monstrous and excessive grotesque character, the character who overwhelms the play and reshapes the dramatic universe in the wake of his actions. Indeed, Atreus seems to escape the tragic law of retribution in a universe devoid of punishing gods. He, significantly, has the last words in the play. His hubristic self-apotheosis ("Now I am god of gods and king of kings" [85]) is never answered by divine wrath. The blithely ignorant words of the chorus that "[k]ings of the earth must bow to a higher kingdom" (71) are mere wishful rhetoric. In the universe that Seneca lets Atreus construct, there is no one above—and no one below—Atreus.

To carry out the deed takes more than an ordinary man as well, and so Atreus goes about the task of systematically turning himself into a monster, first by summoning a "monstrous rage" to fit his disposition and by delivering himself to unnamed chthonic "forces" (56), later by bestializing himself in the simile of a hunting dog sniffing the "scent of blood" (67). His (a)moral reasoning reduces him to the status of an animal; all vestiges of fraternal loyalty are subordinated to beastly instincts. Atreus purposely metamorphoses into the "monstrous double" of his brother, Thyestes, who, returning from exile, is reluctant to emerge from a "green world" (in Frye's term) of harmony with nature, from a "life among the beasts, shared with the beasts" (Frye 63) that, apparently, has transformed and ennobled him. The pastoral world of natural harmony in which humanity coexists with fauna and flora (in which the Wild is merely the assimilable projection of Culture) is then immediately identified as beyond the bounds of the play. Thyestes' ill premonitions are justified, for here, the radical disjunction of beast and man obtains, and he is about to encounter the true beast that knows nothing of the Stoic-pastoral realm. Purely for the sake of dramatic contrast, Seneca has made Thyestes a helpless victim; in the original myth, his guilt equals his brother's. But Atreus's excesses would be rendered less potent if his revenge were visited on too deserving a victim.

There is no doubt that Atreus is a grotesque creature, one of Seneca's "misshapen giants of puppets," as August Wilhelm Schlegel has summarily called them, thereby inaugurating the dim view long held of Seneca's tragic achievements (Watling 9). Schlegel's description, although meant to be disparaging, captures the double nature of Atreus: the gigantic extremity of his volition and his puppetlike reflexes to the excess of his passionate appetite. But in Atreus's case, the movement is *self*-reflexive; it is the movement of a monstrous and deliberate self-dramatization. Atreus's descent into bestiality or biocentricity is recaptured by the messenger in his narration of the murder of Thyestes' sons to the chorus, in which two distinct images interpenetrate: that of the king as a "priest" staging a meticulous and solemn ritual of sacrifice (actually, its ultimate travesty), and that of the rapacious, prowling beast, with "scowling eyes" like the "hungry tiger in an Indian forest" (76), or like a "tawny lion in Armenia / Crouching amid the vanquished carcases / Of a whole herd of oxen," insatiable in his fury (77). Insistent images of hunger and thirst pervade the play's language from the first words of Tantalus to the last lines of Atreus, emphasizing the point that this is a world famished for substance, in which all activity is subject to a rampant voracity, to the "stuffing" of a void that cannot ever be filled.

In this universe Seneca draws, we can recognize a degenerate version of the Stoic dogma of totality and of its determinate ratio of inner to outer life. Microcosm and macrocosm are linked in such a way that the deformed characters are an expression of the blind and violent macrocosmic forces, and the macrocosm is the extension of the amoral constitution of the monstrous characters. Thomas Curley remarks that "the microcosm stands face to face with the macrocosm" in Seneca (210). Such lack of mediation and proclivity toward excess, as I have noted, is the first sign of a grotesquely constituted dramatic system. When Atreus goes to kill Thyestes' boys, he seeks out the ideal place to commit the crime, a *locus horridus* that stands in grim contrast to the *locus amoenus* from which Thyestes has returned. It is an "ancient grove" (or grotto) in a hollow of the palace, the "secret heart of [Atreus's] domain" where black and knotty trees grow unpruned, and in which "trophies of every crime / Committed by this family" are kept (74).

In short, the murder takes place in something resembling the monster-king's unconscious itself, congealed into dramatic (or at least rhetorical) space. Seneca could not make it more apparent that the entire landscape of *Thyestes* is a deictic analogue or "expressionistic" projection of Atreus's interior state. Atreus has uncompromisingly taken over the play; indeed, as the composite god-man-beast as which he has designed himself, he defines its upper and lower limits. Consequently, it only takes Atreus's single deed for day to turn into night, order to be plunged into chaos, East and West to become indistinguishable, and the universe, disjointed, to reel into catastrophe (these are some of the apocalyptic images that the chorus summons). The dramatic world of *Thyestes* has been addressed as "a world turned upside-down" (Calder 190); "inside-out" might perhaps be the more appropriate term.

The grotesque pièce de résistance in *Thyestes* is the moment of recognition Atreus engineers at the culmination of act 5 for his brother, who has just devoured his children. There is scarcely a more horrible scene than this anywhere in dramatic literature, and the entire act carefully builds up to it. Atreus watches his sated and drunken brother with unconcealed glee, anticipating the moment of revelation. But Seneca exacerbates the scene with near unbearable irony; the unsuspecting Thyestes has not only eaten but has feasted with a voracity that seems to run in the family (his meal consists of three boys) and now launches into a vinous "song of jollity" (85). As he calls for his sons to share his festive mood with him, Atreus remarks that they are "already with you here / In your embrace" (87). The Latin is *in amplexu patris,* which, for greater effect, may also be read as "in their father's bosom": Atreus's ultimate villainy hinges on a kind of radical metaphor. But Thyestes is uncomprehending until the very physicality of the deed comes to haunt him:

> *Thyestes:* What agitation in my stomach swells?
> What moves within me? Some protesting burden
> Lies on my heart, and in my breast a voice
> That is not mine is groaning. O my children!
> Where are you? Come! Your ailing father calls you.
> If I can see your faces all my pain
> Will soon be ended. Do I hear them? Where?

> *Atreus [exhibiting the children's heads]:* Embrace your children, father!
> They are here beside you. Do you recognize your sons?
> *Thyestes:* I recognize my brother.
>
> (88–89)

This perverse *anagnorisis* is genuinely grotesque; recognition, moral revulsion, and severe indigestion are one and inseparable. Thyestes is constipated by the abhorrent deed, and he cries out in despair: "My stomach moves; the sin within me strives / To find escape—cannot escape its prison. . . . I press my sons to death—they press their father. / Is sin illimitable?" (90).

The "chain of love" of which the chorus spoke earlier (69) is suddenly no more than an idealized vision of the food chain. Low comedy, which typically derives much of its material from the movement of the bowels, insinuates itself into the horror; the moment vacillates violently between pathos and bathos. It could not possibly have escaped the sophisticated Roman author that this radically materialist condensation of the tragic motif renders the tragic tone untenable. He seems to be deliberately provoking the catastrophe of tragedy in the tragic catastrophe. Into this collapse of the tragic structure rings only the improper laughter of its potential audience—a laughter that seems to have a double nature. It is both a protective laughter of rejection and ridicule and highly self-conscious about its own impropriety. If this is grotesque laughter, we see that such laughter not only *reflects* unease but reflects *on* it, that it is in part a kind of meta-laughter about the impropriety of one's own response. Seen in this light, grotesque laughter is not the opposite of, not a palliative to, grotesque terror but a version of it.

Everything in the play, symbolically and dramatically, "comes down" to Thyestes' constipation with his children (just as everything in *The Tutor* comes down to Läuffer's castration). This is its base moral proposition, the grimmest interpretation of Bakhtin's grotesque degradation in which everything is only an aspect of the body; the entire history of the indignities and trespasses of the House of Atreus is condensed into this rumbling stomach that itself is only the radical form of the metaphorical insight that Thyestes' sons are his own "flesh and blood." Segal finds this instance of "boundary violation" so remarkable because the foreign matter in Thyestes is "both alien and fearfully his own" (332):

> The victim is bloated and distorted in his own flesh by being crammed full of a poisonous feast that he cannot disgorge and must assimilate. The scene's outrage works through its evocation of the primary processes over which we have no conscious control, the digestive absorption of alien substance converted into our very being. . . . We are forced to see ourselves in the context of the corruptible entrails of animals. This ultimate reduction of our being to physical matter, to the fate we share with all living (and dying) things, is profoundly disquieting. (335)

In fact, it anticipates (but graphically surpasses) a familiar medieval topos to which Hamlet still alludes: "We fat all creatures else to fat us, and we fat ourselves for maggots" (4.3.21–23).

Thyestes goes as far as tragedy, as drama, can go: it is a dramaturgical experiment to see how much humanity can be reduced and stripped away before the characters are rendered dysfunctional. It pushes the image of man-as-beast, as insatiable desire or appetite incarnate, to its limits. Thyestes' grotesquely bloated stomach stands in stark contrast to the persistent appetite of Atreus, which even revenge will not sate, but both brothers are exempla of a severely reduced conception of humanity.

Tone and atmosphere of the play are unrelentingly bleak; not even a token attempt at suggesting the possibility of a resurgent moral order is made. Even if the Thyestes myth itself did not forbid such conclusions, they would seem arbitrary and ridiculous in the context of the world the drama projects. The audience[5] is provided with sufficient cause for revulsion, even for pity and fear (if those are indeed the applicable terms here), and also for inappropriate laughter, but it is unequivocally denied all cathartic transport. If Seneca's aim was indeed to present Nero with a political object lesson, as Calder suspects, the offer of catharsis would have been counterproductive. Calder, who calls Atreus the "Richard III of Greco-Roman tragedy"—which is an understatement at best—believes that Seneca conceived Atreus didactically, as a character for Nero to "understand and admire," a character who by example "teaches the art of survival in an impossible situation" (188–90). For this there is no proof, but it is a fearfully plausible reading of a play that nowhere contradicts its co-optation as a political tract advocating utter (self-)abasement as a strategy of survival. *Thyestes,* then, puts the contemporaneous grotesque ornaments of Nero's Golden House into perspective: in each, the transformative facility of humans, of the human body in particular, is emphasized. While one is playful and the other demonic, both belong to the aesthetic undercurrent of a despotic age in which the image of deconstructed man served to considerably loosen the perceptual boundaries and make the unthinkable thinkable.

The only way to interpret *Thyestes* that allows us to think of Seneca as a clandestine subversive rather than as a willing accomplice to Neronian corruption is not by extracting moral lessons from a play that is utterly lacking in them but by regarding as completely deliberate the aporia of the tragic system in *Thyestes* (which to the Romans was associated with Attic humanity and culture). In effect, Seneca would be saying that such an irredeemable view of humanity cannot be contained in the tragic frame; it has dropped out of the bottom. Curley has taken up the theme of the problematic tragedy in Seneca and stressed its metatheatrical or metarepresentational dimension. He contends that it is "not merely the enormity of the crimes but their theatricality which makes their theatrical representation difficult." Seneca's solution, says Curley, was "to write a play which is, in part, a meditation on the nature of drama"; he does this by engineering "certain collapses of the dramatic structure itself, in order to incarnate in the body of the work the chaos described" (184).

This is in essence true, although Curley's position seems to be that Seneca's formal achievement is adequate to the matter, and he appears oblivious to the fact that such a "collapse" of dramatic structure subsequently leaves a representational and cathartic vacuum that the play itself cannot fill. The play thus succeeds (as Curley says), but its success is tied to its failure. I have previously described this success-as-failure as a prerequisite of the grotesque form. We here catch ancient tragedy at a point of crisis—a crisis it is well aware of and exploits by virtue of its tacit intertextual reference to its Greek models (this is most obvious in Seneca's *Oedipus,* which seems a calculated travesty of Sophocles). It is also a crisis that, as Gordon Braden sees it, foreshadows exactly what will make Renaissance drama successful, "a rhetoric of psychic aggression that seemingly allows a character to make himself and his world up out of his own words" (62).

Rhetorical self-invention also abounds in *Titus Andronicus.* As if to advertise itself as the most Senecan play in Shakespeare's canon, *Titus* repeatedly quotes the Roman author. It shares with *Thyestes* a grim attention to the specifics of bodily mutilation, which makes it a source of constant embarrassment to many critics. But although *Titus,* in its explicit violence and savagery, may seem similar to the run-of-the-mill Elizabethan revenge plays (and even seems to reach back to allegorical origins as they do), it possesses what most of them lack: an uncannily sophisticated symbolic and metaphorical undergirding in which it reveals itself to be a tract on language, rhetoric, signs, and epistemology. It is, again, the radical way in which Shakespeare deploys the *mise-en-scène* of metaphor from which the grotesque springs.

I have said before that the grotesque must assure itself of some kind of generic environment in order to contradict it, and *Titus* provides a textbook example. The first act behaves much like a foreshortened, self-contained (tragi)comedy, containing in one protracted scene the exposition and subsequent resolution of Bassianus and Saturninus's succession quarrel; the "sacrifice" of Tamora's son; Lavinia's betrothal to the emperor, which is challenged by Bassianus and culminates in Titus stabbing his son Mutius; and finally the reconciliation of the Andronici and the prospect of a double wedding, Saturninus/Tamora and Bassianus/Lavinia: a "love-day" (1.1.491). The plot material contained in this act is sufficient to equip an entire romantic comedy (and this is likely the intended impression). By establishing a condensed version of crisis and its typical comedic resolution into symmetrical nuptials, the play has hurried us through a conventional set of expectations and generated in shorthand the predictable universe of romance. Significantly, it omits the seal of that genre, the wedding feast itself (which is rescheduled, so to speak, for the last act), and as act 2 opens, we are somewhere beyond romance, in uncharted territory, as it were. We have stepped outside the tight circle of the romance genre into "sixth-phase" realms, where anything, especially anything demonic, is possible. Much like Franz Kafka's Gregor Samsa, Titus awakens from "troubled sleep" (2.2.9) into this transformed universe.

It is no coincidence that Aaron, the play's "dark" soul, is given his first malevolent soliloquy in act 2. But there has not been a clean generic disjuncture (which would in any event be atypical for the grotesque). Several disturbing factors already contaminate act 1. There is the incongruously archaic sacrifice of Tamora's son Alarbus, whose "limbs are lopp'd," as Lucius cheerily explains (1.1.143). This is the first instance of a persistent arboreal metaphor and anticipates Lavinia's "trimming": language is a constant giveaway here, particularly in the unthinking use of physical metonymies (Marcus wants to "set a head on headless Rome" [1.1.186]; Saturninus fears that Titus will rob him of "the people's hearts" [1.1.207]). The Romans' language prefigures the body parts that will be liberally strewn across the stage in the coming action before Marcus finally attempts to pick up the pieces and fuse "[t]hese broken limbs again into one body" (5.3.72). Tamora, who finds herself "incorporate in Rome" (1.1.462), betrays an unusual sensitivity to such discourse.

The first scene of the second act provides a remarkable example of generic and metaphorical corruption that signals the pollution of the "green world." Chiron and Demetrius, Tamora's other sons, enter as contentious suitors, engaged in overheated exchanges and professing their love for Lavinia and their intentions to woo her (which would involve them, were this plot followed through, in a kind of comedic triangle with Titus as the "blocking agent" father). They appear here, in effect, as the amorous youths in a Menandrian or Plautine love plot—even the mock-mythical names, so profoundly un-Gothic, suggest such a lineage.[6] Since they are mute in act 1, this is our first real exposure to them, and it is utterly at odds with the monstrous presence they are soon to become. Their transformation occurs literally by a turn of phrase: Aaron, who (like Atreus in *Thyestes*) is the play's hyperconscious built-in dramaturge, recognizes the given generic setup and adopts, *vis-à-vis* Tamora's sons, the role of the wily slave in Roman comedy who will hatch plans to facilitate the sexual encounter. But in appropriating Demetrius's hunting metaphor (Lavinia as a "doe" to be "borne . . . cleanly by the keeper's nose" [2.1.93–94]), he supplants the image's carnal-erotic connotation with a carnal-lethal meaning: Lavinia not as a prize to be won but as a victim on whom the men may "take [their] turns" (2.1.129).

An actual hunt to celebrate the nuptials is imminent, but Aaron has mapped the forest contrary to the topography of romance; its many "unfrequented plots," he suggests, are "[f]itted by kind for rape and villainy" (2.1.115–16). Indeed, Aaron is "plotting" exactly what is "unfrequented" (because it is generically excluded) by conventional romantic comedy: he becomes an agent of the grotesque. Chiron and Demetrius are easily persuaded to exchange courting for rape; Aaron has tapped into their (unacknowledged) second nature. (When they later explicitly acknowledge what they have become by dressing up as "Rapine" and "Murder," the generic context has already changed.)

The dichotomy of the romantic view of nature and its corruption underscores the entire action of the play. The two halves of this dichotomy are strikingly contrasted in Tamora's two speeches about the forest, one describing it as entirely pastoral and conventional, the other conjuring a brooding and forbidding place:

> A barren detested vale you see it is;
> The trees, though summer, yet forlorn and lean,
> Overcome with moss and baleful mistletoe;
> Here never shines the sun, here nothing breeds,
> Unless the nightly owl or fatal raven;
> And when they show'd me this abhorred pit,
> They told me, here, at dead time of the night,
> A thousand fiends, a thousand hissing snakes,
> Ten thousand swelling toads, as many urchins,
> Would make such fearful and confused cries,
> As any mortal body hearing it
> Should straight fall mad, or else die suddenly.
>
> (2.3.93–104)

The manner in which Tamora "sets the scene" in the woods is proto-expressionistic (in Shakespeare such descriptive passages serve of course very much as the substitute for scenic technology). We already find this use of rhetorical scene-setting in Seneca, whose plays take place in an empty universe, a scenic vacuum filled with excessive characters and created by obsessive tropes. There is a duality of "linguistic and situational contexts" in this scene: "Beneath the seeming idyll in the wood lies Tamora and Aaron's 'obscure plot'" (Hiles 67). It is also a clever piece of mood manipulation, designed as an atmospheric cue for the murder of Bassianus by Chiron and Demetrius. The theatrical landscape, as if at Tamora's behest, accommodates this demonic vision; the forest floor abounds with hell-holes like the one Bassianus's body is dumped into. It is scarred with "detested, dark, blood-drinking pit[s]" (2.3.224), "swallowing womb[s]" (239) and "gaping hollow[s]" (249) where perceived normalcy suddenly caves in and the grotesque underground becomes visible.

As in *Thyestes,* the terrain of *Titus* is a landscape of the unconscious in which the pit is a signifier of death (Bassianus's "grave" [2.3.240]), sex and birth (the "womb"), shame (Lavinia begs to be thrown dead "into some loathsome pit" rather than raped [2.3.176]), and the "wound" of pain and loss that the play graphically searches "to the bottom" (Saturninus's words in 2.3.262). The image of the cavity or pit is dug deeply into the text, from Lavinia's empty mouth to the hole in which Aaron finally is buried "breast-deep" and left, like Tantalus, to starve (5.3.179). This infernal landscape is traversed by nefarious creatures (Tamora and Aaron are verbally associated with tigers, dogs, and other beasts more often than one cares to count), and it gives rise to a Senecan extremity (the Goths' "worse than killing lust" [2.3.175]; Saturninus's promise of "[s]ome never-heard-of torturing pain" for Titus's sons [2.3.285]). Unlike the later comedies, for example *As You Like It, Titus* does not merely play on the notion of a contrast between pastoral-idyllic and untamed nature that is mediated in love but radically asserts a lower order treacherously close to the surface in a world that knows only volition and desire.

The most extreme of the play's extremities is the treatment of Lavinia at the hands of Tamora's sons in act 2, scene 4. As in most premodern grotesque plays, we are not directly witness to the mutilation, but the stage direction presents us laconically with its results: "Enter the Empress' sons with Lavinia, her hands cut off, and her tongue cut out, and ravish'd." This scene allows a full view of the grotesque aspects of the play, not because of the plain horror of the violence or even the coarse jests of Chiron and Demetrius (whom we now perceive to be irredeemable monsters), but because of the manner in which Lavinia's uncle, Marcus, reacts to the sight:

> Speak, gentle niece: what stern ungentle hands
> Hath lopp'd and hew'd, and made thy body bare
> Of her two branches, those sweet ornaments
> Whose circling shadows kings have sought to sleep in,
> And might not gain so great a happiness
> As half thy love? Why dost not speak to me?
> Alas, a crimson river of warm blood,
> Like to a bubbling fountain stirr'd with wind,
> Doth rise and fall between thy rosed lips,
> Coming and going with thy honey breath.
>
> (2.4.16–25)

These are the most notorious lines in a play that otherwise lacks familiar quotations, and they have often been commented on. The discrepancy between exalted language (reminiscent, even to the extent of parody, of the conventional synecdochic figures in which love poetry "dismembers" its object of adulation) and scenic occurrence (the raped and mutilated Lavinia embodying the very opposite of such an object) is both horrible in its verbal misapprehension of the situation and laughable in its inadequacy. It is profoundly grotesque.

Marcus, of course, is a latecomer to the second act (we saw him last in act 1), and he behaves as if he were utterly unaware of the transformations that have occurred. By following the pattern of pastoral romance when confronted with a sight unimaginable in that genre, he becomes a kind of generic anomaly by whom we can measure the distance the play has traveled from its origins. He goes on to indulge in luxurious rhetorical parentheses and a profusion of images, belaboring uncalled-for associations (Lavinia's previous lute-playing and singing) and too-ready mythological analogies (Tereus and Philomela) that contrast with his simple misreadings of his niece's "signs." Or is it conceivable that she, "notwithstanding all this loss of blood" (2.4.29), as Marcus meticulously notes, could be *blushing* in delicate womanly shame? Marcus's very prolixity renders Lavinia's permanent silence horribly palpable; her abused figure disappears under the blanket of his uncomprehending figures.

In *Titus* as in *Thyestes,* rhetoric abets monstrosity and verbal excess mirrors character excess. For the excessive characters of Elizabethan and Jacobean drama, this is a fairly standard equation (as in the "mighty line" of Christopher Marlowe's *Tamburlaine*). But Marcus is not an excessive character; in this instance the problem is more complex. Jane Hiles, asserting that the plot of *Titus* "turns on a series of rhetorical failures," observes that the dominant characters in this play manipulate not only words but also the "contexts in which they occur." Linguistic competence determines who is "in charge" in a given scene (62). The Marcus/Lavinia scene would have to be called an egregious rhetorical failure, but Hiles ignores it because it does not revolve around the question of character power but instead reveals an aporia of representation. Here, and not in the outright display of cannibalism, is the most exorbitant of the grotesque "singularities" in which this tragedy almost consumes itself.

This assertion needs some elaboration. We could claim that it is incumbent upon tragic poetry to turn raw action into symbolic meaning through language; in the choral odes, character speeches, and messenger reports of tragedy, the horrible becomes sublime. The physical geography of the tragic scene in older Greek drama, which is a function of its representational ethos, inherently permits such a transmutation: the horrible (physically violent and wrenching) deed takes place out of sight, offstage or behind the doors of the *skene,* and the interpolation of a messenger or witness assures that it is both re-presented to its audience and infused with the poetic pathos and symbolic significance pure scenic violence would overwhelm. This inbuilt separation of the realms of pure violence and its metaphors—most concretely visible when metaphor is about to become violence (Agamemnon's red carpet) or violence is already metaphor (Oedipus's blind eyes)—ensures the integrity of the sacrifice at the root of the tragic action: the physical act and its symbolic interpretation do not pollute each other. Even Seneca's plays for the most part formally uphold this ethos—although there the language is so strongly charged with the invocation of physical particulars that the verbal mimesis of violence is almost unbearable.

In *Titus Andronicus,* however, and particularly in the Marcus/Lavinia scene, there is a gaping chasm between the unspeakable brutality of the presentation and the language chosen to mirror it. To be precise, that chasm is the very gap between literal and figurative usage I have previously investigated, and it is bridged by an unforgiving irony, for we have here in simultaneity the poetic metaphors, metonymies, and synecdoches of the love sonnet and their radical application to the body. Lavinia's specific mutilation appears as the incarnate lower order or radical metaphor of the routine mutilation of the female body in courtly poetry.

The irony belongs not to Marcus but to Shakespeare—it is inconceivable that he is in dead earnest. For the lapse occurs just at the moment when the play could mine the greatest empathic capital—sweet, innocent Lavinia's rape, properly exploited, would leave nary a dry eye in the house. (We must remember that Shakespeare's plays are, to all intents, acting editions and that the author could and would have purged any scene that did not "work" according to plan.) Even if we allow for strong cultural discrepancies between the Elizabethan spectator and ourselves, the effect of grotesque emotional disparity between what is seen and what is heard (or what is seen onstage and what is "seen" through the metaphors of Marcus's speech) appears most deliberate. The meshing images cause patterns of interference in which some aspects are canceled out, others amplified. Simple empathy is purposely forestalled. Marcus's speech—the longest but one in the play and so already a rhetorical singularity—represents the attempt to recontextualize generically a deed that is no longer emotionally or representationally assimilable. What is grotesque is not Lavinia's mutilation (which is "merely" horrible) but this interpretive gap between the raw barbarity of the act and the civilized rhetoric that, disguised as compassion, in effect obscures it. In the juxtaposition of utter physical cruelty and its immediate verbal sublimation, we are forced to see both as interdependent aspects of the same world.[7]

What is revealed in this scene is the inadequacy of the chivalric-heroic (that is, tragic) attitude of the Andronici toward this transformed world that is no longer their imperial Rome but "a wilderness of tigers" (3.1.54), an attitude that is mirrored in their (mis)use of language. As agents of a grotesque vision, Aaron and Tamora have perfected the invention of radical metaphors like that of the "deer hunt." Aaron, hiding a bag of money to later snare Titus's sons for Bassianus's murder, speaks of "coin[ing] a stratagem" (2.3.5); Lavinia partially seems to summon her fate by protesting coyly to Tamora that rape is a thing "[t]hat womanhood denies my tongue to tell" (2.3.174); Aaron chops off Titus's hand prompted by a play on "lending a hand"; and so on. Only when Titus reclaims that linguistic territory by "play[ing] the cook" for/of Tamora's sons in the cannibal feast (5.2.204), and when Marcus takes Aaron's professed infernal nature literally by burying him in the ground and defeats the satiation of his evil ("O how this villainy / Doth fat me with the very thoughts of it!" [3.1.202–3]) by putting him on a Tantalus-diet, is the game reversed. The Andronici, in other words, must become like the very metaphor-wielding monsters they aim to exorcize: their "monstrous doubles." This is the transformation dictated by the grotesque.

Act 3 delineates the reduction and humiliation of the Andronici that precedes their transformation. Titus must prostrate himself in vain before the judges who have condemned his sons; he sees the mutilated Lavinia; his hand is cut off under a false pretext (in a scene that is choreographed in the spirit of farce); and he is presented with his executed sons' heads. To this "fearful slumber" (3.1.252) that life has become, he can react only with hollow laughter, the very inappropriate laughter that is characteristic of the confrontation with the grotesque. "Why dost thou laugh? It fits not with this hour," remarks the bewildered Marcus (3.1.265). His helpless "Ha, ha, ha!" is more than a little reminiscent of King Lear's howling: as in the later play, the descent into wordlessness here signals the emotional nadir. The Andronici present a freakish tableau that sums up their state of diminution:

> . . . Come, brother, take a head,
> And in this hand the other will I bear;
> And, Lavinia, thou shalt be employ'd;
> Bear thou my hand, sweet wench, between thy teeth.
>
> (3.1.279–82)

The act ends in the exacerbation of the crisis of speech (Titus: "Fie, fie, how franticly I square my talk" [3.2.31]) by the crisis of action. Marcus and Titus are reduced to swatting a "black ill-favor'd fly" (3.2.66) in Aaron's stead.

Shakespeare seems to be arguing that the defeat of the Andronici hinges on their inability to read the literal signals of the grotesque world, on their perceptual crisis, as it were. To surmount the impasse, they must become grotesquely literate; they must "wrest an alphabet" from the uncomprehended signs of their foes, as Titus does from Lavinia's silent gestures (3.2.44). This alphabet is uniquely *literary* or mythical. Thus, the perpetrators of Lavinia's rape are discovered by referring to Ovid's *Metamorphoses;* Titus quotes Seneca and sends the villains "weapons wrapp'd about with lines" by Horace (4.2.27). His greater acuity makes Titus able to "decipher" (4.2.8) the criminals, and he can no longer be fooled by their allegorical disguises. Correct reading calls for correct (and permanent) writing: no more does Titus "write" his grief "in the dust" (3.1.12) or Lavinia her accusation onto a "sandy plot" (4.1.69). The writing instrument will now be a "gad of steel" (4.1.103) instead of words and tears and staffs and stumps. The cannibal feast, finally, is a *coup de théâtre* of the confident playwright Titus, in direct imitation of *Thyestes,* and he sets the last punctuation mark to his writ of revenge with his "knife's sharp point" (5.3.63) by stabbing Tamora.

It is true that *Titus* could be called "a beautiful, luminous meditation on the relationship between language and the body" (Fawcett 272), although the beauty is often wrenching because language and body are thrust into such close proximity as to make our idea of their categorical separation untenable. In the logic of radical metaphor that pervades the play, bodies become texts (compare Lavinia as a "map of woe" [3.2.12]) and texts have an immediate bearing on bodies. In Shakespeare, as in Seneca, this entails an investigation into the function of theatre (that is, bodies) as text and vice versa and into the relation between bodies of texts (that is, genre) and the human bodies that are incommensurable to them.

Titus Andronicus no doubt presents a powerful challenge to commonplace generic notions. In analyzing the use of comic conventions in *Titus,* Douglas Parker argues solidly in the tragicomic vein, noting that "a common stock of comic material is brought to the aid of tragedy in order to enhance its effects" (495). Richard Brucher, however, finds the violence "shocking in its expression of power and evil, and yet so outrageous in its conception and presentation that it causes laughter as it disrupts our sense of order in the world." He denies that the play can "comfortably be called tragic" (73). James Hirsh insists that the play's apparent generic failings are entirely intentional: "*Titus* dramatizes incongruity in the human condition not merely by showing characters who behave incongruously, but by inducing the audience itself to behave incongruously" (66).

Here, if anywhere, the term "grotesque drama" is appropriate. Seen under this heading, the entire play becomes a tract on the adjustment of perceptual and generic categories.[8] Such beings as Aaron and Tamora and Chiron and Demetrius are unimaginable within the imperial honor-code of the Andronici. Indeed, the presence of the Goths in the play signals the encounter between two incompatibles: the barbaric world and the pinnacle of civilization and order, Rome. Shakespeare shocks his audience into the realization that the chasm is not nearly as great as we deem it. In effect, an excluded lower order of humankind (Goths, barbarians, animals) suddenly becomes "incorporate" in the smoothed reality of Rome, which, at least according to the initial generic signals Shakespeare gives, is the reality of romance.

But, as always in Shakespeare, the romantic realm is not entirely pastoral-idyllic. It contains the seeds of its own disruption, not only in the darker character shadings (Saturninus, in his rashness, resembles no one so much as Leontes) but also in such acts of unacknowledged barbarism as the "sacrifice" of Alarbus. The Romans are deceived about their own remoteness from the barbaric stratum, as Saturninus's powerful sexual attraction to Tamora and Titus's instantaneous transformation into the monstrous "cook" will attest. In Aaron and Tamora, they meet the baser version of themselves (again, their "monstrous doubles"), and they can only exorcize them by emulating them. This reverse sublimation results in an uncomfortable paradox for the play's claims to tragic standing. The ending permits a mock catharsis at best, and the final visual image it conjures, the unrepentant figure of Aaron standing (only) half-submerged, cursing with his last breath, strongly underscores this persistent ambivalence.

Modern playwrights have recognized the play's unfinished business and have responded with adaptations of their own. Dürrenmatt, in his liberal reworking of *Titus,* which he called "a comedy after Shakespeare," follows the action of the Elizabethan play in principle, although he omits the Marcus/Lavinia scene. His ending, however, is fully geared to the modern sensibility. Dürrenmatt introduces the Visigoth Alaric as a supplementary character, not, as he says, to situate the play historically, but to connote a "mythical destructive force, a trauma of history" (*Titus* 211).

After Lucius kills Saturninus, Shakespeare's play proceeds, quite suddenly, to clean up the carnage and to reinstate authority and punish the wicked, according to the requirements of the genre. Dürrenmatt substitutes an equally sudden but much bleaker peripety. Here, stabbing follows stabbing in a farcical stichomythia of revenge, until finally Alaric stabs Lucius and, exhorting his Goths to massacre all Romans, leaps up on the banquet table and concludes the play with his verdict of unrelieved cynicism:

> Justice climbed down from heaven and became
> Revenge, which demanded Justice
> Which cried again for Revenge; and so,
> One always giving birth to the other,
> The stupid course of time runs on.
> ....
> Justice what for, what for Revenge?
> They're only names for ugly machinations.
> The globe rolls on into the void
> And dies as senselessly as we all die:
> What was, what is, and what will be, shall perish.
>
> (197)

Heiner Müller's version, *Anatomie Titus Fall of Rome, Ein Shakespearekommentar (Anatomy Titus Fall of Rome: A Shakespeare Commentary)* also recapitulates Shakespeare's text and plot quite faithfully, leaving however no doubt, by way of sundry anachronistic insertions, that Titus's Rome ("GREAT ROME THE WHORE OF CORPORATIONS" [128]) mirrors the postcolonial West of the late twentieth century in which the nefarious Moor Aaron stands for the perceived sexual and cultural threat of Africa, and the marauding Goths are merely the foretaste of paranoically imagined immigrant hordes who

> SWEEP GREEDILY THROUGH THE SUPERMARKET
> THE BOOTY OF THE COLONIES WHICH THROUGH THE YEAR
> THE HOOVES OF THEIR HORSES WILL KISS
> BRINGING HOME TO NOTHINGNESS THE FIRST WORLD
>
> (140–41)

Müller adds such explicatory Brechtian annotations to much of the play, a marginal "Shakespeare commentary" that—taking up the original play's fixation on language, writing, and meaning—becomes foremost a commentary on Shakespeare the writer and on the ethics of art and authorship. In particular, the Marcus/Lavinia scene is preceded by a meditation on violence and art; Müller depicts the mutilated Lavinia, with somber irony, as a "WORK OF ART THROUGH VIOLENCE," her rapists as "ARTISTS" who hope that "THEIR FAME WILL NOT OVERTAKE THEM." But the metaphor of art suddenly becomes serious (or radical) when it engulfs the world of the theatre as well:

> THE WORK OF ART EXPOSED RUNS TO AND FRO
> ON STAGE THE RUNWAY BETWEEN MAN
> AND MAN IN THE SEA OF FEAR THE FEAR
> OF THE AUDIENCE NO HUMAN IS ON STAGE
> MACHINES TALK PLAY WALK THE FEAR
> OF THE ACTORS NO HUMAN SITTING DOWN THERE
> MACHINES LAUGH AND WHISPER RUSTLE WITH THEIR CLOTHES
> AND RATTLE WITH THEIR HANDS FROM TIME TO TIME
>
> (151–52)

In this dystopian theatre, a grotesque place in which mechanical responses have supplanted human emotions and audience and actors regard one another with fear and suspicion, the performance of mangled Lavinia is merely a cover-up for the true performance, that of Shakespeare, who, coolly indifferent to the suffering of his dramatic issue, has his own role to play: "HE SHAMELESSLY TIES TO HIS FACE THE MASK / OF THE LECHEROUS UNCLE CONNOISSEUR OF MANY ARTS" (152). Shakespeare, so Müller's accusation, is really the true voice behind Marcus, and what we identified in the analysis of the play above as deliberately composed rhetorical failure here becomes the author's cruel joke on his characters, his "HUMOR OF THE FLESH" in which Müller, much as he might want to distance himself by commentary, inexorably becomes complicit: "HIS MASK GROWS ON MY SKIN" (152). Müller the playwright, the epigone, by rewriting *Titus Andronicus,* thus enters into a complex Oedipal relation with his master Shakespeare that he portrays as a peculiar psycho-sexual consummation, a kind of authorial matrimony in which Müller, shedding "THE GREY CLOAK OF MY NO MAN'S NAME," vicariously acquires Shakespeare's name and fame:

> YOUR KILLER WILLIAM SHAKESPEARE IS MY KILLER
> HIS MURDER IS OUR WEDDING WILLIAM SHAKESPEARE
> MY NAME AND YOUR NAME GLOW IN THE BLOOD
> THAT HE HAS SPILLED WITH OUR INK
>
> (153)

This too is a gesture of cannibalism—Müller is aware that he is taking Shakespeare's "substance" in the act, that indeed his own intent is murderous. The lines, it appears, are meant to be ambiguous: is the killer Marcus, or Aaron, or is it Müller himself, the "killer" of Shakespeare? Müller knows that his *Titus* is the product of a very different time, an age of simulacra, of imitations and parodies in which an act of (if literary) cannibalism provides the last possibility of authenticity. In an "EPOCH OF TOURISM MURDER / IS REPRIEVE SEEING MEANS KILLING THE IMAGES" (153). But if aesthetic contemplation is already an act of assassination (Müller may be thinking of Brecht's famous dictum that during wartime, even a conversation about trees is a crime because it means being silent about the true crimes), then literature and drama are themselves not exempt from censure. For Müller, indeed, art by virtue of its rapacity, its insatiable hunger for the substance of reality, is a "murderous pit" *(Mördergrube)*: "VERSE IS RAPE / EVERY RHYME A DEATH" (191). At the conclusion of the play, as bodies litter the stage and the Goths, *ante portas,* are ready to seize the crippled capital, they are

> SILENTLY APPLAUDED FROM MASS GRAVES
> IN THE THEATRE IN THE REALM OF ART
> WHILE THE TEXT POUNDS NAILS INTO THE COFFIN
> MADE FROM THE BOARDS THAT SIGNIFY THE WORLD
>
> (223)

In Müller's postmodern aesthetic, there is finally little difference between a grotesque play such as *Titus Andronicus* and the incidents it depicts; and conversely, the slaughter of *Titus* (which stands in for the horrors of the twentieth century) is inseparable from its theatricality. It is no longer possible, so much one learns from being subject to a totalitarian regime, to take safe refuge in "the realm of art" as if it were separate and pristine. Müller understands not only the grotesque nature of modern political reality, the worst excesses of which seem mere imitations of bloody Senecan or Jacobean spectacle, but also the grotesque nature of the theatre itself, which in its powerful images, its vicarious vices and cruel fictions, purveys images to the powerful wherein they might mirror themselves (as Nero is said to have taken solace from Seneca's plays). In his postscript, he writes: "The theatricalizing of reality by politics as outgrowth of technology throws theatre back onto its own reality, which measures time in delayed explosions" (224). The Renaissance truism that the exercise of power is a form of authorship, a graphic writ—hence "authority"—is explored on several levels in Shakespeare's play. Müller uncovers the obverse: that authorship is a form of power, the ability to force a grotesque universe into existence. Through Müller's lens, the theatrical self-consciousness and radical irony of *Titus Andronicus* become consummately modern.

In both Seneca's *Thyestes* and Shakespeare's *Titus Andronicus,* cannibalism signifies a peculiar ethical and linguistic hole—it is what cannot be contemplated nor uttered in society, and thus whenever we arrive at the savage act, the tropes become evasive. In these plays, effusive rhetoric seems to want to deflect and dislocate the intrusion of the horrible, but when the horrible is no longer deniable, it is typically converted into a pun (Atreus's "in their father's bosom," Titus's playing the cook "for" the Goths. For the cannibalistic act is in fact here not the ceremonial eating of others (or "the other") but of *self*—at least in its extension: children. It is a perverse double action, for in it the ultimate and most radical objectification of and separation from the progeny, a familiar psychoanalytic scenario, is enacted (child-as-meal), as well as the greatest closeness imaginable (child-as-sustenance). Opening up in a frightening way our own ontological "paradox of substance" (K. Burke), cannibalism is transferred here from its customary scene of distance and exoticism (primitive savages and headhunters) into the moment of a familiar/familial existential crisis.

4 *Kunstfiguren*
The Grotesque in the Modern Theatre

This chapter traces the modern practices of the grotesque theatre and concentrates on a particular trope, the artificial human figure or, in Bauhaus theorist Oskar Schlemmer's term, the *Kunstfigur.* Modern drama—I take Alfred Jarry's *Ubu* plays as a point of departure—concerns itself far less with genre (except skeptically or parodically) and far more with the integrity of identity and personhood. Georg Lukács, in his brilliantly prescient 1909 essay, "The Sociology of Modern Drama," noted that "[t]he new drama is . . . the drama of individualism, and that with a force, an intensity and an exclusiveness that no other drama ever had" (430). The twentieth-century grotesque, as I hope to show, is located primarily (though not exclusively) in our ambivalent notions of the entity of dramatic character.

In contrast to the "impossible tragedies" of the preceding chapter, which are inscribed into a generic horizon they are on the whole unwilling to abandon, the plays around which the following discussion mainly revolves—Jarry's *Ubu Roi,* Yvan Goll's *Methusalem or The Eternal Bourgeois,* and Michel de Ghelderode's *Chronicles of Hell*—are unconcerned with the preservation of genre, except as a foil for parody. The vision that unites them is that they take place in a puppet universe, and they consequently display a kind of metatheatrical sensibility that should rightly be called *infratheatrical,* because it proposes the representability of human relations in the context of a Punch-and-Judy show gone berserk.

The puppet topos, a conspicuous instance of literalized metaphor, is a particularly fruitful area for the grotesque. Jarry on the one hand, and Goll and Ghelderode on the other, frame a period that was rife with the exploration of the marionette theme in the theatre (and which peaked, for historically self-explanatory reasons, in the European interwar period).[1]

Two strands of inquiry typically interpenetrate in the puppet motif. Early romanticism pictures the marionette as the expression of an unalienated human grace that—in the words of its first theorist, Heinrich von Kleist—escapes the congenital affectation that besets humans because its soul *(vis motrix)* is congruent with its movement; it alone can reproduce movements in their geometric perfection, can overcome the vagaries of the body and the ambushes of gravity and trace "the path taken by the dancer's soul" ("On the Marionette Theater" 239). Kleist's essay, a profound philosophical meditation on the notions of freedom and consciousness, is concerned with puppets only insofar as they stand as ciphers of romantic longing, as tangible reminders of the loss of the Absolute. But throughout the brief piece, the narrator's "astonishment" and "bewilderment" at the claims of his cheerful interlocutor that "it would be impossible for man to come anywhere near the puppet" in grace, that artifice is the precondition of total artistry, is an uneasy echo of our own fears about the superiority of the mechanical over the organic (241).

Gordon Craig builds on Kleist's text in his notorious clamor for a theatre of the *Über-Marionette,* in which all that is accidental to the actor and to acting is suppressed in favor of a "noble artificiality" that is itself a reflection of divinity (86). This strand of inquiry takes the puppet's reiteration of the shape and movement of the human form as a progression toward ideal refinement and sublimity. We could, in our terms, address it as a "transfiguring figuration" of human principles.

But the marionette figure also conversely contains a disquieting otherness; once it is brought into contact with the mimetic-realistic aesthetics of Western theatre and the philosophy of individualism on which that theatre rests, it appears as a mere instrumental reduction of humanity and a graphic metaphor for the illusion of free will and enslavement by external, uncontrollable forces and compulsions. Like automata, puppets are always tinged with the uncanny because they remain ideologically and iconologically suspended in the space between degradation and perfection, which is the space of man, of whom they are a synecdochic representation. In the puppet, human ontology is both reduced and universalized—

it conflates higher and lower orders of being, which gives it preferred grotesque status.

As long as the worlds of man and marionette are separate, there is no danger of contagion. If, however, they are literally or implicitly projected onto and into one another in a way that suggests their compatibility or even interchangeability, the grotesque results. In fact, as Roman Paska observes, the more closely a puppet mimes human form, the more unsettling it may become, "as if the attempt to camouflage its otherness were in fact a subterfuge for displaying it" (412). In the theatre proper, the puppet metaphor formed the foundation of characterology in the short-lived Italian *teatro grottesco,* which is associated with the names of Luigi Chiarelli, Piermaria Rosso di San Secondo, and of course Luigi Pirandello. In a play such as Rosso di San Secondo's *Marionette, che passione! . . .* (*Marionettes, What Passions!,* 1918), a mock tragic plot intersects with a parodic "boulevard" play. The nameless characters, although convinced of the pathos of their existence, are merely victims of their ludicrously exaggerated and futile passions. Maurice Valency writes: "Their grandiose postures and their displays of passion . . . can only move the spectator to laughter, for what seems tragic to the figures in the guignol is merely comic to the objective observer; their tragedy is farce" (95). The products of the *teatro grottesco,* in spite of its name, are grotesque in a very loose sense only, in that they disrupt and parody given aesthetic frames and exacerbate the discrepancy between illusion and reality. In theory, these schizophrenic characters, constantly entangled in the conflict of their private and public personae (see Chiarelli's *La maschera e il volto* [*Mask and Face,* 1916]), are quite compatible with the concurrent findings of psychoanalysis, but their aesthetic models are diverse and include a mixture of the kinetics of *commedia dell'arte* and Grand Guignol with J. M. Synge's and August Strindberg's symbolism.

An immediate predecessor is Arthur Schnitzler, whose *Zum Grossen Wurstel* (1904) is a proto-Pirandellian burlesque in the spirit of the romantic anti-illusionistic comedies of Achim von Arnim and Ludwig Tieck. Schnitzler's piece, one of a series of three one-acts entitled *Marionetten,* uses the plausible situation of the performance of a new puppet play in the "Wurstelprater," Vienna's amusement quarter; but the "Puppets" in this ridiculous melodrama are real actors suspended on visible strings, and they increasingly begin to interact with the world of the onstage "Audience" (from where the "Author" and the "Director" attempt in vain to control them). The compressed play creates a set of Chinese boxes of illusion in which the planes of representation and reality are fiendishly run together: characters from other plays, having "time off," enter to watch the performance; the onstage audience is heckled by a malcontent from the offstage audience; and finally a mysterious character called simply "The Unknown" cuts first the strings of the puppets, then the invisible threads suspending all the other characters, whereupon they collapse, and finally threatens the (real) audience and its "highly questionable reality" with like treatment. "Your whole play is dangerous," the Director admonishes the Author when things begin to go wrong (Schnitzler 142, 135). Indeed, Schnitzler's own play is "dangerous" by virtue of the constant threat that underpins its surface jocularity, the threat to cut the "strings" by which we are suspended in the certainty of our own ostensibly irreducible reality and to open up the horrifying prospect of a potentially infinite regression.

It is not surprising that the major playwrights of the twentieth century have been constantly inspired by and have constantly returned to the puppet theatre in search of analogues for the modern condition and models for modern drama. Ghelderode, who wrote a number of plays for the Toone marionette theatre in Brussels, confided that he owed to puppets "the disclosure of the theatre, the theatre in its pure state, the theatre in its savage state, the original theatre" ("Ostend Interviews" 23). Eugène Ionesco similarly recollected from his childhood visits to the puppet theatre of the Jardins du Luxembourg the simultaneously disturbing and exhilarating ability of the puppets to reveal a baser but more profound vision of life: "It was the very image of the world that appeared to me, strange and improbable but true as true, in the profoundly simplified form of caricature, as though to stress the grotesque and brutal nature of truth" (*Notes* 18).[2]

The leap from humanoid puppets to the puppetlike human form that Craig had anticipated was first made in the dance and theatre experiments of the Bauhaus by László Moholy-Nagy and Oskar Schlemmer in the early 1920s. Schlemmer in particular used his performances of the *Figural Cabinet* and the *Triadic Ballet* to assert the necessity for reconceiving the dancers/actors as pure abstract figures in space as a prelude to "substituting for the organism the mechanical human figure *(Kunstfigur): the automaton or marionette*":

> The Artificial human figure *(Kunstfigur)* permits any kind of movement and any kind of position for as long a time as desired. . . . Endless perspectives are opened up: from the supernatural to the nonsensical, from the sublime to the comic. Precursors in the use of pathos, of the sublime, are the actors of ancient tragedy, monumentalized by means of masks, cothurni, and stilts. Precursors in the comic style are the gigantic and grotesque figures of carnival and fair. (Schlemmer 29)

For Schlemmer, the *Kunstfigur* literally held metaphysical promise: it embodied "symbolically a new faith" (29). Such a phrase is chilling to read, if one mentally summons up the pictures of Nazism's *Kunstfiguren,* as they march in lockstep through the films of Leni Riefenstahl, animated by "a new faith." As critics of modernism like José Ortega y Gasset well knew, the dehumanizing impulses of modernist art and of modern life intersect even where they purport to be wholly inimical.

This clandestine complicity of the subversive or progressive image with repressive ideologies is perhaps one of the most disturbing realizations for the student of modernism. For although the cubist dissolution of the face, which is inaugurated with Pablo Picasso's *Les Demoiselles d'Avignon,* or the fractured figure of Marcel Duchamps's *Nude Descending a Staircase,* or the massing and abstraction of the human form in early theatrical expressionism (Wassily Kandinsky's *Yellow Sound;* Oskar Kokoschka's *Murderer Hope of Womankind*) are meant only to explore and convey novel aspects of representation, they employ the language of the depersonalized *Kunstfigur* in a way that opens other, more immediate avenues of human abstraction. The tacit conversion of the human shape into the artificial, manipulable physique devoid of individual will or personal dignity made possible the horrendous numbers games of the first mechanized and industrialized war and of subsequent totalitarian mass movements. Even meant as a reflection upon technical civilization, as a stinging critique of alienation, the alienated countenance, unable to provide an outlet into transcendence, promoted further alienation.

Thus the *Kunstfigur,* assembled and constructed man, simultaneously becomes the utopian human image through which the optimistic strands of modernism (for instance, Futurism or constructivism) expressed their fervent belief in human perfectibility and the dystopian symbol of humanity's deconstruction and usurpation by malevolent anonymous or malignant social forces. Some of the most striking examples of the theatrical avant-garde in the twentieth century are derived from this doubled human image, the simultaneity of the human and nonhuman, the *homme-machine,* the superposition of the organic and the functional that profoundly affected even the theory of acting—compare in particular Vsevolod Meyerhold's "biomechanical" approach with its avowed derivation from the industrial rationalization efforts of Frederick Taylor. The modernist vision of *Kunstfigur* and *homme-machine* encases the paradox of idealism: that the human ideal is always ready to collapse into its opposite, inhumanity. Indeed, this paradox is nowhere better embodied than in some of the enthusiastically antihumanist tenets of Futurism.

The deformation and re-formation of the human shape onstage takes several avenues. There is the massing of human form, as in Ernst Toller's *Masses and Man;* Max Reinhardt's vision of a monumental mass theatre (which attempted to conflate the mythic choral presence of the Greek *demos* with modern mass society); or Georg Kaiser's abstract masses in *Gas.* Another avenue is the oversizing of the individual form to effect a disquieting scenic disproportion, as in the giants of Kandinsky's *Yellow Sound* (1912); the ten-foot cubist characters in *Parade* by Picasso, Jean Cocteau, Erik Satie, and Sergey Diaghilev (1917); and the looming figures on stilts in Bertolt Brecht's 1931 production of *Man Is Man,* to name only a few of the most salient examples.

This vocabulary of the *Kunstfigur* is present even in the more recent avant-garde theatre. For instance, the figures of Jean-Claude van Itallie's entropic farce *Motel* (1965), composed of primary shapes as if in a travesty of cubism, are "slightly larger than human size," though not gigantic. They skewer human perception in an aggravating intercategorical manner, since they no longer appear to come from the world of the audience and yet cannot simply be assigned to the fantastic realm that is inhabited by the giants of the fairy tale. Manipulated by silent actors and speaking in disembodied voices, the characters of this "masque for three dolls" display movements that possess "the quality of ritual," reminiscent of "a dance or a machine; strictly controllable, humorous sometimes, but increasingly violent and disturbing" (van Itallie 83). Technical progress, finally, has cast another light on the trope of the *Kunstfigur*—in a completely mediatized culture, the distinctions between real and illusory (or hyperreal), here and not-here, and cause and effect (or affect) fall away. Humans are useful only as nodes, switchpoints in a vast circuit in cyberspace. The performance artist Stelarc, in a piece called *Remote Body*

(1995), acknowledged as much: he hooked his body to muscle stimulators that, through the Internet, were anonymously manipulable from anywhere in the world (Warr 12).

I borrow Schlemmer's coinage of the term *Kunstfigur* here and in the following to describe aspects of the modern grotesque, not in order to indict Schlemmer ideologically but because his term encodes this double discourse so potently: "Kunst" is both art and artifice; "Figur" is figure, character, and body all in one.

Ubu Roi and the End of History

Alfred Jarry's *Ubu Roi,* as is by now well known, was originally written for the puppet stage as a schoolboy satire on a pedantic and unpopular physics teacher, Monsieur Hébert, although it has long been recognized, as Frantisek Deak writes, as "an absolute, metaphysical, symbolist comedy, rather than a high-school prank" (241). Even when it came to be performed in the professional theatre, Jarry tried to retain the spirit of puppetry by addressing his actors as "man-sized marionettes." He planned to hang the actors from strings for the first production and relented only because it proved technically too awkward. When Jarry asserts that the marionette is capable of producing "universal gestures," he is thinking in terms of a kinetic eccentricity that has nothing in common with Kleist's romantic concept of grace: "An example of universal gesture is the marionette displaying its bewilderment by starting back violently and hitting its head against a flat" (Jarry, *Selected Works* 73).

In *Ubu Roi,* we face a qualitatively different type of grotesque play. Not only is it *prima facie* not a tragedy but a comedy, but its grotesqueness is also constituted largely intertextually, not contextually. That is to say, Pa Ubu is not so much monstrous *in opposition* to the surrounding dramatic universe (like Atreus) but is rather in essential harmony with it, as its monstrous and excessive epitome. In other words, there is no apparent gaping rift between the actions of the main character and the moral assumptions of the play-world that endangers dramatic representation itself. The grotesque contrast arises instead from a mental comparison with the laws of mimesis and character conduct in the plays that *Ubu* explicitly invokes and parodies—Elizabethan plays (particularly *Macbeth, Julius Caesar,* and *Hamlet*) and the neoclassical high tragedies of Jean Racine that Jarry dismissed as "rosaries of roles" (Jarry, *Selected Works* 89). In *Ubu,* we could speak of "blasphemies of roles." No longer do we see only the internal breakdown of a dramatic system geared toward the removal of an irritant, as in the "impossible tragedies" discussed above; instead the play itself—the mere possibility of writing and staging such a monstrosity—becomes the persistent irritant. When it first appeared, critic Henry Fouquier of *Le Figaro* condemned Jarry's play as "an act of anarchy, reactionary in its nature and outside of culture" (qtd. in Deak 246)—an anxious phrase that affirms the notion of a realm "beyond culture" that secretes the monstrous and grotesque.

This type of grotesque drama might be called an "intertextual grotesque," although any grotesque drama that plays with the conditions of genre is potentially intertextual, since any genre is defined as much by a body of (inter)texts as by given rules. As I have shown, the grotesque only needs a generically defined space, such as the theatre, to effectively set up shop. In Claude Schumacher's opinion, *Ubu Roi* amounts to "a comprehensive and deliberate sabotage of twenty-five centuries of Western theatrical tradition, a tradition based on implicit faith in Graeco-Judaeo-Christian humanism" (61).

The turmoil and invective that Jarry's play provoked on its first night, December 9, 1896, at Lugné-Poe's Théâtre de l'Œuvre, is legend. However, the reports of a great opening-night tumult, from the first "Merdre!" on, much as one might wish them to be true for the sake of theatrical lore, are largely exaggerated (see Deak 235–37). It seems in fact that Jarry's piece, scandalous as it was at first glance with its liberal use of profanity, its crude characters and its confoundingly anticonventional techniques, unfolded its greatest power not in the frontal assault, where it appeared to be little more than a prank calculated for maximum shock effect, but in its after-effects, what we might call its scorched-earth policy toward the pieties of nineteenth-century drama and nineteenth-century art. William Butler Yeats felt himself obliged to support the play out of a sense of artistic solidarity, but he was clearly startled, shaken: "[A]fter all our subtle colour and nervous rhythm . . . what more is possible? After us the Savage God" (430).

Pa Ubu stepped on stage and proceeded to render the categories of conventional dramatic analysis quite meaningless. To say that the character fulfills the Aristotelian desiderata for a tragic personage, since he represents "human nature in general," and his actions are "either . . . necessary [or] probable," and that he therefore "engenders a complex amalgam of 'pity and fear' in the spectator" (Labelle 72), is too far off the mark. For although Ubu, in some warped sense, indeed represents general human traits, Aristotelian ethical-mimetic categories of "goodness" or "badness" are clearly inapplicable. Jarry, in this play, constructs a universe in which the actions taken are just the opposite of "probable" or "necessary": a pataphysical universe.

Pataphysics, which in its dramaturgical application is an ancestor of Goll's "alogic" and "superrealism" and of Stanislaw Witkiewicz's "pure form" and "non-Euclidean" dramaturgy, is simply, in the half-whimsical definition Jarry proposes in his novel *Doctor Faustroll,* "the science of imaginary solutions, which symbolically attributes the properties of objects, described by their virtuality, to their lineaments": "Pataphysics will examine the laws governing exceptions, and will explain the universe supplementary to this one; or, less ambitiously, will describe a universe which can be—and perhaps should be—envisaged in the place of the traditional one" (*Selected Works* 192–93). The supplementary or parallel pataphysical universe, in other words, is highly improbable and confounding from the perspective of the "traditional one," because it reactivates the virtual but unacknowledged properties underlying that conventional scene and gives them shape and outline. Pataphysics is a name for the dramaturgy of the grotesque. In the pataphysical environment—and the "Poland" of *Ubu Roi,* this Nowhere (or, *u-topos*), which is really "a distantly interrogative somewhere" (*Selected Works* 79), is such an environment—lower orders of discourse replace smoothed perceptions of reality, and the exception becomes (and usurps) the rule. Pa Ubu himself is (in his own words) a "celebrated pataphysician." "Pataphysics," he claims in *Ubu Cuckolded,* "is a branch of science which we have invented and for which a crying need is generally experienced" (Jarry, *Ubu* 78).

In the pataphysical realm, moral absolutes and even value judgments have no place—it stretches beyond good and evil and strives for the "identity and reconciliation of opposites (for example, being/living, zero/infinity, plus/minus, day/night)" (Stillman 41). If this sounds in principle like the loftiest aspiration of philosophical Idealism (Georg Wilhelm Friedrich Hegel's "identity of identity and non-identity"), Ubu is the rawest expression, the worst-case scenario of such pataphysical synthesis. "Oh tripe!" he cries when Ma Ubu suggests that the son of the murdered King Wenceslas may have justice on his side; "Isn't injustice just as good as justice?" (*Ubu* 39)—and he proceeds, what is worse, to act on that assumption.

Ubu's character so dominates the first *Ubu* play that there is no plot without him. The putative plot is only the clichéd and parodic refraction of the history play scheme (which Jarry, speaking like his creation in the *pluralis maiestatis,* found "beneath our dignity to construct" [*Selected Works* 79]). The later plays of the canon become even more tenuous in their plot construction. It is Ubu's presence alone that organizes them as theatre (and this preponderance of character over plot in and of itself should clearly advertise the anti-Aristotelian nature of the play). What constitutes Ubu is solely his "strumpot," his stomach. Being first king, then slave (and equally suited to both), Ubu's only fealty is to his stomach, but this stomach is "huger than the whole world." "From now on," he concludes at the end of *Ubu Enchained,* "I shall be the slave of my strumpot" (*Ubu* 178). Jarry has thus reduced the operative logic of his dramatic universe to the mere principle of ingestion.

In keeping with the notion of the primacy of the visual in the grotesque, Jarry felt compelled to establish Ubu's shape and comportment in a series of illustrations showing the monster king in a peaked hood and with an enormous spiral covering the ovoid belly (see fig. 7). This primal shape doubtless holds a key to the character; Ubu represents a kind of super-sign. The oviform body recalls the alchemical symbolism of the egg, just as the pointed (or, in some drawings, beak-faced) head appears like an alembic. Alchemy and pataphysics, in their mutual effort to reconcile opposites, are sympathetic sciences. In *Ubu Cuckolded,* Pa Ubu meditates on the sphere as the "perfect form": "The sphere is the form of the angels. To man is it given to be but an incomplete angel. And yet, more perfect than the cylinder, less perfect than the sphere, radiates the barrel's hyperphysical body. We, its isomorph, are passing fair" (*Ubu* 88). In his own estimation, then, Ubu is only a slightly corrupted transfiguration of angelic perfection. Addressing the audience of the first *Ubu* performance, Jarry reasoned that "embryonic forms" shared with the "most evolved creatures" certain specifics: the primitive forms

> . . . lack any element of accident, protuberance, or special characteristics, leaving them practically a spherical form like the ovule or Mister Ubu; and equally, that the latter possess so many personal attributes that they too take on a spherical form, by virtue of the axiom that the smoothest body is the one presenting the greatest number of different facets. Which is why you are free to see in Mister Ubu as many allusions as you like, or, if you prefer, just a plain puppet,

a schoolboy's caricature of one of his teachers who represented for him everything in the world that is grotesque. (*Works* 76)

Jarry thus not only gives us a perfect example of the lower-order/higher-order dichotomy that he sees conflated in Ubu's polysemic rotundity but also announces a peculiar phenomenon of the grotesque character: the apparent congruence of extreme complexity and universality with the primitive, reduced, and unformed. Ubu's stomach symbolizes both "divinity and monstrosity": "this giant gut symbolizes the process of assimilation and rejection, construction and destruction, upon which all life depends" (Stillman 46).

Fig. 7. Alfred Jarry, *Véritable portrait de M Ubu.* From *Livre d'art* 2 (Apr. 25, 1896).

Yeats captured the essence of the deliberate archaism and roughness of the play when he accorded Ubu his famous epithet of the "Savage God." In the language of myth, we could see Ubu as the degenerate version of the monster-king who is "simultaneously god, man, and savage beast" and as both "the most intimate of insiders and the most bizarre of outsiders" (Girard, *Violence* 252). Although enlarged into a heinous caricature of his dramatic forebear, Ubu in many respects continues in the vein of Atreus: his kingship is defined not by any magnitude or nobility of spirit but by willful violence and utter rapacity. Mercilessly squeezing his subjects for more money, he bellows: "Fork out! Or I'll give you the works good and proper: torture, twisting of the neck, and decapitation. Hornstrumpot, am I or am I not your King?" It is to no avail that Ma Ubu, the sole possessor of wit in the family, admonishes him after he systematically "debrains" the nobles that "kings aren't supposed to behave like that" (*Ubu* 43, 41).

When he goes to extract "phynance" (with that vaguely gruesome instrument of torture, the "phynance hook"), it is not cash he is after but, in Harold Skulsky's term, "substance." Dreaming, Ubu is most candid about his desires: "Debraining, killing off, perforation of nearoles, money grabbing and drinking oneself to death, that's the life for a Phynance-extortioner, and the Master of Phynances revels in such joys" (*Ubu* 63). Ubu's greed is an archaic appetitive greed in its rawest and most pristine form, uncorrupted by guilt or second thoughts. In Kleistian terms, the *vis motrix* of the marionette Ubu is completely congruent with its movements: he exhibits a kind of hideous grace.

It is Pa Ubu's utter mediocrity, the laughable pettiness even of his grandest ambitions, that separates him from such dramatic antecedents as Atreus, Richard III, Macbeth, and Tamburlaine, or even Albert Camus's philosophical monster Caligula, and moves him closer to the "banality of evil" (in Hannah Arendt's charged phrase) of the Eichmanns of the world. He is the signature character of the offhandedly homicidal century that was about to commence. What is most grotesque about him is the seamless manner in which such an agenda fits into the precepts of the comedic character, who habitually seeks the attainment of pleasure and the avoidance of pain. André Breton called Ubu a "magisterial incarnation of the nietzschean-freudian id" (qtd. in Stillman 53). Indeed, Pa Ubu incarnates quite spectacularly the Pleasure Principle gone rampant, "ripping people up because he enjoys the idea," as Jarry says, "and imploring the Russian soldiers not to shoot in his direction because he does not enjoy the idea" (*Selected Works* 80).

Yet Ubu, strangely, exudes a certain innocence. His vices are not clandestine, and he never attempts to excuse them. His guilelessness, as Judith Cooper remarks, is "one of the least objectionable aspects of his character, and at the same time one of the most frightening" (66). Such lack of self-awareness is typical for the archetype of the Jungian Trickster, and Ubu is nothing if not a monstrous Trickster. There may even be a trace element here of the observation that Charles Baudelaire makes concerning the "absolute" (or grotesque) comic: that it "remains unaware of itself" (646). Childlike and clownish in his unconsciousness, Ubu is at liberty to ignore all social and moral restraints (in which respect he vicariously embodies the anarchic freedom afforded the fool for an audience less at liberty). But he is also at liberty to fully enact the cruelty of the fool or the child, a freedom they lack.

It is possible to see Ubu as "man's psychic double," as a "hieroglyph of the discourse of the Other" (Stillman 53, 58), but Jarry put it more simply and to the point when he referred to Ubu as an "ignoble creature" and therefore very "like us all (seen from below)" (*Selected Works* 80). This shift of perspective from higher to lower orders is the fundamental technique of grotesque characterization. *Ubu Roi* imposes a critical impasse: the transparency of the protagonist creates a structure of action that is both absolutely pure (or "classical") and distressingly trivial. By enlarging the antic puppet despot to a size commensurate with the human stage, Jarry endows him with a potentially mythological stature, but he refuses to supply the innate grandeur that such eminence constitutionally demands. The result is a grating disproportion: Ubu's "strumpot" is distended but empty—it needs constant "substance," until what fills it is the entire world. Here is the ultimate exacerbation of Kenneth Burke's "paradox of substance"—the agent *eats* the scene. Jarry seems to be suggesting that in this space of transfiguring figuration, the metaphysical is expressible only through the hyperphysical, which is both an indictment of and a surrender to total materialism. If the progressive social philosophies of the late nineteenth century envisioned the salvation of humanity in the material vein, Ubu, the complete material monster, "pschitts" on such aspirations.

In his construction of a monadic character and a (non)plot—a montage of loose incidents that give the illusion of propelling the action while truly emphasizing the immutability at the center—Jarry promotes the systematic destruction of the history play by positing what is incomprehensible to the pieties of that genre: the annihilation of history itself, its subsumption into an endless cycle of "phynancial," "physical," and "pschittical" ferocity. Ubu's pataphysics obliterates hierarchy, memory, and progress, the mainstays upon which the representation of human history in historical drama is predicated. *Ubu Roi* is a sacrilege to the Hegelian tidiness of historical philosophy in a twofold way: by exposing the tenuousness of the causal nexus (Ubu comes to power randomly, and many actions in the play are without consequence) and by asserting the blunt force of the immutable against the illusion of perfectibility. The play reveals "history" to be an ideological and intellectual construct, barely masking the eternal recurrence of the Savage God. Ubu is product and propagator of the radical presentness of existence, an existence that knows no "before" and no true aim (it would be absurd, for instance, for an actor to search for a prehistory of this character who has always been there and thus, or for a "super-objective" in the teleological sense in which Konstantin Stanislavsky demands it). Being animal, Ubu resembles the animals Friedrich Nietzsche cites in "On the Uses and Abuses of History," tethered tightly, by their short-term desires, to the "peg of the moment" (*Werke* 1:211)—except that Jarry has enlarged the radius of the tether to be congruent with the orb of the world.

Jarry's own theatrical ideas in regard to the staging of *Ubu* are explicated in a loose series of writings that, in a peculiar mixture of the programmatic and the peripheral, contain a kind of pataphysical aesthetics, which is unequivocally an aesthetics of the grotesque in the theatre. Part of the nature of the grotesque in modern drama is that it departs in a rather radical manner from the conventional interaction between author and audience. Implicit in the paradigm of the theatre as democratic organ for the enactment of communal history and myth in the Hellenic period is the notion of a harmonic interest that author and audience share. This is still true for the medieval *teatrum mundi* out of which the theatre-as-world metaphor of the Renaissance evolves, and even for the didactic Enlightenment paradigm of the "theatre as a moral institution" (Schiller), a standard that in turn informs the precepts of naturalism and carries over to Brecht. The didactic theatre may assume that its audience is in error and needful of instruction, but even in its paternalistic strictness it is eternally benevolent. But the modern grotesque play—and Jarry is its avatar—secretly or openly mistrusts its audience, and thus it reviles and assaults it. Jarry expressly thought of the audience as an idiotic "herd" and frankly wrote *Ubu* as a "direct attack on the public," eager to confront the audience with an "exaggerating mirror" in which it catches sight of its "ignoble other self." Citing the critic Catulle Mendès, who had praised *Ubu,* Jarry wrote: "This other self . . . is composed of 'eternal human imbecility, eternal lust, eternal gluttony, the vileness of instinct magnified into tyranny; of the sense of decency, the virtues, the patriotism and the ideals peculiar to those who have just eaten their fill'" (*Selected Works* 84, 83).

Here we are beyond the mere use of satire as a social corrective, as we might find it in the tradition of the French comedy of manners embodied in *Tartuffe*—Jarry was essentially convinced that his audience was irredeemable. By implication, then, the entire comfortable vicariousness of the theatrical transaction, on which the theatre industry of the nineteenth century relied, is canceled and annulled. Benjamin Bennett has defined this type of drama, in the creation of which Jarry figures prominently, as the "drama of assault," a drama in which "the audience is attacked *for being an audience*" (287). It is a drama that can only be written by an author who has placed himself decisively outside the circle of social discourse: a *poète maudit.* In that most social of arts, the theatre, this is an irreducible paradox, but it is a paradox that rapidly becomes the foundation of the modern author-audience relationship. We might call the entire topical complex of which it is part the *criminality of the audience.*

From Jarry to Pirandello, Jean Genet to Brecht and Edward Bond, the audience, enticed to watch, is always on trial for merely watching, and the play is conceived, to quote the title of the piece by Peter Handke that embodies this attitude most purely, entirely as a vehicle for "Insulting the Audience." William Gruber has discovered this attitude inscribed in Friedrich Dürrenmatt's plays as well; he finds that in *The Visit,* Dürrenmatt "transforms his audience from comedic anonymity to full communal responsibility, implicating them ultimately in Alfred Ill's death for their willingness to be spectators only." He detects a "curious antitheatrical bias" in Dürrenmatt's play because the indictment of the spectatorial attitude is presented as "a standard of moral worth" (Gruber 158, 163)—a development clearly prefigured in Jarry. The theatrical avant-garde of the 1960s embraced this casual hostility as fully as did the artistic avant-garde—van Itallie stipulates that the figures in *Motel* wear mirrored eyeglasses, remarking with Jarryesque indifference: "The audience may occasionally catch a glimpse of itself, or be bothered by reflections of light. It doesn't matter; the sensory nerves of the audience are not to be spared" (83). It may be objected that to lay an incitement to the destruction of the audience at Jarry's feet is exaggerated. But if the premodern grotesque plays had cast doubts on the fundamental premises of representation, they had at least remained focused mainly on the corrupted grammar of the stage itself. In the modernist grotesque, the indictment widens to include the entire structure of mimetic exchange between spectacle and spectator, and suddenly the audience—no longer community but merely the inchoate Habermasian "public sphere"—finds itself not only the witness of a *sparagmos* but its object as well.

In stagecraft, Jarry looked for a way of peering beyond (theatrical) surfaces, to reactivate an infantile sense of imaginative seeing. The mask, he realized, is the ideal instrument through which the actors can "depersonalize themselves voluntarily"; it fully envelops the actor's head, "thus replacing it by the effigy of the CHARACTER" and announcing not the emotional state but (as in the *commedia dell'arte*) "the nature of the character" (*Selected Works* 81, 72). Jarry saw the mask as the means to get past "accidentals" to the "essential expression," the "solid structure of the skeleton" under the "surrounding animal flesh" (73). Such blatant, archaically evocative use of the mask as device, which deliberately obliterated the actor's features in the attempt to expel his or her ego, increasingly became part of the theatrical avant-garde (Gordon Craig, Goll, Eugene O'Neill), but Jarry's writings must be seen in the context of (and in ironic opposition to) a naturalistic school of acting that held the meticulous refinement of the close mimesis of surface reality (that is, "accidentals") to be tantamount to truth.

The same aesthetics applies to Jarry's use of scenery—he assailed the "stupidity of *trompe l'oeil*" (*Selected Works* 71) and advocated a type of deliberate dilettantism by employing badly painted decor, placards to announce locale, and the nonchalant decontextualization of scenic elements as props (a door to be broken down is expediently brought in when needed, and so on). The shoestring budget of the *Ubu* premiere even forced a kind of proto-surrealistic scenic instability that is reminiscent of much later René Magritte paintings ("doors opening onto snow-covered plains under blue skies, mantelpieces with clocks on them swinging open to turn into doorways" [*Selected Works* 77–78]) and is not unlike the transformational scenic experiments of Strindberg's *Dream Play* five years later. Jarry argued that his technique "saves the onlooker from being regularly reminded of base 'reality' through a constant substitution of conventional sets which he really only sees properly at the moment the scene is being shifted" (71). In effect, Jarry is saying with some irony, it is the *illusionistic* theatre that, by virtue of its unavoidable perpetual disillusion of the audience in the "shifting of scenes," is truly assaultive, because it attempts to cover up the baseness of existence instead of giving it its due.

Jarry did not invent his dramaturgy out of thin air—although he is believed to have constructed it in opposition to the excesses of naturalism. The broad, violent, and scatological *parades foraines,* which were seen in the French marketplace and on the French stage since the early eighteenth century, constantly ducking censorship, and themselves in burlesque and parodic opposition to the solemnity of high neoclassical tragedy, are the legitimate ancestors of *Ubu.* One could of course play this game of influence-tracing as far back as Aristophanes. Remarkably, Jarry the iconoclast had great respect for Henrik Ibsen (in whose *Peer Gynt* he once performed) and apostrophized Maurice Maeterlinck as a "tragic man" whom he credited with the rebirth of the French-speaking theatre, "an ABSTRACT theater" to rival the "eternally tragic" plays of William Shakespeare and Johann Wolfgang von Goethe (*Selected Works* 86).

But the true model of his pataphysical dramaturgy is perhaps the German author Christian Dietrich Grabbe, whose astonishing play *Jest, Satire, Irony, and Deeper Significance* (1826) Jarry had freely translated as *Les Silènes.* Grabbe's play is primarily a literary satire that breaks all the rules of conscientious playwriting at once. One particular stage direction requires the Devil to tear out his left arm with his right and thrash several scientists, then replace it in the socket; another reads laconically: "A meadow, daybreak. Baron Murdrax is out taking a walk, meets thirteen apprentice tailors, puts on his napkin, and kills the whole lot" (Grabbe 58). Causality is the sacred cow of serious drama, and this grotesque kinetics of a universe utterly indifferent to causal logic in Grabbe's play may have inspired the prevalence of farcical mayhem and *sparagmos* without lasting consequences in *Ubu.*

In production, the text of *Ubu* presents very much the obverse problem of a text such as *Titus Andronicus.* Where in Shakespeare's play the director is faced with the necessity to tone down the grotesque elements and to let what is genuinely tragic in the play speak over their din, they need to be restored and updated in *Ubu,* which nowadays seems aesthetically quite "safe." The key to any modern production of *Ubu* would seem to be to strenuously resist the comedic cues that the play gives in abundance and the desire to indulge in a kind of knockabout hyperfarce with Pa Ubu as a superbuffoon. Jarry himself warned that Ubu's speeches "were not meant to be full of witticisms . . . but of stupid remarks, uttered with all the authority of the Ape" (*Selected Works* 83). The obvious surface comedy needs to appear as the veneer of an unspeakably bestial universe.

An ideal *Ubu,* paradoxically, would be one in which there is almost no laughter (or a great deal of laughter immediately felt to be inappropriate) and in which the generic context seems to be continually giving the signals for hilarity (the expletives, the Grand Guignol slapstick, the manifest cowardice of Ubu the *alazon,* the parody of tragic scenes) but where the actors behave with complete disregard for the kind of complicity with the audience that makes this form of satirical low comedy work. A 1977 BBC television version with Donald Pleasence and Brenda Bruce as the Ubs seems to have fulfilled these criteria:

> [Pleasence and Bruce] underacted, their performances were coarse, they were revoltingly ugly and stupid. There was not a single witticism or piece of comic business in the whole production. . . . Traditional jokes were used in an unfunny, deadpan manner that forced the viewer to reassess his reaction to such pranks and to face the inherent violence of such comedy. (Schumacher 117–18)

In short, the performance purposely refused the conversion of ugliness into something appreciably beautiful or sublime by passing it through artistic refinement so that the distastefulness of the subject would be compensated for by the virtuosity of the presentation. The actors "underacted" and provocatively withheld the aesthetic compensation that is part of the bargain of performance; this is—particularly where the comparatively unsophisticated mass medium of television is concerned—a far graver violation of standards than is apparent, for it means that their actions were no longer measurable in the terms of performance (a measure they rejected) and must thus, by default, be measured in terms of reality.

In the same year, 1977, Peter Brook staged *Ubu* at the Bouffes du Nord in Paris, attempting to liberate this classic of dramatic irreverence from the reverence it is often subjected to. Brook's Ubs were "demythified and humanized," as David Williams found, which made them "more odious for being more recognizable; they were presented as a living reality rather than as symbolic puppets" (*Peter Brook* 282–83). In many ways, Brook was returning to the serendipitous *Ur*-Ubu with this staging, for the original premiere at the Théâtre de l'Œuvre was arranged so hastily that the Ubu-shape familiar from Jarry's drawings could not be copied in costume and mask, and so Jarry had the actor, Firmin Gémier, wear a gray suit and bowler hat instead. He created, quite by default, an archetype of the modern theatre, the *Über*-bourgeois.[3]

Expressionism to Superrealism

The impact of Jarry's oafish king is everywhere in evidence in modern drama, but nowhere more perhaps than in the immortal superbourgeois who is his direct descendant, the protagonist of Yvan Goll's *Methusalem or The Eternal Bourgeois* (1922). Where Jarry engineers the destruction of the history play, Goll simultaneously attacks the tenets of bourgeois drama and the revolutionary fervor of expressionism. Goll's satirical play is admittedly seriously flawed as drama, and it must be understood and analyzed symptomatically in the context of concurrent avant-garde movements, particularly surrealism and expressionism, which in its paradoxical quest for dramatic sublimity made a habit of forcing kitschy pathos and caustic grotesqueness into the closest proximity.

Ernst Toller's play *Transfiguration* (1918), which may here serve as a typical example of postwar expressionism, not only illustrates the critical significance that drama gained as a political and social forum in Germany in the immediate aftermath of the First World War but also reflects with almost complete purity the type of the station-drama, the journey of the archetypally stylized protagonist that Strindberg *(To Damascus)* had first modeled on the passion play pattern. Although revolutionary and chiliastic pathos and grotesque allegorical visions intermingle in *Transfiguration*, the play is not grotesque drama in the sense developed here: the messianic protagonist (and Toller surrogate) Friedrich realizes that political change is the only way to prevent the recurrence of the horror of war, and the drama ends in the ecstatic proclamation of revolution and human brotherhood.

Yet in *Transfiguration*, with its conscious medievalism and wood-cut aesthetics, we find some of the most pointed scenes ever conceived in the grotesque mode. Some are conventional, such as the parade of corpses led by the skeletal figure of Death-by-War, or the *danse macabre* of slain soldiers on the battlefield. But it unfolds its greatest power in the scene in which a medical professor in a field hospital exhibits a procession of maimed war victims who, truncated, march forward "like clockwork figures" with their artificial limbs clicking while the doctor boasts to his students of his success in "regenerating" them:

> Three months ago they were mere passive stumps!
> To-day they stand before you—men!
> Did you observe the pleasing willingness
> With which they carried out my orders?
> To say nothing of the exquisite precision
> Of their synthetic movements.

But what the sinister doctor regards as his "masterpiece" is that he has "restored their procreative powers," which allows them to once again enjoy "the pleasures of the marriage bed" (Toller 76–77). His aim, clearly, is not the restoration of the patients' humanity but the restitution of a cold, functional eros of procreation that will assure a plentitude of manpower for the next war. Arms technology and medical technology, it appears, are merely each other's obverse, replacing the natural dialectics of birth and death. These cripples are artificial human figures, mechanical-organic contraptions, products of a war that promised their victorious "transfiguration" and accomplished only their disfigurement.

But in this inhumanity (which Toller's scathing indictment already casts into grotesque and disturbing images), we cannot help but also perceive a grotesquely parodic refraction of the modernist aesthetics and its own attitude toward the abstracted representation of the human figure. For the obedient "clockwork figures" of *Transfiguration* are virtual Craigian *Über-marionetten,* "all alike and stereotyped" (Toller 76). They are totally disposable *Kunstfiguren.*

The career of the Alsatian Yvan Goll, who wrote in French and German and was equally homeless in both cultures (his poetic alter ego was the peripatetic Jean sans Terre), is symptomatic in several respects of the modernist drama of the grotesque—its possibilities and limitations become visible in his work. Under the impression of World War I, Goll temporarily abandoned poetry for the stage and demanded the establishment of an assaultive drama, antirealistic and anti-illusionistic. By means of "superrealism," the dramatist was called upon to express the "superworld" in a "Superdrama" *(Überdrama).*

The terminological closeness to surrealism is unmistakable, although Goll strenuously objected to the "forgery of Surrealism which was invented by several ex-Dadas to bluff the bourgeois" and which he felt was perpetrating the confusion of "psychiatry and art" (*Dichtungen* 187). However, Goll was an admirer, if not an imitator, of the artist to whom the invention of the term "surrealism" is credited and whose play, *The Breasts of Tirésias* (1918), set the precedent for Goll's own dramaturgy: Guillaume Apollinaire.[4]

Like Goll, a poet-turned-dramatist—his *Calligrammes* are a first foray into concrete poetry—Apollinaire reflects the combined influence of Jarry (he attempted a new edition of *Ubu* in 1914) and of his own obsessive preoccupation with sex (an illegitimate child, he supported himself for a time by publishing erotic novels). His "surrealistic" drama springs from the devastating experience of the war, and in an Aristophanic manner it satirically reverses the roles of the belligerent men and the women who must produce the cannon-fodder for their bloody conflicts. But it also attempts a genuine theatre reform. In his programmatic prologue, Apollinaire paints the prewar theatre as a "slanderous and pernicious art" against which the total freedom of the modern dramatist to be the "creating god," a poetic license unfettered by logic or good taste, must be upheld (Apollinaire 64, 66).

The Breasts of Tirésias is a simple fable of female emancipation in which a woman, Thérèse, transforms herself into a man to join the army and leaves her husband to do the childbearing and rearing. The *mise-en-scène* of this transformation, however, has no parallel in Ibsen or George Bernard Shaw: "She utters a loud cry and opens her blouse from which her breasts emerge, one red, the other blue, and as she lets go of them they fly off, like toy balloons, but remain attached by strings" (Apollinaire 69). Reasoning that they are only a hindrance, Thérèse explodes the balloon breasts by striking a match and spontaneously grows a beard, whereupon she feels "as virile as the devil" (70). Subsequently, she overpowers her husband, exchanges clothes with him, and, reborn as Tirésias, confidently declares through a megaphone: "Now the universe is mine / The women are mine mine is the government" (73).

Apollinaire's stance is not truly progressive; *Tirésias* is not a parable addressing the causes of the war, nor a *pièce à thèse* championing genuine political or social reform, but a stage fantasy in which sexual politics can be resolved simply by discarding the symbols of difference (balls and balloons). Arnold Heidsieck remarks that in Apollinaire,

> the human body seems to consist of individual parts, the mutilating transformation seems like a *démontage:* humans are objects, nothing more. The objectal mechanism of mutilation—that it transpires as easily as "balloons flying off"—demonstrates the matter-of-fact-ness of the process. (20)

But such a judgment quite mistakes the tone of the play and attempts to pry a critique from it that it will not readily deliver, for the "process" is very much a voluntary act, and Thérèse is a character recruited from the tradition of a self-confidently anarchic, androgynous Harlequin, not from that of the grotesque victim Pentheus.

The leitmotif refrain of the play is that Thérèse, emboldened by an aggressive transsexualism that leaves the husband to raise 40,050 (!) children while she goes off to run the world, "carries a joke too far" (Apollinaire 77), and the same was widely held of the play. But there is a genuine aesthetic subversiveness to Apollinaire's drama that belies his somewhat confused social ideas and that Goll, a true leftist, recognized. In his "Letter to the Dead Poet Apollinaire" (1918), Goll took *Tirésias* as a cue to artistic revolt; the play, he remarks, is "no joke, only proclamations intensified to the grotesque-megaphonic, bitterest seriousness, bleeding truth, but realized through the new means of the poet: Superrealism" (*Dichtungen* 44). To Goll, superrealism is primarily an artistic means, not an ideology. It harbors the possibility to "connect the distant parts of reality most directly and swiftly" (*Dichtungen* 186); thus it is an aesthetics of highly compressed symbolism, of radical metaphor. The metaphorical process of super-realism permits both the intensification of lyrical imagery (in the Symbolist vein) and the exacerbation of the grotesque effect. This is the effect Goll actively sought: "grotesque" is the key term of his theatre aesthetics.

The preface to his two short "Superdramas," *The Immortal One (Der Unsterbliche)* and *The Undead (Der Ungestorbene)*, composed in 1918, promulgates the expressionist destruction of form and the rejection of conventional theatrical and dramatic devices as the conditions for the revival of the social and emotional import of drama, following what Goll perceives as the aesthetic bankruptcy of realism and psychologism.

Like most expressionists at the end of the First World War (including Toller), Goll reasons in apocalyptic language, citing the "heavy fighting" that has erupted around the New Drama and placing the dramatist in the front lines of "the final battle, the conflict of man with everything that is thing-like and beast-like in and around him" (*Dichtungen* 64). Human relations in the new theatre are to be shown "naked," under the "magnifying glass." Drama must thus seek to revert to the state in which the stage promoted such extremity: the primitive and archaic childhood of the human race:

> It has been forgotten that the first symbol of the theatre is the mask. The mask is rigid, unique, intense. It is immutable, inescapable, Fate. Every man wears his mask, what the ancients called his guilt. Children are frightened by it and scream. Man, sober and smug, shall learn to scream again. That is the purpose of the stage. . . .
>
> Art does not exist to comfort the fat bourgeois, so that he shakes his head: Yes, that's how things are! Now we're off to the snack bar! Art, insofar as it wants to educate, to improve, or to be effective in any other way, has to knock everyday man dead, to terrify him, like the mask does the child, like Euripides the Athenians, who staggered out of the theatre. Art must make children of men again. The simplest means is the grotesque, but without provoking laughter. The monotony and the stupidity of humanity are so enormous that they can only be countered with enormity. The new drama shall be enormous.
>
> The new drama will therefore employ all the technical devices which today trigger the effect of the mask. For instance, there is the grammophone, the mask of the voice; the electric poster; or the megaphone. The actors must wear oversized face-masks in which the character is already recognizable in a crudely externalized fashion: a magnified ear, white eyes, elongated legs. (*Dichtungen* 65)

The physical enlargement or "enormity" that Goll propagates is the countermeasure of the dramatist to compensate for the loss of the original naïveté of his audience *vis-à-vis* the illusion of the theatre, a spectatorial innocence that he attributes to the Greeks and that he believes could still be found in the theatre of Plautus or Molière. Goll, in other words, wants to elicit, if not exactly the terrified reaction of an ancient audience to Aeschylus's *Eumenides,* in which children purportedly died and women suffered miscarriage, then at least the fainting and cries for water provoked (later) by Brecht's clown play. The preface to his play *Methusalem* takes up the same subject:

> [T]he modern satirist must look for new stimuli. These he has found in [superrealism] and Alogic. [Superrealism] is the most forceful negation of realism. Surface reality is stripped away to reveal the Truth of Being. "Masks": crude, grotesque, like the emotions they express. No more "heroes," just people, no more characters, just naked instincts. (79)

I have noted Jarry's use of the mask for much the same effect. Goll is referring to a twofold function of the mask. One is the conventional summation of salient character qualities (emotion, gender, social rank) and the concurrent disguising of the all too "real" actor behind it; we might label this its histrionic function. But the second is its shock function, the exaggeration and physical enlargement, which attempts to break down the emotional indifference of a jaded audience and to restore in it a childlike state, not of wonderment and illusionistic transport but of vulnerability to unconscious fears, to the "uncanny." Goll would agree with Antonin Artaud who observed that "[n]o one knows how to scream any more in Europe" (Artaud, *Selected Writings* 266); the ideal spectator of his grotesque theatre is captured in that seminal icon of expressionism, Edvard Munch's *Scream*.

It is only logical that Goll avails himself of physiological terms (such as "stimulus") that reflect an essentially behaviorist attitude. The aim of art in this period of the "final battle" is not pleasing subtlety and the sublime. Goll's theatre tolerates no disinterested contemplation; it seeks, in fact, to make what Brecht called the "culinary" attitude all but impossible—although in the final analysis it is emphatically un-Brechtian, since it wants to supplant one purely irrational charge with another.[5] Indeed, Goll's theatre must be called grotesque precisely because its shock effects are (by intention, anyway) not already indentured to an ideological agenda but seek to preserve the free flow of archaic anxiety in the face of the unnameable. Goll's art wants to descend into the realm of the purely and unashamedly visceral where it can compete with the excesses of civilization, the horrors of war on the one side and the drone and drumbeat of the city with its lures of advertising on the other. Grotesque theatre is trying to become what realism forbids: the true emotional correlative of an already assaultive reality with which it is in permanent competition.

"[T]he perturbation of the dramatic discourse," writes Jean-Marie Valentin, "is inseparable from a kind of subversion of social reality. . . . The *Überdramen* are certainly in this respect attempts to reconquer the essence of art" (88). Goll's grotesque drama demands a dramaturgy *ex negativo* that derives its authority from the Enlightenment imperative that the theatre should be instructive, a "moral institution" (Schiller), but recognizes that it is unable to fulfill that mission any longer due to its self-imposed formal restrictions. Goll knows that if the bourgeois ideology is to be annihilated, it must be accomplished by smoking the burgher out of his last refuge, the theatre, in which causal logic, verisimilitude, and probability, the virtues of bourgeois epistemology, are enshrined. It becomes mandatory for the dramatist to destroy the dramatic self-reflection in which the burgher finds repose and catharsis, the theatrical alter ego through which he magnifies his own banality into artistic sublimity. The bourgeois self-image of heroic individuality, as we find it typified in the drama of Friedrich Schiller and Friedrich Hebbel in the nineteenth century, must be exposed as a ridiculous artifact, a *Kunstfigur.*

But Goll is clearly a more eloquent theoretician than he is a dramatist. The two Superdramas he wrote in 1918, before *Methusalem,* are short Apollinaire-style burlesques filled with surreal scenic inventions but with scant inclination toward a serious grotesque.[6] Roundly ignoring his own injunction to avoid easy laughter, he milks the playlets for every conceivable gag. In the first play, *The Immortal One,* the composer Sebastian is exposed to the Faustian temptations of the media-world. A sponsor offers to buy his genius, even to buy his "healthy stomach," while Sebastian pleads to maintain his fashionably tortured existence and "unprecedented lack of recognition." A police officer claims his talents for the public and the state, and his landlord, Lupus, proposes to make him rich by selling him to a "giant American vaudeville" (*Dichtungen* 68).

Lupus is the only character in *The Immortal One* to adhere to Goll's aesthetics of enormity, although the stage direction that characterizes him is puzzling: "He has one small and one hand-sized ear which he always takes off while speaking" (*Dichtungen* 69). He is a stock character of no consequence who "falls out of the window" shortly after appearing, a victim of Goll's breathless dramaturgy. What quality is "externalized" by his detachable ear, and who would feel provoked or frightened by it? The problem here is that Goll seems to confuse the "alogical" and the gratuitous, because he fails to heed Aristotle's eternally valid injunction that dramatic inconsistency must be consistent.

But Lupus is a red herring of Goll's grotesque technique, which focuses instead on the ensuing action. Sebastian's former fiancée Olga returns—she had "fallen/floated out of the window" earlier, this kind of Chagallian levity being endemic to the superreal world. She is now married to the "soul photographer" Balloon from Cairo, who has an offer Sebastian cannot refuse:

> I am a photographer of souls. That means I can immortalize you painlessly. You continue to live in the eyes and memories of mankind. But you yourself vanish, pain vanishes. The monstrous and stupid longing of the artist. You will be immortal in the most chemical sense of the word, silver bromide paper and hydrogen acid. In short: I will film you. Painless, o, painless. You live forever. (*Dichtungen* 71)

Balloon, who intermittently lets a phonograph continue his pitch while he romances Olga, is the grotesque agent of the machine age, a proto-McLuhanite who recognizes the ultimate interchangeability of medium and message. The photographer—whose name signals his inflated emptiness and whose fantastic profession seems the confirmation of primitive superstitions—is after Sebastian's "substance," or, we might say, his "aura." For he is in the forefront of what Walter Benjamin, scarcely twenty years later (1936), would analyze as the mechanical reproduction of the work of art. Having "photographed"—that is, effectively annihilated—Sebastian, Balloon sets up shop in the latter's studio. But public clamor forces him to resurrect Sebastian; his advertisement reads: "WAKING OF THE DEAD! ART LIVES ETERNALLY! SEBASTIAN AS GOD FOR THE BOURGEOISIE!" (*Dichtungen* 74).

Goll's media-apotheosis recognizes the entanglement of religion with commerce born from the new sacrality of the projected image (the resurrected Sebastian is a film projection), and it ironically belies Benjamin's idealistic expectation that the removal of the "aura" will thwart the use of art for cult and ritual, will in fact democratize and politicize art. Indeed, Goll almost anticipates the sober conclusions of Theodor Adorno and Max Horkheimer in the *Dialectics of Enlightenment* concerning the machinations of the star system in the "cultural industry" of Hollywood. As in the case of Greta Garbo or Humphrey Bogart, the image of the artist becomes a cult commodity at the disposal of a bourgeoisie both entranced and cynical. Sebastian is turned into another mechanically animated, mechanically reproduced *Kunstfigur.* Goll, incidentally, remained intrigued with the (essentially romantic) theme of the rift between burgher and artist as it was being transformed, by the invention of film, into the commercial relationship of consumer and consumed. His "film-poem" *The Chaplinade* (1920) features Charlie Chaplin as the archetype of this modern artist, hounded by unfeeling masses, multiplied by posters and projections, and yet always solitary.

The second "superdramatic" one-act, *The Undead,* is similarly satirical in orientation, and here Apollinaire's influence is perceptible even down to the details. Where *Tirésias* had a perambulating kiosk, Goll has an animated poster board and morning paper. Where in *Tirésias* the "People of Zanzibar" were represented by a single choral character, *The Undead* features a personified public in "Mr. Audience," a character designed as an allegorical caricature of prurience with his "long dachshund ears" and "protruding frog-opera-glass eyes" (*Dichtungen* 76). There is "enormity" in the seven-foot briefcase one character carries, and a student tears his brain out and flings it into another's face in a calculated effect of superreal grotesquerie, but this whizzing farcical pandemonium about a commercial prophet promising world salvation is largely topical satire, not in the least horrifying and rarely even very funny. Even its kinetic buoyancy is counter to the dominant kinetic atmosphere of the grotesque, which is often one of chthonic heaviness, of being "bogged down."

Undeterred, Goll attempted a full-length play in *Methusalem.* The present obscurity of *Methusalem* as a post-expressionist satirical farce on the Weimar bourgeoisie stands in contrast to its illustrious production history. The play opened at the Dramatisches Theater in Berlin on November 13, 1924, appropriately under the direction of Wilhelm (William) Dieterle, a man whose later career in Hollywood films included another profoundly grotesque subject, *The Hunchback of Notre Dame.* Artaud himself took part in a 1924 Paris staging (Esslin 385). The play sets dramaturgical precedents as well—its use of film clips for dream sequences is pioneering, and some of its dialogue and scenic style uncannily resembles later works by Ionesco, such as *The Bald Soprano.* Goll's concentration on quasi-cinematic montage and breakneck speed has rightly been called a "dramaturgy of 'rapidity' and surprise" (Mennemeier, "Überraschung" 23). And although the two authors likely knew nothing of each other's coincidentally contemporaneous work, Goll's *Methusalem* can be thought of as a countervariation on Shaw's generally optimistic *Back to Methuselah.*

At the center of this superfarce, designated a "satirical drama" by the author, is the monstrous "original bourgeois" Methusalem, a cigar-smoking, apoplectic caricature of raw capitalism who, more immortal even than his biblical counterpart, survives his own demise. "Eternal" in a twofold sense, he is not only indestructible but also immutable and unteachable, the extreme allegory of a ridiculous petit bourgeoisie come to power and wealth. His lowbrow vulgarity is symbolized by his constant appetite for goulash (as in the case of Ubu or that of the husband in Apollinaire's play who clamors incessantly for "lard," gastric functions override all conscious thought). A figurine by George Grosz for an unrealized production shows Methusalem with an oversized kitchen knife as sword and a wine glass in hand; his face is just an assemblage of planks (the German idiom *vernagelt,* "nailed shut," means obtuse) (see fig. 8).

The underlying fable is pure melodrama: The Methusalems arrange a marriage for their son, Felix; their overwrought daughter, Ida, gets herself pregnant by a revolutionary student; and a worker's rebellion that threatens Methusalem's shoe factory is violently quelled. Goll could easily have borrowed his subtitle from a preceding series of satiric plays by the dramatist Carl Sternheim: "Scenes from the Heroic Life of the Middle Class."

Methusalem, the eternal bourgeois, enacts a travesty of the concepts of bourgeois tragedy, in which the enlightened common man replaces a now corrupt aristocracy as the representative of a progressive moral order. In a satirically pointed manner, the play recapitulates precisely the arguments of Arnold Hauser, who, in his essay on domestic drama, observes that the modern middle class, being more heterogeneous than any other class before it, was always "menaced by the danger of dissolution" and thus "bred a super-bourgeois attitude to life" through which it attempted to "conquer itself and struggle[d] to attain a universally valid humanism" (417–18). Methusalem is the monstrous mockery of such aspirations, the guarantor of a universally valid inhumanity.

Methusalem's conversations with his wife, Amalia, sound like proto-Ionescan patter in which homespun philosophy and trivial romantic attitudes mingle with a disturbingly sadistic voyeurism:

Methusalem [asleep, awakes with a start]: Nothing new. The world's getting so old.

Amalia: Life is hard.

Methusalem: It's much of a muchness.

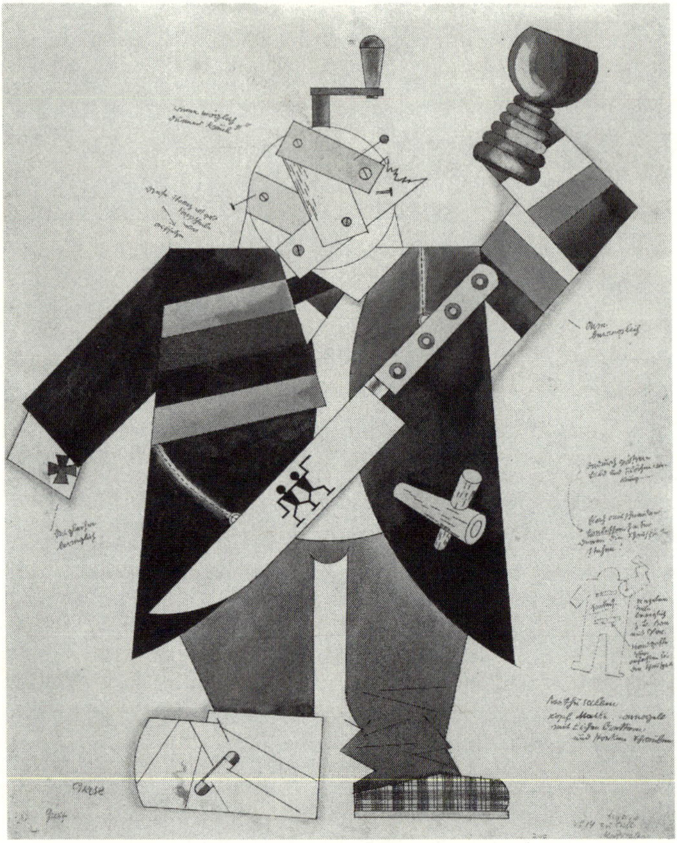

Fig. 8. George Grosz, *Methuselah [Methusalem]* (1922). ©Estate of George Grosz/Licensed by VAGA, New York. Digital image ©The Museum of Modern Art/Licensed by SCALA/Art Resource, New York.

Amalia: No juicy little murder in the paper?

Methusalem: Seven-and-six.

Amalia: Spaghetti?

Methusalem: No, vegetable oil.

. . . .

Methusalem [with paper, turning over the pages]: A robbery with manslaughter!

Amalia: Where? Read it out! Quick!

Methusalem: She was lying stark naked at the door.

Amalia: The cheek of it.

Methusalem: Half an udder cut off.

Amalia: All for love: oh, love!

(82)

The "latest little murder" is discussed in crude detail as an aesthetic experience ("Shakespeare has nothing so fantastic" [97]—an erroneous judgment, clearly) on a par with politics and grocery prices.

Just as *Ubu Roi* is posited on the fundamental plot of the history play, *Methusalem* grounds its plot in bourgeois tragedy and in melodrama. And just as King Ubu's universal reaction to any occurrence is violence (random or retaliatory), Methusalem's single point of reference is commerce. When his daughter, Ida, announces her illegitimate pregnancy, he responds as only *homo oeconomicus* can:

Ida: I have a baby in my body, pink and pure.

Methusalem: We must do something about public opinion. Announce a big Sale.

Felix: 20 per cent reduction.

Methusalem: Ooh my leg, fallen whore of a daughter!

(103)

In fact, Methusalem personifies the industrial nineteenth century's ideal of the new man but flies in the face of the expressionist ideal of the "New Man," found in its most rarefied form in such a figure as Eustache de Saint-Pierre of Kaiser's *Burghers of Calais* (1914). Where Kaiser's character is the glowing avatar of a new self-sacrificing and holy humanity, Goll's is the pompous summation of the pejorative that the epithet "burgher" had become. Kaiser's *citoyen* (because he is tragic) perishes; Goll's burgher (because he is ineradicable and impervious to tragedy) survives. Although he is shot dead on stage in a spurious revolution, he appears unscathed in the last scene of the play. Like Ubu, Methusalem is an unholy cross between Dionysus and an indestructible cartoon character. Equipped with a horrifying, inhuman resilience that bounces them back from every catastrophe and seems unstoppable, both are the incarnation of eternal recurrence. Unable to learn, they will, in the spirit of George Santayana's grim aphorism, repeat history indefinitely.

The insights Goll permits us into Methusalem's psyche (through dream sequences projected as films) confirm his self-absorption, philistinism, and purely mercantile patriotism. But his true nightmare, the most radical threat to this static monolith of wealth-accumulation, is the constant possibility of insubordination, chaos, and revolution (a possibility not at all far-fetched at the time Goll was writing). The most extensive film sequence in the play concerns a "revolution of the beasts" in which the stuffed hunting trophies on the wall come to life in Methusalem's dreams. This Orwellian fantasy is a sarcastic inversion of traditional animal allegories: upon deciding to "establish a spiritual animal republic," the beasts immediately collapse into fractious backstabbing in a pointed caricature of the political cauldron of Weimar—liberal parrot against royalist cuckoo, idealist monkey versus authoritarian bear, and so on.

A real calamity, however, befalls Methusalem in the form of a strike against his shoe factory, led by the very Student who later impregnates Ida and who is a caricature of the rebellious expressionist youth found frequently in the plays of Toller, Walter Hasenclever, Reinhard Sorge, Arnolt Bronnen, and others. His militant pathos ("I will liberate you with my radial mind" [91]; "I am the deed!" [108]) is pure pose, and Goll—no sentimental socialist convinced of the innate goodness of the proletariat—makes his followers out to be mostly half-wits bent on their material advantage, and thus essentially no different from Methusalem. The squelching of this uprising is accomplished in a manner entirely worthy of Pa Ubu. When the crowd begins to press into Methusalem's home, the cowardly burgher pushes a secret button,

> *whereupon a safe fixed on the left opens and six policemen armed with revolvers step out. The mob screams and scatters. While things are quieting down two gold-braided lackeys bring in a lavishly-carved commode, help Methusalem to unbutton his trousers and pull them down and seat him on the afore-mentioned stool. The mob is completely mastered. The policemen stand stiff and respectful. Methusalem smiles and farts. Curtain.* (92)

In keeping with the grotesque ethos of debasement and physicalization, the revolution is expressly likened to a bothersome bout of constipation, the policemen brought in as a laxative in uniform.

This dénouement exposes, in psychoanalytic terms, Methusalem's obvious anal-retentive nature, but it also taps into and effectively reverses a strain of popular theatrical imagery. For in the carnival plays of the fifteenth and sixteenth century, constipated peasants were a perennial figure of fun, and itinerant quacks typically sought to relieve them of their symptoms and their cash. Methusalem is the offspring of these peasants, but he is now the triumphant party, having, in his hamfisted way, taken the place of the doctor/trickster. In the context of the carnival logic invoked here, such a role-reversal heralds far more than is immediately apparent: it signals that the "lower bodily stratum" that Mikhail Bakhtin associates with carnivalistic liberation and autonomous folk culture—indeed, with revolution—has been summarily usurped by the powers of authority. As in Ubu, in Methusalem we have a character in which the lower orders of human behavior become immediately, unmediatedly, transparent, in whom there is "a radical suspension of the difference between deep structure and surface structure" (Mennemeier, "Überraschung" 20). Goll himself perceives the moment as the peripety of the play, allowing: "There can be an interval here" (*Methusalem* 92).

The Eternal Bourgeois propagates his stale ideology of acquisition even via that revolutionary upstart, the Student, who in Goll's play is the satirized cipher of true social ideals. Methusalem is a double father in this play—first to the symbols of the new mercantile age his son, Felix, embodies, then to the Student who is his ostensible adversary (a generational conflict typically found in much of expressionist drama). But the Student, too, is merely a materialist (though, he fancies, with a capital "M"). When Felix shoots him in a duel of honor, he exhales his soul in the "shape of an overcoat" (106), only to rise again. His true concern is the ennui of existence, and he is not excluded from (indeed, he perpetuates) the inexorable cycle of historical revolution and devolution, which is a pale and trivial shadow of the classical history play:

> *Student:* O God, isn't life dull!
> *Ida:* When will the Revolution be finished?
> *Student:* When the others don't have a mansion left.
> *Ida:* And when we have one?
> *Student:* The new Revolution starts.
>
> (112)

This is the cynical co-optation of Leon Trotsky's "permanent revolution," the maintenance of the status quo under the pretense of genuine social change, the unavoidable *embourgeoisement* of the radical. A scene such as this—and indeed, all of *Methusalem*—must be considered in the context of the almost religious fervor that pervaded even the most secular exponents of expressionism. *Methusalem* flatly denies any belief in the imminent social, political, even spiritual salvation of man that propped up the core of expressionist ideology. Measured against the ideological precepts of its time, the play seems far more disquieting—even grotesque—than it does today.

The modernist *Kunstfigur* is present here in several variations. Felix is the most flagrant example, appearing as though he had just stepped out of a dadaist montage: "Felix is the modern mathematical man. For a mouth he wears a copper megaphone, for a nose he has a telephone receiver, for eyes two gold coins, for forehead and hat a typewriter, and on top he has antennae which light up every time he speaks" (*Methusalem* 90). Felix spouts forth stock market quotes and news bulletins in an unrelenting staccato (parodying, incidentally, the familiar speech mannerism of Sternheim heroes, the "telegram style"). Constructed out of the objects that define commerce and communications in the machine age, it is not clear whether he inhabits them or whether they have overwhelmed him—instrumental perfection and dehumanization are indistinguishable, symbolically synonymous. Indeed, the other mechanical presence in the play, the "joke box"—a man-shaped wind-up robot that, to Methusalem's great pleasure, tells anti-Semitic jokes—seems decidedly more human than Felix. Goll could have found inspiration for such a satirical manifestation in *Tirésias*, where the husband makes a reporter of one of his children by giving him ink for blood, a huge fountain pen as a backbone, and glue as "a brain for not thinking with" (Apollinaire 85). But he had to look no further than the art of the German dadaist movement for his *Kunstfigur.* Felix is the character equivalent of a dadaist icon, Raoul Hausmann's famous montage object *The Spirit of Our Times* (1919), a wooden mannequin's head with a ruler and assorted instruments of calculation attached. A dancer in one of Oskar Schlemmer's ballets (*The Figural Cabinet I,* 1922) is similarly described as having "a blabbermouth and a swivelhead and a nose like a trumpet" (Schlemmer 40).

The Student is the other *Kunstfigur,* and in the play's most farcically effective scene, the anti-Freudian Goll uses him to satirize the psychoanalytic model of the mind. In this scene, in which he woos Ida in a park, the Student is represented threefold, each incarnation wearing a hat with an inscription: "I," "You," and "He."[7] These ego-constituents of the Student engage in a fierce contest for attention, a kind of externalized stream of consciousness, in which the "I" worries about money and halitosis, the "You" sings ecstatic lyrical arias to his paramour, and the "He" schemes how to get into Ida's pants. When "He" finally lunges in exasperation at

"I" and gives it the boot, Goll's superrealistic technique has simply converted the metaphor of the psychic apparatus into literal stage reality and reduced the Freudian id to a lecherous bully and the mechanism of psychic economy to a farcical brawl. The character, in other words, lacks a center that can hold—he falls apart. In this he takes precisely—and ominously—the opposite path from a protagonist such as Toller's Friedrich in *Transfiguration,* who "comes together," transfigured from soldier into savior. Even expressionist characterology, Goll seems to be asserting, can represent the modern dramatic subject no more adequately than the traditional drama suffices to reflect the misery of modern a-history.

Yet while it is certainly true that "[t]heatrical modernity . . . resides in the loss of the face and of irreplaceable individuality, in the deformation of the voice" (Valentin 90), Goll seems incapable of sufficiently exploring the dark and fearful side of that modernity. There is not much menace about Felix; he is simply a comical theatrical metaphor of human functionality, a jab at the accountant mentality. Nor is the Student developed to full grotesque potential. We find that "the unmasking of the reality of living beings and of things" (Valentin 90) is often a rather trivial affair and that Goll's dramatic world seldom conveys that powerful sense of grotesque endangerment upon which the radically assaultive artwork thrives. Most critics will agree with John Swan, who contends that *Methusalem* "fails, despite its strengths, to be a truly original modernist farce" (194).

Goll became increasingly disillusioned in the 1920s and convinced that even the drama—which he had hailed only a few years before as an artistic panacea—was no longer effective or even possible. Around the time of *Methusalem,* he wrote in the journal *Die Neue Schaubühne* that the revolutionary drama was dead because the revolutionary impulse had been corrupted: "The word 'Red' has become kitsch. . . . Toller is great in jail, but on stage as boring as a newspaper." In fact, Goll concedes that the spirit of Methusalem has triumphed:

> Our time [is] far too mercantile. . . . What remains? To make fun of the times. Salty, hard, malicious irony. The whip. Being inexorable. Scalpel to the bone. Pulling down the pants. Openly laughing at the indignity. The healthy revenge of children, who throw with stones. *A bas le bourgeois!* Tear apart his umbrella. That is not dramatic, God knows. But we can laugh ourselves to death a bit, and death is the last thrill which can still overcome our boredom a little. (*Dichtungen* 84)

Ghelderode, Rudkin, and the Triumph of Death

The dramatic work of Belgian Michel de Ghelderode represents probably the most sustained canon of grotesque plays by any single author in the modern era. Ghelderode's work is completely idiosyncratic in style, but its substance is composted from the rich soil of six centuries of Central European culture. Although the medievalism of his tone and technique is immediately striking, he is impossible to imagine without the context of modernism and especially of expressionism. But if he confesses an allegiance to the modern, then it is only to those of its exponents who share his sense of the numinous—Edgar Allan Poe and Strindberg—and consequently, he "despises" the rationalist Brecht (Ghelderode, "Interview" 47). Shakespeare, Christopher Marlowe, Ben Jonson, and Lope de Vega are his acknowledged dramatic models; in these Ghelderode grasps a sort of nature different from what he perceives as a passionless present, "[a] total nature—with all the horror and sublimity that this entails" because the Renaissance is set "between two extremes, the ecstasy of living and the horror of living" (Ghelderode, "Ostend Interviews" 18).

Ghelderode's theatrical creed is mystical. "The theatre," he says, "is an art of instinct. . . . The dramatic author must live by vision and divination only, the part played by the intellect remaining auxiliary" ("Ostend Interviews" 20). He is, as David Grossvogel puts it, the oracle "through whom speak the occult voices of the theater," a theatre that "seeks primarily to evoke moods and metaphysical truths" (303, 285). The plays are strongly inspired by extratheatrical religious and popular spectacles such as carnivals, *parades foraines,* masses and holy processions, circuses, music halls, and even films. But Ghelderode also draws upon the Flemish tradition of painting and graphic arts from Hieronymus Bosch and Pieter Breughel to James Ensor. All is steeped in a perception of the universe that is substantially picaresque—the figure of the Flemish trickster Ulenspiegel and Miguel de Cervantes's Don Quixote in particular exert their influence (Beyen 149–50).

In his mystical bent, his attraction to extremity, his veneration of the Elizabethans and sympathy for Strindberg, his invocation of popular forms, and many other details, Ghelderode appears almost as the necessary complement to Artaud, perhaps even the first playwright of the Theatre of Cruelty, although the two were almost certainly oblivious of each other's work. But critical enthusiasm for such seeming fraternity too often overlooks the fundamental divergences between their philosophies of the stage, from Ghelderode's non-Artaudian baroque verbosity to Artaud's reliance on the theatre itself as the metaphysical instrument of salvation, a concept that Ghelderode would have rejected out of hand.

Ghelderode the playwright is essentially *sui generis*. On the occasion of the first production of his *Chronicles of Hell* in 1949, the critic Guy Dornand of *La Libération* found it necessary to invent a special epithet: *ghelderodite aiguë*—the Ghelderodian pain (Beyen 5). This term sums up a fervency of suffering and a plasticity of anguish on Ghelderode's stage that are reminiscent of the Flemish painters. Indeed, his sensitivity seems to grow immediately out of the Flemish landscape and its nightmares.

The force of this *ghelderodite aiguë* caught the postwar Paris audience unprepared; the scandalized bourgeoisie chose to close down *Chronicles of Hell* at Jean-Louis Barrault's Théâtre Marigny after only four nights. (It then transferred to the Théâtre des Noctambules for an extended run to great acclaim.) Ghelderode attributed the scandal to a "misunderstanding"; the audience of the Marigny had mistaken "the work of a moralist" for that of an "anti-cleric." The play had merely "disproportionately inflated a pictorial 'detail' which in other, more 'sane' times, such as those of Rabelais or of our great painters, would have seemed completely normal" (qtd. in Beyen 107).

This uncompromising (but never realistic) attention to detail is the key to Ghelderode's aesthetic, which projects a kind of eccentric semiotics of the object. Indeed, like Bosch's, Ghelderode's world contains neither subjects nor subjectivity. Everything within it (including the characters) is reified, more or less progressively animated, and contingent upon an inscrutable but very manifest divine will-to-revelation. Ghelderode, then, is the true grotesque mystic; his stage is filled with a reflection of the numinous, but it is a reflection that has greatly suffered in its transmission to the material realm and now stands mangled and corrupted, no more true to its transcendent origin than the shadows beheld by the imaginary denizens of Socrates' cave are to reality. In this transmuted realm, the playwright formulates a painful theology of abjection, as indeed his art is grounded first in the sensual, the abject, and the nonabsolute—the "world of shapes," he remarks, preceded the "world of ideas" in his discovery ("Ostend Interviews" 15).

Yet the theatre, the "world of shapes," as both a medium in the full sense of the word and as the primal symbolic art, enjoys a privileged position in his theology. Though it cannot promise salvation, it is uniquely constructed to deliver the raw phenomenal essence of things, a perspective through which the necessity of salvation (in more than a narrowly ecclesiastical sense) becomes apparent. For Ghelderode, the theatre is inevitably amoral and therefore almost inescapably grotesque: "The aim of the theatre—and of mine in particular—is not to comfort, no more is it to grieve. The theatre is a fact. . . . Morals have nothing to do with the matter" ("Ostend Interviews" 26).

His plays are often set in a grotesque world he sometimes calls "Breughelland," in which the modern, the medieval, and the ancient intermingle inextricably; gardens grow wild like the vegetation over the Golden House of Nero. The scene of *Hop, Signor!* is set in "[a]n uncultivated garden. Among the bushes and rank weeds lie carved stones, statues of saints, bas-reliefs, capitals, pillars, sundials that make the garden look like a neglected yard or even some old forgotten cemetery" (*Hop, Signor!* 51). It is a fantastical and enigmatic landscape, essentially Gothic in style, filled with contradictory signs and rife with possibility. Into such an environment *Chronicles of Hell,* too, is placed.

The stage directions of *Chronicles* convey with stark plasticity the divisions of this theatrical world: enveloped by the persistent snarling of a hellish "invisible and threatening crowd" rising from the public square below, the interior walls of a "decaying episcopal palace" are hung with portraits of ecclesiastical dignitaries on tattered tapestries, "very high up." At the base of the walls, on the other hand (and thus at the eye-level of the audience) lie "piles of baroque objects, idols, suns, witches' masks, multicolored devils, totems, stakes, and instruments of torture," seemingly signifying a quotidian life of superstition and brutality (*Chronicles* 238).

Ghelderode's worldview is well summed up in this three-tiered theatrical topography that replicates aspects of the medieval stage but does not, like its model, already encompass the metaphysical. Rather, true to the aesthetics of the grotesque, Ghelderode uses the grammar of transfiguring figuration. The snarling crowd is not literally a mob of demons but a demonic carnival parade of instincts, humanity-as-hell, seen from the perspective of ecclesiastical orthodoxy (the papal legate calls them "freethinking, subversive, yes, violent, unmanageable" [*Chronicles* 252]). The painted clerics are no closer to true divinity for being hung near the firmament; and the middle ground, the palace rooms in which the play proper ensues, represents Ghelderode's concept of a world in which human extremity is the necessary result of such corruption and distance from the ideal—from God.

This attitude colors Ghelderode's anthropology as well. The image of the puppet is the literal or symbolic basis of most of Ghelderode's work in the theatre, and in it are crystallized several complex aesthetic layers that belie the stark simplicity of the medium. Ghelderode's dislike for human actors and his inclination toward caricature are merely the most superficial motivations for his leaning toward puppetry; at the center of his fascination is clearly what we might call the puppet's metaphysicality.

To say that the marionette is symbolic of human existence because man is nothing if not manipulable and constantly in need of direction from above is to fail to get past a kind of vulgar mechanistic theology that severely discounts Ghelderode's profundity. I have previously pointed out the concurrent reduction and universalization of human ontology in the puppet, and Ghelderode, in his "Ostend Interviews," takes up the revelatory and mystical quality of puppetry, to which he claimed to owe the "disclosure of . . . the original theatre." Ghelderode is an animist at heart; objects to him are sensitive, living, magical. While "by their shape and structure marionettes and dolls cannot be other than the objects that are the closest to us," this very closeness is only the reminder of a metaphysical distance or chasm that aesthetically sharpens every aspect of Ghelderode's theatre ("Ostend Interviews" 23–24).

Ghelderode first honed his craft by writing for the Toone Marionette Theatre of Brussels in the 1920s, and from that period on, the image of the marionette became the controlling image of his theatre. The Toone, liberated by the presence of the puppet and its innate eccentricity, was open to the kind of transgression customarily reserved for the carnival; it "traditionally ridicule[d] society's deepest-seated taboos (cannibalism, incest) and fears (death, the powers of evil)" (Botsford 279 n).

Like *Ubu Roi, Chronicles of Hell* is a kind of oversized puppet play that confounds our sense of proportion, character, and place. Particularly the minor characters, priests in the ecclesiastical hierarchy, reflect the author's proclivity for extremity, for a dramatic-caricaturistic amalgam of the *homme-machine,* or puppet, and the *homme-bête.* Outfitted with signifying names such as Carnibos, Duvelhond, or Real-Tremblor, they comprise a subhuman chorus of laughing, heckling, and quarreling minor fiends, beset by deformity, stuttering, and deafness. Degenerate versions of man, they verge on the animal and mechanical (one has a "rat's snout," another a "wooden ear") or the freakish (Krakenbus's ominous hump "contains a second brain" [*Chronicles* 240]). George Wellwarth detects in the characters "this quality of the painted, frozen grimace suddenly animated" (111). They are gargoyles sprung to life.

In this "instinctual" dramaturgy, some of the superstitious medieval attitude toward physical deformation is preserved and exploited. Hunchbacks and dwarves here still signal the presence of evil and abjection. (Ghelderode's liberal use of these figures who had long served the small-minded Central European denizens as convenient scapegoats runs up uncomfortably against contemporary pieties and has no doubt contributed to the flagging popularity of his plays.)

Chronicles is centered around two archetypal figures, Jan in Eremo, the supposedly deceased bishop of Lapideopolis who suddenly and terribly revives while lying in state, and his antagonist and heir designate, Simon Laquedeem. Lapideopolis, the city of stone, which Jan had once saved from a plague like Oedipus saved Thebes, is situated in an imaginary medieval Flanders, which is in truth a para-historical composite of the Catholic realm on the periphery of the Dark Ages (or, as Jarry might say, "a distantly interrogative somewhere"). It simultaneously tolerates the presence of a Vatican-style Swiss Guard and of a populace identified as essentially pagan and barbaric, even cannibalistic (the priests fear to be "grilled like pigs" and to become "bones for their soup" [265]).

Once again, Lapideopolis is the belly-world, and the ethics of ingestion governs all. From the first scene on, the chaplain Carnibos's uncontrollable appetite threatens to lay waste to the funeral table. The dead bishop to him is merely "meat" (241), and this impious ambiguity is deliberately maintained throughout the play. When the guild of butchers (giants all) comes at last to claim the corpse of their patron and remove him from the palace, it could be to bury him or to feast on him—both equivalent and equally sacred acts in the grotesque world.

In the ubiquity of the gastric image, the curious conglomerations of body and world peculiar to the grotesque occur, propounding a scenic instability or amorphism in which the threat of reversal is always imminent, in accordance with the carnival code. Simon, referring to the undead bishop, maintains that "it's the diocese that needs purging of what is obstructing it" (248), but it is the obstruction of the bishop's trachea by the host (Simon's doing) that has brought about this greater obstruction. Moreover, Simon is plagued by an insistent constipation in his "Calvary of a stomach" (249), to which "great belly" the eponymously perverse papal legate Sodomati ascribes the power "to infect all the nearby countries more thoroughly than heresy" (254). Later, the priests cannot distinguish the rumblings of Simon's stomach from "the belly of the storm" that punctuates the action (257). Indeed, the play underscores its own "organic" unity of action by beginning with Carnibos's compulsive eating ("Yum . . . yum . . . I'm nibbling" [239]) and ending with Simon, crouching with an expression of "demoniac bliss" (273), ridding himself of his constipation. In this odd compositing of outside and inside, or macrocosm and microcosm, a medieval ideal of wholeness shines through the sometimes crude physicality of the play, but that physical crudeness is also the scenic equivalent of the central dramatic metaphor of the world-as-body, which is suspended unrelievedly between infection and purgation, poisoning and purification.

Jan in Eremo's unresolved state of suspension, his living death, in particular dramatizes the primary paradox of the play, the inextricable simultaneity of the spiritual and the physical in human existence. Jan is already identified as a monstrous product of chthonic and ethereal forces; it is claimed that he sprang from "the fornication of a monk and a mermaid" (257). His abrupt and starkly theatrical appearance in Lapideopolis resembles an epiphany ("suddenly looming out of the mists, bowed beneath a huge cross made from tarred planks" [258]) that prefigures his horrifying manifestation on the scene as a living corpse ("a dark and heavy mass hieratically sculpted and as though vibrating in the light" [263]). Ghelderode emphasizes his status as an oversized *Kunstfigur,* lumbering like a "jerkily moving athlete" (264), a metaphysical marionette.

The image of the consecrated but poisoned host lodged in Jan's throat, the last sacrament administered by Simon, which, instead of alleviating the burden of death, is its true cause, yields an eminently successful theatrical metaphor for Ghelderode's assessment of the human condition. Jan's suspension leaves him hanging between life and death, suffering and redemption. But the host in his throat—it is the body of Christ he is choking on, the act of officially sanctioned cannibalism—is the pure physicalization of the play's implicit theodicy, namely that the grotesque world resists complete sacralization or transubstantiation. It is out of this insistent material essence of the world in which the carnal aspect obtrudes all, and which is irreducible, that Ghelderode's theatre is constructed.

Jan in Eremo finally accepts his death in a scene of such flagrant psychoanalytic readability that one is amazed to find it in the work of the vehement anti-Freudian Ghelderode. Simon and Jan are locked in mortal combat, "struggling like stevedores," when the sudden entrance of Jan's mother Veneranda brings the entire drama to a standstill, a "fateful" silence and "emptiness" in which "nothing breathes" (269). Veneranda relieves Jan of the offending host, upon which he crumbles to the stature of "a tottering old man" (269). She forces him to absolve the priests and finally leads him to die his long-deferred death. Simon, under the sarcastic pretense of giving her "communion," takes the very host she has extracted from Jan's throat and violently stuffs it down hers, pointedly proclaiming: "Rejoin in eternity him to whom you gave birth" (270). In Veneranda, the old servant woman, Ghelderode produces an echo of Mary (who also witnesses the death of her son), but by bringing the sacred event down into the grotesque world, he reverses it and counters centuries of Catholic hagiography and mythical purification. Veneranda must symbolically eat her son's flesh and die of the poison with which the Church has debased it.

The expulsion of the irritant Jan in Eremo, who can no more be assimilated by Lapideopolis than the symbolic body of the host can be by his own, and his final interment in the "deepest crypt" where "the cathedral will press down with all its weight on his bones" (249) is so urgent because he has summoned something that, like himself, refuses to die or be vanquished. It is embodied in the idols and "grotesque dolls" (266) that he has accumulated as his "only friends," indeed his "court" (251), and that cause great alarm among the clerics: it is the stratum of the archaic, carnivalistic, savage, and pagan. But Ghelderode advances no Bakhtinian argument that paints the carnival sphere as the scene of social liberation and ultimate human freedom; the idols are stolen from "savages" whom Jan had converted by "beating and barking" and delivered to a "hard life" for the Church (251). He himself, in turn, seems to have metamorphosed into a savage god, a looming and sculpted presence. An inexplicable but irreversible transference between the realms of the sacred and profane has occurred, a mutual corruption of lower and higher orders. Jan's missionary triumph is an ethical disaster.

Both antagonists are "grotesque," but again the distinction between higher and lower orders obtains here. Jan in Eremo, reviled by the Church hierarchy as an anti-Christ and celebrated by the populace as a saint, embodies the positive aspect of the grotesque, exemplifying the unmediated and unregulated access to the sacred, even if through profane symbolic representations. Aesthetically suspended halfway between human presence and an apparition, he is a transfiguration of the numinous. Simon Laquedeem and Sodomati, who (barely) disguise their profanity as godliness, are indicative of the truly deviant grotesque. (The principal heresy threatening the Catholic hierarchy in the sixteenth century is the "grotesque" Protestant proposition that ecclesiastic mediation is unnecessary to communion with God. By implication, *Chronicles* is set at the height of that heretical crisis.) But *Chronicles* must be read more generally—or metadramatically—as a parable on the continuing repression of the unorthodox (and on its irrepressibility), a fate the grotesque itself has shared.

How strong a compulsion the grotesque drama creates to search for a cathartic return that is not there is in evidence in an essay on the play by Helen Hellman in the Catholic-leaning journal *Renascence.* Hellman's intelligent reading concludes by asserting that Jan's "merciful death" signals "relief and catharsis" and that, all appearances to the contrary, his is "the ultimate moral victory." Jan, the argument goes, is a "fool of faith" whose ambiguous nature contains a flash of Christ and John the Baptist. His struggle with the "false disciple" Simon reiterates the basic Manichaean struggle of darkness and light (37–38).

These patterns are indisputably contained in the play. But we must, strictly speaking, refer to catharsis as the emotional effect of the restitution of balance in a system or community that is blemished by a single hubristic act, a system that is therefore cleansable. Such a community is nowhere to be found in *Chronicles,* the whole point of the play being the eternal perpetuation of degradation. Catharsis is not a generic option of this *tragédie bouffe;* one critic writes that Ghelderode's drama creates not merely "mixed feelings" but "an unrelieved experience of dissonance" (Janik 227). It is "a very moral play," as the author himself took pains to emphasize (Ghelderode, "Interview" 44), but it asserts this in the manner typical of grotesque morality: by withholding the moral. It is not true, however, that Ghelderode is entirely unsuccessful as a moralist, as Grossvogel asserts (300–301). If anything, Ghelderode's moral stance is comparable to Bosch's, but like the painter, his pictorial immediacy overpowers what there may be of the cathartic or didactic. The French stage director Jean-Luc Dejean has said that although one blasphemes in Ghelderode's theatre, "God is always present" (qtd. in Beyen 188).

The play, indeed, has very little to do with the Catholic Church as an institution, or with any argument against an ineffectual and foolish clergy—this was the fundamental misunderstanding of the scandalized audience at the Théâtre Marigny. Rather, it illustrates in its drastic way the perpetual struggle of the carnival and Lenten forces, the powerful undertow of chaos within the illusion of order. The poles of Ghelderode's universe are Manichaean—he himself confessed to having "an angel on [his] shoulder and a devil in [his] pocket" ("Ostend Interviews" 13)—but on his stage the poles of the sacred and profane are mutually compromised. It is the very ambiguity in the figure of Jan in Eremo that argues most strongly against reading *Chronicles* as a tale of achieved salvation; indeed, it is another illustration of René Girard's "sacrificial crisis."

The manner in which these themes are condensed and fused into a brief *tragédie bouffe* confirms the play's central standing in Ghelderode's canon; it is perhaps his most universal drama, the summation of his theatrical theology. Jean Genet, who attended *Chronicles* several times in 1949, announced: "It's all there, all that will (ever) be done" (qtd. in Beyen 155).

If the *ghelderodite aiguë* finds its home anywhere in the work of contemporary dramatists, it is most likely in that of the Irish playwright David Rudkin (like Belgium, Ireland is a privileged source of grotesque drama). Rudkin's early plays, such as his celebrated debut *Afore Night Come* (1962), reveal the influence of Samuel Beckett, Harold Pinter, and Artaud: out of a context of utter debasement and violence emerges an enigmatic sense of ritual and archetypal myth. But his 1976 play, *The Triumph of Death* (incidentally taking its name—and certainly its atmosphere—from a phantasmagoric Breughel canvas), operates in an allegorical mode very similar to Ghelderode's, although perhaps more graphic. Ghelderode and Rudkin also share a penchant for a blisteringly and intoxicatingly powerful brand of language wielded with sacerdotal fervor. Like Ghelderode's, Rudkin's stance is antirational and antimodern, even mystical and visionary; his writing, which he says comes out of an "affliction of images" (Wilcher 571), is often verbally torrential and symbolically hypertrophic.

Triumph unfolds a loose plot set "ostensibly in the 'middle ages,'" freely mixing prehistoric and biblical motifs. Tableaux reminiscent of the Crusades, the Passion of Joan of Arc, the Inquisition, and the Reformation paint a broad picture of the progress of human corruption. Presiding over the feverish proceedings is the Papatrix (see fig. 9), a monstrous female *Kunstfigur* compositing Pope, God, and Death that appears lifted from an image by Bosch or a *danse macabre:*

> Face a farded skull of cancerous death. Crown a Triple Tower, from which diminished human figures imprisoned scream and reach. Throne . . . a carved wooden Gothic city in like idiom—scream, strain and prison everywhere. Robe a burden of silver, gold. Skeleton hands bulbous with jewels. (Rudkin, *Triumph* 1)

Fig. 9. David Rudkin, *The Triumph of Death.* Birmingham Repertory Theatre, 1981. Photo: Willoughby Gullachsen. By permission of Birmingham Libraries (UK) (Birmingham Repertory Theatre Archive).

Typical of Rudkin's blend of sacred and profane, the Papatrix disgorges dreamlike doomsday prophecies in the throes of rectal spasms (a sacred birth parody) and later elaborates in gruesome detail on the martyrdom of child crusaders. Rudkin's stage is carnivalistic in the Bakhtinian sense—it is no place of subtlety, hiding, coy indication, or mere symbol but the scene of the body in absolute turmoil. Taking his cues from medieval iconography, Rudkin reinvests the body with the allegorical authority it once possessed, and he thus reinstalls it with a vengeance in the presentational vocabulary of the stage: it becomes again the ravaged icon of a ravaged world. The concreteness of allegory is taken to lengths where even expressionists feared to tread: we are confronted in one scene with bodies torn limb from limb ("meat that had been people, rendered into heaps we cannot read" [*Triumph* 34]), in another scene with an onstage auto-da-fé. Rudkin leaves no doubt that he means this to be a drama of pestilence and cruelty: the recurring character of a fanatical monk is appropriately named "Artaud."[8]

Rudkin's world is one of endless metamorphosis. For instance, one character—if that term is not too quaint—turns from a Christlike figure into a version of the pagan god Pan. It is a grotesque world in which such essential instability is possible, even unavoidable, where sublimity and debasement interpenetrate with explosive force. Rudkin's talent lies exactly in the unsparing juxtaposition of such painful extremes—sanctity and degradation, high-flying eloquence and wrenching inarticulacy. His description of a birth (fittingly the child of a woman about to be burned at the stake) is already drenched in the imagery of death: "In chaos and ugliness the child is born, umbilicus bloodily cut, slimed homunculus hung by the heels for [the] traumatic slap" (*Triumph* 46).

As in Ghelderode, humanity's preordained distance from holiness, its inexorable existence as a transmuted, disfigured figuration of divinity, is Rudkin's true theme, and like Ghelderode he is subject to the aesthetic dictates of modernism that preclude a romantic bridging of this divide and demand instead its fierce exposition. The final scene in *The Triumph of Death* belongs to the figure of "Martin Luther," who is found squatting on a closestool and whose morphology of man and genealogy of morals (like Rudkin's) are very much those of anal fixation—*homo erectus* as an erection from the muck, the Fall of man as a fecal fact. Luther puts into drastic words the discrepant nature of man as body and soul:

> Daily I travail in this tower. Martyr to Man. My face strains up to the deathless chastity of Heaven. My old nick arsehole strains over this sulphurous pit. My head and sty perforce are yoked. Oh for a garden again, in which no shitting and no fucking and no dying. Oh for a transcendent life above, where we shall soil not, neither shall we sperm, not yet decay. (50)

But these are idle redemptory dreams. The world is a "construct from shit," and freedom from the "banked pathology" of history, even salvation, is ironically equated in Rudkin's radical stage metaphor with a loosening of the bowels (51). The yoking, perforce, of "head and sty," which Luther laments, is precisely the fundamental premise of the grotesque condition that this world sustains. Thus Rudkin's scatological fixation articulates a history of physical abjection precisely at odds with Bakhtin's ahistorical celebration of the material lower body. Rudkin's characters, often half-consciously perched on the threshold of modernity or the precarious edge of civilization, are *hommes-bêtes* growing dimly and painfully aware of their mortality: "Awareness. Ape shits, and knows it. Ape fucks; now knows it. And now ape knows he'll die. His Eden's lost; and ape is Man" (50). David Ian Rabey calls *The Triumph of Death* "Rudkin's densest and bleakest Song of Experience," an "intense exploration of the mechanics by which the human imagination is driven into self-amputation and self-mutilation" (102).

In Rudkin's world—which exhibits a remarkably similar texture from play to play—the biocentric impulse is always close beneath the surface and will erupt as a consequence of threat or as a result of regression or coercion. In *The Saxon Shore* (1986), set at the time of the collapse of the Roman Empire, a group of Germanic Saxons, abandoned by their Roman masters, find themselves in the hostile territory of the British Celts, barely protected by the crumbling wall erected by Hadrian centuries earlier. Staging their nightly raids on the Celts, the Saxons metamorphose into rapacious wolves, preying on women and children, triumphing in their kills: "I dragged he off among the thorns. I tore the flesh from his bones wi' teeth and claws. I feasted on he all. But 'shoulder and the stomach part" (1). It is a transformation Rudkin neither fully explains nor wants executed by conventional theatrical means. Rather, it is an "acting problem": "These characters *experience* themselves as wolves" (52). This is felicitous advice, for by emphasizing that the wolves must somehow be generated out of the raw material of the *actors'* performance, Rudkin underlines how close the biocentric energy lies to the *characters'* surface; it is, in fact, right "under the skin."[9] The leader, Cambyses, explains: "We are not of one skin, as mere men are. We have wolfhairs, that by day grow inward" (2). When the protagonist, Athdark, troubled by the confusion of identity his wolf-nature creates in him, kills his secret Celtic lover, Ceiriad, he laments: "I have no name when I come this journey, but snout, tooth, fang, claw. . . . Tell me the name of the man I am!" (41). Only at the end of the play does he rise from his dreamlike state of savagery, "the beginnings of a man" (49). Practically all of Rudkin's characters possess this permeable double skin, this uncertain humanity, capable of instant regression into animality.

In his magnum opus, *The Sons of Light* (1965–77), Rudkin constructs a dramatic world whose structure is again very much indebted to medieval ideology, partitioned into heaven, earth, and hell. The play's earth, however, is Skaranay, a far-flung island in the Hebrides, an "abomination of deformity" (Rudkin, *Sons of Light* 27), inhabited by a tribe of rough-hewn islanders awaiting the arrival of a new pastor with his three sons. Heaven is present only in the mysterious figure of Sir Wendell, a remote squire who owns the island and to whom the islanders are devoted in childlike gratitude; God makes no appearance on this impoverished rock. The play's hell is a bizarre subterranean realm called "The Pit," a dystopian underworld seemingly inspired by Fritz Lang's *Metropolis* in which a crazed Teutonic psychologist, Dr. Nebewohl, reigns as *Über*-father to hordes of juvenile delinquents turned willingly emasculated slaves for his vast construction enterprise. To spur his soulless charges to their endless toil, Nebewohl constructs for them an *ersatz* mythology of redemption, an "alchemical scheme" that promises them that they may overcome their base nature by striving to be transfigured into light by the ghostly "King of Love" for whom they continuously build a never-to-be-finished palace. Nebewohl explains:

> These eat still, these excrete still. They still have their anality to wrestle with. Now understand the logic of the process above: that inflammative assault on the dissonance the subject feels, between his narcissist "self" and his lower function. He yearns for elevation upward, all of him. In the myth he is promised that: justification through work; to ultimate sublimation, through his King his Mediator into pure light. (38)

Nebewohl's crudely efficient system grotesquely conflates Christian dogma, psychoanalysis, and a perversely sexualized fascism in the service of functionality and the suppression of individualism; like *The Triumph of Death, The Sons of Light* is an anticapitalist allegory (see Wilcher 579–81). But unlike Luther in *The Triumph of Death* or Athdark in *The Saxon Shore,* Nebewohl does not despair of human anality or bestiality. To the contrary, like any great ideologue, he draws his power from this unresolved dissonance between "head and sty," higher yearning and abject guilt.

His nemesis in this half-parodic, half-reverent retelling of the Harrowing of Hell is Yescanab, an island elder's son and homosexual misfit who descends angellike into the Pit to rescue Gower, a gold-clad soldier-slave and Nebewohl's putative "son," from his atrophied subterranean existence as a depersonalized *Kunstfigur.* In showing Gower the light, Yescanab also condemns him to death: horrible (and explicitly described) vengeance is extracted from the aberrant Gower by the king (who turns out to be no more than another *Kunstfigur,* a crippled islander) and the fearsome "obscenely alarming" Holst, "a pornographic 'black angel,' ikon of bestial malehood" (22). Finally, however, in a section appropriately entitled "Surrection," Rudkin stages the purgation of this island hell and the liberation of the underworld as an ecstatic eruption, narrated by the play's most pathetic character, Sheila Manatond, now no longer a wild and incoherent "uncertain person" (9) but a young woman woken from her nightmarish past. Such openly redemptive imagery is rare in Rudkin's drama.

Rudkin's more recent plays have been met mostly with bewilderment by critics and audiences, and *The Sons of Light* lays open the problem of Rudkin's grotesque dramaturgy. Christopher Innes complains that "the actions of Rudkin's characters appear unmotivated" (425) by dramatic logic, and indeed this play in particular suffers from referential excess, invoking biblical, Freudian, expressionistic, mythical, sexual, and medieval imagery all at once, weaving violently from naturalism to allegory. I do not agree with Innes, however, that "Rudkin's inversion of good and evil becomes so absolute that it loses moral relevance" and that consequently "regressive primitivism [remains] as the only positive value" (Innes 425). Rudkin's drama is an anguished and often grotesquely phrased attempt to come to terms with human abjection, but its foundation is a strong ethical sensibility. If Rudkin's work appears antimodern, given to primitivism, it is because it is historical in the most fundamentally material (as opposed to materialistic) sense in its insistence that history is first a history of the abject body.

In the words of Rudkin's Luther, "The past is another country. The past is not another country. There is no escape from history" (*Triumph* 51). Rudkin sketches his oxymoronic credo—and, indeed, Ghelderode's—in these words that are also the epigraph to *The Triumph of Death.* Both playwrights assert that while we may comfort ourselves that "[w]e're humanists now," the "antique delirium" (54) of heaven and hell, or of grotesque higher and lower orders, is everywhere ready to erupt out of the surface of smoothed reality.

The work of Ghelderode and Rudkin is suffused with the perception of humanity's final abjection. It is Death who is the true main character in most of their plays. Pastor Bengry in *The Sons of Light* speaks of Death almost tenderly: "Our only love for him must be in our destroying him; no? But Death himself: think, Brother: what's Death's love for a man? But to come for him, to take him and to leave him in ruin in his arms? Poor Death, wouldn't you say? For that to be the only love he knows?" (73). Death, says Ghelderode, is "the only person of whose constancy you can be sure. Crown him with roses!" ("Ostend Interviews" 14). For Ghelderode and Rudkin, theatre means learning to accept the rule of abjection, the Triumph of Death.

Williams, Müller, and Grotesque Revolutions

Recalling a moment during a performance of his play *The Local Stigmatic* (1967) when a woman in the audience "had a fit" in reaction to a scene in which a character gets brutally beaten, Heathcote Williams explains that he became afraid of that "infective threshold" and labored to make his second play, *AC/DC* (1970), "totally self-contained, so that it wouldn't leak in any way." "People," he says, "are frightened of the theatre because it's the nearest thing to talking and touching each other, which is the deepest flash. In the ladder of artificiality, theatre is on the bottom rung" ("Interview" 140). This moment of "infection," of reaching past aesthetics into the visceral, has been sought out by the grotesque theatre since long before Artaud invented the metaphor of pestilence as its analogue, and so it is curious to find Williams, who acknowledges the basic radicalism, the mimetic incontinence of theatre, in retreat from it, advocating an hermeticism attributed mostly to the classical stage.

But Williams recognizes that theatrical "leakage" is as much a liability as it is an asset. Written after a decade of increasingly "leaking" theatre (culminating perhaps in the Performance Garage's notorious *Dionysus in 69*), *AC/DC* acknowledges the importance of aesthetic boundaries in the theatre event, just as it argues for the elimination of these boundaries in interpersonal relations (Williams freely concedes the "schizophrenic" nature of the play).

Heiner Müller's *Hamletmachine* (1977), too, is a piece of hermetic theatre, almost insolently unplayable, daring a director to plumb whatever depths it may possess and to reconstruct its deconstructed characters.[10] Müller's play may not actively seek the prevention of "leakage," but it cannot help itself: its conscious self-mystification gets in the way of any possible emotional charge it could engender. The gesture of closure in these two plays, a kind of anxious aesthetic containment strategy, stands in stark contrast to the radical openness (and open radicalness) of their imagery and argument. In the following I will offer a comparative reading of the two plays, taking little account of the fact that Williams's work has (undeservedly) fallen into obscurity[11] while Müller's is (perhaps also undeservedly) now regarded as paradigmatic of the postmodern play—a label it received to Müller's considerable consternation. I regard them both as exemplary of a postmodern grotesque drama, born with its will-to-assault intact into a world that can no longer be assaulted. Part of their mission, then, is to break down this resistance intra-aesthetically while simultaneously asserting that it can only be accomplished outside of art, in the mind or in the streets.

There is a kind of complementarity in these dissimilar plays that establishes a dialogue. Neither has a conventional, summarizable plot. The reaction to both was initially a stunned and puzzled muteness; they resisted both critics and audiences vigorously. Irving Wardle perceives quite correctly that *AC/DC*'s "shell cannot be cracked with the ordinary critical tools" (Williams, "Interview" 139), and John Russell Taylor is amazed at "how far [Heathcote Williams] has managed to write himself out of his work, to . . . leave it absolutely to speak for itself, without explaining, apologizing, hinting by the flicker of an eyelid at what sort of response we are expected to make" (220). To Ruby Cohn, "access into this oxymoronic drama is arduous" (159). Conversely, Müller has so much written himself into his play that it appears a maze of self-reference, particularly to his own earlier work and biography. The enduring success of the play in the United States, especially on college campuses, is slightly puzzling in light of the fact that *Hamletmachine* is something of a dramatic rebus that presumes specific knowledge of the political culture and climate of East Germany in the 1970s.

Both plays are titled with a technical metaphor; Williams's *AC/DC* is an allusion to alternating current and the "plugged in" strategy of an electric play, Müller's *Hamletmachine* a calculated affront to the keepers of a high culture that *Hamlet* embodies. Williams's play is as excessively long as Müller's is short. *Hamletmachine* is a fragment, as are many of his plays, although Müller objects to the term, calling it "a very dangerous word": "I think the most fragmentary thing is a perfect square because you have to exclude so much to make it perfect, to make it not be fragmentary" (qtd. in Zurbrugg 446). The eight pages of *Hamletmachine* are reportedly the condensed remnants of an earlier two-hundred-page drama.

Both plays are about a world of media, a mediated world, the inescapability of which they simultaneously dramatize and embody—their dominant modus operandi being the quotation or montage. Both take place as much inside a consciousness as outside; they are vaguely expressionistic in technique but profoundly post-Freudian in content. Both end on a kind of self-conscious riddle, an enigma announcing their transcendence of the purely theatrical realm. Williams's central character, Perowne, after undergoing a mind-opening trepanation (or, as the author puts it less delicately, being "fuck[ed] . . . in the head with [an] astral dildo" ("Interview" 143), breaks into unintelligible speech, represented in the text by nine lines of indecipherable hieroglyphics. Müller's protorevolutionary Ophelia, quoting the Manson-follower Susan Atkins, declaims: "Long live hate and contempt, rebellion and death. When she walks through your bedrooms carrying butcher knives you'll know the truth" (Müller, *Hamletmachine* 158).

In its frequent use of the mystical babble and tripped-out lingo of the 1960s and its unsparing verbal frankness, it is easy to mistake *AC/DC* either for a shallow play about an assortment of sociopaths coming off their respective drug-induced fantasies or an instance of mere shock theatre. It is, however, very serious drama, "a play," as Katharine Worth writes, "with such virulent power that one feels it must make a significant impact on the modern tradition" (160). It has not. The play's buzzing, hallucinogenic, polyphonic structure imitates unmediated communication only aesthetically. Its acute torrents of language, stacking planes of reference and allusion, are highly dense and complex, but because it is afraid to "leak," it sometimes appears self-referential, self-enclosed, even self-indulgent.

A key to both plays is perhaps contained in the electromechanical metaphor of their titles. *AC/DC*'s characters refer to themselves and others almost exclusively in technical terms: media slang, psychological jargon, chemical formulae, esoterica of particle physics, and the like. Bodies and minds are dissected, reified, alienated, part of a "cybernetic model" of the world (Williams, *AC/DC* 72). Williams's characters, each typographically distinguished in the script so as to underline their "separate resonance fields," are the warped products of the currents and streams of images and information that flow through them, so much so that they seem—or perceive themselves—to exist only as the nodes and conduits of the media environment that possesses them as much as they inhabit it. (Worth finds the term "elements" more appropriate than "characters" and receives the "horrific impression . . . of man as a soft machine" [161–62]). Written long before the Internet became viable technology, the play seems to anticipate some of the intermedial conditions of the early twenty-first century.

The initial stage setting itself, a pinball arcade, is an allegory of the nervous system, and Williams claims explicitly: "One meaning of the play's title is that human beings are convertible; we are AC/DC" ("Interview" 142). In this postmodern environment, the modernist *Kunstfigur* has undergone some redefinition that mirrors the progress of the instruments of alienation. The previous metaphors of mechanical domination (Toller's hydraulic cripples; Goll's megaphone-mouthed Felix) are replaced by the metaphors of a ubiquitous tyranny of the image in a world of blaring nonpresence, of Baudrillardian simulacra, where everything is a copy of something else and "there is no possibility of living firsthand" (Lahr 171).

Williams's characters are still *Kunstfiguren*, humans created, fed, and sustained by artifice, but their violent oppression is not so much adversarial as it is consensual, "brain surgery without anaesthetics" (*AC/DC* 89). It is their "convertibility" that makes them vulnerable to the unceasing assault of imagery, but that also enables their cathartic transformation. The play exacerbates the metaphor of excretion with which the grotesque play is generally obsessed (Sigmund Freud, in his discussions of anal eroticism, has powerfully linked it to sadism and aggression) by transferring it to the psychic realm; *AC/DC,* Williams claims, sprang from a need for mental catharsis, representing "a process of fighting my way out of a clogged psychic environment: 'where's the toilet in my brain, how do I flush it?'" The play itself is an exercise in psychic toilet training:

> All the characters are trying to do some housework: they're trying to clean up their brains. They've all been plunged into the midst of a giant electronic whispering alley. They're trying to regulate their infective thresholds; and if they can't do it, then they'll seal them off. ("Interview" 140–41)

The true aim of this unclogging and brain-catharsis is to find the authentic self, or rather, selves—the convertible, schizophrenic personae within and through which the world becomes survivable. Williams is not interested in revolutionizing the political or cultural landscape, which he sees as given, but in projecting a radical mutation of human consciousness, a "behavioral leap into future pressures, future speech patterns, future resonances" ("Interview" 144). By all lights, he is successful; psychically, although not technically, he seems to anticipate some of the consequences of the current extension of cyberspace into popular culture.

In the second and pivotal act of the play, "Direct Current," Maurice and Sadie, a black girl, attempt to restore the psychic equilibrium in Maurice's lover, Perowne, who has fallen powerfully under the spell of the ambient energy of fame (some two thousand celebrity pictures cover his walls). Like an autist, Perowne is unable to distinguish between the "basic input" (72) of the world and the "random noise" of the "psychic parasites" that captivate him (76). His friend Maurice, a schizophrenic bent only on getting his "juice" (that is, electroshocks), is helpless, and so Sadie, in what John Lahr called "one of the most brilliant scenes in modern English drama" (174), begins to set up a "By Pass Circuit" (81) for Perowne that culminates in his trepanation. Referring to the celebrity photographs, which she dismantles and neutralizes bit by bit, Sadie says:

> The thing to do is to colonise them *(pointing to the wall)* before they colonise you. Right? And that's Maurice's big mistake. They've really eaten into Maurice. Maurice has short-circuited, and that's just what they want. They WANT you to short-circuit, so they can shove another wire up your toes. (85)

This is Williams's vision of the grotesque demand for "substance" in the mediatized environment, the cannibalism of celebrity. Famous people, Sadie theorizes, exude "electromagnetic waste" and therefore upset the "ecological balance": they are "predatory sewage," "hustling Feedback" (89, 92).

A conflict of the public and the private, of inside and out, as I have previously noted, often marks the grotesque constitution. For Ronald

Hayman, *AC/DC* represents exactly a "tug-of-war . . . between individual identity and collective identity" (74). More precisely, it attempts to render either category obsolete. Sadie emerges as the agent of a positive grotesque, a kind of hip shaman (Williams refers to her as a "witch") whose method of restoring a balanced identity is to counterattack, to generate an environment of unmediated "total access" (98). Her resolution is genuine (and genuinely female) in both a psychological and sexual sense; she repudiates Maurice's "territory-sex-adrenaline-bullshit" (109) and finally uses the photographs to "masturbate everybody's reverberations into neutral" (111).

Sadie's prolonged, ritualistic masturbation scene and the trepanation that follows are among the most difficult scenes in the modern theatre to stage (and also, one assumes, to endure). "Good deeds," Sadie finds, "can often be very shocking" (130)—like the play itself, these actions lead into "virgin territory" (126). The metaphor's sexual connotation is no accident.

Hamletmachine, like *AC/DC,* derives its first impulse from the author's need for expurgation and catharsis, to "flush the toilet in his brain." By his own admission, it is Müller's attempt to destroy *Hamlet,* a text that had long obsessed him. Yet the metaphor in the title of Müller's *Hamletmachine* is not merely gratuitous provocation. The play is a "Hamlet-machine" in a twofold sense. The first is its almost mechanical imitation of the five-act play, but as in one of Marcel Duchamps's "ready-mades," the iconic artifacts of modernism, the visible structure of the plundered and dysfunctional (dramatic) machine out of which the play is constructed only underscores the obsolescence of that machine itself. For beneath its façade of orderliness lies an entropic contraption. In terms again reminiscent of *AC/DC,* Robert Wilson refers to *Hamletmachine* as a "labyrinth" and "pinball [machine]" (qtd. in Zurbrugg 447).

As in *AC/DC,* the unfree characters of *Hamletmachine* are confined, obsessed, oppressed by ubiquitous images. Ophelia's transformation from victim to revolutionary in the play begins with the destruction of the "tools of [her] captivity," the domestic environment with bed, table, chair, and window, and lastly "the photos of the men I loved and who used me" (*Hamletmachine* 54–55), the "mugs of the manipulators," as Hamlet later calls them (and among whom the author counts himself—the Hamlet-actor is at one point instructed to tear up Müller's photograph in a gesture that has attained emblematic status for the postmodern theatre). Like Williams's, Müller's cryptic play contains an inordinate amount of references and quotations—at times it is positively overwhelmed by them—as if to advertise both the plethora of connections it purports to make between Shakespeare's play and contemporary history and its own deliberate (artful) inauthenticity, the impossibility of any longer framing history, conceived as the "petrification of a hope" (56), in an autonomous plot. The time span between *Hamlet* and *Hamletmachine* is marked, for Müller, by "the Long March through the hells of the Enlightenment, through the bloody swamps of ideology. Hitler's geographical error: genocide in Europe instead of, as is usual practice today and tomorrow, in Africa Asia America" (Müller, *Gesammelte Irrtümer* 170).

The essence of Shakespeare's *Hamlet* is contained in *Hamletmachine*'s scene 1, "Family Scrapbook," which makes short work, literally, of the model play's plot by transposing it into a postwar/postapocalyptic setting in "the ruins of Europe": Hamlet pries open his father's (Stalin's?) coffin and feeds his flesh to the bystanding "bums"; Claudius and Gertrude fornicate on the coffin; Hamlet taunts the ghost ("you've got one hole too many"). Revenge on Claudius will not be taken. History is stasis; there is no reason for continuation:

> Tomorrow morning has been cancelled.
> SHALL I
> AS IS THE CUSTOM STICK A PIECE OF IRON INTO
> THE NEAREST FLESH OR THE SECOND BEST
> TO LATCH UNTO IT SINCE THE WORLD IS SPINNING
>
> (54)

But Hamlet's insight into the futility of violence is short-lived. Upon the entrance of Horatio, Hamlet reverts to ruinous logic, rapes his mother, and sends her off to her wedding, all the while aware of the contrived nature of his situation. "I knew you're an actor," he says to Horatio (who also doubles for Polonius); "I am too. I'm playing Hamlet" (54). Hamlet is Müller's metaphor for the self-possessed intellectual trapped in his assigned role, whose post-Enlightenment cynicism makes him cognizant of the failings of his conception of (historical) action but who is yet unable to avoid their ceaseless repetition.

Scene 4 (the play's longest) is the exploration of this paradox situation, an extended monologue by "the actor playing Hamlet" about an uprising modeled on Hungary's 1956 revolt (but representing any revolution) in which he finds himself, in schizophrenic dispersion, on both sides of the barricades. The scene—which contains some transparent resonances of Müller's own autobiography—establishes the impossibility of historical progress in the absence of a true countervailing force to the status quo. Hamlet/the Hamlet-actor is confronted always and only by his own countenance; the revolutionary cataclysm reduces to auto-aggressive behavior; all action is condemned to remain purely self-referential: "Choking with nausea, I shake my fist at myself who stands behind the bullet-proof glass. Shaking with fear and contempt, I see myself in the crowd pressing forward, foaming at the mouth, shaking my fist at myself. I string up my uniformed flesh by my own heels" (56). Faced with the cyclical nature of history and his impotence in the face of its eternal recurrence, the intellectual reacts with "nausea," a longing for exile, retreat, self-encapsulation, painlessness, mechanical comforts, the end of history: "I force open my sealed flesh. I want to dwell in my veins, in the marrow of my bones, in the maze of my skull. I retreat into my entrails. . . . My thoughts are lesions in my brain. My brain is a scar. I want to be a machine. Arms for grabbing Legs to walk on, no pain no thoughts" (57). The wish to exchange reflection for function, consciousness for oblivion, to dehumanize oneself and become a *Kunstfigur* instead of an active subject of history, is an essentially grotesque response to the impasse of Enlightenment thinking, as Müller emphasizes by his invocation of physical metaphors. Hamlet's "nausea" seemingly alludes to an existentialist reflex (Jean-Paul Sartre's Roquentin, to wit), but Müller's reference may actually be to Nietzsche's brief but pointed analysis of *Hamlet* in *The Birth of Tragedy*, in which nausea is construed as the irrepressible impulse robbing the hero of any initiative once he has "gained knowledge." Nietzsche confidently produces the antidote: "Here, when the danger to his will is greatest, *art* approaches as a saving sorceress, expert at healing" (*Birth* 60). Clearly, Müller is less sanguine than Nietzsche about the power of art. "I am not Hamlet," he has his actor intone, "I don't take part any more. My words have nothing to tell me anymore. My thoughts suck the blood out of the images. My drama doesn't happen anymore" (*Hamletmachine* 56).

Hamletmachine, in large part, is a confirmation of such skepticism; its images themselves too often fall prey to the vampirism of overwrought cogitation, and its drama refuses to occur. Such is the case when Müller attempts to contrive a scenic analogue summarizing the Hamlet/intellectual's response to the predicament of history. Three naked women appear onstage, representing Marx, Lenin, and Mao. While they quote in unison a famous Marxian precept ("The main point is to overthrow all existing conditions . . ."), the Hamlet-actor slips back into character, verbally transforms himself, Atreus-like, into a "bloated bloodhound," and splits their heads with an ax, whereupon the scene immediately turns into an "ice age," the author's shorthand for late capitalism.

The odd mixture of allegory and virulence is meant to convey Müller's ambivalence about the idolatry accorded the prophets of Communism and simultaneously about the butchery their bourgeois rejection entails. But the image seems both gratuitous and lifelessly calculated, a thundering cliché. Such matings of the self-consciously meaningful and the trivial spike the text of *Hamletmachine.* Designed as radical metaphors, they become didactic allegories and often fizzle. In a transparent borrowing from surrealist imagery, Ophelia's heart in scene 2 is a clock, which she tears out in a bid for self-liberation. In scene 3, dead philosophers, their tombstones turned lecterns, throw books at Hamlet; Ophelia, in the makeup of a whore, steps out of a coffin labeled "HAMLET 1" to do a striptease; a "madonna" with radiant "breast cancer" appears; and so forth.

Nonetheless, grotesque metaphors, particularly those employing the motif of bodily orifices, provide the underpinning of the play's political discourse; they concretize the Hamlet/intellectual's attempt to close the "holes" (gaps, variances) in the catastrophic but continuous current of history, to permit no alternate wellspring. Thus he formulates drastically that "[w]omen should be sewed up—a world without mothers. We could butcher each other in peace and quiet" (53). He mocks his slain father's superfluous hole. He cries, committing incestuous rape, "A MOTHER'S WOMB IS NOT A ONE-WAY STREET" (54). Finally, he despairs of (but does not resist) a teleology that compels his "STUMBLING FROM HOLE TO HOLE TOWARDS THE FINAL/HOLE" (58).

What springs forth from the orifice in Bakhtinian profusion is a suppressed lower order, a threat to smoothed perceptions, quite literally. For, in Müller's startling image, the "poorer inhabitants of the capital"—the *lumpenproletariat* of the coming revolution—dwell in "the spacy [sic] nostrils and auditory canals, in the creases of skin and uniform" of the toppled statue of their once powerful leader (56). As absences, blind spots, unthinkables in the *episteme* of prevailing authority, holes are the perfect signifiers of a revolt about to erupt, for they are the open wounds inescapably created by an economy of oppression. "Somewhere," muses Hamlet, "bodies are opened so I can be alone with my blood" (57).

It is in consequent reaction to Hamlet's construction of the epistemology of the hole and his subsequent gestures of closure that Ophelia, who stands for victimized women, for the oppressed, must emancipate herself from the ca(pti)vity of diminution and absence into which she has been placed (we see her first in an "enormous room" [54]) by creating a fissure or discontinuity in history—a gap—and by inserting herself in it precisely by refusing to submit to any further insertions herself: "I eject all the sperm I have received. I turn the milk of my breasts into lethal poison. I take back the world I gave birth to. I choke between my thighs the world I gave birth to. I bury it in my womb" (58). Indeed, the butcher knife she verbally arms herself with a few moments later, clearly an implement for the production of painful holes, underlines her newfound autonomy in this regard. Here, she has snatched the symbolic Phallus from Hamlet and put an end to all such phantasmal displacements in a manner that would surely intrigue Jacques Lacan, and she intends to "stick a piece of iron into the nearest flesh" (Hamlet's earlier quote) exactly because it is not "the custom." However, Müller's attitude is more ambiguous than this simple gesture of revolt implies. While Ophelia (sitting in a wheelchair and now identifying herself as Electra) takes up arms in "the name of the victims," two men in white coats wrap gauze around her until she is motionless and leave her alone onstage. The lingering image is one of defeat: Ophelia, the victims, the revolt, have been whited out. History has been corrected.

The end of *AC/DC* is similarly concerned with holes, both physical (Perowne's trepanned head) and semantic (his hieroglyphic speech). Both plays in fact conclude with gestures of revolt, but the difference is marked. Trephine and butcher knife are both sharp and violent instruments of catharsis, yet one is directed inward, the other outward. Herein lies the programmatic distinction between Williams and Müller: the first is concerned with psychic (self-)liberation, the latter with revolutionary politics. Still, these agendas exist interdependently, for while Williams colors his metaphor of mental oppression with political language, referring to "psychic capitalism," Müller's bid for social reform is similarly grounded in his rejection of the terrorism of the image:

Television The daily nausea Nausea
Of prefabricated babble Of decreed cheerfulness
How do you spell GEMÜTLICHKEIT
Give us this day our daily murder
Since thine is nothingness Nausea

(*Hamletmachine* 57)

But the "catharsis" effected by knife and trephine is pathological; blissful self-annihilation or indiscriminate murder seem the given alternatives. The audience sitting in Müller's or Williams's theatre is no community that can receive cathartic restoration of its affective balance, at least not yet. However, the apocalyptic language masks a strand of optimism or utopianism in both plays that identifies them as postmodern only in the stylistic sense ("true" postmodernism having dispensed with the notion of history as a meaningful concept, and therefore having little use for optimism).

There is an affective and effective moment of collusion in each of the plays, in the manner in which they attempt to constitute their audience and make it the object and paradigm of a new theatrical transaction, a transaction involving transformation or conversion instead of mere assault. Müller envisions a Dionysian theatre, both "house of pleasure" and "chamber of horrors," which is at the vanguard of a transformation of the audience into a "collective" (the conventional Marxist term takes on a different, almost ecstatic meaning here). Harking back to expressionist terminology, Müller summons up the "alternative of the NEW MAN" who can be born only through a kind of *sparagmos:* the "tearing apart, death, or Caesarian section" of the old individual, for which Ophelia's butcher knife is the tool (Müller, "Brief" 103). Heathcote Williams's New Human is similarly the product of a "Caesarian section" or rather trepanation (another form of *sparagmos*), born in the revolt against the "psychic chauvinism" of the image, against the hegemony of logical and "Linear Man." Williams's re-formed humanity is pan-psychic, schizophrenic, capable of "direct brain to brain contact" ("Interview" 143).

Both plays turn on a fervent desire to find or create a new mythology, to eradicate our obsession with the profusion of ersatz mythologies and to get at the "basic input" *(AC/DC)*, the "truth" murderous Ophelia prophesies. They represent a powerful cultural desire for a breach with past and present orthodoxies that, because it is so inevitably violent and revolutionary instead of evolutionary, finds it has an irresistible affinity for the grotesque image. The first step of this revolt, which the drama must first seek to instigate in aesthetic terms, is the destruction of what obscures our access—historical or psychic parasites. But only Williams's play manages to turn the destructive energy into a regenerative impulse; Lahr even believes that Perowne's trepanning is "a kind of resurrection" in the Christian sense (180). It is certainly a literal metaphor for the opening of the mind, a radical "utopian heresy" (*AC/DC* 123).

Such heresy comes to fruition in the revolt of the victim, as embodied in the victory of woman. Worth notes that the finale of *AC/DC* is "the climax to an elaborate sexual ritual out of which the female principle has emerged triumphant" (166)—although perhaps, minding Williams's pivotal thesis that humans are totally "convertible," terms such as male or female lose their meaning at that point of synthesis. ("AC/DC," after all, is a colloquialism for bisexuality as well.) The play goes full circle in its rearrangement (or redefinition) of sexual relations. What had been attempted by the characters at the beginning of the play (although in a silly, self-conscious, image-hungry way) now becomes possible: a "Mongolian Cluster Fuck" in the photomat of the pinball arcade, initially no more than a carnal stunt, gives way to the complete psycho-sexual liberation of the galactic hermaphrodite Perowne, in whom man and woman, physical and mental coalesce ("every cell of his body" becomes "a brain cell" [136]). Indeed, Sadie's trepanning operation is meant to reopen the atrophied "third eye" of Perowne that allows him the view onto a "Lost Paradise" of universal connections (130).

Here, Müller's play runs sharply contrary. Such a pan-sexual conversion is attempted by Hamlet as well when he begs Ophelia in the scene entitled "scherzo," "I want to be a woman." She obliges, but unlike Sadie she is no shaman. The transformation is purely external: "Hamlet dresses in Ophelia's clothes, Ophelia puts the make-up of a whore on his face" (55). Hamlet poses lasciviously and dances a wild dance with the angelic Horatio; no mystical liberation here, no paradise regained, only a transvestite horror-show. Müller clearly does not regard his characters as simply "convertible."

The marked difference in Williams's and Müller's conception of change is grounded in their divergent views of history. For Müller, the materialist, history remains an objective category amenable to revolutionary transformation, even if it appears, like his play, a jumble of catastrophic occurrences. *Hamletmachine,* he remarks, "is about the results of missed occasions, about history as a story of chances lost. That is more than plain disappointment, it is the description of the petrification of a hope" (qtd. in Teraoka 106).

Williams's idiosyncratic concept of time hinges on his rejection of causality; the more enlightened of his "convertible" humans partake of a schizophrenic simultaneity to which the causal nexus is wholly secondary and trivial. Where Williams spreads out a tableau of futurity characterized by the desirable utopia of "total access," for Müller total access amounts to total barbarity. Müller's brand of sound and stolid progressivism clashes fiercely with Williams's far more radical position, which he admits could easily lead to the detection of "fascistic tendencies" in his play ("Interview" 141). Indeed, the atmosphere of *AC/DC* is marked by the kind of political and ethical ambiguity that is no longer resolvable into preformed ideological categories; it seems the startling preview of a narrative genre that became a quintessential genre of the 1980s: cyberpunk science fiction.[12]

Not coincidentally, *Hamletmachine* and *AC/DC* each aspire to an Artaudian *mise-en-scène,* and they exemplify the principal division within Artaud's legacy quite well—one being true to the spirit of his writings, one to the letter. There is a critical consensus that Williams comes closer; Hayman sees in his play a "genuine example of the Theatre of Cruelty" (76), and Lahr claims that "[i]n the intensity and proportion of the psychic struggle, *AC/DC* assumes the heroic dimensions Artaud wrote about but never achieved" (178). Certainly *AC/DC* provides the ritualistic energy, the incantatory language, the synaesthetic spectacle, and the vision of a human totality ("total man") and of a "direct communication" between audience and action envisioned in Artaud's manifestos.

Herbert Blau credits the "cannibalistic text of *Hamletmachine*" with achieving something close to Artaud's vision, "to the degree that the mutilated body, a finger, a hand, a head, is felt through the mediascape as something more than fantasy, not mere simulation" (*To All Appearances* 81). But for the most part, the play seems unfortunately bent on imitating the weakest link in Artaud's writing, scenarios like *Spurt of Blood* or *The Conquest of Mexico,* which force a measure of imagistic concretion that leads almost inevitably to a certain quaintly surreal transparent obscurantism. The stagings of Robert Wilson have taken Müller's text and often discarded the implied imagery, replacing it with surreal imagery of Wilson's devising that frequently bears little relationship to the meaning; Müller, with a kind of ironic indulgence, endorsed this usage of his texts as theatrical palimpsests as if to signal the exhaustion of theatrical signification altogether.

The radical nature of Williams's and Müller's visions proves ultimately unfulfillable; in fact—much like Artaud with his *Cenci* and *Spurt of Blood*—they have been accused of falling back into the conventionalities of dramaturgy they are most trying to avoid. The British director William Gaskill has compared Heathcote Williams to William Congreve, and John Russell Taylor agrees that Williams is "regarded in some respects as our most advanced dramatist, and yet in his meticulous concern for the written word, his almost painfully acute sense of style, he could also be seen as the most traditional of them all" (222). Nicholas Zurbrugg comments that there is "something surprisingly unsurprising about the obscurity of the monologues and dialogues in *Hamletmachine.*" Müller's text, he claims, "does little more than subvert traditional dramatic rhetoric by converting its well-jointed realist linearity into disjointed surrealist linearity" (Zurbrugg 443, 448). And Müller himself could claim (with some irony, of course) that *Hamletmachine* can be read "as a five-act play, completely classical in its dramaturgy" (qtd. in Teraoka 87).

The plays have fared very differently: *AC/DC* has become invisible; it has disappeared without ever receiving an adequate production; it is out of print; and surveys of modern British drama ignore it. *Hamletmachine* has become the cause célèbre of European dramatic postmodernism and—in the English-speaking world at least—carries the weight of Müller's posthumous theatrical reputation almost single-handedly. While it is incessantly produced, indeed overexposed, the productions seem, by all indications, more troubled by the play than informed by it. (Müller speculated on the popularity of this enigmatic play: "First, it's short. You don't have to read a lot. At least it gives the impression that you don't have to read a lot. Also, the title is very attractive. 'Hamlet' and 'Machine,' that could both be from an advertisement. Add to that that Hamlet is a great symbol for the loss of hope and expresses everything felt by those who are somehow disappointed" [*Gesammelte Irrtümer* 103].)

Both plays take on more than drama can solve. Williams advocates a kind of spiritual liberation that, if taken to its consequent extreme, would render the vehicle of its advocacy—linear, discursive, imagistic theatre—obsolete. Müller constructs a revolutionary hypothesis in which truth and truth-telling, the Enlightenment imperative of the theatre, can no longer be conceived of as an aesthetic function but only as a visceral and violent, extratheatrical act: "When she walks through your bedrooms carrying butcher knives you'll know the truth." Blau writes:

> [T]he self-incriminating ferocity of *Hamletmachine* suggests that the lesions are unlikely to be healed as the site of revolution shifts to preindustrialized parts of the world and to other categories, such as race and gender, in the imbecilic spectacle and bloodbath of history. Which requires its quota of bodies like Jarry's debraining machine. (*To All Appearances* 81)

This ineluctable paradox marks both plays in the last analysis as schizophrenic drama; they may seek closure only as nonclosure, one by self-fragmentation, the other by self-transcendence.

Criminals and Victims

Alas! there were days when all men of action appeared to him as toys in the hands of grotesque madmen; he laughed terribly about this, for a long time.

—Arthur Rimbaud, *A Season in Hell*

The grimness of the grotesque is part of its play; we should not underestimate the pleasure we take in grotesque figures. By casting monstrous criminal characters as agents of the grotesque, playwrights can vicariously transgress against social and aesthetic pieties and transform the fictional realm in the wake of a character who imposes his excessive laws on the world, as may from time to time be our own secret wish. Freud observed, with his customary clinical precision: "In general, it may perhaps be said that the neurotic instability of the public and the dramatist's skill in avoiding resistances and offering fore-pleasures can alone determine the limits set upon the employment of abnormal characters on the stage" (*Standard Edition* 7:310). There appear to be few limits. Daniel Gerould argues that the comedic lure of despotic brutality in the theatre is age-old and proven (among other plays, he mentions *Ubu Roi,* Witkiewicz's *Gyubal Wakazar* [1921], and Brecht's *Arturo Ui* [1941]): "The arbitrary exercise of absolute power by a deranged tyrant can be a source of comic pleasure to an audience—and comic, not in spite of the arbitrariness, but precisely because of it. The ridiculous and the terrifying coalesce" (4). But the comic impulse is not triggered by the utterly and meaninglessly bizarre. Grotesque violence, in fact, must never be arbitrary, though it may seek, for greater effect, to hide its directedness behind an apparent absence of motive.

Atreus's criminal self-fashioning, his ambition to become perpetrator of the perfect amoral crime, must be so understood; so also Iago's teasing justification for his villainy, or that of Marlowe's Barabas. All have sufficient motive for retribution but aspire to—or construct—a motiveless malignity by means of an excess of criminality. In denying causality and motivation, those staples of dramatic logic, the grotesque character opens avenues for the manifestation of what I have called radical ironic metaphor—the startling presence of what should not be there in a moral (that is, just) universe but must be in a grotesque one. In the case of Thyestes and Othello, the crime is essentially inflicted by the victim upon himself within the bounds of a logic of events completely designed *for* the victim; there is a self-referential, ontological inevitability to it that is both deeply horrifying (because it is fused with the identity of the victim and thus impossible to distance) and farcically funny in the manner of a predictably self-destructing machine.

Far from being arbitrary, then, the grotesque crime is indeed most acutely logical. What seems arbitrary can be merely a petty impulse monstrously magnified. Pa Ubu's shocking "debraining" of the Polish noblemen, for instance, though excessive, is not at all inconsistent; it is quite the logical action of a despot endowed with sparse intellectual power himself. Such a sudden shift from one perfectly acceptable logic of action (the diurnal or "normal") to another logic (the nocturnal or grotesque) that is more insidious but equally incontrovertible generates a certain formal, if horrific, pleasure. And perhaps the pleasure of these displays emanates too from the fact that such grotesque crimes restore a logic and an imagery, however warped, to proceedings that have become ever more unspeakable, because they are unattainable to mimesis—proceedings of power. The imagery of political power now by and large eludes a drama whose symbolic vocabulary descends from the Renaissance. "Art," says Dürrenmatt, "penetrates only to the victims, if it penetrates to people at all; it can no longer reach the powerful" (*Theater* 60).

Although the comical tyrant is a special case of the grotesque figure, in his realm we find preformed that particular segregation of the grotesque world by which its characters are always defined: the inbuilt dichotomy—which is also a perverse symbiosis—of criminals and victims. In modern drama, says Lukács, the "realization of personality will be achieved only at the price of suppressing the personalities of others (which, in turn, require for their realization the ruin of the personalities of others)" ("Sociology" 439).

If Lukács is right, it stands to reason that modern patterns render a strict separation of the two categories, oppressor and oppressed, to some degree arbitrary. Every victimizer also seems victim within the horizon of moral relativity. By implication, criminal and victim are one and the same. Here too the principle of isomorphy, of the monstrous double, rules. (Who could deny that antagonistic pairings such as Pentheus and Dionysus or Atreus and Thyestes are symbiotic in such an intimate way that they form a kind of dramatic biotope?) Certainly the distinction is not moral, for the grotesque display apparently thoroughly obliterates the grounds of moral thinking. Who is attacker, who prey, is not determined by any superiority of principle but merely by temporary advantage. In an entirely grotesque universe, the one brutalized is always ready to brutalize in turn. There is no appreciable ethical difference between Pentheus and Dionysus, or Atreus and Thyestes, or even, in the end, between Aaron or Tamora and Titus. There are only strategic advantages. Innocence is merely a sentimental term for ignorance, as decorum is for the absence of biocentric wit. This fundamental pattern of grotesque characterology is already inscribed into the double physique of Jarry's Ubu. Linda Klieger Stillman comments on this mixed message of Ubu's body:

> Circles and spheres serve often, in Jarry's oeuvre, as metaphor for the self shielded in its pure, primeval essence from exterior vicissitudes. Ubu's sharply pointed head, however, in the shape of a cone, adds another dimension to his body. Sharpness, in Ubu's case, corresponds to the function of sadistic penetration. (45)

We are reminded of Nietzsche's controversial dichotomy between *Herrenmoral* (master morality) and *Sklavenmoral* (slave morality) and his stipulation that in "all the higher and more mixed [that is, modern] cultures," these two ostensibly distinct categories can "occur directly alongside each other—even in the same human being, within a *single* soul" (*Beyond* 260). The grotesque criminal, or agent, strives for the total autonomy of his crime, but the assertion of that "master" autonomy is paradoxically tied to an ethos of enslavement, for the purview of his actions is defined by its very lack of freedom: he may only decide whether to dominate or to submit, to be brutalizer or brutalized. Ubu, who is both king and slave, fully confirms this observation.

Throughout this study, I have been pursuing mainly two variants of the grotesque character, the biocentric character and the *Kunstfigur,* or the man-as-animal and the man-as-puppet. These variants, which are the extremes of the classical (centrifugal) and of the romantic (centripetal) concept of character, often appear conflated in modern drama. Georg Büchner's Woyzeck, suffering an instrumental reduction of his human potentiality, is both puppet and monster. Or compare a modern counterpart to Woyzeck, Howard Brenton's serial killer, Christie, in *Christie in Love,* who confirms Hannah Arendt's Eichmann stereotype: a "feeble, ordinary man blinking through his pebble glasses" (Brenton 2). The inspector who arrests Christie observes, with mounting disappointment: "Why can't a mass murderer be just a bit diabolical? Why can't a pervert like you, already in the annals of nastiness, have fangs or something?" (20). The reason is that this monster, as Brenton takes pains to illustrate, is also a victim of a prurient and repressive society; thus he lets Christie make his first appearance wearing "a grotesque mask, a papier mâché head that distorts his features," but immediately contradicts the Gothic expectations of "nice shivers, easy oohs and aahs" (13, 2).

Indeed, in the modern grotesque, the division between criminal and victim, although not arbitrary, is mainly allegorical. One may think, for instance, of Boris Vian's parable *The Empire Builders* (1959), with its archetypal victim (and putative *pharmakos*), the "schmürz," and the tyrannical father who abuses it, only to finally be himself revealed as the play's true *pharmakos.* This dichotomy fulfills the structural requirements of fiction, especially drama (in which conflict can best be shown as an opposition of characters), but in truth in the modern grotesque play, one may have to speak more accurately of victimization as the preeminent ontic quality of the dramatic environment—the way the dramatic world is indisputably set up. Or, to paraphrase Max Scheler's insight into the phenomenology of the tragic, mutual subjugation is an essential element of the (grotesque) universe itself. This is the universe the grandmother in Büchner's *Woyzeck* so painfully invokes in her grim fairy tale, in which the moon is "a piece of rotten wood," the sun a "wilted sunflower," the stars "little golden flies stuck up there like the shrike sticks 'em on the blackthorn," and the earth, finally, an "overturned pot" (Büchner 218).

Since historically the grotesque character may be construed as an extension of the allegorical "vice" figure, stage tradition has it that we recognize this character by a limp or physical deformation. There is a consistent trope or archetype in literature of the "unfinished man," as expressed perhaps most forcefully in the lines of Richard III, who finds himself "[d]eform'd, unfinish'd, sent before my time / Into this breathing world, scarce half made up" (*Richard III* 1.1.20–21). Richard is what I referred to earlier—in regard to the imaginary humanoid monsters of medieval folklore—as an "allegory of want." Edmund Burke had observed that "*deformity* is opposed not to beauty, but to the *complete common form.* If one of the legs of a man be found shorter than the other, the man is deformed; because there is something wanting to complete the whole idea we form of a man" (75). Even King Ubu's "hyperphysical barrel body" is incomplete in its grandiosity—it is the *manqué* shape of the sphere, the perfect angelic form. But in this state of want, the character almost inescapably becomes the impersonation of an appetite.

Ubu, tyrannical as he appears, is so not out of a genuine inner impulse (the Nietzschean will-to-power) but precisely out of the *absence* of one. He is purely reactive in a creaturely way; his is a ferocious passivity, and in him we recognize the archetypal formation of that modern character whose will is in truth want and in whom what appears as appetite is the absence of "substance." He can be measured best in opposition to the true classical character in whom essence, impulse, and action are completely congruent. The grotesque agent perennially wants, in the double sense of the verb, what he lacks.

In one of his seminal essays, Erich Auerbach speaks of the concept of the *figura,* in the sense not only of rhetorical figures but also of the "figurative" use of that term in connection with the medieval biblical exegesis that assumed that sacred history takes place in a series of prefigurations and fulfillments (Adam-Noah-Christ, and the like). "Figural interpretation," says Auerbach, "establishes a connection between two events or persons, the first of which signifies not only itself but also the second, while the second encompasses or fulfills the first." Thus both the prefigurer and the fulfiller, like the components of a sign, are thinkable only in combination, as signifier and signified. Individually, they have "something provisional and incomplete about them" (53, 58).

The grotesque topos of "unfinished man" may be thought of in reference to this teleological concept of the *figura.* The character of lack is in search of a salutary counterfigure to whom he stands in a position of inferiority, of whom he is, as it were, a lower order or monstrous double. The specific notion of the grotesque character enters not only where this fulfillment is unattainable but also where the deficiency is compensated for in excess, by the act of excessive self-fulfillment, which is identical to an act of self-filling, or consumption of "substance" (in the sense of both Skulsky and Kenneth Burke). In other words, the grotesque figure (or *figura*) makes up for that missing other, in whom it could find itself completed, by the excessive assertion of self; or else it finds the *figura* it seeks and projects itself toward in its victim, accounting for the conspicuous "doubling" of victimizer and victim (Dionysus and Pentheus, Atreus and Thyestes, and so on).

Geoffrey Harpham finds evidence of the grotesque specifically where "the substitution of an object or a representation" occurs, in which the substitute is "analogous to a perfect original in every way, but in all points inferior, low, or structurally simpler, so that [it] stands in an inverse relation to the original" (125). But only when the "shades of meaning between copy and archetype" (Auerbach 49) in the *figura* build to a tension that needs release, when the inferior usurps the superior and the deformation of the archetype *becomes* the archetype, does the grotesque figure appear.

Such a potentially aggressive inversion, in particular of heroic and holy archetypes, is the mythical figure of the Trickster, a ubiquitous and ambivalent presence in the lore of most cultures. In Carl Jung's words, the Trickster is "[g]od and animal at once. He is both sub-human and superhuman, a bestial and divine being" (143). Like the fool, the Trickster maintains an unequivocally marginal position in the stratification of the literary universe—a marginality that simultaneously emboldens him, for he is given the license to transgress by virtue of his putative powerlessness. As such, the Trickster is a generically containable figure whose transgressions are subject to a certain regularity and function (as are fools in Shakespeare); but if the Trickster breaks out of this archetypal box and tyrannically takes over a play, the result is the grotesque character in the sense in which I have described it. Designated by convention as the outcast *(pharmakos)*, he turns the tables in a bold move of self-empowerment. This is the case with Atreus, Aaron, and finally Titus, who are (or become) Tricksters, but also with Pa Ubu, Methusalem, Simon Laquedeem, and Sadie.

Michael Goldman has seen a parallel between Jarry's Ubu and a popular Trickster figure in the dramatic performances of the Orokaiva tribesmen of New Guinea, the *samuna,* who is an equal mixture of the antic, clownish, violent, and menacing (41–43). The two principal elements that distinguish the Trickster, a "cunning form of intelligence" and a "grotesqueness of the body imagery," often seem to obtain in the case of the grotesque figure as well (Koepping 194). Dürrenmatt's visiting Trickster, Claire Zachanassian, for instance, could not be more aptly described. There may be some argument about the "intelligence" of figures such as Ubu or Methusalem, but it is difficult to deny their native cunning—call it biocentric wit.

It is possible to establish a difference between the grotesque *figure* and the grotesque *character.* The hallmark of this distinction is that (in the simple but substantially accurate terms of E. M. Forster) one is "flat," the other "round." Round and flat characters are usually relegated to fixed positions within the generic spectrum; tragic fate and tragic empathy demand a complex (round) character, while comic action inevitably thrives on the single-minded, almost abstract flatness of its protagonists. In the grotesque drama we often find these attributes disturbingly commingled or redistributed: the (flat) grotesque figure is the dominant, brutalizing, ultimately victorious presence. Its one-sided, manic determination to find figural self-fulfillment does not subject it to ridicule (as the Bergsonian comic code would demand) but is instead the true source of its amoral energy. The grotesque figure, such as Atreus, Tamora, Aaron, Ubu, and so forth, has either systematically dehumanized himself or herself or is unendowed with humanity in the first place. Dürrenmatt describes Claire Zachanassian as moving "outside the human pale": "[S]he has grown into someone unalterable and rigid, contains within herself no further possibility of development and she, in consequence, is cast in a mould of stone, she is the one to be represented as a stone idol" (*The Visit* 106–7). The grotesque figure's intrinsic agenda of dehumanization demands that it bring the victim to its level, that is, reduce and flatten the character of the victim until it becomes purely figural and empathy is forestalled. This is the force that makes Alfred Ill a bargaining chip for economic recovery in *The Visit,* Galy Gay a "human fighting machine" in Brecht's *Man Is Man,* or the soldiers of Toller's *Transfiguration* "clockwork figures."

Flat and round may also appear in odd and disquieting mixtures, as in Brenton's *Christie in Love.* Brenton describes his style as a "fundamental dislocation," a description that also applies to the construction of his characters, in which disjunctions and gaps between flat and round being become visible. The Inspector and the Constable in this play, says Brenton, are conventional "stage coppers": "But they have 'sudden lights,' unpredictable speeches beyond the confines of pastiche. As if a cardboard black and white cut-out suddenly reaches out a fully fleshed, real hand. It's a bathos technique. . . . It is very cruel" (3). Brenton might just as well be calling this cruelty an "alienation technique," for the peculiar British pairing of Brechtian and Artaudian precepts is formidably embodied in his work.

Grotesqueness in a character or figure announces itself in a certain disproportion it assumes or occupies in regard to its host play. Any dramatic world is implicitly equipped for a certain "size" of character; its act-scene-agent ratios are ascribed to it by style or genre. A grotesque monster-figure like Atreus, Tamburlaine, or Ubu is *in excess* of his play (act and agent, agent and scene are configured in an irrational relation). But there is also the opposite of such excess, the irrational disappearance of the character, as in Büchner's *Woyzeck* (which for that reason alone stands as one of the earliest examples of genuinely modern drama).

What we find in this *démontage* of the modern grotesque character is the shocking absence of a vital center in which the intangible quality of personal identity is preserved and maintained. Identity is revealed as elusive and illusory, a mere amalgam of contextual forces and circumstance. While the Greek tragedians, strictly speaking, needed no concept of the character as a separate entity because the shape of character was outlined and thrown into relief with sharp precision in the interstices of the tragic action (thus Aristotle's lack of interest in character as such), the fundamental passivity of the grotesque victim-character dissolves any thrust of ethos based on action. It is, in truth, the naturalist conception of milieu taken to extremes.

Naturalism, sick of pallid neoclassical abstractions traversing ideal stage-spaces and of romantic soul operas, clamored for physiological truth. The grotesque character answers this demand: it is fully and terribly physiological, and it can everywhere be reduced to the body because it cannot retreat beyond it. There is no monadic cohesion of personal traits, no essence that cannot be displaced or dispersed by the virulent adversarial irony wielded by the grotesque tyrant-figure. Like the Student in *Methusalem,* the grotesque character is psychoanalytically presliced into id, superego, and ego. Describing the psychic condition of modernity, Schnitzler observes:

> The soul of some people seems in a sense to consist of single floating elements which never group around a center and thus are unable to form a unity. So the core-less person leads his life in a monumental solitude which, however, he never fully and consciously perceives. The vast majority of humans is core-less in this sense.

The existence of such people, Schnitzler notes, "seems only to consist of a succession of isolated moments" (qtd. in Offermanns 9). Indeed, the disintegrated and fragile sense of self is the main point of attack for the characterology of the grotesque. Several playwrights of the early twentieth century, such as Schnitzler, Ödön von Horváth, or—most notoriously—Pirandello, tend to rest their case on the argument that personal identity is irredeemably suspect as a construct. That suspicion is firmly inscribed into the narratives of Franz Kafka as well. James Rolleston comments that "nothing is harder than to evolve an image of the 'character' of a Kafka hero" (140).

Futurism and expressionism, especially in their dystopian variety, argue the converse: that a true unified and forceful will, a ruthless will-to-power, is attainable only in the form of the beast or the automaton and that man's transformation into either, regrettable as it may seem from the standpoint of a sentimental humanism, is the inevitable price of progress. It is little wonder that the Futurists as well as a certain fringe of the German expressionist movement (Bronnen, Hanns Johst) felt themselves powerfully attracted to the Fascist regimentation of human forces that seemed to exemplify this attitude only too well.

The *démontage* of the character can (and must) be taken to an extreme in the grotesque work, that is, either to its physical obliteration or to its aesthetic disappearance. This second is the more subtle and modern variant, for modernism itself, as has frequently been argued, is built around the notion of pauses, silences, absences—symbolic deaths. Countless modern plays are composed around this very principle: a central character who is symbolically "dead" but who functions as the still eye of a chaotic storm, who is a vortex, a singularity, who has collapsed into the utter interior and then beyond, into nothingness, but whose absence, paradoxically, remains the driving force of the action, such as Jan in Eremo in *The Chronicles of Hell.* These characters are only the logical extension of the romantic-centripetal anthropology, and they are the artistic reflection of a modern condition—the dissolution or dispersion of the subject, the slipping grasp on the figure of the self.

It is because dramatic character has always been practically synonymous with substance, presence, and volition that its presence-as-absence, its substance-as-void, its will-as-passivity is so disconcerting. Rudolf Arnheim, reflecting on general compositional principles, writes:

> Only when the center is potentially there does its denial become an artistic statement. Emptiness and homogeneity as positive presentations of a desirable or undesirable state of being are sharpened and strengthened when a rallying point is potentially available. The psychological connotations of floating in the nowhere, in a space where no one place differs from the next, exert their bliss or terror artistically when an anchorage is explicitly represented as being denied. (*Power* 107)

Since the introduction of the term "protagonist" to designate the character around whom the action is organized, the dramatic figure has always provided such anchorage. Yet it is fairly easy to think of some signature plays of modernity (including most of Beckett's and Pinter's) in which this notion is challenged and finally dispensed with.

It is in the vortex of this absent center that the character wavers before our eyes and the categories of criminal and victim intertwine. Büchner's Woyzeck is primarily a victimized character (victimized, notably, in the most typical grotesque manner: by being turned into a mere bladder and digestive tract in the service of medical research). The play is so structured—and its fragmentary, almost erratic nature underscores this—that Woyzeck virtually disappears as a character. Downtrodden by his circumstances, hampered by his inarticulacy, confused by feverish visions, all of the attributes of the classical character—eminence, expression, clarity of purpose—are denied him. The only recourse to self-assertion is the pure criminal act—the killing of Marie. Such an analysis, of course, overlooks the social and psychological motivating factors that the play also puts forth. I am, however, not in search of extenuating circumstances but rather of a precedent for the reshaping of character in the direction of the grotesque, which *Woyzeck* seems powerfully to supply.

Frank Wedekind's mysterious Lulu is another character whose apparent vapidity—her lack of "substance"—creates moral chaos and death, and who terrifyingly (but logically) falls prey at the end to the criminal archetype, Jack the Ripper, who in a perverse manner becomes her fulfilling *figura.* Lulu submits to her own creation by the coterie of her lovers, to the projection of their desire that she desires, exhibiting the same "unconscious criminality" Strindberg attributed to many of his own heroines: a criminality impervious to moral judgment and practically indistinguishable from victimization. At the end Jack, grotesquely, cuts out her uterus, symbol both of her sexual allure and her vacant center.

On the other hand, Brecht's Galy Gay in *Man Is Man* is systematically deprived of his moral center, his identity, the better to turn him into a "fighting machine," a figure equipped with nothing more than an overriding will to survive, harnessed by imperial interests and thus converted to a criminal instinct. Brecht's title, it turns out, is ironic: far from assuring us of the inviolability of personality, it argues its interchangeability. Galy Gay is "convertible."

In consequence, the profoundly modern exacerbation of the romantic-centripetal character model enables the creation of a new character type, a vacant *Kunstfigur* lacking the discriminatory grid of ethos that makes tragic action meaningful. This character is in itself double *because* it is nothing: being, as Ubu might say, "de-cored," it is victim, but its victimization that has left it "outside the human pale" is the very prerequisite for its criminality. Because it inserts into the figural equation of drama a zero where a cipher should stand, it wreaks havoc on the outcome; the exchange of energy becomes an unstoppable descent into entropy.

Witold Gombrowicz's *Ivona, Princess of Burgundia* (1935) is one of the slyest modern plays that thematize the absent character center. Ivona, an unattractive girl whom the Burgundian Prince Philip marries against his better instincts and merely to satisfy his taste for the bizarre, only to see her cause utter chaos in his family and court, is the modern grotesque an-agonist par excellence. In her passive stupidity and uncouthness, Ivona becomes the focal point for the entire submerged pathology of the court of Burgundy. Although not truly deformed, this "monstrous scarecrow" and "universal irritant" appears to exist only to try everybody, to hold up a warped mirror to the barely hidden baseness of the other characters. "Do you know," the prince says to her, "that the moment one looks at you, one is tempted to harm you in some way?" (Gombrowicz 9). Because of this aura of victimization that irresistibly surrounds her, because "you can do absolutely anything you like with her" (51), as Philip blithely assures his father, the king, she catalyzes the complete breakdown of social norms. As her vacant image intolerably confronts each person with his or her own inadequacies, she inspires the eruption of unprecedented barbarity and murder-lust. Her violent death inevitably concludes the play.

The measure of a character's congruence with or alienation from the scene, or contextual dramatic universe, is also expressible by means of a peculiar kinetic and temporal discrepancy that Gaston Bachelard brilliantly addresses in his book on the Comte de Lautréamont. Bachelard contrasts the representations of character metamorphosis in Lautréamont and Kafka and observes that in the writings of Lautréamont (particularly *Maldoror*), the bestial transformation is an act of complete volition that catapults the character into an energetic state of aggression, a "vital acceleration" of the will-to-attack; it is the "conquest . . . of a new kind of time." Kafka's hero Gregor Samsa, on the other hand, lives—in Bachelard's inspired phrase—"in moribund time." Gregor exists "in a coagulated world, in viscous temporality" in which all action is unbearably retarded and ineffectual (6–7).

This may remind us of a familiar dream state frequently experienced in anxiety dreams—that of finding ourselves in a situation in which action is urgently demanded but where we are prevented from acting or restrained by an invisible force. Freud has associated this kind of motor inhibition in dreams with a "conflict of will" and with the inhibition of the libido (*Standard Edition* 4:336). In fact, we could see it as a kind of castration anxiety translated into temporal-kinetic terms. Humans are, in the neologism Ionesco coins in *Jack or the Submission,* "chronometrable"—hostages of time.

We find analogues of "moribund time" everywhere in the grotesque drama: the satiety of the cannibal feast makes Thyestes drunk and slow(-witted), even as Atreus runs up to the top of his bestial form. Titus Andronicus seems trapped in two acts' worth of "viscous" time before he launches into the final cataclysmic attack on his tormentors. Läuffer of *The Tutor,* following his actual castration, succumbs to "moribund time." The ever accelerating rhinoceroses in Ionesco's play strand Berenger in a retarded and deficient time frame while the biocentric impulse usurps his environment. In *The Visit,* Alfred Ill finds himself prevented by some unknown internal force from boarding the train that could deliver him from his nemesis after his symbolic alter ego, the black panther, is shot (which eliminates all his animal resistance). He remains in a state of motionless paralysis as his train departs. In many of Beckett's plays, particularly, for instance in *Endgame,* "moribund time" is finally the only type of time there is.

We find the obverse—but not the opposite—in a play like *Woyzeck,* in which the main character is infected with a feverish but undirected energy that makes his captain "quite dizzy." But Woyzeck's manic drives are counteracted by a time frame reflecting sheer cosmic indifference; the Captain remarks: "Woyzeck, it frightens me to think that the earth rotates in one day—what a waste of time, what will come of that? Woyzeck, I can't look at a mill wheel anymore or I get melancholy" (Büchner 206–7). Almost unequivocally, the grotesque character is recognizable by a kind of disparate, proprietary temporality that underlines that he is at odds with his dramatic environment.[13]

A correlative to this temporal anatomy of the grotesque character might be found in an early essay by Wedekind, entitled "Zirkusgedanken" ("Thoughts on the Circus," 1887). In this characterological piece, written long before his mature plays but extremely pertinent to their theme, Wedekind metaphorically projects the dialectic of success and failure, survival and defeat into the kinetic venue par excellence: the circus arena. The preeminent principle in this venue, Wedekind asserts, is "elasticity"; the presence (or lack) of elasticity in the acrobat serves as a kind of "plastic allegory" of human life. Those who, because of their rigidity, are incapable of bouncing back must perish; the "wild hunt, howling and barking, passes heedlessly over them." The character capable of survival is the one who is endowed with "fabulous virtuosity"—the perfect artiste, or in our terms the perfect beast (Wedekind 881–82). (Note that in the prologue to Wedekind's *Earth Spirit,* the circus director introduces the exceptionally elastic Lulu as the "wild, true, beautiful animal.") The circus stands for an amoral realm in which self-assertion ("egotism") is the driving force and flexibility the highest virtue. In Wedekind's later plays, circus directors will appear almost exclusively as agents of doom, and circus metaphors will habitually signal the site of the most cruel competition for survival.

Wedekind, like Lautréamont, is prominently a part of what Margot Norris, in her *Beasts of the Modern Imagination,* has dubbed the "biocentric tradition": an artistic strain of modernism that seeks to resurrect an animal(istic) discourse and confront the ingrained anthropocentricity of Western art. This discourse is present in the contemporary postmodern theatre as well. In the plays of Sam Shepard, for instance, the possibility of an archetypal transformation, of the sudden assertion of the biocentric impulse, is never far from the surface. Shepard diagnoses an effectively unstable sense of a separate self in modern American mass society that occasions the search for and resurrection of a mythical past or a mythical identity frequently expressed in animal terms.

In *La Turista* (1967), Shepard lets space, time, and identity waver, reverse, and interpenetrate in ways that are all but unrecountable. Near the end of this play set in Mexico, Kent, the American tourist struck with the rabid dysentery invoked in the title, transforms (reverts?), under the influence of his feverish imagination, into a "monster," a hunted beast. In the form of a beast, Kent becomes free to break the restraints of theatrical representation—the actor is instructed to leave the stage and run into the audience. The last tableau of the play startlingly summarizes the nexus of grotesque dehumanization and the assault on conventional aesthetic contexts: the Kent-monster, swinging Tarzan-like on a rope, crashes through the upstage wall "leaving a cut-out silhouette of his body in the wall" (300). In this cartoonish act of transcendence, both the box set and the immutable character boxed in by it are simultaneously ridiculed; to the beast there are no theatrical or mimetic pieties, no inviolable perimeters.

Such acts of mystical transformation occur repeatedly in Shepard's early plays—the entire cast of *Back Bog Beast Bait* (1971) metamorphose into animals of the swamp and prairie. Slim, who is transformed into a coyote, is given the final soliloquy, an inner meditation on (and in) animal consciousness:

> I devour my young. I am the beast. The beast is me. I'm feeling your blood now. It's thinner. Your heart beats faster. You look to the right and the left with quick jerks. Afraid to be eaten yourself. Small animals crawl through your skin. You're infected with desert life. Your loneliness is beyond what humans know. You've given yourself to the ground and I give myself to you. It's only fair. It's only fair. (333)

The bestialization of the character here is an instrument of instinctual survival in a hostile environment, just as in Seneca's *Thyestes* or in *Titus Andronicus*. In this respect, the biocentric motif has undergone little change. But in Shepard we also note an absence of the cultural pessimism that colors the earlier plays (the coyote is of course one of the most prominent Trickster figures of Native American mythology).

To Shepard, the amoral realm of the animal spells a possibility of freedom unattainable in civilization (although he is altogether too skeptical, too ironic, to qualify as a true vitalist). The exchange and mutual transmutation between beast and human is "only fair," as Slim says; it is part of the psychic and energetic economy of the living world in which balances are restored. In Shepard, theatrical possibilities that Seneca or Shakespeare could not begin to contemplate are opened up. Shepard is not content to leave the transformation of his characters in the metaphorical sphere: he laconically demands that "Slim howls and turns into the coyote" (333). Such unmediated stage presence of the animal by virtue of a radicalized metaphor ("I am the beast. The beast is me") fits in exactly with the biocentric agenda as Norris has described it for the modernist movement:

> The literary equivalent to the ontological recuperation of the animal was achieved by turning metaphor on its head: repressing its abstract meaning and retrieving the material reference, the literal residue, that is treated as the symbolic equivalent to unconscious animal life. (224)

The stage is exactly the place of the literal residue (or resuscitation) of the animal metaphor. Shepard's argument can thus be pitted precisely against that, say, of Ionesco in *Jack or the Submission*. When Ionesco's characters, including the subjugated Jack, turn into crawling animals at the end of that play, the author takes care to stipulate that "[a]ll this must produce in the audience a feeling of embarrassment, awkwardness, and shame" (110). The characters in *Jack* may seem like animals, but they are still, in Bachelard's term, "moribund," and the shame they induce is that cultural shame of the animal side, that pervasive guilt that drives civilization into ever-deepening discontents, which Kafka's insect Samsa, too, projects. Sam Shepard's animals, however, are truly biocentric, for they are shameless. But the biocentric urge harbors a terrible paradox, for the true motive for the metamorphosis must be seen in the *security of identity* that the animal provides as a closed and stable category that gives refuge from the bewildering, crisis-prone ontology of humanness. No demands are made upon the animal but solely that to survive, and its desires are never complicated by ambiguity. The category is dissolution-proof; the tiger, as Ortega remarks, "cannot be de-tigered." Thus biocentricity amounts to an attempted escape from the ubiquitous threat of a dehumanizing environment through willful self-dehumanization.

If Shepard's convertible characters stand partially for a rehabilitation of biocentricity, which now appears to hold the promise of a more authentic existence, we find conversely that an erstwhile Enlightenment character ideal, the cogitating protagonist, becomes a grotesque anathema in modern drama. The grotesqueness of this character, the ideologue, springs from the increasing problem with the concept of heroism itself, as Lukács has observed in his *Theory of the Novel.*

Lukács describes the early modern period, around the time of Cervantes, as "a period of great confusion of values in the midst of an as yet unchanged value system." Such confusion was bound to affect most profoundly the literary figures in which the age sought to define its objectives. Heroism collapsed into its opposite: "[T]he purest heroism is bound to become grotesque, the strongest faith is bound to become madness, when the ways leading to the transcendental home have become impassable" (*Theory* 104). In other words, there existed (and increasingly exists) a disturbing similarity between heroic steadfastness and monomania, tenacity and psychosis, because the teleological assurance of the hero, his connection to a divine aim, has been replaced by pure self-assertion. In a horizon of accruing doubt, the absolute becomes freakish. We could speak of a figural deficit in the grotesque character, a missing correlative that if present would ensure that the deed of self-assertion is accorded heroic "sense" in the actual world. (Sophocles' Ajax suffers from a version of this deficit.)

The solution for the characters of the nineteenth century—so runs Lukács's quite irrefutable conclusion—was to withdraw from seeking a sense of self-fulfillment in the world into the absolute interiority of the narrow soul, indeed, into the utter narrowness of ideology. Such ideologues (Lukács mentions Ibsen's Brand, Stockmann, and Gregers Werle) tolerate no irony, which would immediately render them comical, because it would confront their closed minds with an open world:

> Grotesquely depicted characters either become innocuously comic, or else the narrowing of their souls, their all-devouring concentration upon a single point of existence, which no longer has anything to do with the world of ideas, produces pure demonism, and the characters, however humorously treated, become

> representatives of the "bad" principle or of the pure absence of ideas. (Lukács, *Theory* 106)

Such characters are all but a hallmark of the early-twentieth-century German theatre. There are Wedekind's fanatics, like Karl Hetmann of *Hidalla* (1904), who offers an uncanny preview of Hitler; Sternheim's dogmatic middle-class heroes; or the ranting ideologues of the expressionist stage. They become, as Wellwarth has remarked about Ghelderode's characters, "monsters, persons who have become so obsessed by one of the more perverse possible phases of human character that they become in fact dehumanized personifications of it" (116). We can find a marked tendency toward this monomaniacal character behavior in recent German drama as well. The plays of Thomas Bernhard in particular seem little more than single-minded misanthropic tirades, in which a cranky central character (often a philosopher or an actor, like Kant in *Immanuel Kant,* or Minetti in *Minetti,* or the nameless "world-improver" in *Der Weltverbesserer*) rails against a hateful world that he nonetheless requires as his captive audience:

> The world is a cesspool
> From which it stinks into our face
> This cesspool needs to be cleaned out
> That is the content of my treatise
> But when we clean out the cesspool completely
> It is empty
> . . . .
> Then nothing remains for us
> but to vault headlong into it.
>
> (Bernhard 938)

Reduced to the oratory of impotence, these characters are not so much threatening per se; their horror derives from the fact that they are Alcestes and Tartuffes treated without irony or humanity—they are insufferable and irrefutable. The ranting monomaniacs and sterile ideologues of the contemporary theatre could be summarized in a description that Bernard McElroy proposes as the key to the modern grotesque character, using the hero of Dostoyevsky's *Notes from the Underground* as his model: "Underground man." This subterranean figure, says McElroy, embodies "not alienated man, but *humiliated* man":

> Underground man's real problem is not that he cannot find a home in the world; in fact, he finds one of sorts: the mousehole. But what makes him writhe in his mousehole is that he can neither accept the self-confident, materialistic world, nor reject the humiliating appraisal that world makes of him. On the contrary, he fully agrees. Having been taught since childhood that he is contemptible, even repugnant, he seizes repugnance as his banner and forces it upon the world with defiance and spite as an act of self-assertion. (22–23)

Of course, such a description brings to mind a number of older characters, including Aaron, Richard III, or Bosola, and one may have to conclude that the modernity of the trope lies not in the mere fact but more in the unrelieved nature of the humiliation and in its normative rather than exceptional literary status. Albert Innaurato's monstrously fat Benno Blimpie (in *The Transfiguration of Benno Blimpie*) is a version of such an underground character, and (typically) his self-assertion also becomes his self-destruction. Assaulted by other children, reviled by his cruel parents, neglected by his lecherous grandfather, Benno attempts in vain to compensate for his grossness with the study of art. Finally convinced that "nothing alters anything" and "all that matters is the taste of our own flesh," Benno takes that grotesque underground creed to its furthest consequence. He locks himself into a tiny room, nails shut all apertures, and proceeds to eat himself to death, a "mountain of flesh," a sacrificial offering to the rats: "These rats will find Benno beautiful. They will long for him. He will be a sexual object to them. They will make the devouring of Benno's body an erotic act" (Innaurato 158, 164). In this last "supper of self," Benno recognizes the paradoxical possibility of a transfiguration, echoing a scene of utter self-abasement that, as a child, had first allowed him to feel "totally free of myself" (174, 176). As underground man, in a parodic turn on Christian transubstantiation, Benno can regain his substance only by relinquishing it and retain his dignity only in embracing completely his humiliation.

A variant type of the grotesque character is the monster-as-victim, or the pathetic monster. This character is relatively rare in recent literature, I suspect because it is difficult to make it deliver worthwhile dramatic goods without succumbing to melodrama. The pathetic monster is victimized by its own monstrosity; although it appears horrible and offensive at first glance, it clearly assumes the position of moral authority measured against which all other, "normal" characters seem monstrous. There is an obvious mythological lineage: "Mutilation or physical handicap . . . is often the price of unusual wisdom or power, as it is in the figure of the crippled smith Weyland or Hephaistos, and in the story of the blessing of Jacob. The Arabian Nights are full of what may be called the etiology of mutilation" (Frye 193). The only ancient tragedy in which such a constellation occurs is Sophocles' *Philoctetes,* where the putrescent presence of the hero with his magical bow puts Ulysses' evil plotting to shame. But Philoctetes' undeserved fate has often riled critics who found that the play fails as tragedy. Like Ajax, Philoctetes is the protagonist of a sacrificial crisis never fully resolved. Updating the myth in his *Philoktet,* Müller puts strong emphasis on what we may call the "semiology of mutilation." Philoctetes' wound, to Müller, is "ornament, burden, booty":

> Identity, too: during the time that belongs to pain, the man becomes a footnote, screaming commentary of the sick appendage. The wound can be deployed as a weapon, because the foot marks the hole in the net, the gap in the system, the always newly threatened and newly to be conquered interstice between animal and machine, in which the utopia of a human community appears. ("Brief" 104)

Gregor Samsa too may be thought of as a pathetic monster. In Kafka's tale, the human magnitude of Gregor's suffering and the concomitant animality of the family are made quite apparent, and in his stage adaptation of the story, Steven Berkoff strongly emphasizes the latter aspect when he calls for the scenic image of "a giant beetle composed of the FAMILY, the arms moving in stiff staccato rhythm, and bodies twist and join together in agonized conflict," or when he gives the lodgers synchronized, exaggerated *commedia dell'arte* movements and pig masks: their monstrous inhumanity could not be more manifest. Gregor's transformation, on the other hand, is merely mimed; he is the indisputable human presence on stage (Berkoff 112).

The preeminent modern dramatic version of the pathetic monster is David Merrick in David Pomerance's *Elephant Man.* This play shares with Berkoff's *Metamorphosis* adaptation the stipulation that the protagonist's deformation be mimed (thus visually preserving, even emphasizing, the true human form underlying it), and both echo that archetypal cry of the pathetic monster: "I am not an animal!"[14] In Bruce Wilshire's reading, the central motif of *The Elephant Man* is a mutual play of recognition between Merrick and the actress Mrs. Kendal, in which he recognizes himself through her and she recognizes "aspects of herself that she has more or less successfully repressed," namely "the socially unacceptable and self-unacceptable in *her:* her moments—or more than moments—of not fitting in; the monstrous aspects of *her* life." Mrs. Kendal, says Wilshire, "is fully natural, fully herself, only with the monster" (9). This, presumably, is also the effect on the audience. The perceived, but deceptive, monstrosity (for the monster is the *true* human here) kindles our human self-recognition. The pathetic monster, by playing deftly on a switch of figure and ground, thus effects an empathic inversion by shifting our point of view to the outcast and revealing normalcy to be essentially "grotesque." This is a kind of moral illusion in which the ideal is visualized by the most aggressive use of the nonabsolute (the wound or deformation being the gap through which, as Müller says, the "utopia of a human community" may appear).

Pathetic monsters, however, are most often the stuff of melodramatic or romantic genres that can assure their eventual apotheosis (the Frankenstein monster, Quasimodo, the Phantom of the Opera). Pomerance's *Elephant Man* is in truth a kind of secular mystery play. The grotesque play shares only formal similarities with such drama, much as it does with conventional tragedy.

Even where the grotesque play maintains vestiges of the tragic structure, it rejects the categories on which tragic characterization is founded. It repeals not only the Aristotelian formula for the adverse fate that befalls a hero "neither good nor bad" but also the variants that deviate from tragedy proper, the moral structures of melodrama (the wicked person brought to justice) and of the martyr play or the absurd (the good person unjustly destroyed). The grotesque nexus between character and fate or character and action simply bypasses these explicit questions of guilt and moral substance, which are the contrivances of Western theatre, by reconfiguring character relations in essentially nonmoral terms. Simply put, if drama is a form of moral discourse, a dialectical disquisition on individual action in a social context, the grotesque valorizes this form by invalidating it. The grotesque character conceives of himself or herself as "beyond good and evil." Horváth, commenting on his play *Faith, Hope and Charity,* writes:

> As in all my plays, I've made it a point with this little dance of death, to focus on man's animal instincts. If his acts are brave or meek, if his choices are fight

or flight, it's up to the animal instinct in him to choose the action. Good and evil don't enter into it at all. (94)

If comedy is structured on the codification of social ethos and tragedy on the exploration of individual ethos, and both form the interpretive context for conventional dramatic action, grotesque character action and grotesque character fate display a pure, autonomous, and amoral dynamic that appears unconscious and atavistic and against which any ethical consideration—such as the audience might struggle to maintain—is thrown into relief. Grotesque characters move in a world that often resembles the dramatic world constructed by moral vision, and yet their fundamental relations can be expressed only in the primitive metaphors of power and desire. Calling this relation one of criminals and victims, as I have, is perhaps already tingeing it with a moral hue it explicitly rejects (unless we add that the surrounding universe itself abets this criminality and provides no instance for its redress). It is the relationship of hunter and prey, eater and eaten. The biocentric will-to-power of the grotesque figure can be thought of as the concept of hubris (a patently moral concept) translated into purely energetic terms, as excess energy.

The dramatic world of the grotesque is filled with mere objects and objectal relationships, and what is more (and more horrific), it immediately and matter-of-factly reduces anything within its purview to the object level and thus "proves" the futility and illusoriness of any higher or more sublime aspiration. It is a baldly appetitive world, a biocentric world, to which the amoral, "natural" movement of acquisition and ingestion gives the basic thrust and where the surest sign of dehumanization is to become a perpetrator or victim of such ingestion or objectification. The only way to preserve one's humanity against the odds is, conversely, to refuse complicity with the consumptive logic, as in Kafka's *Hunger Artist,* that parable of extreme sublimation, where the act of not eating becomes the correlative of a fragile but defiant humanity on its paradoxical path to extinction.

The most extreme reflection of this aesthetics and ethics of victimization that the grotesque exploits is perhaps to be found beyond the conventional stage or the realm of conventional characters, in the machine theatre of Mark Pauline's California Survival Research Laboratories (SRL). The cyberpunk performances of this loose group with vaguely threatening titles such as *Epidemic of Fear: The Relief of Mass Hysteria Through Expressions of Senseless Jungle Hate* (1984) or *A Carnival of Misplaced Order: Calculated to Arouse Resentment for the Principles of Order* (1990) and should perhaps be called neo-Futurist; they are in a sense the apex of the Futurist "drama of objects." In the words of Pauline, the founder and director-mechanic of the group, an SRL show consists of "a set of ritualized interactions among machines, robots, special effects devices, and computers, with humans present only as operators or audience" (287). SRL employs bizarre remote-controlled machines reassembled out of hydraulic discards, occasionally with parts of animal carcasses strapped to their frames, which publicly enact cataclysmic scenarios of mutual kinetic violence. Because the large, loud, and terrifying machines seem to operate by themselves and often appear to be on the verge of losing control (an illusion encouraged by the meticulous Pauline), the performances are imbued with a sense of visceral threat. When during the Balkan conflict SRL performed in the placid town of Graz, Austria, near the Croatian border, residents thought Serbian war planes were attacking.

In a 1985 performance, *Extremely Cruel Practices: A Series of Events Designed to Instruct Those Interested in Policies That Correct or Punish*,

> [an] SRL epic of cruel, incomprehensible and unexplained acts, a Walk and Peck Machine performed delicate cat mummy drops and burns; the Screw Machine tore at, picked up, pursued and pulverized helpless Sneaky Soldiers; a catapult lobbed steel darts, gasoline bombs, and exploding missiles; an oversized Flip Book repeatedly presented 3 scenes of doom; and the Tower of Power finally focused its threatening arms on an undulating Bottle Man, later meeting its match in a flaming confrontation with The Big Man. On the sidelines was the Pig Pull, a carousing Spiky Roller Machine that completely flipped over, and the rolling Buzz Saw. The conclusion of festivities was marked by the release of several parachute flares, which attracted an LAPD helicopter to the scene. ("SRL Performance Chronology")

An excerpt of another performance is recounted by Theodore Shank:

> A five-foot-high dog-like Jumping Machine powered by an internal combustion engine periodically crouches and jumps several feet into the air apparently attempting to crush a small four-legged piece of squirming raw meat (meat skewered on a motorized metal armature). Over a period of 40 minutes,

> other events are taking place, the Jumping Machine stalks the piece of squirming meat. Finally, the jumper succeeds in landing on the squirming meat, breaking it into pieces. Part of the victim continues to "live" as its motor continues to turn until the performance is over. (225)

Pauline deliberately divides his machines into classes; the most complex and versatile robots, his "flagship devices," he thinks of as "real actors": "They have multiple functions, they are much more dexterous, they have fairly sophisticated control circuitry in them." The second class of machines is more simple and passive, unable to manipulate objects: "They're controlled just by switching them on and off, sometimes with a timer. These machines provide a sort of backdrop or are victims for the other machines to destroy or tear to pieces or just shove around or whatever" (qtd. in Shank 233–34).

This kinetic-hydraulic theatre lays bare the essence of victimization far more clearly than the conventional theatre can, for the moral dimension is purposely excluded from its displays, and the victim-machines are already constructed to be taken advantage of by the sophisticated criminal-machines. Pauline's theatre sets into scene a bleak mechanical ontology; it is bereft of all content other than a robotic allegory of rape, and yet, perversely, it delivers an aesthetic thrill by the virtuosity of its invention and execution. It is all the more provocative because it plays on the tension between its framing as a performance (a genuinely human and communal occupation) and the total absence of human actors or characters. In an illustration of the mainstream's incessant recycling of avant-garde energies, SRL's technical achievements have recently been emulated in television shows that pit teams of remote-controlled robots against each other, but these programs have typically sanitized all of the elements that make Pauline's art so disturbing.

Pauline's kinetic-robotic performances, quintessentially postmodern in their straightforward but pervasively ironic brutality, seem indifferent to any aesthetic or political categories. I would not hesitate to call these displays "grotesque," however—not merely because of their actual or implied conflation of the mechanical and the organic, or because they are the most sophisticated example of the grotesque topos of animation I know of, but also because they are clearly "anthropic," that is, concerned with humans, even if in a backhanded way. Pauline's stance is avowedly political, his intentions didactic and ethical, but his attitude is all grotesque criminality. SRL performances are the carnivals of the late industrial age. Pauline gloats that "SRL enjoys nearly unlimited freedom to engage in both decadent technical extravagance and unapologetically acerbic commentary" (287).

> If you take the human elements out of a situation, it redraws from a perspective that gives you a different look. . . . People desperately need a new perspective on some of the confusing things in our culture, one of which, the main one, is the intense, horrible things that we can now do to each other. (qtd. in Shank 246)

It is perhaps legitimate to question whether Survival Research Laboratories' machines, these furthest extensions of the notion of the *Kunstfigur,* deserve the title of "characters" at all, and yet what else could one possibly call them? Free of all psychological accretions or cultural gestures, they are the purest characters imaginable in the sense in which Aristotelian theory demands them: as acting nodes of a violent plot within an absolute conflict (or what Pauline describes as "unrestrained action" [288]). Like the carcasses affixed to SRL's robotic contraptions, in the last analysis the humanity of Aristotle's characters is merely incidental to their purpose, a meat suit hung on the gleaming skeleton of ethos. Thus—and this is the operative paradox of grotesque characterization in general—the quality of humanness comes most sharply into focus where the work most vehemently appears to withhold it.

First, this theatre must exist.

—Antonin Artaud, "First Manifesto of the Theatre of Cruelty"

Conclusion
The Paradoxes of a Grotesque Theatre

The grotesque plays with Western concepts of binarity by hosting them and then exploding their inner balance. It takes advantage of our preoccupation with symmetry, with the syllogistic logic and the dialectical pursuit of synthetic truths that are the legacy of antiquity, reinvigorated by scholasticism and refined by idealist philosophy. Binary thinking and dialectics are pervasive habits of Western culture, of the Western mind—so much so that we long entrusted our lives to them (the politics of mutually assured destruction, for instance, was a global syllogism). The grotesque undermines these assumptions of truth-production that structure virtually everything we do, casting drastic doubt upon them, for it presents the mind with defective dialectics, bizarre binarities, mangled metaphors, aborted syllogisms, fearful symmetries. I believe that it is this assault on the undergirding of our cognitive and epistemological faculties that makes the grotesque so effective as a shape of refusal, a species of dissonance. This holds equally true for the relation of the work of art to its referent; Georg Wilhelm Friedrich Hegel's dismissal of the grotesque artists on the grounds of symbolic incompetence may thus be reread as a kind of mastery of symbolic indeterminacy that, in its extremism, questions the assumptions of symbolic signification itself.

The final aim of the grotesque, if it can be stated in separation from its individual manifestations, is the liberation of interpretation (by first arresting and confounding the interpretive movement) for the production of a certain type of knowledge—knowledge of the absences and gaps, of suppressed and sublimated warps in our conventional perception of actuality. As Barbara Johnson remarks in *The Critical Difference,* "[I]t is not . . . what you don't know that can or cannot hurt you. It is what you don't *know* you don't know that spins out and entangles 'that perpetual error we call life'" (xii).

Poststructuralist thought has paid a great deal of attention to decentering strategies, to the necessity of assailing comfortable vantage points; the grotesque, if it succeeds, is an ally of such projects. There is a splendid passage in Luigi Pirandello's *On Humor* that tells of a kind of near-mystical self-apprehension that he ascribes to "certain moments of inner silence" in which "we see ourselves in life, and life in itself, as if in a barren and disquieting nakedness." Caught off guard (or, decentered) by such insights, we attempt to recover a previous certitude:

> With a supreme effort then we try to recapture the normal consciousness of things, to renew our usual relationship with them, to reassemble our ideas and to feel alive again in the usual way. But we can no longer trust this normal consciousness, these newly recollected ideas and this habitual sense of living because we now know that they are deceptions which we use in order to survive and that underneath them there is something else which man can face only at the cost of either death or insanity. (Pirandello 138)

This disquieting "underneath" that Pirandello finds in quiet reflection is the same substratum that the art of the grotesque—with greater vehemence, albeit—exposes in the lower orders of being.

At all levels of expression, the grotesque can be seen as an attempt to erase deferral, the "reign of abstractions," sanctioned by which, in Friedrich Nietzsche's potent metaphor, "man rests on the pitiless, the greedy, the insatiable, the murderous in the indifference of his ignorance, as if lost in dreams on the back of a tiger" (*Werke* 3:108–9). It attempts to reconstitute, in a fashion, the origin that according to the precepts of poststructuralist criticism is "always already lost"—thus its recourse to the body, which is the substance of origin. But in a world of confirmed differences, sharp chasms between interior and exterior, this design is vigorously futile. The grotesque always fails, because art can never liberate itself from the symbol and become pure essence, but it is the dynamics of failure that nourishes it, which makes it aesthetically successful.

What is grotesque is not, strictly, the aesthetically present *product* (the deformed body, Gregor Samsa as bug, the monstrous or dehumanized character) but the *process:* the very act of metamorphosis, of transference, and the obligation—which the grotesque strategy imposes—to think this metamorphosis possible, even necessary. Drama, as Aristotle has taught us, is the art of necessary processes, and so it invites the grotesque. Thus the grotesque lodges neither in the object of contemplation nor in the subject but in the infection and decay of an epistemological space that appears to have always been constituted in a certain way between subject and object, until the grotesque proves otherwise. This epistemological space is external to subject or object; it is "metaphysical" even if the grotesque expresses it in physical terms. In the theatre, which is the site of a controlled metamorphosis in which (ideally) the physical and the metaphysical rub shoulders, the epistemological space is always endangered as a matter of course. We may transfer to the theatre an observation that Julia Kristeva makes about all literature: that it "represents the ultimate coding of our crises, of our most intimate and serious apocalypses" (*Powers* 208).

In the stipulation of "coding," however, lies both the triumph and the problem of art. Art theory in the West established a dialectical position concerning the treatment of the fictitious and the real early on. Augustine speaks of the "inevitable falsehood" that marks a "true work of art," declaring with unimpeachable logic: "[H]ow would the picture of a horse be a true picture, if the horse in it were not a false horse?," or how would Roscius, for that matter, be a true tragedian "if he did not want to be a false Hector . . . ?" (qtd. in M. Barasch 62–63).

An argument such as this, designed to emphasize the autonomy of art and particularly its independence from the moral demands for simple veracity, would seem to rebut the insistent literal-mindedness of (for instance) Tertullian's antitheatrical diatribes. It also helped prepare the ground for a type of Occidental aesthetics that ascribes to life and to art two separate standards of truth, one ontic, the other metaphorical-representational, which do not anywhere intersect: the real horse is true by being, and thereby being true; the painted horse is true only by not being real, and thereby being false. Tautology and paradox exclude each other.

This state of affairs is assailed by the grotesque. For while Roscius may be sublime as the false Hector, another Roman actor, Paris, approaches the realm of the grotesque when he is "slain in earnest" while acting in sport (in Massinger's *Roman Actor*). In the "performance" of Paris, whose moment of death combines the aesthetic truth of tragic falsehood with the final, irreversible ontic truth of dying, paradox and tautology meet. Massinger's play, of course, eludes serious consequences by being a falsehood itself (in which the actor *playing* Paris remains alive) as well as by being generically conceived as a tragedy rather than a farce, but it is informed by actual historical circumstances that leave nothing to be desired in their grotesqueness.

By nature, it is far more difficult for the pictorial arts to close the binary gap between false (truth) and true truth Augustine posits, for there is never a real horse made of paint, nor an image of a horse composed of flesh. In the theatre, though, *the medium is reality,* albeit one temporarily sequestered and declared off limits to the dictates of true truth. As Bert States observes, "In theater, image and object, pretense and pretender, sign-vehicle and content draw unusually close" (20). Thus it is here, in the theatre, arguably the most conservative of arts, that the fundamental dialectics of Western art (and art criticism) are most likely to be abolished, for the theatre provides that dangerous "liminoid" space in which the fusion of true truth and false (truth) may take place. But its paradox is that the fusion is in fact impossible and that this impossibility redoubles the cultural ambition to arrive, as David George writes, "at last at some state beyond paradox":

> The suspect status of the theatre and all paratheatrical performances throughout our history is that they consistently subvert this whole ambition, endlessly creating new "doubles" and thus new doubts, restlessly exposing the world as one which is dynamic and creative only in being clefted. (74)

The grotesque theatre is a reaction against that theatre that has betrayed the sanctified mission of the medium to be an agent and a site of revelation, of, as James Joyce would say, "epiphanies," and that has instead catered to salons and surfaces, facile psychology and futile naturalism. The most general characteristic of the theatre of the grotesque can perhaps be described as its inherent desire to overcome the stricture of representation enforced by Augustine's binarity, its desire to resolve the paradox; it is at every moment pressing to surpass and destroy the "deadly," somnolent, fossilized theatre that is merely endless doubles.

Elemental grotesqueness in the theatre is almost always concerned with dismantling the theatre event's grip on the illusionary, with making play serious. Conventional theatre enjoys an established accord with its audience that permits it to safely and vicariously indulge in even its danger zones and excesses so long as both uphold the distinction between stage fiction and external reality. Grotesque theatre, to use Heathcote Williams's metaphor, will "leak" into actuality, straining at the seams of the fiction that can barely contain it and generating a lawless realm of threat and endangerment. It is the theatre that defies the shackles of representation and the constriction of boundaries, that longs to permeate. It utilizes to the full extent that professional hubris of the theatre: that it always wants to be world. Thus theatrical grotesqueness seeks a revival of the sharpness of ritual (which is the coincidence of false [truth] and true truth) in a social order for which simulation has so much become endemic that it governs even its bona fide rituals.

But the stage is a schizophrenic place, the product of two competing and irreconcilable impulses—one connected with the terms of drama, the other with those of theatre; one an Apollinian product of the discursive-dialectical Socratic tradition, a part of the great omnivorous sense-making machine that converts reality into ever-growing structures of symbols, the other the subterranean counterimpulse of the Dionysian that reconverts symbol into reality and symbolic reality into the immediacy of ritual. Their point of contact is mimesis; mimesis (especially acting) is the act of transference in and through which symbol and reality become practically indistinguishable from one another, the moment of utter danger at which either impulse may triumph. In "Theatre and Science," Artaud writes:

> True theatre has always seemed to me the exercise of a dangerous and terrible act. . . . Because theatre is not that scenic parade where one develops virtually and symbolically—a myth: theatre is rather this crucible of fire and real meat where by an anatomical trampling of bone, limbs and syllables bodies are renewed. (*Artaud Anthology* 169)

Artaud himself is a kind of grotesque character, not so much by dint of his manifest insanity as because he stands as a victim, a "victim of Western metaphysics" (Thiher 506), that tyrannical and ubiquitous system of referentiality that deforms and subjugates his longing to be free of the shackles of text and representation, to reinaugurate a nontheological theatre of pure presence. As Jacques Derrida paraphrases Artaud in his brilliant essay on "The Closure of Representation," that quest can only be seen in terms of an act of metaphysical aggression: "The origin of theater, such as it must be restored, is the hand lifted against the abusive wielder of the logos, against the father, against the God of a stage subjugated to the power of speech and text" (*Writing* 239). But lifting a hand against God, even this imaginary god of speech, will draw retribution; Artaud becomes in Derrida's reading a tragic figure condemned to death by repetition, a visionary to whose vision "fidelity is impossible," sufferer of a perpetual unfulfilled passion: "There is no theater in the world today which fulfills Artaud's desire" (248). But, as Patrice Pavis remarks, this dilemma is what constitutes the avant-garde in the first place:

> The avant-garde distrusts and tries to free itself from the sign, but always succumbs to it in the end: such is the attraction-repulsion movement that was best personified by Artaud in his criticism of the theatre founded on the text and psychology. . . . [The] double movement of Artaud—the search for and rejection of a specifically theatrical language—is characteristic of the avant-garde. (182–83)

The "hieroglyphs" Artaud seeks to replace the logos with are reminiscent of the "new world of symbols" Nietzsche demands in *The Birth of Tragedy* but can never attain. Artaud's own scenarios work hard at extricating themselves from symbolizing overtly and attempt to pass into the realm of the hieroglyphic, the realm where the sign signifies only itself and its teasing illegibility or obscurity and repels its interpretive transference to any other, ordered, context of meaning. Artaud hopes, obviously, that the hieroglyph may become the forebear of pure phenomenon; that its hermeticism may engender a phenomenal reading by discouraging a significative one.

Of course, even a cursory reading of *The Spurt of Blood* or *The Conquest of Mexico* reveals their closeness to surrealist imagery (particularly, for instance, Apollinaire's *Mamelles de Tirésias*) and their derivative and capricious usage of Freudian metaphor. What may be working against Artaud's aesthetics of the hieroglyph is the mere fact that there are few, if any, stageable or even imaginable images left that have not in some manner been integrated and made to serve in some semantic corpus somewhere; that the appropriation of symbolic systems progresses faster than their invention; and that even borrowings from alien cultures (in Artaud's case the Balinese dance theatre, among others) tend to be quietly usurped and rendered useless for a language of hieroglyphs. Postmodern culture is, in fact, the most voracious appropriator of hieroglyphs; it seems to ever escalate the movement from image to symbol, from presence to representation, which Derrida construes as inevitable in any case: "Presence . . . has always already begun to represent itself, has always already been penetrated" (*Writing* 249). Most devastating of all perhaps is Jacques Lacan's apodictic construction of the relation of symbol to desire in which the objectal, concrete world disappears behind the infinitude of signification: "[T]he symbol manifests itself first of all as the murder of the thing, and this death constitutes in the subject the eternalization of his desire" (104). The play, then, can *never* be the thing.

It is not the theatre Artaud *desires* that would be grotesque: the true Theatre of Cruelty is a theatre of total congruence with reality or nature, to the extent that no part of nature is external to it and that the very notion of hierarchical orders of meaning or representational crises becomes moot. On the contrary, the theatre of the grotesque is constructed of the continuance of Artaud's desire, his failing, that vigorous perpetual catastrophe of the avant-garde that Pavis describes as "attraction-repulsion." It is the constant reinscription of this failure to exceed the merely represented in the representation itself that gives the grotesque theatre its particular power. The Artaudian imperative is as strong in the theatre as is the countervailing force; even in their most pallid and attenuated forms, there remains in the acts of performance an umbilical connection, a space of possibility for the locus of origin "whose inextinguishable re-occurrence," as Derrida writes, "has never not been maintained by the metaphysics of Western theater" (*Writing* 240). Thus the theatre, in a sense, *must* be grotesque, but this is not so much the source of its abjection as of its primary strength. We remember Vsevolod Meyerhold's notion of the theatre that is irrevocably "outside of nature" and therefore "essentially an example of the grotesque": "Arising from the grotesque of a ritual masquerade, the theater inevitably is destroyed by any given attempt to remove the grotesque—the basis of existence—from it" (qtd. in Gorchakov 69). Meyerhold's formula, we recognize now, is the obverse of Artaud's: since it cannot be inside nature, nor nature inside it (if we take "nature" to be unrepresented, unrepeatable presence), it must be "outside of nature": self-contained, but not content with this containment. This deep discontent of theatre with itself, indeed, is also its ethos.

Though often understood as the epitome of the marginal and subterranean in the cultural code, grotesque art and theatre are in fact precise indicators of the lines of demarcation for representation within a culture; acting out the grotesque is both a challenge to a culture's order and, ultimately, the affirmation of certain ethical principles that it recognizes (if obliquely) as its own. Thus, the grotesque displays a kind of civilizing extremity and, in its strongest forms, even a transhistorical ethos always at odds with the unsettling quality of its images. Certainly there is at the basis of grotesque theatre the perception of an ethical contradiction, the "produced disfigurement of man, the inhumanity perpetrated by man," as Arnold Heidsieck has stipulated (17). But this reading limits the grotesque too strictly to social protest; instead, in art or even in perception, every grotesque is already a "produced disfigurement," and it is always the indicator of an imminent or already transpired dehumanization. As soon as we ascribe a higher value to humanity than to nonhumanity, we are subject to a kind of "moral vision" without which there can be no grotesque; even what we perceive as pure cognitive or logical paradox is predicated on the fact that the categories of cognition are inscribed with a privileging of the human over the mechanical or bestial, with a foregone, unexamined distribution of the roles of self and other. In the context of such a moral vision, the grotesque is always a form of protest not only against purely social injustice but also against the totality of an amoral realm in which the category of humanness itself is put into question. Just as by "scandalizing" genre it revalidates the generic vision, the grotesque finally subscribes in an impious manner to the very pieties it appears to demolish.

In other words, the production and perception of grotesque art rest, in a general sense, on an ethical or moral ground; it can, as Geoffrey Harpham says, "perhaps only be defined as the art of moral extremes" (184). But the knowledge the grotesque produces is not primarily practical, didactic, even moral knowledge; its principal aim is not to point out what in reality should not exist but what is *possible* alongside, underneath, above, and despite our fortifications of morality and logic. Since morality and logic are in turn—at any given time—the arbiters of representation (pictorial, poetic, theatrical), the grotesque is always on the verge of declaring representation questionable where it follows vested interests, orders, powers. Grotesque theatre is ethical, not by *representing* ethical standards (by signifying moral terms or precepts) but by *bodying forth* an ethics of boundaries in their most egregious violation.

That is perhaps the ethical nature of the grotesque: that its impieties are always the clandestine reflection of pieties, its criminality not a rejection but an invocation of the laws it violates. The deformed body is always doubled by the body intact; the scandalized genre revalidates generic vision. *Thyestes* is not the destruction of tragedy but tragedy's extremity thrown into relief. *Ubu Roi* does not declare history dead but necessary. *The Bacchae* makes the crisis of representation representable. Whatever it consumes or is consumed by, the theatre never eats itself. As Eugène Ionesco has said, "There is a crisis in the theatre only when the theatre fails to express a crisis" (*Notes* 29).

Notes
Bibliography
Index

Notes

Introduction

1. See the detailed study by Nicole Dacos, *La découverte de la Domus Aurea et la formation des grotesques à la rénaissance.* The attachment of the term "grotesque" to this particular fashion spurred by the Neronian decoration should not blind us to the fact that this is merely the etymological root. For, as Dacos remarks, "much as they are fundamental to the further development of the grotesques, the explorations of the Golden House did nothing but favor a tendency which manifested itself already in the second half of the 15th century" (57). Indeed, it is a tendency which may, albeit not without gaps, be traced as far back as art history extends.

2. The summaries of criticism on the grotesque that in my view are the most consistently enlightening are these: Arthur Clayborough, *The Grotesque in English Literature* (an inclusive overview, although sometimes lacking in accuracy); Philip Thomson, *The Grotesque* (a marvel of brevity and even-mindedness, this book has become a standard point of reference precisely because it does not advance a strong opinion); and Geoffrey Harpham's *On the Grotesque.* Also central to any understanding of the modern grotesque is the study by Wolfgang Kayser, *The Grotesque in Art and Literature* (1957), on whom most subsequent critics in some manner rely. Whatever the shortcomings of his book, it is fair to say that Kayser as much as single-handedly invented the modern critical inquiry into the grotesque. Mikhail Bakhtin's book *Rabelais and His World* will be discussed later; his terminology has very specific connotations, although it has in recent critical usage become the default reference for any discussion of the grotesque.

3. Here and subsequently, unless otherwise stated, all translations from foreign language sources are my own.

4. The grotesque is also, in broad terms, a deconstructive mode, if deconstruction is taken to mean the inclusion of "a phase of *overturning*" of hierarchy. Says Jacques Derrida:

> [I]n a classical philosophical opposition we are not dealing with the peaceful coexistence of a *vis-à-vis*, but rather with a violent hierarchy. One of the two terms governs the other (axiologically, logically, etc.), or has the upper hand. To deconstruct the opposition, first of all, is to overturn the hierarchy at a given moment. (*Positions* 41)

Insofar as it perceives hierarchies and inverts or erases them, the grotesque maintains a link to the deconstructive project. But the latter is in effect a philosophical inquiry, while the grotesque is an aesthetic strategy. It posits not the incomprehensibility or undecidability of the world-as-text in general, but only at that point at which the grotesque representation collides with a consciousness that is not equipped or ready for it.

1. The Sense of Disorder

1. Vitruvius's reference is not precisely to the style of decoration found in the Domus Aurea and later called *grottesche* (or, what art historian August Mau described as the Fantastic or Intricate Style) but to a style of ornamentation slightly preceding that, also known as the Ornate Style, which is found until about 63 C.E. See Frances Barasch, *The Grotesque* 29 n.

2. Lester Burbank Bridaham, in his *Gargoyles, Chimeras, and the Grotesque in French Gothic Sculpture,* suggests that the devil figure of the early mystery plays inspired the subjects for a number of grotesque sculptures (x).

3. Another animal analogy is the familiar Pavlovian dog. Having conditioned his canine to the symbols of a circle (= food forthcoming) and an ellipse (= food not forthcoming), Ivan Petrovich Pavlov presented it with an intermediate shape, a sort of flattened circle, upon which the dog suffered an "experimental neurosis" or nervous breakdown. See Pavlov, 290–92.

4. In Andreas Gryphius's *Catharina von Georgien oder Bewährete Beständigkeit* (*Catharine of Georgia or Constancy Rewarded,* 1657).

5. Gombrich speculates that there is an apotropaic (demon-repelling) function inherent in visual ambiguity, most of all in the lines and patterns that allow us to read a face into a complex ornament. These ornaments are always to a degree undecidable: where is the limit of their ornamental and where the beginning of their representational character? Such perceptual contradiction, where the eye's search "can never come to rest" (*Sense* 267), is said to confuse and thus ward off demons, which are thought to be rather simple-minded creatures.

6. Compare how Michel Foucault sees the historical and teleological development of the trope in connection with the problem of madness:

> In the thought of the Middle Ages, the legions of animals, named once and for all by Adam, symbolically bear the values of humanity. But at the beginning of the Renaissance, the relations with animality are reversed; the beast is set free; it escapes the world of legend and moral illustration to acquire a fantastic nature of

> its own. And by an astonishing reversal, it is now the animal that will stalk man, capture him, and reveal him to his own truth. Impossible animals, issuing from a demented imagination, become the secret nature of man; and when on the Last Day sinful man appears in his hideous nakedness, we see that he has the monstrous shape of a delirious animal. (*Madness and Civilization* 21)

7. Such "irruptions of subjectivity" are by no means limited to the "new canon" of bourgeois private physicality but speak through the emblematic language of medieval and Renaissance art as well. The National Gallery in London, for instance, contains a portrait entitled *A Grotesque Old Woman,* attributed to the sixteenth-century artist Quinten Massys. Possibly meant as a satire of the vanity of age, its arresting ambiguity transcends any didactic purpose. The attributes of youth, expressed in the headdress and finery, the supple hand grasping a budding rose, and especially the tightly corseted breasts which almost seem to make sexual overtures to the viewer, are contradicted by an incongruously spent and ugly (wistful, not laughing) face of uncertain gender. But Massys's picture is rather more disturbing than Bakhtin's ancient terra-cotta figurines, because it is not "pregnant" with possibility; it does not celebrate the cyclical renewal of all things in the universal, dialectical rhythm of fertility but mourns, even in ridicule, individual decay.

8. The O. M. Theatre clearly can trace its lineage to the O. K. Theatre, that is, the radical theatrical experiments of Viennese *peintre maudit* Oskar Kokoschka who in 1907 got himself ejected from the art academy for proto-Actionist activities surrounding his shocking expressionist play *Murderer Hope of Womankind.*

9. Nitsch, in his *Blood-Organ Manifesto,* proclaimed: "Through my art-production . . . I take upon myself that which appears to be a negative, perverse and obscene lust and the sacrificial hysteria resulting from it, so as to spare you the defilement and shame of a descent into the extreme" (qtd. in Loers 12).

10. Certain "endurance art" comes close to emulating the peculiar framing of the freak sideshow; Joseph Beuys, for example, was caged with a coyote for a week, and Tehching Hsieh, in one of several yearlong performance pieces, had himself locked in a cage in his loft, refusing to speak, read, watch TV, etc. Freak shows themselves, long thought distasteful and obsolete, have recently revived as well, and the dividing line between high art and low culture has become almost negligible in this respect: the Jim Rose Circus, avatar of a new "postmodern" freak show movement, insists on the integrity and autonomy of its artists as much as performance art and indeed draws on some of the same audiences.

11. Body art has perhaps now entered a kind of baroque phase of self-referentiality that seems to jettison the claim to authenticity entirely and embrace the pose. This phase is marked by repetition of exactly those acts that seemed unrepeatable, unique. Abramovic, for instance, is repeating Burden's *Transfixed,* while other epigones are reperforming her own pieces, as if they were

no more than texts or plays (Abramovic 22–23). Stelarc has retreated from live performances into cyberspace, spinning sci-fi scenarios of artificial bodies.

2. Theories

1. It should be remarked, however, that the antigrotesque attitude of the neoclassical aesthetic theories helped defer the recognition and production of several notable "romantic" works that exhibit grotesque or disturbing features, though perhaps *Cromwell* is only technically to be counted among them. Shakespeare's plays, especially *King Lear,* already had a history of being sanitized (compare Nahum Tate's 1681 macaronic morality of the text) and fared no better under the attentions of Mr. and Mrs. Bowdler. Caliban's fate in the Restoration version of *The Tempest* by John Dryden and Sir William Davenant is typical of the trivialization of ambivalent grotesqueness into the merely ugly, against which decorous beauty may shine. As Willard Farnham puts it, Caliban's "transformation is from a monstrous underling capable of strange nobilities of spirit into a monstrous underling pure and simple" (159). There was considerable resistance to Shakespeare's dramatic disciples as well; the *Sturm und Drang* movement achieved its true canonical position only in the twentieth century, beginning with its reception by German expressionism. Although for example Jakob Michael Reinhold Lenz's *Tutor* (1774) was already produced by Friedrich Ludwig Schröder's company in 1778, it was Bertolt Brecht's 1950 adaptation that restored it to its rightful place. Heinrich von Kleist's *Penthesilea* (1808) was first seen on stage in 1876, the same year as Christian Dietrich Grabbe's burlesque *Jest, Satire, Irony, and Deeper Significance* (1822). And Georg Büchner's *Woyzeck* (1837) remained unstaged until 1913.

2. Such laughter can also be self-reflexive, that is, it displaces one's own abjection; Arthur Schopenhauer, in his theory of the ludicrous, speaks of a type of "bitter laughter":

> Our own bitter laughter when the terrible truth by which firmly cherished expectations are shown to be delusive reveals itself to us, is the vivid expression of the discovery now made of the incongruity between the thoughts entertained by us in our foolish confidence in men or in fate, and the reality unveiled. (99)

3. The notion of jokes or laughter in the service of the psychic economy is of course Sigmund Freud's, who contends that "'economy in expenditure on inhibition or suppression' appears to be the secret of the pleasurable effect of tendentious jokes," among which I would count the jokes of the macabre, since they aim to evade an "external obstacle," death. Freud does not explicitly consider either the macabre or the grotesque ("Jokes," *Standard Edition* 8:117, 119).

4. The modern fate of the tragic drama or of the eighteenth-century genre of the *bildungsroman* are cases in point. Neither modern realist drama, from *Uncle Vanya* to *Death of a Salesman,* nor existentialist drama is thinkable without the undergirding pattern of tragedy to play against, and yet tragedy is con-

sensually considered to have expired as a viable genre (note George Steiner's thesis of the "death of tragedy"). Likewise, most of the formative novels of modernity, *Remembrance of Things Past, Ulysses, The Castle, The Man Without Qualities,* and *The Magic Mountain,* capitalize on the genre of the *bildungsroman* even as they cannibalize it.

5. "Genres are precisely those relay-points by which the work assumes a relation with the universe of literature" (Todorov 8).

6. In my metaphor of healing, I play on the idea of the *pharmakos,* the scapegoat, through the expulsion of which the social body in tragedy heals itself "pharmaceutically"—the antidote to impurity is the tragic hero who must himself become impure in order to purify. The strong formal similarity between the civic ritual and the generic structure of tragedy is apparent and has often been discussed. In the context of an unsolved "sacrificial crisis" as the grotesque presents it, however, the efficacy of the *pharmakos* is put in question. Compare my discussion of *The Bacchae* in chapter 3.

7. To Walter Benjamin, that act of nomenclature makes Adam "the father of philosophy": "Adam's action of naming things is so far removed from play or caprice that it actually confirms the state of paradise as a state in which there is as yet no need to struggle with the communicative significance of words" (*Origin* 37).

8. There are of course jarring poetic metaphors, particularly in the modernist poetry that descends from Arthur Rimbaud or Baudelaire, some of which produce "grotesque" effects. A well-known example are the first lines from T. S. Eliot's *Love Song of J. Alfred Prufrock:* "Let us go then, you and I / When the evening is spread out against the sky / Like a patient etherised upon a table" (although this is, in truth, a simile). Compare also much of the early patho-poetry of expressionist Gottfried Benn, such as his *Kleine Aster,* in which a drowned beer delivery man is metaphorically transmuted into a vase for a small aster that inadvertently slips into his body during an autopsy.

9. The German word Kafka uses for Samsa, *Ungeziefer*—usually translated as "vermin"—is related to the Old High German root *zebar,* which means "sacrificial animal." *Ungeziefer* is thus what is "unclean and unworthy of being sacrificed." The prefix *un-* is, as Freud would say, the "token of repression." In the metaphor-sacrifice analogy, what is unworthy of sacrifice is also unworthy or inappropriate as the substitute "vehicle"; in this aspect, Samsa's fate is a radical catachresis. As the improper and unclean, but also as that "which disturbs identity, system, order," the Samsa/vermin is paradigmatic of the "abject" in Kristeva's sense of the term (*Powers* 4).

10. In *A Grammar of Motives,* Burke writes:

> [T]he word "substance," used to designate what a thing *is,* derives from a word designating what a thing *is not.* That is, though used to designate something *within* the thing, *intrinsic* to it, the word etymologically refers to something *outside* the

> thing, *extrinsic* to it. Or otherwise put: the word in its etymological origins would refer to an attribute of the thing's *context,* since that which supports or underlies a thing would be a part of the thing's context. And a thing's context, being outside or beyond the thing, would be something that the thing is *not.* (23)

11. A similar problem of having to "smooth" perspective to avoid the grotesque turns up whenever an insect becomes a protagonist in an animated film and is subjected to casual anthropomorphizing. The animator Ward Kimball, who designed the character of Jiminy Cricket for Disney's *Pinocchio* (1940), relates his effort to systematically disguise the lower-order provenance of the character:

> I had a lot of problems with the Cricket. Normally, an artist caricatures an animal by learning to draw it correctly—then the caricature becomes a simple problem of degree. But with an insect, you're in trouble, because insects are very ugly and unappetizing. A cricket looks like a cross between a cockroach and a grasshopper. . . . I did twelve or fourteen versions, and gradually cut out all the insect appendages. I ended up with a little man, really, wearing spats and a tail coat that suggested folded wings. . . . The audience accepts him as a cricket because the other characters say he is. (qtd. in Solomon 6)

3. Classical Grotesque

1. In his "Attempt at a Self-Criticism" of 1886, the preface to *The Birth of Tragedy,* Nietzsche tries to expunge what he realizes to be the inherent "romanticism" of *The Birth of Tragedy,* and he counters the "metaphysical comforts" some might be tempted to seek in his essay with a dose of pessimistic laughter, laughter of "that Dionysian monster" Zarathustra, laughter perhaps of the grotesque (26). Throughout this section, all Nietzsche quotes are from *The Birth of Tragedy.*

2. I am locating Richard Wagner aphoristically here, aware that the Bayreuth Festspielhaus did not open until ten years after the publication of *The Birth of Tragedy.*

3. See my discussion of the Schaubühne production in *Theatre Survey* 40.1 (1999): 31–49.

4. Some other examples of *sparagmos* in modern plays: In Frank Wedekind's *Hidalla,* the grotesque protagonist, Karl Hetmann (whom Wedekind oxymoronically labels a "dwarf-giant" ["Zwergriese"]), the ugly and crippled avatar of an incongruous ideology of beauty, intends to have himself torn apart by disappointed admirers. The sacrifice, of course, is comically unsuccessful. In Ghelderode's *Hop, Signor!,* the protagonist, Jureal, suffers "burlesque torture" and a "ludicrous end" at the hands of a Dionysian crowd that groans with anger and lust. Stanislaw Witkiewicz's *Madman and the Nun* concludes cataclysmically with an imbroglio in which only a "churning pulpy mass of bodies" remains discernible. Earlier, the madman-poet Walpurg had made a Dionysus-like comeback from the dead. The *sparagmos* incident in Tennessee Williams's *Suddenly*

Last Summer, in which Sebastian is torn apart (and cannibalized) by a horde of street urchins, is present only in Catherine's narration in this play, at the heart of which is a grotesque and archetypal "Terrible Mother" (Mrs. Venable). The infamous stoning of the baby in scene 6 of Edward Bond's *Saved* is likewise a version of the *sparagmos.*

5. That Seneca's plays were intended merely for reading and as rhetorical exercises is a common tenet of theatre history. A newer study by Dana Ferrin Sutton, however, arguing on the basis of both internal and external clues, concludes that "the weight of evidence indicates that Seneca intended his plays for production in a normal Roman theatre" (61). The intention, of course, does not prove the existence of any actual productions.

6. In fact, Chiron, the wise centaur, and Demeter, after whom Demetrius may have been called, were both children of Kronos. Perhaps Shakespeare intended a mental association between Tamora and Kronos, or wanted to suggest a spiritual kinship between Tamora's sons and the emperor Saturninus (the Roman god Saturn being equivalent to the Greek Kronos). On the other hand, Tamora's sacrificed son, Alarbus, bears what could pass for a Latinized Gothic name. Shakespeare may have been thinking of the Visigoth Alaric, who sacked Rome in 410 C.E. (This would by implication position the "historic" time of *Titus* shortly before the fall of the Roman empire, appropriately a point of crisis and transition.)

7. Marcus's speech has posed a problem to most who have wrestled with it, either in production or adaptation. Peter Brook's famed 1955 staging of the play in Stratford-upon-Avon (Sir Laurence Olivier playing Titus, Vivien Leigh Lavinia, Anthony Quayle Aaron) cut it entirely, substituting instead the powerful image of the mutilated Lavinia, statuelike and immobile, crimson streamers symbolizing her flowing blood. This cut circumvents the problem of tone and reinstates the pathetic thrust the moment seems to demand. Dürrenmatt's adaptation (see below), which suppresses all lyricism in favor of a laconic harshness, completely omits the scene. In the film version directed by Julie Taymor (*Titus,* 1999), the speech is pruned of its discordant lyricism but underlaid with a musical score signaling pity; it is treated almost as an inner monologue by Marcus (Colm Feore), intercut at one moment with a graphic image of Lavinia (Laura Fraser).

8. In a parallel to my reading, Heather James has analyzed *Titus* as imitating a shift from Virgilian to Ovidian literary strategies and values:

> Re-enacting literary history, Shakespeare first invokes the *Aeneid* as the epic of empire-building, order, and *pietas,* and then allows Ovid's *Metamorphoses* to invade, interpreting the fundamental impulses of Virgil's poem as chaotic, even apocalyptic. Simply put, the founding acts of Empire turn out to contain the seeds of its destruction. (123)

She too sees a "shift in genre" as key to the meanings of the play (131).

4. *Kunstfiguren*

1. Two relatively recent books, Harold B. Segel's *Pinocchio's Progeny* and Scott Cutler Shershow's *Puppets and "Popular" Culture* take up the theme of the human-puppet nexus. Segel's study is wide-ranging and historiographic but lacks a particular theoretical undergirding, whereas Shershow reads puppet imagery and themes broadly through the lens of "the historical intersection of representations and material practices" (2). I point to them as valuable resources on the topic without wishing here to duplicate their efforts.

2. Even Eugene O'Neill felt compelled to explore the possibilities of the puppet topos in a 1931 scenario that, however, never got beyond the conceptual stage. The notes for this "Rabelais Play," a dramatization of *Gargantua and Pantagruel,* call for a "Gargantuan pantomime prologue with gigantic marionettes (?)" (Floyd 224).

3. In 1993, the Rumanian director Silviu Purcarete toured with an *Ubu* adaptation entitled *King Ubu and Scenes from Macbeth,* which played in tandem with his production of *Titus Andronicus,* a kind of bookending of the totalitarian era of Eastern Europe by neoclassical and modern Grand Guignol. Purcarete's Ubus were, transparently, portraits of the recently deposed and executed Ceauçescus. See my review in *Theatre Journal* 46 (1994): 262–67.

4. I have translated Goll's term *Überrealismus* as "superrealism," although it is plainly derived from Guillaume Apollinaire's usage of *surrealisme.* This is to distinguish it from the term used by the later Paris surrealist movement around André Breton. I have also substituted "superrealism" where English translators of Goll have used the more conventional term.

5. Brecht, however, admired Goll's dramatic writings. He remarked, regarding the two *Überdramen* of 1918, that Goll had already overcome expressionism (a mode Brecht himself strenuously objected to) by using its own rules against it, and he praised the "eerily clear ideas" of this "expressionist Courteline." See Brecht, *Gesammelte Werke* 15:34. Brecht's remark is also paraphrased by Martin Esslin, who believes that Brecht himself "came nearest to the realization of a theatre as cruel and grotesque as the one Goll had postulated" (375).

6. In the following, I rely on my own translation of the plays, but an English translation is available in Walter Sokel, ed., *Anthology of German Expressionist Drama: A Prelude to the Absurd* (Ithaca: Cornell UP, 1984).

7. The translator, J. M. Ritchie, tacitly acknowledging the derivation of the terms, has taken some perhaps unwarranted liberties here. In his version we find "EGO, SUPEREGO, ID" (Goll, *Methusalem* 92). However, the German original merely has "ICH," "DU," and "ER," which, although clearly alluding to psychoanalysis, is also the given sequence of singular personal pronouns.

8. *The Triumph of Death,* moreover, is dedicated to Carl Theodor Dreyer, the Danish silent film director in whose *La Passion de Jeanne d'Arc* (1928) Artaud played a fanatical monk. *Jeanne d'Arc* is famous in the history of cinematogra-

phy mainly for its close-ups that deconstruct and displace conventional cinematic space. Rudkin, similarly, dissolves dramatic space and narrative continuity into a dreamlike progression of scenes. The texture of Rudkin's play, though, may even owe a debt to Dreyer's earlier Griffith-influenced film *Blade af Satans Bog* (*Pages from Satan's Book,* 1919–21), which charts the progress of Evil in the world.

9. Gerard Murphy, who played Athdark in the 1986 Almeida Theatre production, notes that the problem of Rudkin's play was not so much uncovering the "deep animal root of the character" but mediating between the character's abjection and the operatic "heights" of Rudkin's writing: "[F]inding the balance between blood and guts, mind and technique, to achieve something new . . . *The Saxon Shore* remains the most daunting play I've ever been faced with, and the most exhausting play I've ever done" (qtd. in Rabey 192–93).

10. The projected premiere of *Hamletmachine* in Cologne in 1978 did not take place; the cast and director, unable to come to terms with the text or their divergent interpretations of it, scrubbed the production several weeks into rehearsals. See the interviews with the participants in Theo Girshausen 46–78. However, Müller himself directed the play successfully several times, as did Robert Wilson.

11. In fact, more than twenty years after its first production at London's Royal Court Theatre, Ruby Cohn still considered *AC/DC* "a major work that has never been appreciated" (15).

12. Darko Suvin's description of the world of Norman Spinrad's *Little Heroes* (to Suvin a "central cyberpunk novel") can make the analogy comprehensible: "[A] cheerless future world, tough, gritty, and disillusioned protagonists, streetwise future slang, erasing of 'hard' vs. 'soft' boundaries or melding of personal experience and politics with biochips and the entertainment industry . . ." (41). *AC/DC*'s schizophrenic location in which mental constructs and reality are mutually inextricable seems to foreshadow cyberspace. Novelist William Gibson defines cyberspace (the term is his coinage) as a "consensual hallucination," a "graphic representation of data abstracted from the banks of every computer in the human system . . . in the nonspace of the mind" (qtd. in Suvin 44). Suvin is well aware of the ideological ambivalence of cyberpunk, its simultaneous embracing of the spirit of revolt and cynical confirmation of the status quo, which he describes as "adolescent" (50).

13. Without wishing to press the analogy too far, I am reminded of a corresponding psychophysical abnormality that illustrates the Lautréamont/Kafka discrepancy very well. In his book *Awakenings,* the psychiatrist Oliver Sacks reports the case of a woman who was struck with *encephalitis lethargica,* a malady that caused her to be arrested in a permanent state of catatonic immobility, "held motionless in the motionless 'eye' of a vortex . . . intensely still, yet perpetually moving, in an ontological orbit contracted to zero" (89). After being

put on a course of the psychopharmakon L-dopa, however, she experienced a fantastic "awakening" following which she fell into the opposite extreme, an unremitting hyperkinesia: "Her threshold of reaction was now almost zero, and all her actions were instantaneous, precipitate, and excessively forceful." In this state, she conveyed the impression of a "speeded-up film" (93), as Sacks comments. Both kinetic states are inhuman extremities that suggest the grotesque. The fact is, our visceral sense of normalcy is extremely biased against such abnormal temporal patterns.

14. To give precision its due, the line occurs in Berkoff 117. It does not occur in Pomerance's stage play but in the film version (dir. David Lynch, 1979) that Pomerance did not script, which is based on the same sources as the play.

Bibliography

Abramovic, Marina. "Interview with Marina Abramovic." With Chrissie Iles. *Performance Research* 1.2 (1996): 20–24.

Apollinaire, Guillaume. *The Breasts of Tirésias: A Surrealist Drama.* Trans. Louis Simpson. *Modern French Theatre: An Anthology of Plays.* Ed. Michael Benedikt and George E. Wellwarth. New York: Dutton, 1966. 56–91.

Aristotle. *The Nicomachean Ethics.* Trans. David Ross. Rev. ed. Oxford: Oxford UP, 1980.

———. "On the Art of Poetry *[Poetics].*" *Classical Literary Criticism.* Trans. T. S. Dorsch. Harmondsworth: Penguin, 1965. 31–75.

Arnheim, Rudolf. *Entropy and Art: An Essay on Disorder and Order.* Berkeley: U of California P, 1971.

———. *The Power of the Center: A Study of Composition in the Visual Arts.* Berkeley: U of California P, 1988.

———. *Toward a Psychology of Art: Collected Essays.* Berkeley: U of California P, 1966.

Artaud, Antonin. *Artaud Anthology.* Ed. Jack Hirshman. San Francisco: City Lights, 1965.

———. *Selected Writings.* Ed. Susan Sontag. Trans. Helen Weaver. Berkeley: U of California P, 1988.

———. *The Theater and Its Double.* Trans. Mary Caroline Richards. New York: Grove, 1958.

Auerbach, Erich. *Scenes from the Drama of European Literature.* Trans. Ralph Manheim and Catherine Garvin. Minneapolis: U of Minnesota P, 1984.

Bachelard, Gaston. *Lautréamont.* Trans. Robert S. Dupree. Dallas: Dallas Institute of Humanities and Culture, 1986.

Bakhtin, Mikhail. *Rabelais and His World.* Trans. Hélène Iswolsky. Bloomington: Indiana UP, 1984.

Baltrusaitis, Jurgis. *Aberrations: An Essay on the Legend of Forms.* Trans. Richard Miller. Cambridge: MIT P, 1989.

Banes, Sally. *Greenwich Village 1963: Avant-Garde Performance and the Effervescent Body.* Durham: Duke UP, 1993.

Barasch, Frances K. "Definitions: Renaissance and Baroque, Grotesque Constructions and Deconstructions." *Modern Language Studies* 13.2 (1983): 60–67.

———. *The Grotesque: A Study in Meanings.* The Hague: Mouton, 1971.

Barasch, Moshe. *Theories of Art from Plato to Winckelmann.* New York: New York UP, 1985.

Barker, Francis. *The Tremulous Private Body: Essays on Subjection.* London: Methuen, 1984.

Barthes, Roland. *Mythologies.* Trans. Anne Lavers. New York: Hill and Wang, 1975.

———. *The Responsibility of Forms: Critical Essays on Music, Art, and Representation.* Trans. Richard Howard. New York: Hill and Wang, 1985.

Baudelaire, Charles. *Selected Writings on Art and Literature.* Trans. and intro. P. E. Charvet. Harmondsworth: Penguin, 1992.

Baudrillard, Jean. *Simulations.* Trans. Paul Foss, Paul Patton, and Philip Beitchman. New York: Semiotext(e), 1983.

Beaune, Jean-Claude. "The Classical Age of Automata: An Impressionistic Survey from the Sixteenth to the Nineteenth Century." *Fragments for a History of the Human Body Part One.* Ed. Michael Feher, Ramona Nadaff, and Nadia Tazi. New York: Zone Books, 1989. 431–80.

Benjamin, Walter. *Illuminations.* Trans. Harry Zohn. Ed. Hannah Arendt. New York: Harcourt, 1968.

———. *The Origin of German Tragic Drama.* Trans. John Osborne. London: NLB, 1977.

———. *Reflections: Essays, Aphorisms, Autobiographical Writings.* Ed. Peter Demetz. Trans. Edmund Jephcott. New York: Schocken, 1986.

Bennett, Benjamin. *Modern Drama and German Classicism: Renaissance from Lessing to Brecht.* Ithaca: Cornell UP, 1979.

Bentley, Eric. *The Life of the Drama.* New York: Atheneum, 1967.

Bergson, Henri. "Laughter." *Comedy.* Ed. Wylie Sypher. Garden City, NY: Doubleday, 1956. 59–190.

Berkoff, Stephen. *Metamorphosis. The Trial, Metamorphosis, In the Penal Colony: Three Theatre Adaptations from Franz Kafka.* Oxford: Amber Lane, 1988. 71–121.

Bernhard, Thomas. *Der Weltverbesserer. Die Stücke 1969–1981.* Frankfurt: Suhrkamp, 1983. 887–962.

Bernstein, Michael André. "'These Children That Come at You with Knives': *Ressentiment,* Mass Culture, and the Saturnalia." *Critical Inquiry* 17.2 (1991): 358–85.

Beyen, Roland. *Ghelderode: présentation, choix de textes, chronologie, bibliographie.* Paris: Seghers, 1974.

Blau, Herbert. *Blooded Thought: Occasions of Theatre.* New York: Performing Arts Journal Publications, 1982.

———. "The Surpassing Body." *TDR* 35.2 (1991): 74–98.

———. *To All Appearances: Ideology and Performance.* New York: Routledge, 1992.

Blöcker, Günter. *Heinrich von Kleist oder Das absolute Ich.* Frankfurt: Fischer, 1977.

Bohn, Willard. *Apollinaire and the Faceless Man: The Creation and Evolution of a Modern Motif.* Rutherford: Fairleigh Dickinson UP, 1991.

Bompiani, Ginevra. "The Chimera Herself." *Fragments for a History of the Human Body Part One.* Ed. Michael Feher, Ramona Nadaff, and Nadia Tazi. New York: Zone Books, 1989. 365–409.

Botsford, Antoinette. "The Toone Marionette Theater of Brussels." Diss. UCLA, 1980.

Braden, Gordon. *Renaissance Tragedy and the Senecan Tradition: Anger's Privilege.* New Haven: Yale UP, 1985.

Bradley, A. C. *Shakespearean Tragedy: Hamlet, Othello, King Lear, Macbeth.* Greenwich, CT: Fawcett, [n.d.].

Brecht, Bertolt. *Gesammelte Werke.* 20 vols. Frankfurt: Suhrkamp, 1967.

Brenton, Howard. *Christie in Love. Plays One.* London: Methuen, 1986. 1–30.

Breton, André. *Manifestoes of Surrealism.* Trans. Richard Seaver and Helen R. Lane. Ann Arbor: U of Michigan P, 1969.

Bridaham, Lester Burbank. *Gargoyles, Chimeras, and the Grotesque in French Gothic Sculpture.* 2nd ed., rev. New York: Da Capo, 1969.

Bristol, Michael D. *Carnival and Theatre: Plebeian Culture and the Structure of Authority in Renaissance England.* New York: Routledge, 1989.

Brown, Frederick. *Theater and Revolution: The Culture of the French Stage.* New York: Viking, 1980.

Brucher, Richard T. "'Tragedy, Laugh On': Comic Violence in 'Titus Andronicus.'" *Renaissance Drama* 10 (1979): 71–91.

Büchner, Georg. *Complete Works and Letters.* Trans. Henry J. Schmidt. Ed. Henry J. Schmidt and Walter Hinderer. New York: Continuum, 1986.

Burden, Chris. *Documentation of Selected Works, 1971–1974.* Video Collection of the Museum of Modern Art, New York. 1975.

Burke, Edmund. *A Philosophical Inquiry into the Origin of Our Ideas of the Sublime and Beautiful.* London: Bell, 1889.

Burke, Kenneth. *Attitudes Toward History.* 1937. 3rd ed. Berkeley: U of California P, 1984.

———. *A Grammar of Motives.* New York: Prentice Hall, 1945.

———. *Permanence and Change: An Anatomy of Purpose.* 2nd ed., rev. Los Altos: Hermes, 1954.

Burwick, Frederick. *The Haunted Eye: Perception and the Grotesque in English and German Romanticism.* Heidelberg: Winter, 1987.

Calder, William M., III. "SECRETI LOQVIMVR: An Interpretation of Seneca's 'Thyestes.'" *SENECA TRAGICVS: Ramus Essays on Senecan Drama.* Ed. A. J. Boyle. Berwick, Victoria, Austral.: Aureal, 1983. 184–98.

Camille, Michael. "Play, Piety and Perversity in Medieval Manuscript Illumination." *Mein ganzer Körper ist Gesicht: Groteske Darstellungen in der europäischen Kunst und Literatur des Mittelalters.* Ed. Katrin Kröll and Hugo Steger. Freiburg: Rombach, 1994. 171–92.

Campbell, Joseph. *The Inner Reaches of Outer Space: Metaphor as Myth and as Religion.* New York: Alfred van der Marck, 1985.

Carr, Cynthia. *On Edge: Performance at the End of the Twentieth Century.* Hanover: UP of New England, 1993.

Churchill, Caryl. *The Skriker.* London: Nick Hern, 1994.

Clayborough, Arthur. *The Grotesque in English Literature.* Oxford: Clarendon, 1965.

Cohn, Ruby. *Retreats from Realism in Recent English Drama.* Cambridge: Cambridge UP, 1991.

Coleridge, Samuel Taylor. *Lectures 1808–1819 on Literature.* Ed. R. A. Foakes. Vol. 5.1 of *Collected Works.* 16 vols. Princeton: Princeton UP, 1987.

Cooper, Judith. *Ubu Roi: An Analytical Study.* New Orleans: Tulane UP, 1974.

Corngold, Stanley. *Franz Kafka: The Necessity of Form.* Ithaca: Cornell UP, 1988.

Craig, Edward Gordon. *Craig on Theatre.* Ed. J. Michael Walton. London: Methuen, 1983.

Crozier, W. Ray, and Antony J. Chapman, eds. *Cognitive Process in the Perception of Art.* Amsterdam: Elsevier, 1984.

The Crucifixion of Christ. Medieval Drama. Ed. David Bevington. Boston: Houghton Mifflin, 1975. 569–79.

Cunningham, Karen. "Renaissance Execution and Marlovian Elocution: The Drama of Death." *PMLA* 105.2 (1990): 209–22.

Curley, Thomas F., III. *The Nature of Senecan Drama.* Roma: Edizioni dell'Ateneo, 1986.

Dacos, Nicole. *La découverte de la Domus Aurea et la formation des grotesques à la rénaissance.* London: Warburg Institute, U of London, 1969.

Davidson, Arnold I. "The Horror of Monsters." *The Boundaries of Humanity: Humans, Animals, Machines.* Ed. James J. Sheehan and Morton Sosna. Berkeley: U of California P, 1991. 36–67.

Davis, Michael. "Politics and Madness." *Greek Tragedy and Political Theory.* Ed. J. Peter Euben. Berkeley: U of California P, 1986. 142–61.

Davis, Natalie Zemon. *Society and Culture in Early Modern France: Eight Essays.* Stanford: Stanford UP, 1975.

Deak, Frantisek. *Symbolist Theater: The Formation of an Avant-Garde.* Baltimore: Johns Hopkins UP, 1993.

Derrida, Jacques. *Margins of Philosophy.* Trans. Alan Bass. Chicago: U of Chicago P, 1982.

———. *Positions.* Trans. Alan Bass. Chicago: U of Chicago P, 1981.

———. *Writing and Difference.* Trans. Alan Bass. Chicago: U of Chicago P, 1978.

Diel, Paul. *Symbolism in Greek Mythology: Human Desire and Its Transformations.* Trans. Vincent Stuart, Micheline Stuart, and Rebecca Folkman. Boulder, CO: Shambhala, 1980.

Dürrenmatt, Friedrich. *The Physicists.* Trans. James Kirkup. New York: Grove, 1964.

———. "Problems of the Theatre." *Playwrights on Playwriting.* Ed. Toby Cole. New York: Hill and Wang, 1961. 131–44.

———. *Theater: Essays, Gedichte und Reden.* Zürich: Diogenes, 1980.

———. *Titus Andronicus: Eine Komödie nach Shakespeare. König Johann, Titus Andronicus: Shakespeare-Umarbeitungen.* Zürich: Diogenes, 1980. 115–97.

———. *The Visit: A Tragi-Comedy.* Trans. Patrick Bowles. New York: Grove, 1962.

Eagleton, Terry. *Walter Benjamin, or Towards a Revolutionary Criticism.* London: Verso, 1981.

Eco, Umberto. *Art and Beauty in the Middle Ages.* Trans. Hugh Bredin. New Haven: Yale UP, 1986.

Edmundson, Mark. *Nightmare on Main Street: Angels, Sadomasochism, and the Culture of Gothic.* Cambridge: Harvard UP, 1997.

Eliade, Mircea. *The Sacred and the Profane: The Nature of Religion.* Trans. Willard R. Trask. San Diego: Harcourt, 1959.

Eliot, T. S. *The Complete Poems and Plays, 1909–1950.* San Diego: Harcourt, 1952.

———. *Elizabethan Dramatists.* London: Faber, 1963.

Esslin, Martin. *The Theatre of the Absurd.* 3rd ed., rev. Harmondsworth: Penguin, 1980.

Euripides. *The Bacchae.* Trans. William Arrowsmith. *Euripides V.* Ed. David Grene and Richmond Lattimore. The Complete Greek Tragedies. Chicago: U of Chicago P, 1959. 141–220.

———. *Electra.* Trans. Emily Townsend Vermeule. *Euripides V.* Ed. David Grene and Richmond Lattimore. The Complete Greek Tragedies. Chicago: U of Chicago P, 1959. 1–66.

Farnham, Willard. *The Shakespearean Grotesque: Its Genesis and Transformations.* Oxford: Clarendon, 1971.

Fawcett, Mary L. "Arms/Words/Tears: Language and the Body in 'Titus Andronicus.'" *ELH* 50.2 (1983): 261–77.

Felman, Shoshana. "Turning the Screw of Interpretation." *Yale French Studies* 55/56 (1977): 94–207.

Fingesten, Peter. "Delimitating the Concept of the Grotesque." *Journal of Aesthetics and Art Criticism* 42.4 (1984): 419–26.

Fischer-Lichte, Erika. "Performance Art and Ritual: Bodies in Performance." *Theatre Research International* 22.1 [Supplement] (1997): 22–37.

———. *Semiotik des Theaters: Eine Einführung.* 3 vols. Tübingen: Narr, 1983.

Floyd, Virginia, ed. *Eugene O'Neill at Work: Newly Released Ideas for Plays.* New York: Ungar, 1981.

Forster, E. M. *Aspects of the Novel.* New York: Harcourt Brace, 1927.

Foucault, Michel. *The Archaeology of Knowledge and The Discourse on Language.* Trans. A. M. Sheridan Smith and Rupert Swyer. New York: Pantheon, 1972.

———. *Madness and Civilization: A History of Insanity in the Age of Reason.* Trans. Richard Howard. New York: Random House, 1965.

———. *The Order of Things: An Archaeology of the Human Sciences.* New York: Vintage, 1973.

Frazer, James George. *The Golden Bough: A Study in Magic and Religion.* New York: Macmillan, 1963.

Freud, Sigmund. *Standard Edition of the Complete Psychological Works of Sigmund Freud.* 23 vols. Trans. and ed. James Strachey et al. London: Hogarth P, 1953–74.

Frye, Northrop. *Anatomy of Criticism: Four Essays.* Princeton: Princeton UP, 1957.

Genette, Gerard. *Figures of Literary Discourse.* Trans. Alan Sheridan. New York: Columbia UP, 1982.

George, David. "On Ambiguity: Towards a Post-Modern Performance Theory." *Theatre Research International* 14.1 (1989): 71–85.

Gerould, Daniel. "Tyranny and Comedy." *Comedy: New Perspectives.* Ed. Maurice Charney. *New York Literary Forum* 1 (1978): 1–30.

Ghelderode, Michel de. *Chronicles of Hell: A Tragedy Bouffe in One Act. Seven Plays.* Vol. 1. Trans. George Hauger. New York: Hill and Wang, 1960. 235–73.

———. *Hop, Signor! Seven Plays.* Vol. 2. Trans. George Hauger. New York: Hill and Wang, 1960. 47–94.

———. "An Interview with Michel de Ghelderode." With Samuel Draper. *Tulane Drama Review* 8.1 (1963): 39–50.

———. "The Ostend Interviews." *Seven Plays.* Vol. 1. Trans. George Hauger. New York: Hill and Wang, 1960. 1–26.

Girard, René. "Lenz ou l'inquiétante étrangeté." *Études Germaniques* 43.1 (1988): 15–23.

———. *"To Double Business Bound": Essays on Literature, Mimesis, and Anthropology.* Baltimore: Johns Hopkins UP, 1978.

———. *Violence and the Sacred.* Trans. Patrick Gregory. Baltimore: Johns Hopkins UP, 1977.

Girshausen, Theo, ed. *Die Hamletmaschine: Heiner Müllers Endspiel.* Köln: Prometh, 1978.

Goldman, Michael. *The Actor's Freedom.* New York: Viking, 1975.

Goll, Iwan [Yvan]. *Dichtungen: Lyrik Prosa Drama.* Ed. Claire Goll. Darmstadt: Luchterhand, 1960.

———. *Methusalem or The Eternal Bourgeois.* Trans. J. M. Ritchie. *Seven Expressionist Plays.* Ed. J. M. Ritchie. London: Calder, 1968. 79–112.

Gombrich, E. H. *Art and Illusion: A Study in the Psychology of Pictorial Representation.* Princeton: Princeton UP, 1969.

———. "The Mask and the Face." *Art, Perception, and Reality.* Ed. Maurice Mandelbaum. Baltimore: Johns Hopkins UP, 1972. 1–46.

———. *Meditations on a Hobby-Horse and Other Essays on the Theory of Art.* London: Phaidon, 1963.

———. *The Sense of Order: A Study in the Psychology of Decorative Art.* The Wrightsman Lectures. Ithaca: Cornell UP, 1979.

Gombrowicz, Witold. *Ivona, Princess of Burgundia.* Trans. Krystyna Griffith-Jones and Catherine Robins. New York: Grove, 1970.

Gorchakov, Nikolai A. *The Theater in Soviet Russia.* Trans. Edgar Lehman. Columbia Slavic Studies. New York: Columbia UP, 1967.

Grabbe, Christian Dietrich. *Jest, Satire, Irony, and Deeper Significance: A Comedy in Three Acts.* Trans. Maurice Edwards. New York: Ungar, 1966.

Greenblatt, Stephen. *Shakespearean Negotiations.* Berkeley: U of California P, 1988.

Grossvogel, David. *20th Century French Drama.* New York: Gordian P, 1967.

Gruber, William E. *Comic Theaters: Studies in Performance and Audience Response.* Athens: U of Georgia P, 1986.

Guthke, Karl S. *Modern Tragicomedy: An Investigation into the Nature of the Genre.* New York: Random House, 1966.

Harpham, Geoffrey Galt. *On the Grotesque: Strategies of Contradiction in Art and Literature.* Princeton: Princeton UP, 1982.

Hassan, Ihab. *The Postmodern Turn: Essays in Postmodern Theory and Culture.* Columbus: Ohio State UP, 1987.

Hauser, Arnold. "The Origins of Domestic Drama." Trans. Stanley Godman. *The Theory of the Modern Stage.* 2nd ed., rev. Ed. Eric Bentley. New York: Penguin, 1976. 403–19.

Hayman, Ronald. *British Theatre since 1955: A Reassessment.* Oxford: Oxford UP, 1979.

Hegel, G. W. F. *Aesthetics: Lectures on Fine Art.* Trans. T. M. Knox. 2 vols. Oxford: Clarendon, 1975.

Heidsieck, Arnold. *Das Groteske und das Absurde im modernen Drama.* Stuttgart: Kohlhammer, 1969.

Hellman, Helen. "'Splendors of Hell': A Tragic Farce." *Renascence* 20.1 (1967): 30–38.

Hiles, Jane. "A Margin for Error: Rhetorical Context in 'Titus Andronicus.'" *Style* 21.1 (1987): 62–75.

Hirsh, James. "Laughter at 'Titus Andronicus.'" *Essays in Theatre* 7.1 (1988): 59–74.

Holinshed, Raphael. *Holinshed's Chronicles of England, Scotland, and Ireland.* Vol. 4. London, 1587. 6 vols. Reprint, London: [J. Johnson], 1808.

Hoppe, Hans. *Das Theater der Gegenstände.* [Basel:] Basilius; Bensberg-Frankenforst: Schäuble, 1971.

Horace. "On the Art of Poetry *[Ars Poetica]*." *Classical Literary Criticism.* Trans. T. S. Dorsch. Harmondsworth: Penguin, 1965. 79–95.

Horváth, Ödön von. "Author's Note [to *Faith, Hope and Charity*]." Trans. Paul Foster and Richard Dixon. *Four Plays.* New York: Performing Arts Journal Publications, 1986. 94–95.

Huet, Marie-Hélène. *Monstrous Imagination.* Cambridge: Harvard UP, 1993.

Hugo, Victor, "Preface to 'Cromwell.'" *Revolution in the Theatre: French Romantic Theories of Drama.* Ed. and trans. Barry V. Daniels. Westport, CT: Greenwood, 1983. 152–91.

Huyssen, Andreas. *Drama des Sturm und Drang: Kommentar zu einer Epoche.* München: Winkler, 1980.

Ibsen, Henrik. *The Complete Major Prose Plays.* Trans. Rolf Fjelde. New York: New American Library, 1978.

Iden, Peter. *Die Schaubühne am Halleschen Ufer 1970–1979.* Frankfurt: Fischer, 1982.

Ilie, Paul. "Gracian and the Moral Grotesque." *Hispanic Review* 39.1 (1971): 30–48.

Innaurato, Albert. *The Transfiguration of Benno Blimpie. The Best Plays of Albert Innaurato.* New York: Gay Presses of New York, 1987. 146–77.

Innes, Christopher. *Modern British Drama, 1890–1990.* Cambridge: Cambridge UP, 1992.

Ionesco, Eugène. *Jack or the Submission: A Naturalistic Comedy. Four Plays.* Trans. Donald M. Allen. New York: Grove, 1958. 80–110.

———. *Notes and Counter-Notes.* Trans. Donald Watson. London: Calder, 1964.

———. *Rhinoceros.* Trans. Derek Prouse. New York: Grove, 1960.

James, Heather. "Cultural Disintegration in *Titus Andronicus:* Mutilating Titus, Virgil, and Rome." *Violence in Drama.* Ed. James Redmond. Cambridge: Cambridge University P, 1991. 123–40.

Janik, Dieter. "Die theatralischen Effekte des Michel de Ghelderode." *Drama und Theater der europäischen Avantgarde.* Ed. Franz Norbert Mennemeier and Erika Fischer-Lichte. Tübingen: Francke, 1994. 215–29.

Jarry, Alfred. *Selected Works of Alfred Jarry.* Ed. and trans. Roger Shattuck and Simon Watson Taylor. New York: Grove, 1965.

———. *The Ubu Plays.* Trans. Cyril Connolly and Simon Watson Taylor. Ed. Simon Watson Taylor. New York: Grove, 1969.

Jauss, Hans Robert. *Aesthetic Experience and Literary Hermeneutics.* Trans. Michael Shaw. Minneapolis: U of Minnesota P, 1982.

———. "Zum Problem der Grenzziehung zwischen dem Lächerlichen und dem Komischen." *Das Komische.* Ed. Wolfgang Preisendanz and Rainer Warning. München: Fink, 1976. 361–71.

Johnson, Barbara. *The Critical Difference: Essays in the Contemporary Rhetoric of Reading.* Baltimore: Johns Hopkins UP, 1980.

Joyce, James. *A Portrait of the Artist as a Young Man.* Frogmore: Triad/Panther, 1977.

Jung, Carl Gustav. *Four Archetypes: Mother, Rebirth, Spirit, Trickster.* Trans. R. F. C. Hull. Princeton: Princeton UP, 1973.

Kant, Immanuel. *Critique of Judgement.* Trans. J. H. Bernard. New York: Hafner, 1951.

Karl, Frederick R. *Modern and Modernism: The Sovereignty of the Artist, 1885–1925.* New York: Atheneum, 1988.

Kayser, Wolfgang. *The Grotesque in Art and Literature.* Trans. Ulrich Weisstein. Gloucester, MA: Smith, 1968.

Kern, Edith. "Molière and the Tradition of the Grotesque." *Molière and the Commonwealth of Letters: Patrimony and Posterity.* Ed. Roger Johnson Jr. et al. Jackson: UP of Mississippi, 1975. 507–20.

Kerr, Walter. *Tragedy and Comedy.* New York: Da Capo, 1985.

Kirby, Michael, and Victoria Nes Kirby. *Futurist Performance.* New York: Performing Arts Journal Publications, 1986.

Kleist, Heinrich von. "On the Marionette Theater." Trans. Christian-Albrecht Gollub. *German Romantic Criticism.* Ed. Leslie Willson. New York: Continuum, 1982. 238–44.

———. *Penthesilea: A Tragedy.* Trans. Humphrey Trevelyan. *Plays.* Ed. Walter Hinderer. New York: Continuum, 1982. 165–268.

Klotz, Volker. *Geschlossene und offene Form im Drama.* 10th ed., rev. München: Hanser, 1980.

Knight, G. Wilson. "'King Lear' and the Comedy of the Grotesque." *Shakespeare, the Tragedies: A Collection of Critical Essays.* Ed. Alfred Harbage. Englewood Cliffs, NJ: Prentice-Hall, 1964. 123–38.

Koepping, Klaus-Peter. "Absurdity and Hidden Truth: Cunning Intelligence and Grotesque Body Images as Manifestations of the Trickster." *History of Religions* 24.3 (1985): 191–214.

Koestler, Arthur. *The Act of Creation.* London: Hutchinson, 1964.

Kott, Jan. *The Bottom Translation: Marlowe and Shakespeare in the Carnival Tradition.* Trans. Daniela Miedzyrecka and Lillian Vallee. Evanston, IL: Northwestern UP, 1987.

Kristeva, Julia. *Desire in Language: A Semiotic Approach to Literature and Art.* Ed. Leon S. Roudiez. Trans. Thomas Gora, Alice Jardine, and Leon S. Roudiez. New York: Columbia UP, 1980.

———. *Powers of Horror: An Essay on Abjection.* Trans. Leon S. Roudiez. New York: Columbia UP, 1982.

Kubiak, Anthony. *Stages of Terror: Terrorism, Ideology, and Coercion as Theatre History.* Bloomington: Indiana UP, 1991.

Kuryluk, Ewa. *Salome and Judas in the Cave of Sex. The Grotesque: Origins, Iconography, Technique.* Evanston, IL: Northwestern UP, 1987.

Labelle, Maurice Marc. *Alfred Jarry: Nihilism and the Theater of the Absurd.* New York: New York UP, 1980.

Lacan, Jacques. *Écrits: A Selection.* Trans. Alan Sheridan. New York: Norton, 1977.

Lachmann, Renate. "Bakhtin and Carnival: Culture as Counter-Culture." *Cultural Critique* 11 (1989): 115–52.

Lahr, John. *Astonish Me: Adventures in Contemporary Theater.* New York: Viking, 1973.

Lenz, Jakob Michael Reinhold. *The Tutor, or The Advantages of Private Education: A Comedy.* Trans. Betty Senk Waterhouse. *Five Plays of the Sturm und Drang.* Lanham, MD: UP of America, 1986. 1–55.

Lessing, Gotthold Ephraim. *Laokoon, and How the Ancients Represented Death.* Trans. E. C. Beasley and Helen Zimmern. London: G. Bell, 1914.

Lever, Maurice, and Frédérick Tristan. *Le Monde à l'envers.* Paris: Hachette, 1980.

Linker, Kate. *Vito Acconci.* New York: Rizzoli, 1994.

Loers, Veit. "When Pictures Learned to Walk: The Aesthetics of Early Viennese Actionism." *From Action Painting to Actionism, Vienna 1960–1965.* Ed. Museum Fridericianum, Kassel; Kunstmuseum Winterthur; and Scottish National Gallery of Modern Art, Edinburgh. Klagenfurt: Ritter, 1988. 11–25.

Lukács, Georg. "The Sociology of Modern Drama." Trans. Lee Baxandall. *The Theory of the Modern Stage.* 2nd ed., rev. Ed. Eric Bentley. New York: Penguin, 1976. 425–50.

———. *The Theory of the Novel: A Historico-Philosophical Essay on the Forms of Great Epic Literature.* Trans. Anna Bostock. Cambridge: MIT P, 1971.

MacRitchie, Lynn. "Marina Abramovic: Exchanging Energies." *Performance Research* 1.2 (1996): 27–34.

Magli, Patrizia. "The Face and the Soul." *Fragments for a History of the Human Body Part Two.* Ed. Michael Feher, Ramona Nadaff, and Nadia Tazi. New York: Zone Books, 1989. 86–127.

McElroy, Bernard. *Fiction of the Modern Grotesque.* Houndmills, Basingstoke, Hampshire (UK): Macmillan, 1989.

Mennemeier, Franz Norbert. "Bertolt Brechts 'Theater der Grausamkeit': Anmerkungen zum 'Badener Lehrstück vom Einverständnis.'" *Der andere Brecht II/The Other Brecht II.* Ed. Marc Silberman et al. The Brecht Yearbook 18. Madison: The International Brecht Society, 1993. 73–83.

———. "'Das wichtigste Element in der Kunst is die Überraschung.'—Iwan Goll als Theaterautor." *Drama und Theater der europäischen Avantgarde.* Ed. Franz Norbert Mennemeier and Erika Fischer-Lichte. Tübingen: Francke, 1994. 1–28.

Meyerhold, Vsevolod. *Meyerhold on Theatre.* Trans. and ed. Edward Braun. New York: Hill and Wang, 1969.

Motto, Anna Lydia, and John R. Clark. "Grotesquerie Ancient and Modern: Seneca and Ted Hughes." *Classical and Modern Literature* 5.1 (1984): 13–22.

Müller, Heiner. *Anatomie Titus Fall of Rome: Ein Shakespearekommentar. Shakespeare Factory 2.* Berlin: Rotbuch, 1989. 125–223.

———. "Brief an den Regisseur der bulgarischen Erstaufführung von 'Philoktet' am dramatischen Theater Sofia." *Herzstück.* Berlin: Rotbuch, 1983. 102–10.

———. *Gesammelte Irrtümer 2: Interviews und Gespräche.* Ed. Gregor Edelmann and Renate Ziemer. Frankfurt: Verlag der Autoren, 1990.

———. *Hamletmachine and Other Texts for the Stage.* Ed. and trans. Carl Weber. New York: Performing Arts Journal Publications, 1984.

Nietzsche, Friedrich. *Beyond Good and Evil: Prelude to a Philosophy of the Future.* Trans. Walter Kaufmann. New York: Vintage, 1966.

———. *The Birth of Tragedy and The Case of Wagner.* Trans. and ed. Walter Kaufmann. New York: Vintage, 1967.

———. *Werke.* Ed. Karl Schlechta. 5 vols. Frankfurt: Ullstein, 1969.

Norris, Margot. *Beasts of the Modern Imagination: Darwin, Nietzsche, Kafka, Ernst, and Lawrence.* Baltimore: Johns Hopkins UP, 1985.

Offermanns, Ernst L. *Arthur Schnitzler: Das Komödienwerk als Kritik des Impressionismus.* München: Fink, 1974.

Ogibenin, B. L. "Mask in the Light of Semiotics—A Functional Approach." *Semiotica* 13.1 (1975): 1–9.

Ortega y Gasset, José. *The Dehumanization of Art and Other Essays on Art, Culture, and Literature.* Trans. Willard R. Trask, Helene Weyl, et al. Princeton: Princeton UP, 1968.

Palmer, Jerry. *The Logic of the Absurd: On Film and Television Comedy.* London: British Film Institute, 1987.

Paré, Ambroise. *On Monsters and Marvels* ["Des monstres et prodiges," 1573]. Trans. Janis L. Pallister. Chicago: U of Chicago P, 1982.

Park, Katherine, and Lorraine J. Daston. "Unnatural Conceptions: The Study of Monsters in Sixteenth- and Seventeenth-Century France and England." *Past and Present* 92 (1981): 20–54.

Parker, Douglas H. "Shakespeare's Use of Comic Conventions in 'Titus Andronicus.'" *University of Toronto Quarterly* 56.4 (1987): 486–97.

Paska, Roman. "The Inanimate Incarnate." *Fragments for a History of the Human Body Part One.* Ed. Michael Feher, Ramona Nadaff, and Nadia Tazi. New York: Zone Books, 1989. 411–12.

Pauline, Mark. "Survival Research Laboratories Performs in Austria." *Flame Wars: The Discourse of Cyberculture.* Ed. Mark Dery. Durham: Duke UP, 1994. 287–95.

Pavis, Patrice. *Languages of the Stage: Essays in the Semiology of Theatre.* New York: Performing Arts Journal Publications, 1982.

Pavlov, Ivan Petrovich. *Conditioned Reflexes: An Investigation of the Physiological Activity of the Cerebral Cortex.* New York: Dover, 1960.

Pietzcker, Carl. "Das Groteske." *Deutsche Vierteljahrsschrift für Literaturwissenschaft und Geistesgeschichte* 45 (1971): 197–211.

Pirandello, Luigi. *On Humor.* Trans. Antonio Illiano and Daniel P. Testa. Chapel Hill: U of North Carolina P, 1960.

Plato. *The Dialogues of Plato.* Trans. B. Jowett. Vol. 1. New York: Random House, 1937.

Poggioli, Renato. *The Theory of the Avant-Garde.* Trans. Gerald Fitzgerald. Cambridge: Harvard UP, 1968.

Pomerance, David. *The Elephant Man.* New York: Grove, 1979.

Rabey, David Ian. *David Rudkin: Sacred Disobedience.* Amsterdam: Harwood, 1997.

Ricoeur, Paul. *The Rule of Metaphor: Multi-Disciplinary Studies on the Creation of Meaning in Language.* Trans. Robert Czerny. Toronto: U of Toronto P, 1977.

Rimbaud, Jean-Nicolas-Arthur. *Complete Works, Selected Letters.* Trans. and ed. Wallace Fowlie. Chicago: U of Chicago P, 1966.

Roach, Joseph. "Carnival and the Law in New Orleans." *TDR* 37.3 (1993): 42–75.

Rolleston, James. *Kafka's Narrative Theater.* University Park: Pennsylvania State UP, 1974.

Rudkin, David. *The Saxon Shore.* London: Methuen, 1986.

———. *The Sons of Light.* London: Methuen, 1981.

———. *The Triumph of Death.* London: Methuen, 1981.

Ruskin, John. *The Stones of Venice.* Vol. 3. New York: Merrill and Baker, n.d. [1853].

Sacks, Oliver. *Awakenings.* New York: Summit, 1987.

———. *The Man Who Mistook His Wife for a Hat and Other Clinical Tales.* New York: Harper, 1987.

Sayre, Henry M. *The Object of Performance: The American Avant-Garde since 1970.* Chicago: U of Chicago P, 1989.

Schama, Simon. *The Embarrassment of Riches: An Interpretation of Dutch Culture in the Golden Age.* Berkeley: U of California P, 1988.

Scheff, Thomas J. *Catharsis in Healing, Ritual, and Drama.* Berkeley: U of California P, 1979.

Schiller, Friedrich. "Reflections on the Use of the Vulgar and Low Elements in Works of Art." *Dramatic Theory and Criticism: Greeks to Grotowski.* Ed. Bernard F. Dukore. New York: Holt, Rinehart, 1974. 468–71.

Schlemmer, Oskar. "Man and Art Figure." *The Theater of the Bauhaus.* Trans. Arthur S. Wensinger. Ed. Walter Gropius and Arthur S. Wensinger. Middletown, CT: Wesleyan UP, 1961. 17–46.

Schmidt, Henry J. *How Dramas End: Essays on the German* Sturm und Drang, *Büchner, Hauptmann, and Fleisser.* Ann Arbor: UMI, 1992.

Schneegans, Heinrich. *Geschichte der grotesken Satire.* Strassburg: Trübner, 1894.

Schnitzler, Arthur. *Zum Grossen Wurstel: Burleske in einem Akt. Das dramatische Werk.* Vol. 4. Frankfurt: Fischer, 1978. 119–42.

Schopenhauer, Arthur. *The World as Will and Representation.* Trans. E. F. J. Payne. Vol. 2. Clinton, MA: Falcon's Wing P, 1958.

Schumacher, Claude. *Alfred Jarry and Guillaume Apollinaire.* Grove Press Modern Dramatists. New York: Grove, 1985.

Schwarz, Dieter. "Chronology." *From Action Painting to Actionism, Vienna 1960–*

1965. Ed. Museum Fridericianum, Kassel; Kunstmuseum Winterthur; and Scottish National Gallery of Modern Art, Edinburgh. Klagenfurt: Ritter, 1988. 91–345.

Segal, Charles. *Interpreting Greek Tragedy: Myth, Poetry, Text.* Ithaca: Cornell UP, 1986.

Segel, Harold B. *Pinocchio's Progeny: Puppets, Marionettes, Automatons, and Robots in Modernist and Avant-Garde Drama.* Baltimore: Johns Hopkins University P, 1995.

Sell, Rainer. "The Comedy of Hyperbolic Horror: Seneca, Lucan and 20th Century Grotesque." *Neohelicon* 11.1 (1984): 277–300.

Seneca, Lucius Annaeus. *Thyestes. Four Tragedies and Octavia.* Trans. E. F. Watling. Harmondsworth: Penguin, 1966. 41–93.

Shakespeare, William. *The Riverside Shakespeare.* Ed. G. Blakemore Evans. Boston: Houghton Mifflin, 1974.

Shank, Theodore. "Mark Pauline: Machine Mayhem." *Mime Journal* [spec. issue on California performance, vol. 1] (1989/1990): 222–59.

Shershow, Scott Cutler. *Puppets and "Popular" Culture.* Ithaca: Cornell UP, 1995.

Shepard, Sam. *Back Bog Beast Bait. The Unseen Hand and Other Plays.* New York: Bantam, 1986. 303–33.

———. *La Turista. Seven Plays.* New York: Bantam, 1981. 255–300.

Sidney, Sir Philip. *A Defence of Poetry.* Ed. Jan van Dorsten. Oxford: Oxford UP, 1966.

Silver, Nicky. *Fat Men in Skirts. Etiquette and Vitriol: The Food Chain and Other Plays.* New York: Theatre Communications Group, 1996. 217–300.

Skrade, Carl. *God and the Grotesque.* Philadelphia: Westminster, 1974.

Skulsky, Harold. "Cannibals vs. Demons in 'Volpone.'" *Studies in English Literature 1500–1900* 29.2 (1989): 291–308.

Sloterdijk, Peter. *Thinker on Stage: Nietzsche's Materialism.* Trans. Jamie Owen Daniel. Minneapolis: U of Minnesota P, 1989.

Solomon, Charles. *The History of Animation: Enchanted Drawings.* New York: Knopf, 1989.

Sophocles. *Ajax.* Trans. John Moore. *Sophocles II.* Ed. David Grene and Richmond Lattimore. The Complete Greek Tragedies. Chicago: U of Chicago P, 1957. 1–62.

"SRL Performance Chronology," date unknown. 9 Feb. 2003 <http://www.ca-nuck.com/Srl/history.html>.

Stafford, Barbara Maria. *Body Criticism: Imagining the Unseen in Enlightenment Art and Medicine.* Cambridge: MIT P, 1991.

States, Bert O. *Great Reckonings in Little Rooms: On the Phenomenology of Theater.* Berkeley: U of California P, 1985.

Steinweg, Reiner, ed. *Brechts Modell der Lehrstücke: Zeugnisse, Diskussion, Erfahrungen.* Frankfurt: Suhrkamp, 1976.

Stillman, Linda Klieger. *Alfred Jarry.* Twayne World Authors Series. Boston: Twayne, 1983.

Stoppard, Tom. *Rosencrantz and Guildenstern Are Dead.* London: Faber, 1968.

Sutton, Dana Ferrin. *Seneca on the Stage.* Leiden (Holland): Brill, 1986.

Suvin, Darko. "On Gibson and Cyberpunk SF." *Foundation* 46 (1989): 40–51.

Swan, John. "Yvan Goll: Profane and Sacred Farce." *Farce.* Ed. James Redmond. Cambridge: Cambridge UP, 1988. 184–200.

Szondi, Peter. *Theory of the Modern Drama.* Trans. Michael Hays. Minneapolis: U of Minnesota P, 1987.

Taylor, John Russell. *The Second Wave: British Drama of the Sixties.* London: Methuen, 1978.

Teraoka, Arlene Akiko. *The Silence of Entropy or Universal Discourse: The Postmodernist Poetics of Heiner Müller.* New York: Lang, 1985.

Thiher, Allen. "Jacques Derrida's Reading of Artaud: 'La Parole soufflée' and 'La Clôture de la représentation.'" *The French Review* 57.4 (1984): 503–8.

Thomsen, Christian W. *Das Groteske und die englische Literatur.* Darmstadt: Wiss. Buchgesellschaft, 1977.

Thomson, Philip. *The Grotesque.* London: Methuen, 1972.

Todorov, Tzvetan. *The Fantastic: A Structural Approach to a Literary Genre.* Trans. Richard Howard. Ithaca: Cornell UP, 1975.

Toller, Ernst. *Transfiguration.* Trans. Edward Crankshaw. *Seven Plays.* London: Bodley Head, 1935. 55–106.

Tuchman, Barbara W. *The Distant Mirror: The Calamitous 14th Century.* New York: Ballantine, 1978.

Valency, Maurice. *The End of the World: An Introduction to Contemporary Drama.* New York: Oxford UP, 1980.

Valentin, Jean-Marie. "'Das neue Drama sei enorm!': Surréalité et grotesque dans le théâtre d'Ivan Goll." *Études Germaniques* 43.1 (1988): 82–95.

Van Alphen, Ernst. *Francis Bacon and the Loss of Self.* London: Reaktion Books, 1992.

Van Itallie, Jean-Claude. *Motel: A Masque for Three Dolls. The Off Off Broadway Book: The Plays, People, Theatre.* Ed. Albert Poland and Bruce Mailman. Indianapolis: Bobbs-Merrill, 1972. 82–84.

Vernant, Jean-Pierre. "Ambiguity and Reversal: On the Enigmatic Structure of 'Oedipus Rex.'" Trans. Page du Bois. *New Literary History* 10.3 (1978): 475–501.

Warr, Tracy. "Sleeper." *Performance Research* 1.2 (1996): 1–19.

Warren, Robert Penn. "The Dramatic Version of 'Ballad of a Sweet Dream of Peace: A Charade for Easter.'" *The Grotesque in Art and Literature: Theological Reflections.* Ed. James Luther Adams and Wilson Yates. Grand Rapids, MI: Eerdman, 1997. 243–74.

Watling, E. F. "Introduction." *Four Tragedies and Octavia.* By Lucius Annaeus Seneca. Trans. E. F. Watling. Harmondsworth: Penguin, 1966. 7–39.

Wayman, Alex. "The Human Body as Microcosm in India, Greek Cosmology, and Sixteenth-Century Europe." *History of Religions* 22.3 (1982): 172–90.

Weber, Carl. Introduction. *Hamletmachine and Other Texts for the Stage.* By Heiner Müller. Ed. and trans. Carl Weber. New York: Performing Arts Journal Publications, 1984.

Wedekind, Frank. *Prosa Dramen Verse.* Vol. 1. München: Langen-Müller, 1964.

Wellwarth, George E. *The Theater of Protest and Paradox.* New York: New York UP, 1964.

White, Hayden. *Tropics of Discourse: Essays in Cultural Criticism.* Baltimore: Johns Hopkins UP, 1978.

Wilcher, Robert. "The Communal Dream of Myth: David Rudkin's 'The Triumph of Death.'" *Modern Drama* 35 (1992): 571–84.

Williams, David. "Wilgefortis, Patron Saint of Monsters, and the Sacred Language of the Grotesque." *The Scope of the Fantastic: Selected Essays from the First International Conference on the Fantastic in Literature and Film [1980].* Ed. Robert A. Collins and Howard D. Pierce. Westport, CT: Greenwood, 1985. 171–77.

Williams, David, ed. *Peter Brook: A Theatrical Casebook.* London: Methuen, 1988.

Williams, Heathcote. *AC/DC.* London: Calder; New York: Riverrun, 1983.

———. "An Interview with H. W." With Irving Wardle. *Gambit* 18/19 (1971): 139–44.

Wilshire, Bruce. *Role Playing and Identity: The Limits of Theatre as Metaphor.* Bloomington: Indiana UP, 1982.

Wittgenstein, Ludwig. *Tractatus Logico-Philosophicus.* Ed. and trans. C. K. Ogden. London: Kegan Paul, 1933.

Worth, Katharine J. *Revolutions in Modern English Drama.* London: Bell, 1972.

Worthen, William B. *The Idea of the Actor: Drama and the Ethics of Performance.* Princeton: Princeton UP, 1984.

Yeats, William Butler. *Autobiographies: Reveries over Childhood and Youth and the Trembling of the Veil.* London: Macmillan, 1926.

Young, Katharine. "'Still Life with Corpse': Management of the Grotesque Body in Medicine." *Bodylore.* Ed. Young. Knoxville: U of Tennessee P, 1993. 111–33.

Zurbrugg, Nicholas. "Post-Modernism and the Multi-Media Sensibility: Heiner Müller's 'Hamletmachine' and the Art of Robert Wilson." *Modern Drama* 31.3 (1988): 439–53.

Index

Ralf Remshardt is an associate professor of theatre and dance at the University of Florida where he directs and teaches theatre history and dramaturgy.